BURNING STEEL

Peter Hart was the oral historian at the Imperial War Museum for nearly forty years. A distinguished military history author, he has acted as an army guide, runs his own battlefield tour company and has a successful weekly podcast series, *Pete & Gary's Military History*. His most recent books for Profile include *At Close Range* and *The Great War*.

PETER HART

BURNING STEEL

A TANK REGIMENT AT WAR, 1939–45

P

PROFILE BOOKS

This paperback edition first published in 2023

First published in Great Britain in 2022 by
Profile Books Ltd
29 Cloth Fair
London
ECIA 7JQ

www.profilebooks.com

1 3 5 7 9 10 8 6 4 2

Typeset in Garamond by MacGuru Ltd
Printed and bound in Great Britain by
CPI Group (UK) Ltd, Croydon CR0 4YY

A CIP catalogue record for this book is available from the British Library.

ISBN 978 1 78816 640 9
eISBN 978 1 78283 760 2

CONTENTS

MAPS

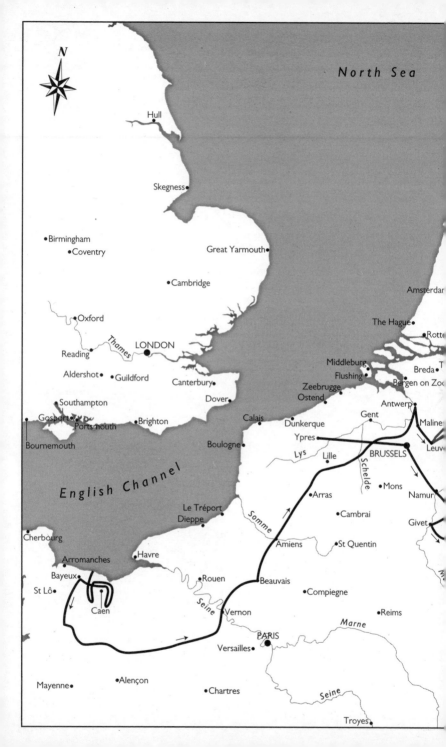

2nd Fife and Forfar Yeomanry,
1944/45

→ 1944
→ 1945

0   20   40   60   80   100   120 miles
0 20 40 60 80 100 120 140 160 180 200 kilometres

Flensburg
Husum
Schleswig
Baltic Sea
Neustadt
Neumünster
Lübeck
Wismar
Hamburg
Schwerin
Harburg
Laurenburg
Emden
Lüneburg
Elbe
Bremen
Rötenburg
Soltau
Ulzen
Celle
Lingen
Hannover
Rheine
Osnabrück
Minden
Magdeburg
Wesser
Aller
Munster
Arnhem
Emmerich
Wesel
Essen
Halle
Duisburg
Kassel
Leipzig
Düsseldorf
Jülich
Cologne
aastricht
Duren
Aachen
Rhine
Luxembourg
Metz
Nancy
Strasbourg

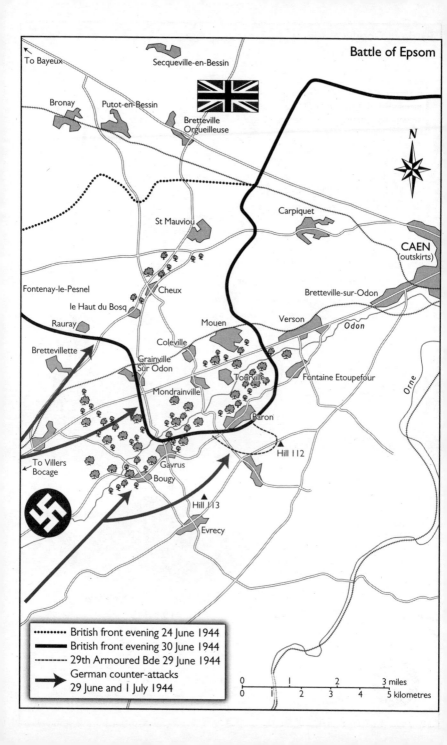

Battle of Epsom

To Bayeux

Secqueville-en-Bessin

Bronay   Putot-en-Bessin

Bretteville
Orgueilleuse

N

St Mauviou

Carpiquet

CAEN
(outskirts)

Fontenay-le-Pesnel

Cheux

Bretteville-sur-Odon

le Haut du Bosq

Rauray

Mouen

Verson

Odon

Brettevillette

Coleville

Grainville
Sur Odon

Tourville

Fontaine Etoupefour

Orne

Mondrainville

Baron

To Villers
Bocage

Gavrus
Bougy

Hill 112

Hill 113

Evrecy

.... British front evening 24 June 1944
━━━━━ British front evening 30 June 1944
- - - - - 29th Armoured Bde 29 June 1944
⬌ German counter-attacks
29 June and 1 July 1944

0   1   2   3 miles
0   1   2   3   4   5 kilometres

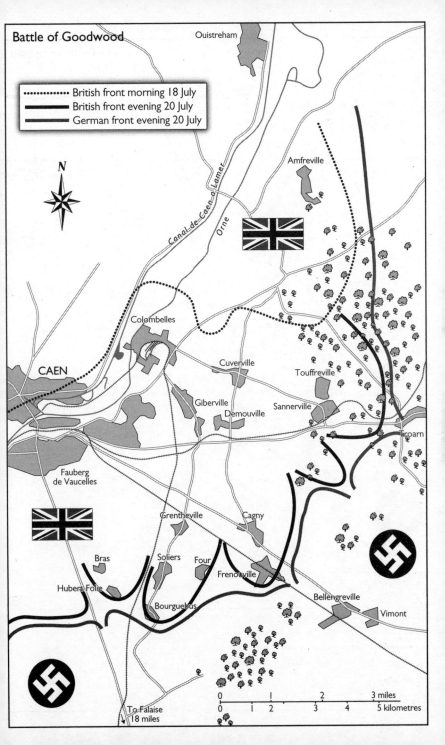

Battle of Goodwood

Ouistreham

Legend:
.... British front morning 18 July
▬▬▬ British front evening 20 July
▬▬▬ German front evening 20 July

N

Canal de Caen à l'Ornet
Orne

Amfreville

Colombelles

CAEN

Cuverville

Touffreville

Giberville
Demouville

Sannerville

Troarn

Fauberg
de Vaucelles

Grentheville

Cagny

Bras

Soliers

Four

Frenouville

Hubert-Folie

Bourguebus

Bellengreville

Vimont

To Falaise
18 miles

0   1   2   3 miles
0   1   2   3   4   5 kilometres

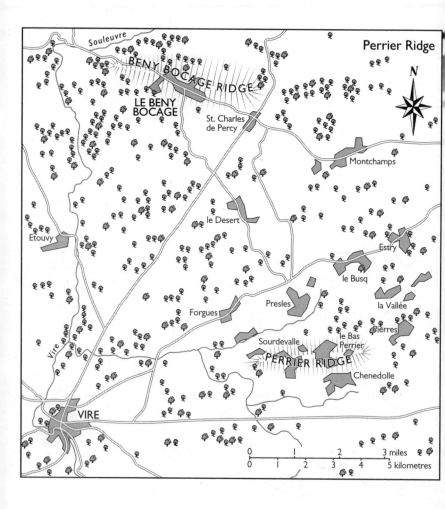

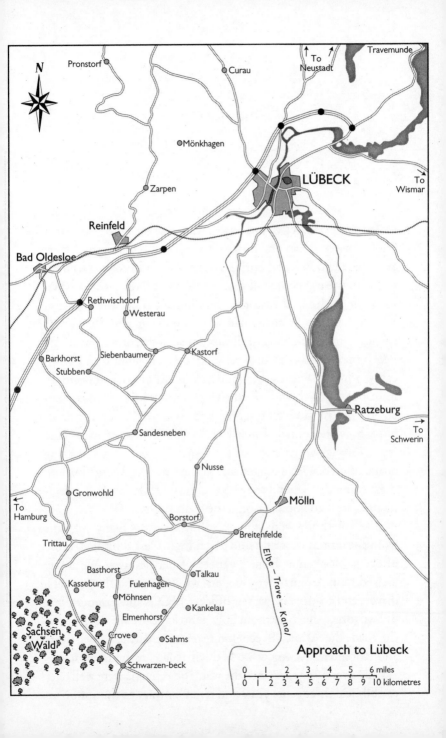

Approach to Lübeck

PREFACE

IT SEEMS EONS AGO, but once it was 'all of our yesterdays'. This book is based on an oral history project interviewing the veterans of the 2nd Fife and Forfar Yeomanry (2nd F&FY), which I began in the last couple of years of the twentieth century when working as the oral historian for the Imperial War Museum Sound Archive. A combination of events meant that I was spending a lot of time in Edinburgh, conveniently close to the F&FY heartlands of Dundee, Cupar, Dunfermline and Kirkcaldy; while I had the great good fortune when back in London, to be put in touch with the thriving 'South of the Border' association for all those who served with this proud Scottish unit, but who were actually English or Welsh. Wherever they came from, interviewing them was a pleasure. They were an amazing group of men, with a quiet pride in their personal contribution, their comrades, and all they had achieved collectively as a regiment. They had good reason to be proud.

Our methods were simple: to interview as many veterans from the unit as we could find to get the widest possible picture of events, looked at from a variety of perspectives. We interviewed tank commanders, loaders/wireless operators, gunners, drivers and co-drivers; we saw officers, NCOs and troopers; nor did we forget the 'backroom boys' who kept the whole show on the road: the 'A' and 'B' echelon fitter/mechanics, lorry drivers and storemen. We knew we had left it late, as by then, it was already over fifty years since the war. The veterans were well over the biblical three score years and ten. Contrary to the aphorism that 'Old soldiers never die, they just fade away', veterans do indeed die – and before that they face declining health and memory problems that can render interviews an impossibility. It was therefore imperative to complete the interviews as quickly as possible. In this I was greatly assisted by several other IWM interviewers including Conrad Wood, Richard McDonough, Nigel de Lee and Lindsay Baker. Collectively, we shared a determination to pay tribute to what these men had done for us in the fight against Nazi Germany in the best way we could – by preserving their incredible memories that would otherwise be lost.

When I was growing up, it seemed that Second World War veterans surrounded me wherever I went. For people of my generation, the veterans were our fathers and uncles, our teachers, the 'old buffers' we encountered in our first jobs. Now, in 2022, with very few exceptions, they are gone – and it is the turn of my generation to 'feel our age' after a life that has thankfully never been tested by war. I wish I had spent more time talking to them as a boy, more time interviewing them when I was working at the IWM. After all, I had plenty of opportunity – I could certainly have worked harder. It is now too late; they are gone. Most of all, I am sorry I never had the chance to interview the outstanding figure of William Steel Brownlie, who had sadly died in 1995 before we started the project. But we are fortunate that he left a wonderful memoir '*And Came Safe Home*', which can be consulted at several museums. Nevertheless, despite such regrets, we have still secured an amazing collection of some fifty interviews which range in length from an hour to fifteen hours, many of which can be listened to on the IWM website.

This is the story of a tank regiment told by the men themselves, in their own words. Raw and visceral recollections of some of the most dramatic and horrific scenes that I ever heard described in nearly forty years of talking to veterans. The sheer nerve-wracking tension of serving in the highly inflammable Sherman tank, said to be known to the Germans as the 'Tommy Cooker', and certainly known to the lads as 'the Ronson', after the cigarette lighter which was boasted by the manufacturer to 'always light first time'. The impact of a German ani-tank shell or panzerfaust missile, the desperate scramble to bail out, the awful fate of those who couldn't. Even if they made it out of the tank, they were still vulnerable to being brutally cut down by the machine guns and hand grenades of German infantry. These were moments of horror recalled by far too many of them. Although able to duel on equal footing with the German Mark IV Panzer, the Sherman was totally outclassed by the Panther and Tiger tanks. And most of all they feared the German 88mm guns. All they had in their favour was sheer numbers as the Shermans rolled off the production lines in their thousands. New tanks and crews would usually arrive almost immediately to replace losses.

This book charts as honestly as possible what the men thought had happened, checked against the facts as far as they can be established. Sometimes the stories do not entirely match, but there is enough agreement to make this a worthwhile exercise. This is as close as we can now get to a sense of 'what it was like' at the sharp end of armoured warfare. They were involved in titanic battles that were far too big, too complex, to allow me to do more than sketch out a rough outline of how the regiment fitted into the 'bigger picture'. I am painfully aware that trying to include too much detail would merely obscure what is the real importance of this book – the story of an amazing group of soldiers. Hence, we rarely get much of a look at the German perspective, nor the chance to pay tribute to the forces of the Soviet Union who were battling against some 200 German divisions on the Eastern Front.

The 2nd F&FY played a full role as part of the 11th Armoured Division which earned a reputation to match or exceed even the 7th Armoured Division that had so excelled in North Africa. But their achievements came at a terrible cost, with some 10,000 casualties and over 2,000 dead – higher than any other British armoured division in that war. The men who make this book were at the epicentre of this fighting, suffering the casualties, losing friends in circumstances which would scar their memories for life. At times I felt almost guilty to be sharing such traumatic memories, but surely it is important that we appreciate what they suffered and what they achieved as part of the vast armies that collectively defeated Nazi Germany. They were ordinary men, performing extraordinary deeds, in a noble cause. We should remember them.

1

FLEETING IMPRESSIONS

IT SEEMED AS IF WAR would never reach the men of the 2nd F&FY. They had trained for so long, year after year, mastering their military skills in readiness for the ultimate test. But nothing in their training could prepare them for the awesome shock of war, the dreadful noise, the confusion, the sudden death and overwhelming visceral horror of it all. They could only try their best to do themselves justice and not to let down their comrades fighting to survive alongside them. The interviews made a big impact on me. Indeed, long after I had finished the interviewing project I still remembered the chilling stories told me by Charlie Workman. He lived in Musselburgh, just south of Edinburgh, and had already lived a full life when I met him, rising to be a senior officer in the Intelligence Corps. But he always maintained his links with the 2nd F&FY. And he never forgot what they had experienced together in the fields of Normandy.

His first impressions of action were those of frenetic chaos, as his Sherman trundled into action on 26 June 1944, attacking strong German positions around the village of Cheux in Normandy.

> The wireless traffic was going like mad! There was an 88mm at so and so; there was something else at so and so. For the first time in my life, I saw German troops – advancing towards us! They would be panzer grenadiers, part of 12th SS Panzer

Division. This was quite a strong defensive line – and we'd hit it! We put the machine gun onto them. We were told the Germans never led with officer, they regarded that as a waste. You could see who the officer was, because people were looking at him – you had to try and kill the officers. Then their tanks opened up; we couldn't see them at all, they were 'hull down'. Cheux was a shambles, the whole village was ruined, it was difficult to tell where the road was. We kept losing tanks – hey we lost seven that day in 'C' Squadron. I could see them being hit, there would suddenly be a flash and the tank on your left, or right, would go up. You saw the flames as they brewed up – and you thought that was just what happened. It was only later on you began to realise that these Shermans were 'brewers'. We were firing – now and again you would see a German tank moving and you would engage that tank. It was such a confusion – it was our first day in action. There was burning tanks, wounded men, constant shells going off all around you – it was pretty noisy. We couldn't get any further forward. Such a confused scene. One was never aware of being afraid – I think that was because we had so much to do![1]

Lieutenant Charlie Workman, 1 Troop, 'C' Squadron, 2nd F&FY

One of his most moving memories of the Normandy fighting was that of young crippled Scottish soldiers, scattered about the battlefield. There was almost nothing that could be done for them.

They never mined the roads, mainly because the Germans themselves were using the roads. But they certainly heavily mined on either side of the road. We were doing a dawn attack, going up a narrow road with infantry on either side. The tank ahead of us slipped over into the ditch and they set off a whole stream of mines on the side. My memory is of seeing these young infantrymen lying – some of them with legs off, some with arms off. One young bloke, with no legs, saying, 'I

want my Mammie, I want my Mammie, I want my Mammie!'
He died. You would often find infantrymen, dead, dying or
wounded, just lying around. Morphine was just a little tube
with a little needle at the end – you just squeezed it into the
person somewhere.[2]

Lieutenant Charlie Workman, 1 Troop, 'C' Squadron, 2nd F&FY

After a period in reserve the next 'big' attack they faced was in
the Operation Goodwood push towards Caen on 18 July. Before
the battle, one of Workman's friends, Major Chris Nicholls, who
was in command of 'C' Squadron, had an ominous premonition
of death. As a desert veteran he had been 'to the well' on many
occasions. His courage seemed undimmed, he just seems to have
believed that his luck had finally run out – that this was the end
for him.

When we were going into action, he handed me a letter and
said, 'Will you make sure my wife gets this?' I said, 'Well why
should I give it her; you give it to her yourself.' He said, 'I'm not
coming back today.' 'Well, if you're not coming back, I'm not
coming back!' 'No,' he said, 'I want you to give it to her.' I took
it and he was killed an hour later.[3]

Lieutenant Charlie Workman, 1 Troop, 'C' Squadron, 2nd F&FY

After the battle Charlie Workman met with another young
officer, Lieutenant Steel Brownlie, to talk over what had happened; who had lived – and who had died. It had been an
unbelievably bad day for the 2nd F&FY.

We discussed what the life expectancy of a troop leader was! We
could see it wasn't very long! We were all young and I suppose
more malleable. I don't think anybody minded being killed – it
was how you were killed! The thing I always had was I didn't
want to lose my eyes. I could accept losing an arm or a leg –
and we saw plenty of that. The Sherman had its ammunition
exposed in the top – there was no lid on the bin. So, when a

Sherman was hit it blew up and very often the tank commander
had his legs away. That's what happened to Chris Nicholls[4]
exactly like that – I saw his tank was brewed up – I saw him
try to get out – and then he fell back in again – and that was
it. In action one never had any fear – a tank commander was
too busy. You were watching your map, looking at your own
troop, you were talking to your own driver, 'Go slow, turn left,
stop!' You were telling your gunner, 'Traverse left, traverse right,
pick up the target!' Your wireless operator would be giving you
instructions. You were so busy! But the worst of it was when
you came out and you were looking round to see who was still
there – what friends you had left. Then you would be told who
had gone – that was the worst bit – afterwards.[5]

Lieutenant Charlie Workman, 1 Troop, 'C' Squadron, 2nd F&FY

But Workman's most terrible memory he left deliberately
vague in his interview; I suspect he did not want the individual
involved to be identified for the sake of any grieving family and
their descendants. During an advance, Workman's Sherman was
suddenly hit with a shattering force.

We were advancing through a cornfield. There was a 'BANG!'
and I was brewed up. I'm not sure if it was a tank or an 88mm
– it was probably an 88mm. The tank wasn't on fire but I was
literally blown out of my tank! I came to on the ground – I
was quite uninjured. The sun was shining, the cornfield all
around. There was a 'sack' lying beside me! My troop sergeant
came up, his tank was just behind me, and this 'sack' of 'stuff'
started screaming at me, 'Shoot me! Shoot me, Sir! I've been a
good soldier, please I can't stand this agony, please, please shoot
me!' This was my driver who had been very badly burned up,
there was a fire in the front of the tank. I took out my revolver
and I couldn't find a face. I couldn't find anything – there was
nothing left of 'him' except a voice – I was prepared to shoot
him. In the end, luckily, the voice died away and he died.[6]

Lieutenant Charlie Workman, 1 Troop, 'C' Squadron, 2nd F&FY

Workman, his wireless operator, the co-driver and the gunner had all managed to get out relatively unscathed. But the tank had caught fire behind him, trapping the driver in among the flames. Somehow, he had managed to crawl out, but it was far too late. 'A sack lying beside me.' Just a phrase, but what horror those mundane words hide. It may now be a fleeting impression for you here on the page; but for Charlie Workman the hideousness of his driver's terrible death never really left him.

2

START AT THE BEGINNING

We were under canvas. They started with the old army sort
of discipline of laying out your kit. The bell tents were all in
perfect long lines and we laid out the kit in lines. The boots and
the blankets and everything all had to be dead in line. It was
really worth seeing! You wouldn't believe that about fifty tents
and boots all dead in line! It was really wonderful![1]

Trooper Ron Forbes, HQ Squadron, 2nd F&FY

THE FIFE AND FORFAR YEOMANRY (F&FY) was a tradi-
tional county territorial unit in the 1930s. The officers were
drawn from the 'great and the good' of society across the Fife
and Forfar regions: the landowners, the factory owners, the
businessmen. The NCOs were either former regular soldiers,
long-standing 'old' territorials, or men with some standing,
such as factory foremen or bank clerks. The men worked on the
farms, the estates, the shops and in the factories, many of them
owned by their officers. Although socially disparate, they were
collectively proud of their 'Scottish' heritage and their unit's tra-
ditions. The formation of the F&FY was triggered originally by
the fear of mass popular uprisings following the French Revolution. Thus, in 1794, the Forfar Yeomanry were raised, alongside
the Fifeshire Light Dragoons which mutated into the Fife Yeomanry Cavalry. Various volunteer formations came and went
on a regular basis, but they finally came together in the 1870s.

During the Boer War, the 20th Company, Imperial Yeomanry was recruited from the regiment and served with some distinction in South Africa, 1900–1901. On the formation of the Territorial Force in 1908 the regiment became formally known as the F&FY. In the Great War they fought dismounted against first the Turks at Gallipoli, then against the Senussi in Egypt. They were then formally converted into infantry, becoming the 14th Black Watch, which again served against the Turks in Palestine, 1916–17, before being brought back to face the Germans on the Western Front for the denouement of the war in 1918. All in all, they had a busy war and emerged with considerable credit.

Having originally been a cavalry unit, it was considered good news when they discovered that under the post-war reorganisation of the territorial forces they were to be reincarnated in 1919 as the 20th Armoured Car Company (F&FY), Tank Corps. Many similar yeomanry regiments suffered the perceived indignity of being converted into artillery batteries as it was evident that there was no longer any need for squadrons of cavalry.

The local F&FY drill halls were based on the main centres of recruitment at Cupar, Dunfermline and Dundee. In the early 1930s, the officers were recruited largely by personal recommendation from within the upper echelons of local society. One such was John Gilmour of the Montrave Estate in Levan, the son of the local MP, Sir John Gilmour, who had commanded the F&FY during the Great War. Gilmour was educated at Eton, passing his Certificate 'A' with the Officers' Training Corps there before studying history at Trinity Hall College, Cambridge between 1931 and 1934. While there he led an active sporting life and was part of the winning team in University Boat Race in 1933. He also found the time to follow in his father's footsteps and joined the F&FY in 1931. He was a tall, good-looking chap who seemed to have a natural air of command about him – he could be seen as an ideal officer type.

I was put in touch with the then honorary colonel, who was Colonel Carnegy of Lour. I went to see him, and he agreed to give me place in the regiment. I went in as a commissioned officer straight away. We were then the 20th Armoured Car Company, Royal Tank Regiment (Fife and Forfar Yeomanry). The company was commanded by a major and there were three troops and a regimental squadron headquarters troop. One troop was based in Dunfermline, one troop in Cupar and one troop in Forfar, and one troop and the headquarters were in Kirkcaldy – in Hunter Street. There was an officer called Ian Williamson, who was the troop commander, a captain and two subalterns, myself and Alastair Spencer Nairn. Williamson wasn't very efficient, not a great personality at all. Nairn was fine. The commanding officer was Major Black, he had served in the First World War and won a Military Cross. He was one of the directors of Michael Nairn and Company, the linoleum manufacturers in Kirkcaldy. Most of the men came from Kirkcaldy town and the farms inland.[2]

Second Lieutenant John Gilmour, No 2 Troop, 20th Armoured Car Coy (F&FY), Royal Tank Corps

His territorial commitments were not particularly onerous in the pre-war years. But they did carry out some low-grade military training, much hampered by shortages of equipment and the overall financial constraints placed on the Territorial Army by government parsimony.

We had a permanent hut at a place called Annsmuir outside Ladybank. We used to go for weekends there. We did a certain amount of rifle shooting – there was a rifle range there. We had one Rolls Royce armoured car, that was kept in Kirkcaldy. They were beautiful machines, with wonderful Rolls Royce engines! They were fitted with a Vickers machine gun – they weren't very heavily armoured! We drew armoured cars for training at annual camp each year. These were kept in a pool at Catterick and shared out among the regiments. The first camp I went to was at Scarborough, 1933. Apart from going to the firing range, which we did at a place south of Scarborough, the training was very difficult because there was no other unit for you to train with. You simply had to train against an imaginary foe all the time. There was no actual 'enemy' to practise on![3]

Second Lieutenant John Gilmour, No 2 Troop, 20th Armoured Car Coy (F&FY), Royal Tank Corps

The Munich Crisis in 1938 made it obvious that war was imminent, and the Territorial Army was swiftly increased in strength. The 20th Armoured Car Company doubled in size and in December 1938, it became the 1st F&FY, with 'A' Squadron at St Andrews, 'B' Squadron at Dunfermline, 'C' Squadron at Kirkcaldy and the Headquarters (HQ) Squadron at Dundee.

When it came to recruitment, the F&FY was very much a family regiment and John Walker, who had a job in the printing department of Nairn's linoleum factory in Kirkcaldy, found he had caused considerable offence when he strayed away to join a local Royal Artillery unit instead of the F&FY.

I joined the 'Terriers' artillery. My grandfather was my guardian, and he says, 'If you're going in the Terriers, you're no going in the artillery, you're going to the Fife and Forfar!' I'd never actually heard of it, because they were called 'The Tankies' here. He says, 'I thought you'd have known that – it was your father, your uncle and your grandfather's regiment!' I had to go and get an application form from them and he filled it in.[4]

John Walker

Suitably chastened, Walker joined the 1st F&FY at Hunter Street Drill Hall in Kirkcaldy in January 1939.

Although the 1st F&FY expanded in size from its former status as an armoured car company (12 officers, 175 men) to a full divisional cavalry recce regiment (32 officers, 403 men), this was still not enough – an indication that war was no longer knocking at the door; it was hammering it down. In April 1939, the

F&FY was required to double in size again. This involved an enormous effort in both recruitment and training, resulting in the formation of the 2nd F&FY under the command of Lieutenant Colonel A. H. McIntosh, a local businessman who ran a successful furniture manufacturing business in Dunfermline. He was widely considered a charming, charismatic and enthusiastic officer with a lovely touch of humour which could help soften the demands and pressures of military service. He was intensely attached to the regiment and took a great pride in the use of a piece of his own family tartan behind the 2nd F&FY badge. All told, he would prove a popular choice as the first colonel of the new regiment.

The 2nd F&FY were recruited from the same social strata as the parent body. One new young officer recruit who joined at this time was Douglas Hutchison. His family ran a prosperous flour milling business and he had attended OTC while at the Loretto School in Edinburgh. Hutchison had neither the appearance nor the inclinations of a natural soldier, despite his family tradition of service in the F&FY. As war approached, he was studying agriculture at Clare College, Cambridge University, but the long shadow of war made him realise that the time had come to act, so he joined 'C' Squadron, 2nd F&FY, based at the Hunter Street Drill Hall in Kirkcaldy in 1939. He explained his decision:

> One was aware of the likelihood of becoming involved in a war. My brother then being in the Black Watch I decided that I would go in something different, so I joined the Fife and Forfar Yeomanry, I knew a good many of the officers in the regiment, in fact several of them were members of my family – the regiment had indeed been commanded by a cousin of my father's. They were kind enough, on the strength of the OTC experience to give me a commission – to which I was certainly not entitled otherwise![5]

Second Lieutenant Douglas Hutchison, 'C' Squadron, 2nd F&FY

By this time, John Gilmour was an acting major. He was working in civilian life as a trainee manager with brewery James Calder and Company Ltd in Alloa, so he found it convenient to transfer from the 1st F&FY to the newly formed 'B' Squadron, 2nd F&FY based at the Drill Hall in Dunfermline.

> I was in the squadron which became the 2nd Regiment, which was 9th Division – the duplicate of the Highland Division. We went from being a very close-knit unit as a company to being a whole regiment with four squadrons. This completely changed the atmosphere altogether. Each squadron was two troops of tanks and four troops of carriers.[6]
>
> Major John Gilmour, 'B' Squadron, 2nd F&FY

Everywhere young men were watching the daily fluctuations of the international situation in the newspaper, as they pondered what to do for the best. First it was war, then no war, then war again. It was difficult to know what to do for the best, but many of them took the plunge.

> I met various friends, chaps, who all went about together, went to house parties together, went with the girls together, sometimes went on short holidays together. During this time there was always this threat in the air about Hitler and Nazism. In 1938 when it came to the Munich Crisis there was a big sigh of relief – there was going to be no war. But I'm afraid we were a bit brighter than that in those days – we kind of saw through people like Neville Chamberlain and we decided there was definitely going to be a war. I don't know why we decided this. We hummed and hawed about what we should do – and finally on 26 April 1939 the whole bunch of us joined the territorials. We were just asked our name and address and who your parents were, were you interested in the army and did you have any ideas of about what you would do – things like that. You got a 'health check' by an old doctor, who simply said, 'My God,

you're a fine-looking laddie – I knew your father!' And we were in![7]

Alexander Frederick

Ron Forbes, who was working in the art department of a printing firm in Dundee, had a similar experience when he reported for his medical on volunteering in April 1939.

We had to go for a medical – going to this doctor – Buchanan his name was. I went in and I sat down. He said, 'Your name is Forbes?' I said, 'Yes!' He said, 'I must know your father? Has he got something to do with the TA?' I said, 'Yes!' Then he said, 'How do you feel, do you feel OK?' I said, 'Yes!' 'A1!' So that was the medical! You were A1![8]

Ron Forbes

That April, the recruits were pouring in through the doors of the drill halls. Tommy Wilmott was working as a salesman at Lawsons departmental stores when he signed up to join the HQ Squadron of the 2nd F&FY based at the Thistle Street Drill Hall in Dundee. Willmott was no fool and he wanted to retain some control over his destiny.

We worked it out that we would be far better to join the Territorial Army and therefore avoid conscription. Because if you lived in Dundee the Black Watch was automatic and my father served through the 14–18 War in the Black Watch. Being tall and skinny – and I didn't like the kilt very much – I was determined not to join the Black Watch. What would we join? We found out the Fife and Forfar were doubling up 'A' Squadron in Dundee – we all decided to go up and join.[9]

Tommy Willmott

A few days later Jack Wann, an apprentice architect in Dundee, took the plunge and joined the HQ Squadron. He had no fixed plans, but he knew it was the right time to enlist.

There was an excitement in the air. The thought of war. Your friends were joining. There at the table was a Corporal Jack Knowles, he took my name and address – he was in my class at school, so fine he knew my name – he was a great buddy of mine! The next person was my family doctor, Dr W. E. A. Buchanan, who was also in the territorials, a full colonel in the RAMC. He just looked up and said, 'Jackie, I know you, you're all right!' That was my medical![10]

Jack Wann

Alex Gilchrist also signed up. He was a lively young chap, who had been working in various clerical jobs, but now he was swept away by the friendly blandishments of the tall, well-built figure of Quartermaster Sergeant Nelson Taylor – a former army boxer who had settled in Dundee.

Sergeant Nelson Taylor lived just round the corner from me. I saw him going out in a uniform – and I had the cheek to ask what the hell the uniform was! He told me it was the Fife and Forfar Yeomanry – was I interested in coming along? I said, 'Not really!' He said, 'Oh, it's a wonderful life, you're interested in cars, we've got little tanks, we've got motorbikes, it's just up your street!' Knowing that I had to join something, I decided to go along with Nelson Taylor![11]

Alex Gilchrist

Overall, the recruitment drive proved a great success, and the F&FY claimed a record second only to the London Scottish across the whole of Britain for the numbers signed up. The new recruits' training focused round the weekly drill night. Here they learnt basic foot drill, the time-honoured foundation of military discipline. At this stage, the differences between the two regiments – the 1st F&FY and 2nd F&FY – were blurred. Except for a few old stagers, almost everyone was 'new'.

To the recruits it seemed as if some drill instructors shouted, some shouted a lot, and some never stopped shouting. Once they had mastered drill, then the brighter ones were moved on to signalling, while a lucky few got to start familiarising themselves on the Vickers machine gun or learning to drive. In a mechanised 'cavalry' regiment there was a demand for a large number of drivers, but at this time very few had driving licences. At the weekend they would go to the Annsmuir camping grounds near the town of Ladybank. Here, Alex Gilchrist found himself giving instruction in driving the Mark VIB tank and Daimler Steyr armoured car.

> We had one or two vehicles; I don't know where they came from! There was two Mark VIB light tanks, with a Meadows engine in it, I was interested in that. A driver, wireless operator/ gunner and a commander. Beautiful to drive – the thing with driving a car, you had to watch where you went, but for the first time in my life you got the thrill of going over bracken and everything else with tracks. We used to take these chaps out to teach them to drive on these things. Also, a Daimler Steyr armoured car, it could drive backwards at the same speed as forward. I used to get to drive this thing! I thought it was great fun – it always amused me to think, if you were going into battle one way, and things didn't go right you turned the seat round and drove back the other way.[12]
>
> Trooper Alex Gilchrist, HQ Squadron, 2nd F&FY

With such a paucity of vehicles to train on, and the pressing shortage of qualified – or unqualified – instructors, this was very much a work in progress.

In July 1939, both the 1st and 2nd F&FY went on their annual camp to the Waitwith Lines at Catterick. Here, many of the recruits spent a great deal of time learning how to drive, but given the unimpressive nature of their tanks there was also considerable discussion among the ranks as to the nature of the armoured opponents they might encounter in action if and when the 'real' war broke out.

We were told not to worry about all those massed German tanks that you saw in the Gaumont British News, the Pathé News in the cinemas, they were all made of wood. Some of us thought they must be because our fathers had told us they'd thumped the Germans in 1918 and there was nothing left in Germany – and they couldn't possibly have built all those things up again. We were a wee bit innocent of the capabilities of Herr Krupp and his vast machinery plants in the Ruhr.[13]

Trooper Alexander Frederick, 'B' Squadron, 1st F&FY

Despite it all, the camp served an important function. It bound them together and for the very first time the 2nd F&FY could gain a sense of their own identity. Not just as the isolated squadrons, but as a single entity.

That camp was the real binding together of the regiment, it made us proud of this semi-Fred Karno-type army we were in at that time! It made us proud to be in the Fife and Forfar.[14]

Trooper Jack Wann, HQ Squadron, 2nd F&FY

3

TINY STEPS

I was actually shooting with a friend of my father's: the butler came out with lunch, with the announcement that the Germans had gone into Poland that morning, the 1st of September. I finished my day's shooting and then motored home and reported to the Kirkcaldy drill hall in my uniform the next morning. That was it![1]

Second Lieutenant Douglas Hutchison, 'C' Squadron, 2nd F&FY

MOBILISATION FOR WAR came in stages. From mid August 1939 it was evident that war was unavoidable, and the territorial key parties were called up on 25 August. It was their job to carry out all the multifarious administrative tasks in preparation for the influx of soldiers when full mobilisation was triggered. The main body was mobilised on Friday 1 September. All over Fife and Forfar men reported as quickly as possible to their drill halls: 'A' Squadron in St Andrews, 'B' Squadron at Dunfermline, 'C' Squadron at Kirkcaldy and the HQ at Dundee. One of their first jobs the next day was to sandbag the façade of the drill hall. Various scares in the inter-war years had led to a popular acceptance of the disturbing idea that the 'bomber must always get through', causing unimaginable destruction. Consequently, air raid defence and emergency schemes naturally took priority. It was certainly hard work.

Our job was filling sandbags down at Broughty Ferry beach. Taken down by truck with haversack rations – and we filled sandbags, and filled sandbags, and filled more sandbags! Further along were the corporation workers filling sandbags – and we were rather peeved because we were on two shillings a day and we knew they were getting more doing exactly the same job as we were doing. It grated just that wee bit! I think we shifted half of Broughty Ferry beach. If you put too much in, you couldn't lift the damn thing! It strengthened us![2]

Trooper Jack Wann, HQ Squadron, 2nd F&FY

Most of the men and the officers were billeted at their own homes during that first week. It is worth remembering that for the first couple of days after mobilisation they were still in an artificial state of peace – a kind of strange vacuum. Everyone thought they knew what was going to happen, but the formalities of declarations of war had yet to be observed. A few optimistic souls even thought that perhaps it would all blow over – after all, it had during the Munich Crisis in 1938.

One of those waiting eagerly to find out what was happening was James Dowie, who had been called up from his work as a linen mill weaver to report to 'B' Squadron at the Campbell Street Drill Hall in Dunfermline.

John Gilmour, the officer commanding 'B' Squadron, he said, 'We'll go into our office now and we'll listen to the Prime Minister Neville Chamberlain. This will determine whether it's going to be peace or war, but I have no doubt it will be the latter!' Of course, he was right. Chamberlain said, 'I've had no communication from the German Chancellor Herr Hitler, and therefore a state of war now exists between Britain and Germany'. And a corporal fell in a dead faint at my feet! Then another, oldish chap, he started to cry, because he'd been in with the Fife and Forfar Yeomanry in the First World War, and now his son – who was 18 – was in it. That was the emotion he had thinking of his son going to war. I said, 'My God, this is great this! One chap falls in a faint and the other one's crying!' I was quite happy; we were young and silly at that time! 'Oh, this is great, we'll be going to Paris, we'll meet the Mademoiselles!' Nobody envisioned a long war.[3]

Trooper James Dowie, 'B' Squadron, 2nd F&FY

Military training began in earnest with early priority given to route marching to raise basic fitness levels. There was also trench digging and work assisting in the local farmers' harvest to help toughen up any of those men who may have been unused to hard physical labour in their civilian lives.

In those early days, the problems must have seemed almost overwhelming. The unit as recruited consisted of eighteen officers and 393 other ranks. But not all proved to be fit for service. The rushed and inadequate medicals undertaken during the enlistment process now came back to haunt them. Properly conducted medicals revealed several undiagnosed cases of tuberculosis, all of which had to be discharged. Then there were numerous problems with the accommodation, as the men moved into hastily improvised billets. As an example, when 'B' Squadron moved into tannery billets in Dunfermline, they found they were overrun with a biblical plague of rats. In addition, not all the officers coped that well with the numerous practical challenges they faced. Increased contact after call-up meant that the men also got a close look at their officers – and sometimes did not think much of what they saw.

On 1 October, the 1st F&FY moved south to Beaumont Barracks at Aldershot, prior to deployment as the recce regiment with the 51st (Highland) Division which was to join the British Expeditionary Force fighting the 'Phoney War' in France in January 1940. This proved a blessing for the 2nd F&FY as it freed up space in the drill halls for the 'junior' regiment and allowed them to move into some of the better billets which had now been vacated. Although 'B' Squadron remained at Dunfermline, 'A' Squadron moved from St Andrews to Cupar, while the HQ Squadron from Dundee moved to join 'C' Squadron at

Kirkcaldy. Here they moved into the Adam Smith Hall, which was soon filled to the brim with soldiers' beds. They were not there long, but there was plenty of time for two idiots to arouse the wrath of the imposing figure of the newly arrived Regimental Sergeant Major Jones.

> Two of my friends, Willie Fenwick and Arthur Schofield had their heads shaved – completely! They did this just for sheer devilment. Until their hair grew again, they had to wear their berets at all times! Arthur Schofield was lying in the next bed to me in the Adam Smith's hall and that evening the number of people who came along to see Arthur's head of no hair – I couldn't get to sleep – everybody came along and lifted his beret up to see his head! He was a wild one Arthur![4]
>
> Trooper Jack Wann, HQ Squadron, 2nd F&FY

During this period, the 2nd F&FY managed to miss a famous event in the skies above their home counties. On 16 October 1939, the Luftwaffe launched the first ever raid of the war over Britain when German bombers struck at the Forth Bridge and the Royal Navy base of Rosyth close by. It was carried out by some twelve Junker 88 bombers. On arrival over the Firth of Forth they dropped some bombs, missing three Royal Navy warships, but getting close to the Forth rail bridge. Anti-aircraft guns engaged them to little effect, but then Spitfires intercepted with some success. But all this drama went right over the heads of the 2nd F&FY, as despite all the excitement, hardly anyone in the regiment seems to have been aware of the raid; certainly none made much of it in their interviews. Typically, although there had been many air raid sirens sounded during false alarms, during this actual raid all was silent.

*

THE TIME WAS RIGHT to concentrate the regiment in one

locality in the heart of their Fife homeland. In late October, the 'C' and HQ Squadrons moved to Leslie, while 'A' and 'B' Squadrons found new homes just a mile or so away at Markinch. There was considerable amusement that 'B' Squadron, under the command of the patrician figure of Major John Gilmour, made the journey by train from Dunfermline, whereas the rest endured the pleasure of stiff route marches. This sense of slight injustice was increased when Gilmour's squadron was billeted in relative luxury at Howiegate Hall. More importantly, the regiment was now together at last, able to work on their training and adding in regimental exercises to practise their official role as an anti-invasion force. Although an actual German landing was considered unlikely, there was always the possibility of a German raid on Scotland's vulnerable east coast. Theoretical lines of defence were mapped out, although there was no chance of them taking physical form on the ground at this early stage of the war.

There were continued delays in equipping the squadrons with the required Mark VIBs. In the interim makeshift training measures were adopted which were frankly surreal.

Tank training was laughable. It was practically non-existent! We were taken down to spare ground near the gasworks in Leslie. We ran around in groups of three: one person was the tank driver, one was the tank commander, and the third was the gunner. You had two groups of three people on the right and left 'wings', and the third group was 'centre half' as it were. Supposedly 'two tanks up and one behind'. We ran around without tanks, without vehicles, but we were a 'tank' and the troop commander shouted orders to the tank commanders – waved flags! And we all veered to the right; or veered to the left. To make it more interesting we had anti-tank gunners, who lay down on the ground and said, 'BANG! BANG! BANG!' You hoped your 'tank' was put out of action so that you could all sit down and enjoy a smoke. It may sound farcical, it *was* farcical to look at, but it did teach us that you were dependent on the other two people. That you were getting some sort of drill so that when you did get a tank, you would know what to do.[5]

Trooper Jack Wann, HQ Squadron, 2nd F&FY

At last some deliveries of tanks began to trickle in. The Vickers Armstrong Mark VIB light tank was not a serious weapon of war in 1939, but it was the only tank then available to the British Army. It had been a success when employed in policing the outer reaches of the Empire, but it was inappropriate for a continental modern war. However, there were no medium or heavy tanks ready for production. Tanks cannot be 'magicked up' off the drawing board and the cupboard was bare. All they had were a thousand Mark VIBs that had been produced between 1936 and 1939. It was not an imposing tank, about 13 feet long, 7 feet wide and just over 7 feet tall. Sadly, the armour was a negligible, 4–15mm in thickness, which provided minimal protection for its three-man crew. It was armed with one .303 Vickers and one .5 Vickers gun.

During this period there were several false alarms that the Germans were launching an invasion, however unlikely that may have been. At first there was little effective response that could have been mounted. When at last a few more tanks, Bren gun carriers and a couple of Rolls Royce armoured cars had been gathered together, Colonel 'Sandy' McIntosh decided to test the battle readiness of his all-unsuspecting men. In great secrecy an 'emergency' turnout was planned. With no advance notice whatsoever, the regiment was awoken early one cold December morning to hear that a German invasion was 'on'. The men's reactions were splendidly varied, ranging from the excited yet determined, to the – rightly – incredulous. 'Most were merely sleepy.'[6]

Their training intensified. More and more men were taught to drive, either on lorries, the Mark VIB, or the Bren gun carriers that had begun to arrive. Men were sent on maintenance and fitters' courses, to ensure that they could keep their vehicles on the road as far as possible. Some were lucky enough to be selected for motorcycle training and became dispatch riders (Don-Rs) used to maintain communications and police convoy moves. Then, of course, there was always more drill, PT, weapons training, route marches and guard duties to keep the men occupied.

The officers' mess was located in Leslie. In the main they seem to have been a pleasant but somewhat eccentric grouping of individuals.

> We had a mess there, where I lived, a house called 'Flubbers'. It was all right, rather fun. The married officers tended to stay at home and appeared during the day. We made ourselves as comfortable as possible – with reasonable success. The mess bills were fairly low. On a day-to-day basis it was very friendly and quite informal in the mess. I used to play bridge with Fergus MacIntyre after dinner. No standoffishness about rank. We had mess nights where we wore blue patrols, otherwise we were wearing service dress.[7]
>
> Second Lieutenant Douglas Hutchison, 'C' Squadron, 2nd F&FY

Major Fergus MacIntyre, the son of an Episcopalian minister from Perth, was the unit's second in command and generally considered a cosy old bachelor. He did not cut a very soldierly appearance as he was heavily built – the eternal euphemism for fat. He was popular, but his role was difficult to discern, in fact he seems to have been 'kept out of the way' for the most part. Stories abounded of his cheerful insouciance in the face of high command.

> When the regiment was in camp near Barry in Forfarshire it was warned to prepare for inspection by some general. Fergus having been told to make himself scarce went off with an NCO and a Lewis gun, ostensibly to undergo a little instruction in the sand hills. It being a fine day, the general decided to take a ride. He was somewhat surprised to come across an officer asleep in the dunes with a Lewis gun pointing to heaven. Fergus having

been prodded awake, the general demanded what he was doing. 'Well, since you ask,' Fergus replied, 'we're hiding from you!'[8]

Second Lieutenant Jo Grimond, 'B' Squadron, Fife & Forfar Yeomanry

Jo Grimond himself was something of a character. Already an aspiring Liberal politician, he had been 'biding his time' training as a barrister in London after a privileged education at Eton and Oxford. Three days before the outbreak of war he had – in his own words – been 'smuggled' into the Fife & Forfar Yeomanry by dint of the influence of his brother-in-law, Brigadier William Black, who had previously commanded the regiment. Grimond found that his public school education had not equipped him for some of the challenges of military life. As a quiet, fairly studious type, he needed a great deal of help.

I was, as are most amateur commissioned officers, largely dependent upon NCOs. At one time in the Fife and Forfar Yeomanry my troop sergeant was a Sergeant [Bob]Wann. Sergeant Wann had been a farm servant. Wann was splendidly organised. Everything was done in the right order. He knew where every tool was to be found and when found they were in apple pie order. It was a pleasure to see him doing anything. Our tanks at night were covered with large and heavy tarpaulins. I never could fold them. Wann, even in a high wind, would fold them as though they were handkerchiefs. He never had a classical education but for economy of effort and logical marshalling of what he had to do, no classicist could beat him. He had worked with horses and had been a ploughman at one time. Perhaps the routine of feeding, watering and grooming horses, the need to understand their characters and capabilities, the pride in them, and the care of their harness, had made Wann the even-tempered, skilled and economical worker that he was. My father, who was meticulously neat, never had a classical education. I suspect that some discipline other than the classics should be taught to most boys.[9]

Second Lieutenant Jo Grimond, 'B' Squadron, Fife & Forfar Yeomanry

Alex Gilchrist certainly found Grimond to be a quite remark-
able individual.

> Jo Grimond was a most peculiar fellow, a distinguished looking
> man, but he couldn't wear a uniform at all because he looked so
> awkward in it. Jo went off on a gas [training] course and [when]
> he came back he had to go round each squadron. He stood up
> and he said:
>
> *If you have a funny feeling and a smell of musty hay,*
> *You can bet your bottom dollar that there's phosgene on the way.*
> *If for garlic or for oranges you've a cultivated taste,*
> *If you smell this in wartime, please leave the area in haste.*
>
> I can see Jo standing up reciting this thing. He was a
> character![10]
>
> Trooper Alex Gilchrist, HQ Squadron, 2nd F&FY

This was the common perception of Grimond – as Ron Forbes
would testify.

> His batman said he was the slovenliest officer he'd ever worked
> with. You know how your beret is pulled down at the side, well
> Jo's was like a big dumpling! He never pulled it down, he just
> stuck it on. He was slovenly, but he was such a nice man![11]
>
> Trooper Ron Forbes, 4 Troop, 'B' Squadron, 2nd F&FY

Collectively the officers, NCOs and men were learning. They
were by no means ready for war, but they were improving fast.
Then, in the depths of winter, they found they were bound for
the land of a Scotsman's oldest enemy – England!

*

ON 18 JANUARY 1940 the 2nd F&FY found themselves *en route*
for Beaumont Cavalry Barracks in Aldershot, which they took
over from their comrades in the 1st F&FY who were on their

way to France with 51st (Highland) Division. The barracks was totally unfit for the accommodation of troops.

> Beaumont Barracks had been condemned for years before the war, they just never got around to demolishing it – when the war came along it was needed! It was a Victorian cavalry barracks, so that all the stables were underneath the living accommodation. The floors were all tar pitch, so if you swept the floor you raised a cloud of black dust! Very often everybody had a sort of black around their mouth. It was an ancient place. That was where we were introduced to the three biscuits. Previously you had a straw mattress on your bed, but this time you got these three square hard padded things that you put on your bed – not very comfortable![12]
>
> Trooper Ron Forbes, HQ Squadron, 2nd F&FY

The barracks were not really that old, having been built in the late 1850s; but the freezing cold weather certainly exposed the many inadequacies of military plumbing. On the more positive side, they were now getting a full complement of Mark VIBs topped up with a fair number of the Bren gun carriers.

> Each squadron had two troops of Mark VIBs, I had one of those, and four troops of Bren gun carriers. We were supposed to be divisional 'cavalry'. They later evolved into what they called a reconnaissance regiment for the infantry divisions. The Mark VI were pretty useless tanks. They had a sort of co-axially mounted heavy machine gun, very light armour and were pretty unreliable mechanically. They were unimpressive. We always lagged behind the Germans in our tank design; I don't know why that should be. The Bren gun carriers were a bit more reliable, but you couldn't be impressed by a Bren gun carrier! You had a little bit of protection from ordinary bullets, but that was all. You had one Bren gun, which you dismounted to fire; the others had rifles.[13]
>
> Second Lieutenant Douglas Hutchison, 'C' Squadron, 2nd F&FY

The regiment were only at Aldershot for a few weeks, but one strange discovery was the talk of the regiment for many years. The severe weather prompted the rapid erosion of the coal stores in the barracks cellars. Then, suddenly, Colonel McIntosh got an urgent summons – a cannibalised tank had been discovered in the coal cellar. Everything of any use had been stripped off and the skeleton remains had been buried under mounds of coal. Many of the regiment thought this was just an old wives' tale, but I interviewed some who remembered it well.

> We heard about it when it happened – and we saw it. I think it was a Mark II or Mark I, it was one of the old tanks. But you could hardly recognise it; it was just a shell by the time they'd found it. It was treated like a mystery – it was an exhibition piece! There were all sorts of stories went around about how somebody had lost their tank on training and somebody else had hid it in the coal cellar and covered it with coal. This cellar must have been filled with coal before we arrived, and it was only by us using it that it was revealed. I saw it![14]
>
> Trooper Ron Forbes, HQ Squadron, 2nd F&FY

Among the other witnesses was Harold Brown, previously an apprentice moulder at the steel foundry, whose father had been a groom to John Gilmour on his Montrave Estate in Levan. After joining the army, Harold followed in his father's footsteps and was acting as Gilmour's batman.

> I saw it! It was in a coal store – it must have been an old gun carriage shed. The coal had been thrown over this tank – which apparently had been 'cannibalised'. It wasn't one of the 1st Regiment's – the previous unit had dumped it – according to the 1st Regiment anyway![15]
>
> Trooper Harold Brown, 'B' Squadron, 2nd F&FY

There is no unanimity as to what the tank actually was or who had been guilty of leaving it. Dark rumours swirled around that it had belonged to the 1st F&FY, but the balance of likelihood was that it had been there for years.

*

ON 16 FEBRUARY 1940, to the great relief of all, the regiment moved to billets in the nearby villages of Farnham and Runfold. It may have been only two to three miles away, but it made a world of difference to the men. They were in comfortable billets and far from both the glowering disapproval of the military police and the pugilistic menace of the Black Watch and Highland Light Infantry. As in Scotland, they had an anti-invasion role, but it had shrunk to carrying out regular anti-parachutist patrols along the road running along the spine of the Hog's Back Ridge that stretched for some 10 miles between Farnham and Guildford as part of the North Downs. However, their main priority remained armoured-car training, which gained momentum as the weather improved, and they readied themselves for a possible deployment as the 'divisional cavalry' with the 9th Highland Division, on active service in France. The troops carried out regular exercises in the local woods and on the North Downs ridges, practising the recce role they would be expected to fulfil in France.

As part of the preparations most of the 'under-19s' were posted away to other units which were not intended for imminent deployment. To replace them came drafts of older recruits. As might be expected, many of these new arrivals were English.

> From then onward it was a continuing process as recruits came in: they tended to be more English than Scottish – simply because there are more people in England. It was inevitable – and a very good thing too. In the First World War when they had these appalling casualties and people were all recruited in the same place you got great lumps of people being killed from small towns of villages at the same time. At least that was

mitigated to some extent. Right up to the end the Scottish nucleus in the regiment was dominant – but not aggressively so. I think we were a very happy regiment.[16]

Second Lieutenant Douglas Hutchison, 'C' Squadron, 2nd F&FY

There was naturally – this was the British Army – a great deal of banter between the English and the Scots. But it was mostly all in fun.

The first batch of English fellers arrived at Farnham. They arrived there – we got on with them very well. I remember a chap I couldn't make out what the hell he was saying! He was a cockney! You'd hear the odd, 'You're a bloody Englishman!' But all in good fun. There was never any real resentment against them. They seemed to mix in very, very well, to accept us all right. They got into the thing and joined in with us![17]

Lance Corporal Alex Gilchrist, HQ Squadron, 2nd F&FY

In truth, they were never really regarded as interlopers as they blended almost seamlessly into the unit.

Yet even as the regiment was approaching the 'start line', the whole world was changing around them. On 10 May, the 'Phoney War' came to a crunching end when the full might of the German 'Blitzkrieg' broke on Gort's Army. The combination of tanks, mobile infantry and screaming Stuka dive-bombers seemed to revolutionise warfare. Neither the British nor their French allies were able to withstand it. As the Germans crashed through and round the Allies' lines, Jo Grimond and many others were in a state of shock as they pored over depressing newspaper reports.

Places familiar from previous wars cropped up in the news, Sedan, Arras, Mons. The German advance was unbelievable. Surely it would be stopped! Or was it possible that the Nazis had sparked off a new era in which the old countries of the west would be annihilated? That it was alarming was undeniable. Alarming is too mild a word, it hit one in the pit of the stomach. It was not a simple fear of military defeat. As far as I remember the feeling was compounded of several fears, one ingredient in the shock we suffered was a fear that the Nazis with all their cruelty and imbecilities might be the harbingers of a new politic destined to rule Europe. We had watched corruption and despair wax in the politics of France, while clarity of purpose waned in our own. Democracy seemed to have grown distracted and feeble. Might the Nazis, like the Goths or the Moslems, be the scimitar which could cut through the floundering politics of the West? Had they not the 'unconquerable will and study of revenge, immortal hate'? But no one contemplated surrender. This was not heroism but simply that there was no reason for it. Britain still seemed to have troops and guns, birds sang, larks and British aeroplanes flew overhead. The collapse of France shattered the dream on which our superiors had fed us: the invincible French Army and the impregnable Maginot Line.[18]

Second Lieutenant Jo Grimond, 'B' Squadron, Fife & Forfar Yeomanry

Many of the officers and men of the 2nd F&FY had hopes – or fears – that they might soon be deployed overseas to help stop the rot – to France, Belgium, or even Norway. But it was not to be. Troops were not going out to the fray; they were coming back home as fast as the Royal Navy could evacuate them. There was literally nothing the 2nd F&FY could do to help. Dunkirk was a marvel, but it was also a cataclysmic defeat. All they could do was stiffen their resolve, attend diligently to their training, and wait for the time when it was their turn to face this terrifying Nazi war machine. They little knew how long that would be.

*

WHATEVER THEY HOPED OR FEARED might happen, the British Army managed to surprise the men of the 2nd F&FY

when, without any warning, they were posted to Dungannon in Northern Ireland in June 1940. No one had predicted this; indeed, the regiment were preparing themselves to go for a firing camp at Linney Head in Pembrokeshire. The news came smothered with an all-too-transparent veil of secrecy.

> I was duty officer one night, because we were always on stand-by at nights in case of invasion. A man arrived on a motorcycle with a message which said, 'Prepare to move to unknown destination at 24-hours' notice!' And underneath it said, 'Copy to Northern Ireland District, Belfast!' Which rather gave it away![19]
>
> Major Sir John Gilmour, 'B' Squadron, 2nd F&FY

This triggered the usual mad rush of preparations before they departed by a combination of road and rail to Stranraer. By 22 June, most of the men of the 2nd F&FY were aboard a train bound for the delights of Dungannon in County Tyrone. The train was heavily overladen with all their goods and chattels; indeed it proved to be too much for the struggling locomotive in the final stretch from Coalisland to Dungannon. There were repeated failures to make the climb, culminating in one classic comic moment when the driver was seen soundly thrashing the side of the engine with his hammer. Eventually another engine was dispatched to help them up the hill.

There had been some speculation as to how they would be received by the local inhabitants. As it happened, they needn't have worried, as was evident right from the start.

> We got quite a surprise when the first civilian we met had a tray of coffee cups, biscuits and things! The ice was broken – we never looked back after that. If you didn't turn up each night for tea, they came up looking for you! At 2 o'clock in the morning you might be on guard and walking about – and suddenly a civilian would appear with a flask of coffee. They just looked after us. We had so many friends in Northern Ireland.
>
> Trooper Ron Forbes, HQ Squadron, 2nd F&FY

The men of the regiment were a real 'hit' in Dungannon. Families soon invited them into their homes and treated them like part of the family.

> Excellent – I had four houses I could go to! We used to get
> lovely suppers and things like that. Some of the boys even used
> to take their equipment to the houses – and sometimes the
> daughter would blanco your equipment and polish up your
> brasses for you![20]
>
> Trooper James Dowie, 'B' Squadron, 2nd F&FY

The officers' mess was set up in a house called Killymeal. They had been warned that there might be a threat or open hostility from local members of the Irish Republican Army (IRA), or their sympathisers, but all seemed calm. The neighbouring pubs were a great attraction to young officers of the regiment. In the bar they even found themselves mingling at close quarters with the members of the IRA.

> The subalterns discovered, much to their delight, that the
> licensing laws in Ireland were entirely different from what they
> are in England. We were making full use of this! There was a
> very nice barman there – he was a keen member of the IRA!
> Dungannon was very much a mixed community – about half-
> and-half Protestant and Catholic. With quite a strong IRA
> contingent. I don't think we regarded it as very serious, but all
> weapons and rifles had to be chained up when they weren't being
> handled, so that they couldn't be stolen very easily. But one wasn't
> aware of unpleasantness. There was one remark I remember very
> well which brought me up with a jolt. I used to buy my cigarettes
> from a little shop, this fellow, he was a nationalist, said to me,
> 'You know, I was talking to my wife this morning and saying
> to her there's a very nice lot of boys in your regiment, I was just
> saying we do hope your side wins!' It shows the remoteness.[21]
>
> Second Lieutenant Douglas Hutchison, 'C' Squadron, 2nd F&FY

The locals also bestowed upon Hutchison a nickname that seemed so apposite that for the rest of his life he never lost it.

'Pinkie', that came from when we were stationed out in Ireland. The daughter of the house, she started calling me 'Pinkie' – a fresh-faced young man – so that became my regimental name and people from the general downwards would call me 'Pinkie' to my face! The men called me, 'Sir!' But they referred to me as 'Pinkie'.[22]

Second Lieutenant Douglas Hutchison, 'C' Squadron, 2nd F&FY

At times, the officers would even mingle with their own soldiers – after all, as a territorial unit they had often known each other in civilian life. This did not always end well for the men concerned.

We had been in the hotel Dan Wherry's, playing snooker. Coming downstairs, the officers were all in the cocktail bar – they introduced us to 'Very Lights' a drink where the liquor is lit on top. The idea is to drink this while the flame is still going up! We stood there drinking with them, we were all having our go at these 'Very Lights'. When we got back to the billets in Dungannon, the sergeant major, standing outside, put us all on a charge, because we were late! We'd been drinking with the officers. The following morning, we were up in front of Major Powell. We were put on 'pack drill'![23]

Trooper Jack Wann, HQ Squadron, 2nd F&FY

Major John Powell (pronounced Pole) had been a rowing blue for Cambridge in the team that had triumphed in the 1935 university boat race. By this time, he was in command of HQ Squadron, a quietly efficient officer who proved a popular figure in the regiment – with whom he was universally known as 'Joe' as a sign of affection. He tended to speak 'man to man' and although he was reasonably strict, he was considered fair – always an important consideration with soldiers.

Having got to Ireland, the question was why on earth had the regiment been detached from the 9th (Highland) Division and sent there? What were they meant to be doing?

> Our role was to rush down to wherever the Germans landed and sweep them back into the sea! Trouble is our Mark VIBs would never have got there I shouldn't think – they would have all broken down. Some of the Bren carriers would have got there I dare say, but it would be a long way to drive to get down there presuming they landed in County Wexford or something like that! I couldn't for the life of me see why the Germans should want to come via Ireland when they would have a double jump to get at England.[24]
>
> Second Lieutenant Douglas Hutchison, 'C' Squadron, 2nd F&FY

Possibly the most valuable action carried out by the unit against the Germans came as a result of a commendable initiative by some junior ranks.

> About four of us used to go down to Dublin by train in civilian clothes. We used to walk past the German Embassy and do 'V-Signs' to the Germans on guard! [25]
>
> Lance Corporal Alex Gilchrist, HQ, Squadron, 2nd F&FY

Given such a nonsensical role, the regiment busied itself with training. There was a great deal of concentration on good map reading – always useful when patrolling in a border area if embarrassing diplomatic incidents were to be avoided. Convoy driving and drills were practised relentlessly, until map reading and wireless control became second nature. Firing ranges were organised so they could practise with the feeble armaments they possessed on the Mark VIB and Bren gun carrier, but at least they were showing willing. Tactical exercises and battle drills tested their potential response to a landing by German parachutists and various other equally unlikely emergencies. More prosaically, they were dispatched on a series of route marches – a pastime that was rarely popular in an armoured unit, but it was all a matter of instilling a basic level of fitness in all of the men, ready for the trials that lay ahead of them.

In December 1940, the 2nd F&FY lost their colonel: Lieutenant Colonel 'Sandy' McIntosh had raised the regiment, and few could imagine him leaving. However, he was also seen to have done well by those in higher authority. He was consequently promoted to full colonel and dispatched as second in command of the 27th Armoured Brigade, before a further posting to take over a secret special reconnaissance unit, the GHQ Liaison Regiment – appropriately known as 'PHANTOM'. His departure left the somewhat hapless figure of Major Fergus MacIntyre in charge, pending the appointment of a new colonel.

This was combined with the news that the 2nd F&FY were to leave their new 'home' at Dungannon on 19 December. This somewhat insensitive timing created considerable ructions with the local inhabitants, who collectively had spared no effort in organising Christmas celebrations for the soldiers in their midst. Irate telegrams were dispatched by local dignitaries to the highest in the land.

> There were big objections in the town, everybody had their plans for parties and things. They wrote to Winston Churchill and some member of his staff answered and said they couldn't do anything about it, but when we got to Bessbrook and Christmas time came over, he would see that the maximum amount of weekend leave was given to the regiment. So, every taxi and bus was commandeered in Newry to go up to Dungannon for Christmas.[26]

Trooper Ron Forbes, HQ Squadron, 2nd F&FY

The 2nd F&FY duly moved to their new billets in the village of Bessbrook in County Armagh. Bessbrook had the appearance of a 'model' village, but the Nissen huts occupied by the regiment were not popular. Overall, Bessbrook was nowhere near as welcoming to them as the good folk of Dungannon had been. The soldiers were taken aback by the levels of religious bigotry and sheer venomous hatred that existed between the Protestant and Catholic communities.

> I got to know a family called Smith very, very, well, and I just about lived there! I went in one day and I thought, 'Things are very chilly in here!' I said to the lady of the house, 'Have I done something to offend you, because I'd hate to think I'd done that!' She said, 'Well, I saw you speaking to Mrs Black!' I said, 'Yes, because one of my friends goes to Mrs Black's. What's wrong with that?' 'They're Catholics!' 'So what, they're just like you and I, ordinary people!' 'Oh, but we don't talk to Catholics!' Bessbrook, it's a lovely little village, beautiful, but I have never met such bigotry in all my life.[27]
>
> Trooper Leslie Gibson, HQ Squadron, 2nd F&FY

Many of the men preferred to spend their recreational time in the livelier environs of the neighbouring town of Newry.

In January 1941 there were several changes among the officers. Most important was the arrival of the new commanding officer in the form of Lieutenant Colonel Edward Sword, formerly of the 13/18th Hussars. For a dyed-in-the-wool regular officer like Sword, replacing a popular territorial officer with deep local roots was always going to be a difficult task, not helped by his slightly phlegmatic and aloof manner, based, some thought, on an underlying shyness – although one must beware of amateur psychology. His harsher critics thought Sword was overly concerned by 'bull' and lacked intelligence. For some unknown reasons, he 'took against' Joe Powell and replaced him with Major Robert Bruce in command of HQ Squadron, which did not increase his popularity among the officers. At around the same time Jo Grimond's organisational talents had been recognised and he was swiftly spirited away to be a junior staff officer at the headquarters of the 53rd (Welsh) Division.

Winter storms had badly disrupted training, but tactical schemes resumed with the spring, though even as they polished and refined their reconnaissance role, the ground was moving beneath their feet. It had been decided that the 2nd F&FY should be converted into an armoured regiment, which meant a move back to England. Their Ireland sojourn was at an end.

WHY ARE WE WAITING?

We were told we were leaving Ireland and going to Yorkshire.
We then discovered at the same time that we were giving up
being a divisional cavalry regiment as a reconnaissance regiment
for a division to become part of an armoured brigade. When
we arrived in Whitby, we became part of the 29th Armoured
Brigade. We got a Valentine tank, which was a British made
tank, made in Leeds.[1]

Major Sir John Gilmour, 'B' Squadron, 2nd F&FY

THE 2ND F&FY MOVED LOCK, STOCK AND BARREL to
England on 5 July 1941. The seaside town of Whitby in Yorkshire was their new home from home. Any hopes or fears of an
immediate active service deployment were thwarted or allayed
by this change, as it meant that in effect their training would
have to start again almost from scratch in their new role, with
new weapons of war – a mixture of Valentine and Matilda tanks.
They little knew at this point that this training would carry
on for a further three long years. The whole 29th Armoured
Brigade was centred around Whitby (the 23rd Hussars, 24th
Lancers, 2nd F&FY – all newly formed wartime regiments –
and the motorised infantry of the 8th Rifle Brigade); the 30th
Armoured Brigade gathered at Helmsley (22nd Dragoons, 2nd
Lothian and Border Yeomanry, 2nd County of London Yeo-
manry and the 12th King's Royal Rifle Brigade), while the 11th

Support Group was located at Malton (13th Regiment, Royal Horse Artillery, 75th Anti-Tank Regiment, Royal Artillery, 58th Light Anti-Aircraft Regiment, Royal Artillery and the 12th Green Howards). These units, plus the armoured cars of the 27th Lancers and various ancillary units, together formed the 11th Armoured Division, a relatively new formation only created in December 1940. In all they would deploy some 350 tanks, and three motorised battalions of infantry. They were commanded by Major General Percy Hobart.

Percy Hobart was an inspired but controversial choice as divisional commander. Born in 1885, he passed through the Royal Military Academy, Woolwich, before being commissioned into the Royal Engineers. He served in pre-war India then saw active service in the Mesopotamia campaign and Waziristan. After attending Staff College in Camberley in 1920, he became convinced that the future lay with armoured warfare, and in 1923 he transferred to the Royal Tank Corps. In 1934, he would become the brigadier in command of the first ever permanent British armoured brigade and develop his own theories of the practice of armoured warfare. However, although clearly a competent soldier, Hobart had acquired the reputation of being 'difficult' – characterised by both his unconventionality and an evil temper. He was prone to expressing his views abruptly and with a wounding level of insubordination, which led to several prolonged 'feuds' with senior officers which would return to haunt him. After a period as Inspector Royal Tank Corps, he took on increasingly high-profile staff positions, before in 1938 being dispatched to form and train the Mobile Force (Egypt), which on the outbreak of war would mutate into the 7th Armoured Division. However, a series of disputes with high command meant that he was shuffled off into premature retirement early in 1940. His reaction was to join the newly formed local defence volunteers as a lance corporal. As the Blitzkrieg raged in France and the Low Countries in May 1940, Britain's foremost expert in tank warfare was busy preparing for the defence of his home town of Chipping Campden.

In August 1940, the journalist Basil Liddell Hart had begun a press campaign against the decision to retire Hobart, which reached the ears of Prime Minister Winston Churchill. Despite opposition from General Sir John Dill, the Chief of the Imperial General Staff, Hobart was re-enlisted and posted to the 11th Armoured Division in 1941. He soon made his mark. Although not always in good health, he had energy and commitment to spare, driving his division onwards and upwards to attain new heights of efficiency following the usual pattern of training in the British Army: individual training, then small-scale troop exercises, building up to squadron, regimental and divisional exercises.

The 'A', 'B' and 'C' Squadrons were equipped with the new Valentine tanks, although a few of the Matildas were issued to the Headquarter troops of each squadron. The Valentine was a typical British tank of the period in that it was designed in a rush by Vickers-Armstrong as a stopgap when the British finally realised, with war looming, that they lacked any medium tanks. Manufactured in haste from 1939 onwards, the first version was delivered in May 1940. On the plus side, it was good-looking tank, a bit quicker than the Matilda, quite spacious and comfortable for the three-man crew. It also had reasonable armour protection, at least by the standards of the early war, although it was soon overtaken by more modern designs. Best of all, it was very mechanically reliable. The big negative was the totally inadequate 40mm (2-pounder) gun, which left it out-ranged and out-punched by its German contemporaries. Yet compared to the visibly obsolescent Mark VIB, the Valentine was a 'real' tank. It exuded, at least to the uninitiated, an image of untrammelled power. Ron Forbes was posted as a Valentine driver and he was excited at the prospect.

> There's something about driving a tank – you feel as if you've got a powerful vehicle under you! On these schemes you were driving over rough ground – and it was like being on the big dipper sometimes – I just enjoyed it. They were good to drive –

you were on your own – you didn't have a co-driver. You were
sitting in the middle of the tank. Your view was fairly restricted
– as it always is in a tank! You just had your two levers, your
gear lever, your accelerator. Only a 2-pounder gun and Besa
machine guns. Useless as far as a modern weapon goes – against
the stuff the Germans had they were useless.[2]

Trooper Ron Forbes, 4 Troop, 'B' Squadron, 2nd F&FY

That summer the 2nd F&FY were all kept busy training in their
new roles. Individual skills had to be acquired and thoroughly
mastered. Then the Valentine commanders, gunners and drivers
had to mould themselves into efficient tank crews, working
together as a seamless whole. It wasn't just 'tank battles'; they
also had to practise going into laager at night where they could
be resupplied. Wireless training was given particular emphasis
as the 'remote' control of armoured formations in battle was of
particular concern to General Hobart.

*

AUTUMN BROUGHT A RECKONING. In early September they
attended a nine-day firing camp at Pembroke Ranges, where the
overall standard was poor, although one 'B' Squadron gunner
excelled to such an extent he reputedly got the highest score in
the whole 11th Armoured Division. Their progress through the
whole training regime was being closely monitored by the commander of the 29th Armoured Brigade, Brigadier Chris Peto, a
Great War veteran, who served with great distinction in France
in 1940 as commander of the 9th Queen's Royal Lancers until he
was badly wounded in the right hand. Peto blended his evident
military abilities with a wry sense of humour. Above him was
the ever-restless eye of Percy Hobart, committed to driving his
division to new heights. After a series of small-scale exercises on
the Yorkshire Moors, the annual training peaked in October
1941, with the eponymous Exercise Percy.

We did some wonderful schemes, and I became aware of what it was like to go into battle. We were properly organised. We were taking commands coming down the chain of command. When the umpires told you your tank had been knocked out because you had taken up a silly position of the moors, when you should have gone 'hull down' so that the tank commander could see but they couldn't see you – when the umpire came along and said, 'You're out – you're killed!', for the first time you began to realise what it was all about.[3]

Sergeant Alex Gilchrist, HQ Squadron, 2nd F&FY

However, overall the 2nd F&FY did not shine on Exercise Percy and as a result, shortly afterwards both Lieutenant Colonel Edward Sword and his second in command, Major Fergus MacIntyre, were abruptly 'moved on'. Douglas Hutchison explains the brutal truth of what had happened.

Brigadier Chris Peto had commanded the 9th Lancers in 1st Armoured Division. Shot in the hand – still visible scars. Didn't think much of Colonel Edward Sword. We did a lot of training on the Yorkshire Moors, which weren't very suitable for tanks; we were always getting the tanks bogged on the soft moors. An autumn exercise was a pretty average shambles, and it finally decided Chris Peto that Edward Sword had got to go – that he was not in control of the situation. MacIntyre went at about the same time, because quite frankly he would have been fortyish at that time and he wasn't really sufficiently militarily competent to be second in command of a regiment – after all that means he should be fit to command! From then on he was in administrative jobs in the army.[4]

Lieutenant Douglas Hutchison, 'C' Squadron, 2nd F&FY

In October 1941, Lieutenant Colonel George Cooper, who had previously been on the staff at the divisional headquarters, took over command of the 2nd F&FY. Cooper was another regular officer, a big man, over 6 feet tall and an ex-army boxing champion, which had left him with a distinctive damaged nose. He proved a real character, as he had also been a pre-war racing driver and would race about in his Humber staff car – indeed he was arrested for speeding! Cooper was a strict disciplinarian, who brought in guardsmen instructors to improve the standard of the regiment's discipline and drill, but he was nevertheless popular with the men, who appreciated his idiosyncrasies. Fergus MacIntyre was replaced as second in command by Major George Trotter, formerly of the Scots Greys, who proved to be of somewhat limited ability, while unlike MacIntyre, he was hampered by a lack of the social skills that might have made him popular. He was somewhat aristocratic in nature and some of the junior officers considered he only 'accepted' them rather as he 'accepted' household servants in his home.

Bigger changes were afoot as the whole of the 11th Armoured Division was recast and reorganised to reflect the lessons learnt up to that point in the North African campaign. It had become evident that the format of the existing armoured divisions was not suitable for the multitude of roles they might have to carry out. More armoured divisions were needed, but there needed to be a change in their composition. The Germans had already reduced the armoured element within their panzer divisions and the British followed suit. More infantry was needed close at hand to deal with any strong German defensive positions that might bar their way, or to establish bridgeheads across rivers. And far more artillery was needed, as it was increasingly realised that concentrated artillery fire was the real key to a control of the battlefield. As a result, the 30th Armoured Brigade was dispatched to form the nucleus of a new armoured division and a whole new lorried infantry brigade, the 159th Brigade (3rd Monmouthshire Regiment, 4th King's Shropshire Light Infantry and 1st Herefordshire Regiment) was added – they had previously been with the 53rd (Welsh) Division. The Support Group was disbanded with the departure of the Green Howards to pastures new and the formation of a more powerful divisional artillery with the addition of the 151st Field Regiment (Ayrshire Yeomanry) Royal Artillery.

*

IN MAY 1942, THE 2ND F&FY MOVED SOUTH to Hove and Stanmer Park in Sussex, taking over the billets of the 8th Armoured Division which had been sent to the Middle East. They were gradually being re-equipped with the Crusader cruiser tank, another typically British series of tank design compromises. It represented one step forward and two steps back from the Valentine. As a 'cruiser' it was certainly faster, but it had even thinner armour, and still had only the 2-pounder 'pop' gun as a main armament, although some 6-pounder versions did begin to appear later that summer. The fact that it was far less mechanically reliable really put the cap on it! Nevertheless, the regiment simply had to make the best of it. They also received some of the Covenanter tanks which were even less prepossessing, and indeed which were eventually classified as unfit for overseas active service and only to be used for training purposes.

The regiment was based in Sussex to undergo a continuous programme of armoured brigade and divisional training all across the South Downs. Not only were they training as a tank regiment, but also practising their liaison with the infantry, artillery and recce regiments. The officers were encouraged to get to know each other, not only as fellow professionals, but also to develop friendships that would bind them together in the 'bad times' in action against the Germans. Much of this was not apparent to the ordinary soldiers. It culminated in the fourteen-day extravaganza of Exercise Tiger, the creation of Lieutenant General Bernard Montgomery of South Eastern Command. It was the largest exercise held in Britain up to that date and involved over 100,000 troops, stretching its tentacles all across southern England. It was a hard rations exercise where the troops were forbidden to supplement their basic rations by purchasing food from local shops or farmers. By the end of these exercises there was a growing confidence that they were at last ready for deployment to the 'shooting war'. Yet still no active service seemed to be on the horizon for the 2nd F&FY – or indeed for the rest of the 11th Armoured Division.

*

FROM AROUND THIS TIME in the history of the regiment, the number of English drafts began to swell rapidly. This triggered quite a lot of good-natured humour, for most of the Scots in the unit were quite prepared to accept such reinforcements as a necessary 'evil'.

> Gradually we were getting more English influences coming into the ranks! A few English officers had come into the regiment. I never had any problems with them at all. We were becoming, instead of 90 per cent Scottish, we were becoming about 60 per cent Scottish to 40 per cent, it didn't matter to me at all, as long as they were good chaps.[5]

> Sergeant Alex Gilchrist, HQ Squadron, 2nd F&FY

One of the many new arrivals was Geoff Hayward, an insurance clerk who had been working in London and Harpenden before he volunteered to join up in June 1941. After lengthy training as a fitter and motor mechanic he was posted to the workshops attached to the HQ Squadron. It was a rude awakening for the quiet and somewhat reserved Hayward.

> In the workshops, apart from one chap, they were all Scottish. All very much in it right from the start, 1939. I thought they were quite a wild crowd, probably because of the Scottish accent, some of which I couldn't understand at the time – and the frequent swearing that took place. It was more powerful than the swearing we'd heard at Catterick Camp! A lot of 'effing' and 'blinding', that sort of thing. It was the frequency

with which the swearing went on that I had to get used to! Which I did eventually, although I didn't indulge in it much! I think they found me a bit strange at first – another 'Sassenach' I suppose they would call me. Some of them were quite friendly, but when it came to an 'issue' they would all support each other and leave you high and dry. It was difficult to integrate at first. I didn't feel part of the 'family'.[6]

Trooper Geoff Hayward, HQ Squadron, 2nd F&FY

In August 1942, the 2nd F&FY moved into a proper Nissen hutted camp at Fornham All Saints in Suffolk, where they were blessed with concrete roadways and a proper hardstanding area for the tanks. It now seemed clear that they were ready to be mobilised for an active service deployment.

By this time, some of the original Scottish NCOs were being considered for a commission after a further brief training at an officers' cadet training unit. One such was Alex Gilchrist, who found they had to go through a rigorous selection process, which may cause a wry smile to those who recall how the pre-war officers of the F&FY were chosen.

John Powell was the first one to say, 'I'm sure you should take a commission!' Then I saw Colonel Cooper, 'I think you'd make a bloody good officer! But that's up to you whether you want to do it or not!' He sent me off to a two-day interview. Two of us went. We were tested on our initiative, you had to think what you would do on a certain occasion. Four of you in a group, one had to become a leader and you had to cross a 'river'. This was assessing as to your potential as an officer. I was told I would very shortly be picked to go to Officer Training Corps. I was sorry in many ways because I was leaving so many of my friends. But nevertheless, I felt that I would like to be an officer – quite frankly without being conceited – I felt I knew a bloody sight more than half the young officers who had been posted to the regiment. I felt I could do the job as well or better![7]

Squadron Quartermaster Sergeant Alex Gilchrist, HQ Squadron, 2nd F&FY

Gilchrist went off to attend the Royal Military College, Sand-hurst, and in May 1943 was commissioned into the 12th Lancers. As some of the Scots departed, more and more English drafts came flooding in, including Roy Vallance, who came from Suffolk but had worked as a printer in London pre-war. He was initially posted as a spare crew member to 'A' Squadron. It would become his 'home' but this was not immediately obvious.

> They were all Scotsmen, there were very few Sassenach
> members there at all. I was the only English chap in my troop!
> So, life was quite difficult! I didn't know what they were saying
> half the time! I hadn't heard many Scotsmen talking in my
> young life then. They seemed to talk very rapidly, and they
> had a lot of slang which I'd never been acquainted with. They
> seemed to not really welcome Sassenachs! Naturally, my leg was
> pulled a bit! Quite friendly, provided you take it with a smile
> on your face![8]
>
> Trooper Roy Vallance, 4 Troop, 'A' Squadron, 2nd F&FY

*

BY LATE 1942, it was thought that the 11th Armoured Division would be sent out as a reinforcement to North Africa. As there were still some questions over Percy Hobart's state of health, he found himself under pressure from his many 'enemies' at the War Office, who said he could not possibly cope with the physi-cal demands of active service. Churchill once again intervened, and although Hobart would have to leave the 11th Armoured Division, he was assigned to raise and train the 79th Armoured Division. His replacement in command of 11th Armoured Divi-sion was Major General Montagu Burrows, who had served with the 5th Inniskilling Dragoons and been a POW in the Great War before serving with the North Russia Expeditionary Force. A true 'all-rounder', he had even played cricket for Surrey County Cricket Club in the 1920s, had held various instructional and staff postings and was for a period the military attaché in Rome. Since the outbreak of war, he had had some valuable experience when commanding the 9th Armoured Division. The appointment of this new commander seemed to be a final indication that the division were 'on their way' to war. There were several other changes afoot in the high command. Thus Brigadier Chris Peto moved from the 29th Armoured Brigade, to be replaced by Brigadier Otho Prior-Palmer, who had served with the 9th Lancers during and after the Great War. In 1940, Prior-Palmer had been given command of the 2nd Northamptonshire Yeomanry, then had a brief interregnum in command of the 30th Armoured Brigade.

On 16 September, the regiment – and indeed all the units in the 11th Armoured Division – were given the long-expected orders to mobilise. Everyone presumed the moment of truth was upon them. But, despite this mobilisation and all the preceding changes in divisional and brigade command, with all the intensive training preparations for posting overseas, it was once again not to be. Once mobilised, all they did was pay another visit to the firing camp at Linney Head, after which they returned to Fornham All Saints. To many of the men this was getting beyond a joke, others were secretly pleased that their war could wait a while yet.

In mid October 1942, instead of North Africa, they moved to Chippenham Camp near Newmarket. On 20 October, the 2nd F&FY got their new commanding officer with the arrival of Colonel Alec Scott, previously of the 5/6th Inniskilling Dragoon Guards. Scott was considered an intelligent officer, although he was slow to make up his mind while he assessed the situation. Yet he was still more than capable of making decisions and taking firm action when required. His personality was perhaps dogged by a slight shyness, as some of his men considered him not to be a 'mixer' and overly conscious of his rank.

Another of the new officers attached to the regiment who joined at this time was Charlie Workman. Originating from

Glasgow, Workman had been working as a law apprentice before serving as a ranker with a searchlight battery. His officer potential had been recognised and he was commissioned into the Royal Armoured Corps after attending Sandhurst. Here he learnt not only the tactical and technical requirements for being an officer, but had also been inculcated with the universal qualities expected from all British officers. At the end of the course, he had to pick a unit and decided to take a commission into the F&FY. His welcome was slightly eccentric and in some ways was a reminder of the pre-war regime.

> I was wheeled in to meet Alec Scott, the colonel. His first words were, 'Well, welcome to the regiment, you've had a long journey, have a drink!' I drew myself up and said, 'I don't drink, colonel!' I saw a little smile – I wonder how long this will last! 'Oh,' he said, 'have tea or something!' I was then posted to 'C' Squadron. Alastair Nairn, who was the squadron leader, and he said, 'Do you ride?' I said, 'No!' and he said, 'Well, what are you doing here?' 'Well, I'm interested in the horses in that engine!' I didn't take it amiss, one of the great things about Sandhurst was that it gave you a terrific self-assurance – I reckon I could have run the army by this time![9]
>
> Second Lieutenant Charlie Workman, 1 Troop, 'C' Squadron, 2nd F&FY

He was posted to command 1 Troop, 'C' Squadron, where he was under Nairn's watchful eye.

> The more I got to know Alastair Nairn the more I admired him. He had estates up in the north and he was a great deer hunter. Most of the men came from Nairn's Linoleum. They knew him. I think he was a fairly hard man; I wouldn't say he was a Yorkshire mill owner, but he was that kind of type! I've never known anybody read a map like him, never. He was very, very efficient. 'What is the task for the day?' There was no such thing as nothing to do! Every squadron had a big board up that said, 'The task for the day is'. It could either be domestic, or it

could be technical. 'Has every man got an extra pair of socks?
Has every man got a proper pair of gym shoes? Has every man
got a clean spare shirt? Have you inspected the gun? Have you
checked that you have all the ammunition? Have you checked
every man has his sidearms? Have you checked every man has
cleaned his sidearms?'[10]

Second Lieutenant Charlie Workman, 1 Troop, 'C' Squadron, 2nd F&FY

Perhaps even more important was the influence of Workman's
senior NCOs within his troop. They had far more practical
experience and guile than any callow young officer, wet behind
the ears and fresh out of Sandhurst.

My two sergeants, Christie and Hutton, were both real 'Fifers'.
A Scotsman who is a 'Fifer' is a particular brand, rather like an
Englishmen would regard a Yorkshireman: a sort of craggy type
with a very particular approach to life? Both of them had been
in the Fife and Forfar Yeomanry for years. They were older than
I was. I could see when they got on a tank, and the way they
handled their tanks, that these guys knew what was what. We
were out in a wood and I was in my tent and I heard Christie
say to wee Hughie Hutton, 'Oh, where's that young Charlie
fellow, he's a new officer, aye we'll have to train him – same as
the rest!' I don't think tact is a feature of a 'Fifer'. They are not
into tact; they are into blunt truth.[11]

Second Lieutenant Charlie Workman, 1 Troop, 'C' Squadron, 2nd F&FY

*

THE CHIPPENHAM CAMP LAY in the parkland of a country
house, within which the officers were billeted. For the men, the
rows of grim identikit Nissen huts were hardly a home from
home.

That camp sticks out in my memory because it was infested
with rats. These Nissen huts were built with a double 'skin'.

They had two layers of corrugated iron and there was a gap between them, probably for insulation purposes. The rats could live in that space. At first we didn't realise this, until one night, one fellow woke up in his bed, having left a bar of chocolate under his pillow and he woke up with a almighty scream – woke us all up – switched his torch on and found there was a rat in his bed! Climbed up the post of the bed. That wasn't very nice! We learnt the lesson that you mustn't leave anything eatable in your bed! For a sport we used to sit on the messroom tables with our legs dangling, with a suitable brick or stone in our hands, waiting for the rats to pop up in the crevices – then we'd all let fly! [12]

Trooper Geoff Hayward, HQ Squadron, 2nd F&FY

Training was now just more of the same.

More and more English drafts were joining the 2nd F&FY at Chippenham, one of whom was Len Newman, previously a junior clerk with a telephone cable manufacturer from Eastleigh. Posted in as an electrical fitter, he soon felt that he fitted in.

It was the first unit I'd ever been in the army where you had a sense of belonging. It was like a big family. They'd been together since before the war: there was a load of Scottish fellows there, the originals; there was a load of people who had joined up and gone straight to them and never been anywhere else. They'd been together and there was a real community feeling there. You felt you belonged to something; you didn't feel you were just 'tacked on'. We were all working together, and we all worked with each other. The other people who joined us who came from other regiments, they said exactly the same thing. It was a different feeling in the Fife and Forfar Yeomanry; there was a family feeling. [13]

Trooper Len Newman, 'B' Squadron, 2nd F&FY

One fairly difficult-minded new recruit was John Gray, who had worked in a Co-operative store in London. Gray was a convinced

Labour Party activist who had imbibed left-wing views from his trade union activist father, indeed he had been encouraged by him to be a conscientious objector based on his experiences in the Great War. However, Gray put aside this option when he was called up himself, although things did not go as he planned.

I got a card inviting me to join His Majesty's Armed Forces. I went to the Labour Exchange, with this card, was given a medical, and you were asked what service you what like to go into! I said, 'I would like to go in the Navy! If I can't go in the Navy, I'll go in the Air Force, I'll even go as a rear gunner! But if I have to go in the Army I don't want to go in the tanks!' The fear I had all the time – of burning to death! That was what frightened me! Where did I finish up! If I had said, 'Please put me in the tanks – I would have been in the Navy as a cook or something!'[14]

Trooper John Gray, 2nd F&FY (Doesn't know first squadron)

He was posted in as a gunner/mechanic and was happy enough with the reception he received on arrival at Chippenham.

They were quite decent to you. You were just somebody else that was going to take a seat in a tank – and that was it! We were among the first English that were going to go in. The problem was they'd all come from Scotland, around Cupar and Fife, where the Scots language was fairly broad. It was difficult to understand them! You'd get an instruction over the radio and sometimes you hadn't got the foggiest idea what they were talking about! Like everything else in the army, you soon learnt.[15]

Trooper John Gray, 2nd F&FY

Although he was obviously a bright lad, Gray had no desire for promotion and had deliberately failed an interview for a possible commission while with his training regiment.

I didn't want to become an officer. I didn't want any kind of rank! I was too much of a human being, I think! In other words, I didn't want any responsibility. Although I might get killed myself, because of some other stupid bugger, there was no way I was going to get anyone else killed giving him instructions – it was never in me! I didn't want to get killed; I wanted to stay alive. I wanted a nice quiet life in the army! That was me![16]

Trooper John Gray, 2nd F&FY

Another new English arrival was Jack Edwards, from Droylsden in Manchester, who before the war was working as a laboratory assistant testing and producing dyes at Courtaulds, then switched to factory work in the manufacture of camouflage nets and machine-gun belts. After training as a gunner and wireless operator he was sent to join the 2nd F&FY at Chippenham. Like many of the English, he found much merriment in the thorny question of porridge: to salt or not to salt, that was the question.

The first morning I walked into the mess hall, it was porridge the first course. This chap ladled some nice thick porridge on to my plate – I thought, 'That looks nice!' He says, 'Do you want some more?' 'Oh, please!' He gave me some more. When I tasted it, it was salty! I'd never had salted porridge! Anyway I ate it – and was glad of it! I got used to their salted porridge.[17]

Trooper Jack Edwards, 4 Troop, 'B' Squadron, 2nd F&FY

Then a few Welshmen arrived to join the regiment. Of these, the one who made the most dramatic initial impact was Len Harkins, the son of a horse dealer and farmer from Pontypridd. Harkins had boxed as a middleweight and had been in frequent but minor trouble with police – mainly for fighting, which was something he clearly enjoyed.

I got put on a charge before I even signed in – I laughed, that's all! We got there as they were mounting the guard and there was a man on guard with the biggest head in the British Army. We didn't have the old helmets, we had the same helmets as the paratroopers, no brim, they came straight down over. I can see him now – ginger head! The biggest head and the smallest tin hat in the British Army I reckon on his head – it looked like Laurel and Hardy – stuck on top! I started to laugh, and I got put on 'fizzer' before I'd even been signed in! All the bagpipes playing! I said, 'Some handy mob this is!' A voice came out, 'If you don't like it you know what to do – get out!' And then it came to fighting talk and I said, 'Well fair enough, there's plenty of room outside, let's go out!' He said, 'No, you're good enough for us!'[18]

Trooper Len Harkins, 'A' Squadron, 2nd F&FY

Scottish, English or Welsh, they all began to mould together as a unit. Real, or imagined, grievances were gradually smoothed out as they realised that they had far more in common than the minor cultural differences that divided them.

*

TRAINING, TRAINING, TRAINING – it never seemed to end. Gradually the scale of the exercises built up once again from troop to squadron, to regiment, until the whole of the 29th Armoured Brigade was manoeuvring under the direction of Brigadier Otho Prior-Palmer.

Chippenham, if you look at a map, you're lucky if you get a 15-foot contour. It was all very flat. The whole brigade was there, and it was very, very impressive to see three regiments of tanks milling around. I wasn't into criticising. I was new to tanks and I was loving it – I thought it was great. When the regiment was moving off, the tank crew would assemble in front of their tanks on the tank park. Then the order would be given, 'Mount!' It was done as a drill and everyone leapt into the tank. Then the order, 'Start up!' Then the CO would hold his hand up and say: 'The order of march will be 'A' Squadron, Regimental HQ, then 'B' and 'C' Squadrons follow!' Everyone would turn and move. The noise, the roar of the engines revving, it really was quite something.[19]

Second Lieutenant Charlie Workman, 1 Troop, 'C' Squadron, 2nd F&FY

The exercises were as realistic as they could manage and there was often scant respect paid to local farmers' crops and fences.

Attack such and such a village, the opposing enemy will be another regiment. You were given an indication of where they were – and their idea was to ambush you. That meant reading a map! Am I in a valley? What do I find across the hill? You literally went where you wanted to go – if that meant knocking down a wall and planting yourself in the middle of a corn field – that's precisely what you did. At that stage you didn't have to respect walls.[20]

Second Lieutenant Charlie Workman, 1 Troop, 'C' Squadron, 2nd F&FY

There were however moments of great comedy value, normally triggered by the wireless system, which demanded extreme care if individual wireless operators and tank commanders were not accidentally to broadcast their ribald comments over the air to the whole regiment.

Coming back in from an exercise, the whole regiment was on the net and the CO came over the air to the squadron leaders and said, 'Practise picking up targets on the way back – to practise the gunners!' Then you heard 'A' Squadron leader telling his squadron to do this, 'B' Squadron, 'C' Squadron, a very lengthy business. Then at the end you heard a Scottish voice come over saying, 'Swing the effing turret round a bit Jock, the silly old bastard wants us to practise gunnery!' The commander, thinking he was speaking on the intercom, was speaking on the 'A' set, which everybody heard! The air was blue from the colonel after that![21]

Trooper Roy Vallance, 4 Troop, 'A' Squadron, 2nd F&FY

Then came the news that their long wait was over. After a series of frustrations, they were informed that they would be leaving on 22 February 1943. Parties of men were sent on embarkation leave and then the tanks were dispatched to Glasgow ready for the long voyage on transport ships to the Middle East. The 2nd F&FY were on their way to war – at last.

> It was the first time we had put these tanks on the low-loaders on the train. There was only about half an inch on either side from the tracks to the edge of the loaders. And we were doing this at night. It wasn't funny – it was very difficult for the drivers. The tanks were all loaded, and all went away from Chippenham, except about eighty of us in the rear party to tidy up. We were all ready to go and some of the tanks were already aboard a ship in Glasgow.[22]
>
> Lance Sergeant Jack Wann, Recce Troop, HQ Squadron, 2nd F&FY

The 'A' and 'B' echelon lorries and support vehicles were also on their way to Glasgow.

> I moved the 'soft' vehicles up from Chippenham. We stopped at Doncaster and it was then pretty obvious we were going north to Glasgow. Then we were turned back! The tanks actually went on the ship. Well according to the brigadier we were disappointed, but I don't think the men were all that disappointed. He gave us seven days leave to let us do what we wanted to 'hide' our disappointment![23]
>
> Trooper Leslie Gibson, AA Troop, HQ Squadron, 2nd F&FY

Although the regimental historian refers to the regiment as 'subsiding like a deflated balloon',[24] the men were far more ambivalent.

> You did feel unwanted! A bit annoyed. We always said they were keeping the Fife and Forfar to 'bull up' the tanks and drive into Berlin! These are the sort of thoughts that went through your mind. Why was it that four years after we were mobilised that we'd never got into any action at all? Personally, I was quite

happy! I'd have been quite happy driving round the Yorkshire Moors for the whole of the war! I'm not one of these types bursting to win a VC![25]

Trooper Ron Forbes, 4 Troop, 'B' Squadron, 2nd F&FY

The question has to be put: did they really want to get into action? My view is that, one way or another, these men had joined the army and they needed a concrete collective purpose to justify the endless training. They may not have sought a desperate series of battles against crack German troops, but they were willing to play their part in the war against Hitler.

Everybody was getting bored with the continuous training, doing the same thing over and over again. There was some rejoicing at the idea of going overseas. Especially when they found it was the Middle East, where the campaign was going quite well for us at that time. We thought, 'Oh well, that's a good point to go out there!' I was quite looking forward to doing something different. Only vaguely nervous. I think they'd trained us up to the extent that everybody had got a certain amount of confidence that we were going to do the right thing and be on the winning side. We didn't mind the idea of going into action as a regiment – it was something novel, new and exciting![26]

Trooper Geoff Hayward, HQ Squadron, 2nd F&FY

What had happened? Why was the deployment cancelled? In fact, it wasn't a vendetta against the 2nd F&FY, it was a change in policy as regards the whole 11th Armoured Division. They had indeed been intended for North Africa, but the fighting in Tunisia in early 1943 had indicated that what was really needed in that theatre of war was more infantry, and not another armoured division. The decision had been taken late, far too late, with the result that some advance parties of men had actually left and were soon swallowed up by other units to replace casualties suffered in Tunisia.

Whatever the reason for the cancellation, Colonel Alec Scott and all his officers now had to face up to the realisation that they were not going to be deployed overseas any time soon. For James Dowie, a serious soldier, it was not enough. He had had enough training and had the commitment to demand a posting to a unit that would guarantee him active service as soon as possible.

> I volunteered for overseas service. I got an interview with Sir John Gilmour and said, 'I would like to be put on draft, Sir!' He said, 'Are you a bloody fool, Dowie? You're [serving] beside your own people from Dunfermline and you want to leave here?' 'Well, Sir, I think there's a war on and we've been training all these years, and I think we're grossly over trained. I feel I want to do what I joined up to do and take part in this war. We're always going abroad and going abroad – and we've never been sent abroad! I would like to go abroad, Sir!' 'Well, we don't want discontented people here!'[27]
>
> Trooper James Dowie, 'B' Squadron, 2nd F&FY

Dowie was soon on a draft to Algiers where he served with the 142nd (Suffolk) Regiment, Royal Armoured Corps first in Tunisia and then in Italy from 1943 to 1945.

The majority of the men had to settle down to a return to routine training. But more and more men were beginning to wonder: what was the point of it all? In such circumstances their minds could easily begin to 'wander' into non-military pursuits.

> We were pretty fully trained and apart from some big exercises it was a job to know what to do with us all the time! We had a competition to see who could produce the best garden around their Nissen hut. They would give us some food and send you off as a tank crew for three days. The only stipulation was you weren't to live in a house! We went to a farm near Cambridge and lived in a barn! We'd go down to Cambridge and have a punt on the river. Silly things like that to pass the time away.[28]
>
> Trooper Roy Vallance, 4 Troop, 'A' Squadron, 2nd F&FY

One almost unnoticed excitement was the arrival of a couple of the American General Sherman M4 medium tanks, better known as the Sherman. This, it turned out, would be their real future.

5

SHERMAN TRAINING

It was a lovely feeling to see this tank, which we thought was the 'be all and end all' of tanks. The novelty of it was something as well. We thought this was something new and something grand! The thickness of the turret, the engines, everything was so different from any British design.[1]

Trooper Ron Forbes, 4 Troop, 'B' Squadron, 2nd F&FY

IN MID JUNE 1943, THE 2ND F&FY MOVED once again in their seemingly never-ending tour of Britain. This time they settled in a camp just outside Rudston, a small village some five miles from Bridlington in north Yorkshire. Once again, they were in the Nissen huts. But the really important change was the arrival of a full complement of Sherman tanks. Any tank is always a compromise as the designer strives to attain a balance of the desirable, but incompatible, concepts of firepower, armour protection, speed, manoeuvrability and mechanical reliability. The British had got themselves into a state of confusion in their twin desires for a fast cruiser tank with anti-tank armour-piercing (AP) firepower and a heavier infantry close-support tank with heavy armour and a high explosive (HE) shell compatible gun. However, some, including Montgomery, based on his experiences in the Western Desert, did not see the need for such a dichotomy and demanded a single tank capable of fulfilling both roles – and saw the mechanically reliable American

Sherman M4 with the 75mm dual purpose gun as the nearest thing to that 'ideal' then available. He considered the British-designed Churchill tanks designed for an infantry close-support role to be too slow for an exploitation role. Unfortunately, the Sherman fell between the two stools: the armour was rather too thin for a true infantry close-support role, while in any tank versus tank duel, it ended up being both under-gunned and under-armoured in comparison to the rather more 'complete' new German tanks such as the Panther and Tiger. But this was all in the future for the 2nd F&FY. As they gathered round their new Shermans the overall reaction was positive.

> The Crusaders went, and we got the new American Sherman tanks. We had one or two per squadron and we all did training on them. Our first impression was that it was a giant tank – much bigger than what we'd had in the past. For a start, the crew was five and it was very high to climb up on until one got used to it. It was very modern looking compared with our old Crusaders, more streamlined and smoother lines. The 75mm gun looked much, much more powerful than the old 2-pounders we had been used to, with a co-axial Browning .30 and a hull Browning .30 in the co-driver's compartment. On the cupola was a .50 machine gun. It had the usual 2-inch bomb thrower in the roof for the smoke. Very comfortable inside, quite spacious, one could stand up quite easily, the seats were adjustable. The engine was a five-bank Chrysler, very reliable.[2]
>
> Trooper Roy Vallance, 4 Troop, 'A' Squadron, 2nd F&FY

It represented a qualitative step forward from the Crusader and many men felt an increased sense of security as they gazed at their new Shermans. It was indeed a 'big beast' more than 8 feet high, weighing in at up to 34 tons, but capable of a reasonable top speed of around 26 miles per hour. The gunners certainly appreciated the destructive potential of the medium velocity 75mm gun which boasted a range of over 10,000 yards and had some genuine hitting power. Certainly, it was a veritable monster compared to the 2-pounder 'popgun' that had equipped the Crusader, Valentine and Matilda. Internally, the Sherman was a spacious and comfortable tank in comparison with the somewhat cramped and functional British tanks they had become accustomed to. As to the 2-inch frontal armour and 1½-inch side-armour – well, Gordon Fidler, who had previously been an electrician's apprentice in Newbury, was one of many blissfully unaware of the penetration capabilities of German guns and who thus felt a sense of real security in his magnificent new tank.

> I felt that being in a tank was marvellous – nobody could get me in here – this is really why I wanted to go into tanks. Nobody would touch me in here. We'd heard of bigger guns, but I could never imagine AP (armour-piercing) shot penetrating a tank. At the beginning I was quite happy to be in a tank regiment because I thought we were immune from being knocked out. I don't think you could imagine an AP shell going through one side – out the other – or setting fire to it.[3]
>
> Trooper Gordon Fidler, 'A' Squadron, 2nd F&FY

Collectively the crew dealt with the day-to-day maintenance of the Sherman, each of them dealing with their own speciality, but helping each other as required on some of the bigger tasks. It was a reliable tank, but like most machines it needed regular tender loving care if it was to give of its best.

Once they had mastered their individual roles and welded together as a crew, they began the usual series of troop and squadron exercises building up to Exercise Blackcock, where they had the pleasure of playing the 'enemy'. They were meant to be realistic, testing not only their military skills, but their endurance levels, so the men were on iron rations in field conditions.

> Blackcock was realistic – they got us all together and they explained that in this exercise we would do exactly what we

would do for real. In other words, if we had to go through a wall, knock down the side of a barn and site our tanks in the middle of a field of wheat, that was precisely what we would do. They explained the maximum damage that could be inflicted by the division – you're talking about two hundred tanks milling around – had been calculated, and they had arranged for that amount of extra food to be brought from America. So that one should have no compunction about putting your tanks where they should be.[4]

Second Lieutenant Charlie Workman, 1 Troop, 'C' Squadron, 2nd F&FY

They were learning all the time, with the older, more experienced officers passing on their knowledge to callow young subalterns.

You refuelled with jerry cans. That was one of the things I learnt from Alastair Nairn. We did a big exercise in Yorkshire, where we had a very tricky navigational problem: we had to move right across country, and I was lead tank. I worked out on the map where we were going, and I did it by my compass. It was getting dark and I took a compass bearing on a tree or a farmhouse, then I took another compass bearing. When the regiment got – successfully – to this place I was very proud of myself – very pleased. Alastair Nairn came up and he said, 'Well done, Charlie, you did very well! Have your tanks been petrolled?' At that moment I was basking – everyone was saying how marvellous I was! He said, 'The first thing you do is make sure your tanks are re-petrolled and re-ammunitioned!' That lesson always stayed with me. The first thing we did when we pulled out of action was fill up and replace any ammunition.[5]

Second Lieutenant Charlie Workman, 1 Troop, 'C' Squadron, 2nd F&FY

Workman was upset when Nairn was subsequently removed from the regiment as a result of a general edict from Montgomery on the need for active service experience among the officers. To him it was an example of the inflexible application of a sound policy as its application meant the ejection of a perfectly good squadron leader.

> Montgomery had taken over and issued an edict that every regiment should get rid of one squadron leader or company commander who hadn't battle experience and replace him with a battle-hardened officer. We had therefore to get rid of one squadron leader – and as Alec Scot and Nairn didn't get on, he replaced him with a chap called Chris Nicholls who came to us from the Staffordshire Yeomanry and was an Eighth Army 'Desert Rat'. Nairn took it very badly. He was the Fife and Forfar Yeomanry, and 'C' Squadron was 'his' squadron, the men almost entirely came from the Nairn linoleum factories in Kirkcaldy. He was almost in tears at the farewell from the squadron when we lined up.[6]

Second Lieutenant Charlie Workman, 1 Troop, 'C' Squadron, 2nd F&FY

Major Chris Nicholls, the replacement, was another excellent officer, and he had acquired considerable experience during the North African campaign. However, some considered that he had perhaps had his fill of war and, while never negative in his attitude, he was considered to be not overly enthusiastic at the prospect of yet more active service.

The 11th Armoured Division were undergoing a series of changes. The most important was in December 1943, with the arrival of a new divisional commander in the form of Major General Philip ('Pip') Roberts. Born in 1906, Roberts was a relatively young and vigorous officer, who after attending Sandhurst had been commissioned into the Royal Tank Corps in 1926. Although only an adjutant of the 6th Royal Tank Regiment when the war broke out, he had rocketed through the ranks and commanded the 22nd Armoured Brigade during the Battle of Alam el Halfa and the Second Battle of El Alamein, before taking over the 26th Armoured Brigade for the Tunisian campaign. After being posted back to Britain, he briefly commanded the 30th Armoured Brigade under Major General Percy Hobart in the 79th Armoured Division. His unparalleled expertise in armoured warfare was recognised by his promotion as acting major general at just 37 years old to command the 11th Armoured Division. The division would be part of VIII Corps, under the command of desert veteran, Lieutenant General Richard O'Connor, freshly returned from a two-year incarceration in an Italian POW camp.

The 29th Armoured Brigade also had a change as Brigadier Charles 'Roscoe' Harvey took over command from Brigadier Otho Prior-Palmer. Roscoe Harvey was commissioned in 1920 into the 10th Royal Hussars, who were then still a horsed cavalry regiment. He devoted much of his time as a subaltern to his stellar career as a jockey, even participating in the Grand National at Aintree. It was then, when riding overweight, he picked up and subsequently adopted the nickname of 'Roscoe' after Roscoe 'Fatty' Arbuckle, the film star of the 1920s. As a mad keen horseman, Roscoe Harvey was initially slow to accept mechanisation, but he soon knuckled under and took to it like a duck to water. He was with his regiment in France in 1940, but then promoted to colonel and later commanded them to great effect in the Western Desert in 1941–2. His 'cavalry dash' was much remarked upon. Promoted again, he commanded first the 4th Light Armoured Brigade, and then the 8th Armoured Brigade during the successful Tunisian campaign. On arriving at the 29th Armoured Brigade, he made his presence felt in no uncertain fashion.

> The first day in my office I was surprised that nobody came to see me, and I told my Brigade Major so. He said, 'Well, Sir, the red light was on outside your door.' I asked him what the hell he meant by a red light. He told me that when the light was on, it meant that the brigadier did not want to be disturbed. So I said, 'You will now smash that red light. Anybody who wants to

visit me can always do so. If for some reason I don't want to see them, I'll tell them to fuck off!'[7]

Brigadier Roscoe Harvey, 29th Armoured Brigade

The battle order of his brigade was slightly juggled as the 3rd Royal Tank Regiment were brought in to replace the 24th Lancers, who had been posted to the 8th Armoured Brigade.

One significant new arrival to join the 2nd F&FY was a young officer who would become the most renowned tank commander the regiment ever produced. William Steel Brownlie was born in Greenock in 1923 and had been educated at the Greenock Academy. As a schoolboy he had falsified his age to join the local defence volunteers on their formation in June 1940, indeed he was even promoted to the dizzy heights of lance corporal – where he found himself giving orders to his science master who was a mere private. He went to study engineering at Glasgow University, where he soon found himself struggling to keep up. It was a 'sandwich course' so he was attached to an engineering factory helping manufacture landing craft. In August 1942, he volunteered to join the Royal Armoured Corps. After the usual basic training he went to Sandhurst and was commissioned as a second lieutenant. Steel Brownlie (he rarely used his first name) was a real live wire, bright and cheerful, with a dry sense of humour. He chose the 2nd F&FY as they were the only Scottish RAC regiment requiring officers at the time. He joined them at Bridlington on 13 February 1944.

I was wheeled in to see the CO, Colonel Alec Scott, who sat at his desk and looked me in the eye for a full minute before saying anything. I looked straight back. At least, that's my version. After all the training and the bullshit, it was great to be in a real regiment. Moreover, everything was aimed at being ready to cross the Channel, as part of 11th Armoured Division, and help put an end to the ghastly war.[8]

Lieutenant William Steel Brownlie, 4 Troop, 'A' Squadron, 2nd F&FY

He tended to be fairly easygoing with his tank crew, usually leaving them to their own devices, although like any good officer he made sure they were 'looked after'. There was a pernicious rumour that he preferred an 'all Scottish' crew: this was believed by some I interviewed and repudiated by others. Whatever the truth of it, he was certainly a proud Scot.

Under this new bevy of commanders, the 2nd F&FY took part in the huge Exercise Eagle, which was designed to be as realistic as possible in recreating active service conditions.

> To toughen us up, there was Exercise Eagle, everyone on half-rations for a fortnight as we manoeuvred over the Yorkshire Wolds. It was nae bother to me; fresh from Sandhurst, but it did accustom everybody to living in a tank day and night. It also taught the value of scrounging, and I often defeated the half-rations notion by going off on a motorbike and bringing back goodies for the troop – like, believe it or not, loaves of bread. Luxury![9]
>
> Lieutenant William Steel Brownlie, 4 Troop, 'A' Squadron, 2nd F&FY

During one of these exercises, James Donovan, from Swanley in Kent, who had been working as a garage fitter at a laundry before being called up, would have good reason to remember the system by which the umpires determined casualties.

> We were sitting in this field, waiting to advance on this scheme. I got out of the tank and was lounging on the front having a smoke. All of a sudden, the umpires who operate these manoeuvres, came flying along in a jeep and threw a thunder flash – that went 'BANG!' and then they came over and said, 'You're wounded!' They put a label on me that I was wounded, and the medics have to come and 'attend' to me. They put dressings on as if you are really wounded to make it all realistic. Then you're put on a stretcher, put in the ambulance, they take you to the field hospital. Ironically enough, on mine they put, 'Injuries to face and damage to nose'. This is a coincidence

because in real action I got my nose blown off! So, the exercise came true in real life for me![10]

Trooper James Donovan, 'B' Squadron, 2nd F&FY

The tanks also went a couple of times to conduct a live firing practice at Kirkcudbrightshire ranges.

We would trundle out to the ranges and pick up Shermans. Either firing inland at old tanks or firing out to sea. It was always envisioned that the tank would be stationary when it was firing, because tanks firing on the move wasn't a very satisfactory set-up. It was a question of judgement and experience by the naked eye as to what you thought the range was. You put down a ranging shot to see how far out you were – usually it would be short of the targets and then you increased. It varied enormously the standard of shooting.[11]

Second Lieutenant Charlie Workman, 1 Troop, 'C' Squadron, 2nd F&FY

Here their gunnery was initially judged to be below the standard required, which prompted some intensive remedial training. As a result, a second live range-firing visit ensued, which was much more successful. During the firing, Jack Edwards was given a first inkling of what lay ahead for so many of them.

One of the Shermans caught fire. Why I don't know – whether it was oil on the engines, lack of cleaning or what, I don't know, but the engine caught fire. They were messing about with fire extinguishers. They couldn't get out of the tank because it was about 18 inches deep in mud everywhere. Another tank ran alongside, and all the crew jumped off. The order was move at least 20 yards away from the burning tank. So, we did. That's when I saw my first brewed up Sherman. All the ammunitions started burning, bursting, exploding – it was a terrible sight. I didn't realise the same sort of thing might happen when a shell came through.[12]

Trooper Jack Edwards, 4 Troop, 'B' Squadron, 2nd F&FY

The regiment also got a number of specialist tanks, some of which proved successful and some not. The most important was the Sherman Firefly variant which had a much more powerful 3-inch calibre gun (the 17-pounder), with a four-man crew as the increased size of the gun left no room for a co-driver. The intention was to provide a gun capable of knocking out the latest German tank designs, but also capable of firing HE shells some 10,000 yards.

> We were equipped with one Sherman Firefly per troop with these 17-pounder guns, which were a very decent gun and just about a match for a Panther's long-barrelled 75mm gun. We had to learn to use those and we went up to ranges in Cumbria – everybody that was going to be involved firing these Firefly guns had the opportunity to fire it.[13]
>
> Captain Douglas Hutchison, 'A' Squadron, 2nd F&FY

A Recce Troop was also formed as part of the Headquarter Squadron. They were equipped with the Honey tank which was the British name for the rather inadequate light tank M3 Stuart, armed with only a 37mm gun and machine guns. Its armour was thin and almost tokenistic. John Gray was one of those posted to a Recce Troop Honey.

> The Honey had a radial Witney-Pratt engine in the back. It used more oil than petrol – it used to leak out – it was something you could never stop. We just kept pouring oil in. It had hydramatic gearbox, an automatic gearbox. The tillers were the same, but you didn't have to change gear on it. You could fix it in third gear, so it didn't go above third. This was vital when you were running away, because if you just left it in normal automatic, as soon as you hit a slope, you'd be down to two to three miles per hour with a German chasing you! We had a crew commander, a wireless operator, a co-driver and a gunner – until they took the turrets off![14]
>
> Trooper John Gray, Recce Troop, HQ Squadron, 2nd F&FY

Slowly but surely the regiment was once again almost ready for the long-overdue active service. The Second Front was surely beckoning.

*

RUDSTON CAMP WAS ADORNED with the rows of Nissen huts set in some woodland clearings. It was here that George Cozens, in civilian life a trainee-chartered surveyor from Willesden, but now reinvented as a sergeant clerk, arrived to join the regiment. He was given an amusing reception.

> I went into the sergeants' huts and I said, 'Can I get a shower?' 'Yes, down there, get a nice hot shower!' I went down there, stripped, had a hot shower, came out – and a very nice chap came out and said, 'Who are you?' I said, 'I'm the sergeant clerk!' He said, 'Oh, well I'm Lieutenant "So and So". You know you're in the officers' quarters!' I said, 'Sorry, I've just been sent here!' It was quite all right! But that was the sort of trick that they naturally played on me as soon as I arrived![15]
>
> Sergeant George Cozens, HQ Squadron, 2nd F&FY

A couple of the squadron officers' messes were originally located in a local pub to their great satisfaction, but the powers that be soon put a stop to that, and they were given a Nissen hut to share between them.

> The 'A' Squadron had a Nissen hut at Rudston in the corner of a nice grass field, which was where we slept and had our mess. We'd learnt how to make ourselves comfortable. There was the most marvellous crop of mushrooms in that field! I used to go out first thing in the morning and collect them – a basket full of mushrooms – without any difficulty. Then regimental headquarters found out about these mushrooms, so sent their mess sergeant out to collect mushrooms – all that meant was I had to get up a bit earlier![16]
>
> Captain Douglas Hutchison, 'A' Squadron, 2nd F&FY

As the weather got worse, the regiment moved into civilian billets in Bridlington for the winter of 1943.

> It was very popular, because the men were billeted in houses. The tanks were just in the street. My troop were in a row of terraced houses. They were pretty basic. What people don't realise about the war is how drab it all was. You couldn't buy paint; nobody went round painting the outside of a house and if they did it was khaki. It was the drabness. If we took over a house and moved in there was no lampshades, naked lights, the carpets had all been moved away. If there was any question of a curtain, it was just a blackout. There was no colour at all. It was a pretty drab outlook.[17]
>
> Second Lieutenant Charlie Workman, 1 Troop, 'C' Squadron, 2nd F&FY

As a seaside holiday resort, there were plenty of recreational facilities even in wartime.

> There was a big dance hall, dancing was a big craze in the country; from the Hammersmith Palais in London to the Locarno in Glasgow. The girls and the men went in – they were great fun – jiving and all that sort of stuff! There was never ever any booze for sale inside these dance halls. What you had to watch was when you put your hat in the cloakroom – they would nick your badge – our badge was very attractive – a man on a horse – that's the Thane of Fife. One of the great things was the cinema, they changed the films every two or three days. All the young blood like myself, we were great boys for going to the cinema. The squadron leaders, who were all living out, would say, 'Well, no gentleman should have dinner before seven!' Now the cinema started at half past six. We wanted dinner at six! Not seven![18]
>
> Second Lieutenant Charlie Workman, 1 Troop, 'C' Squadron, 2nd F&FY

As they moved into 1944, they were well aware that the long-delayed launch of the Second Front in Europe was imminent

– and that as part of the 11th Armoured Division, they would almost certainly be involved. The men were still ambivalent. They were mostly content with their lot at Bridlington, but at the same time they were bored stiff with training; they were also wanting to test their training against the ultimate foe. Overall, there was certainly a willingness to fight if that was the price that had to be paid before they could return to a normal civilian existence.

> There were lots of rumours we were moving. We were quite happy there and we were in no hurry to leave, but at the same time, most of the regiment had been training, training, training since 1939, and the feeling was, 'Well, let's get it over, get it done and get back home!'[19]
>
> Trooper Roy Vallance, HQ Troop, 'A' Squadron, 2nd F&FY

One sure sign of impending death and destruction was a formal visit by George VI in March 1944.

> The king, the queen and the two princesses were coming to inspect us in March. Some chaps trained up as guard of honour at the station – they were going to come by train. We spent a week cleaning the tanks up! Scrubbing all the mud off and painting the new divisional signs on everything – that's where Ron Forbes came in handy, because he was in the troop and he could do these signs a treat! They were due on Friday, and on the Thursday, our squadron was sent out to do some shooting on the ranges. We came in about teatime and the tanks were absolutely covered in mud from the ranges. After tea, everybody turned out, we got stirrup pumps and yard brushes. We had bucket chains from the various houses, some of the civilians were joining in with buckets and supplying water. There was a bloke scrubbing with yard brushes, blokes pumping stirrup pumps! We worked at that till it went dark – all the tanks were lined up in the street. We went to bed with the tanks all scrubbed and washed. We got up next morning, had to put on

all our best battledress and everything on. Went to breakfast and when we looked at the tanks, they'd all dried dirty, streaky dirty. We had to line them up on the main road and the side of the tank that was going to face the road, where the king and queen were going to drive past, we were all rubbing away with bits of cotton waste trying to smarten up the side they were going to see. When they came, they were in the limousine and they just drove slowly past with an escort of Household Cavalry in armoured cars. We all had to stand, and the troop commander saluted as they drove past![20]

Trooper Jack Edwards, 4 Troop, 'B' Squadron, 2nd F&FY

It would be soon. The men of the 2nd F&FY were officially ready for war.

6

ON THEIR WAY AT LAST

I didn't really know what to expect, I'd never been in a war before or anything like that. I was apprehensive. I had a feeling inside myself that I wouldn't come back. I'd just have to take my chance.[1]

Lance Corporal Peter Young, 3 Troop. 'B' Squadron, 2nd F&FY

IN MARCH 1944, IT WAS BACK TO THE FUTURE when the 2nd F&FY once again moved into a cavalry barracks at Aldershot, just as they had in 1940. The only difference was that this time it was the Warburg Barracks. The opening of the Second Front was obviously nigh, but of course they didn't really know where they were going – or when.

Every possible kind of preparation was made, in the knowledge that D-Day was not far off, so much so that I could think of nothing for my troop to do except to get into the tanks and give them another clean-up. Trooper Vallance said that they were as clean as they would ever be – and refused. I couldn't have that, so gave him a direct order. He told me to 'Fuck off!' I couldn't have that either, so put him on a charge. He got seven days confined to barracks. Later, he proved himself as a superb tank commander.[2]

Lieutenant William Steel Brownlie, 4 Troop, 'A' Squadron, 2nd F&FY

As the days went by, a somewhat fevered atmosphere developed.

After a period of wild rumours, they finally got a real clue as to what the future held for them.

> We were issued with French money. We were throwing this money in like confetti playing pontoon. You've never seen so many notes flying about. So, we knew we were going to France! Inside you're a bit nervous. You knew it was going to come sometime, so you were glad it was now – and let's get it over and done with! You were apprehensive, but you also look at your mates next to you and you say to yourself, 'Well, I'm not going to let myself down in front of them!'[3]
>
> Trooper James Donovan, 'B' Squadron, 2nd F&FY

A big clue that it would be soon was the accelerated waterproofing programme for the Shermans, the Honey tanks and all the regimental lorries, halftracks and jeeps, a huge programme that had commenced in May 1944. This was not a popular task.

> The worst thing we were ever put on was when we were waterproofing the tanks. All the engine plates, which amounted to about twelve of different sizes – some of them took two men! All the plates had to be lowered and for each plate there was a gasket. The main thing was Bostik – we were supplied with tubs and tubes of this. When we put it on it hardened. I'm still taking Bostik out of my fingers now! We had weeks and weeks of it![4]
>
> Trooper Gordon Fidler, 4 Troop, 'A' Squadron, 2nd F&FY

Geoff Hayward explained the process in more detail, as by this time he had been posted away from the workshops and was then a co-driver to the Sherman commanded by Lieutenant John Darke of 'B' Squadron. It is evident he was no more enamoured with the whole laborious, sticky, messy process.

> There were two basic ingredients we had to use for the waterproofing. There was a black bitumen-like substance called Bostik, which was difficult to get off your hands – it was a very

messy, sticky product. The basic idea was to seal off all welded joints on the tanks, anywhere where there was a bolt through the metalwork to the interior. You smeared this stuff around very thickly where water might penetrate. You would need several men to do one tank – it would take literally days. You'd start at one end and work through. You started with the outside, then go on to the interior, so you'd do both sides. Some of the places were very difficult to reach. Then there was a kind of sticky material, which was rather thicker in composition, light green in colour, you could almost mould it like plasticine. You could stretch it and mould it, but the idea was to seal off any electrical components and wiring against water penetration. The exhaust had to be dealt with specially, sealed all the way along, but when it came to the tail of the exhaust where it emerged then they had to fit an extra tail-pipe on pointing up into the air, high enough to be poking out of the water. If you'd done the thing properly, you could have the tank swimming in water, and it wouldn't get in anywhere vital to stop the engine working.[5]

Trooper Geoff Hayward, 'B' Squadron, 2nd F&FY

The final touch was to ensure that should they land in a dangerous situation, then they could immediately get rid of enough of the waterproofing to allow the tank to function relatively normally.

We put explosives around the waterproofing of the turret, the gun and the chute over the exhaust. The theory being that if we landed and were opposed, we could blow off the waterproofing that was sealing everything up without getting out – and fight![6]

Trooper Roy Vallance, HQ Troop, 'A' Squadron, 2nd F&FY

*

BARRACK-ROOM CYNICS might scoff, but by this time it was obvious that the 11th Armoured Division – and hence the

2nd F&FY – were destined to take part in the Second Front operations. On 25 May, a party of seventy men had the pleasure of joining an inspection parade for the VIII Corps, at which General Dwight Eisenhower, the Supreme Allied Commander for D-Day operations, gave what the regimental history claims was an inspiring speech. None of the men seemed to remember it. Next, the whole regiment was put on six hours' notice to be ready to move. Final preparations were made, all equipment was checked and any faulty items replaced. They all knew it would be soon, but even though the clock was ticking down that was all they knew. Secrecy was paramount. Facing up to the prospect of going to war for the first time, it is not surprising that many of the men fell into a maudlin or sentimental frame of mind. Some of the old Great War songs were recycled for another generation facing death far from home.

> There was quite a lot of people had quite good singing voices and they'd start singing at the drop of a hat. We knew, although we were never told, we were coming up to D-Day. We were all writing our last letter home. We were very quiet in this billet. Somebody started singing, 'Old Australian Homestead':

In an old Australian homestead
With the roses round the door,
A girl received a letter,
Just newly from the war.
With her mother's arms around her
She gave way to sobs and sighs
For when she read that letter,
The tears came to her eyes.
Why do I weep? Why do I sigh?
My love's asleep so far away.
He played his part that August day
And left my heart in Suvla Bay.

It's a very poignant song about the girl receiving a letter from the war. This went on for a few minutes – then somebody lobbed a boot at him! Which broke the spell![7]

Trooper Doug Hayes, MT Section, 'A' Squadron, 2nd F&FY

There was however no uniform reaction to the imminence of action. For some, anything was better than the endless tedium of training for a war that never seemed to come. And, of course, there was the eternal optimism of youth, confident, as so many young soldiers had been before them, of their own immortality.

Why would you be nervous? It wasn't going to happen to you! The fellow sitting next to you – yes! But it wasn't going to happen to you! I think we all felt like that.[8]

Trooper John Gray, Recce Troop, HQ Squadron, 2nd F&FY

Then, on 6 June, came the news that D-Day had finally dawned – the Second Front had been opened in Normandy. Next morning, at a briefing for divisional officers, the overall operational plans were explained in outline and maps were distributed. Now they knew it was to be Normandy. The 11th Armoured Division was to spearhead the reinforcements arriving in the second week as part of VIII Corps. This meant just a few more days to wait. Charlie Workman remembered their last night in Aldershot.

The night before we actually moved, we were told in secrecy. There was a dance – we were told make your arrangements to meet these girls, we went to this dance, it was almost like Waterloo, we had this big dance. We weren't allowed to say, 'Well, I'm sorry, we're off tomorrow!' There was no mention of that at all. When the dance finished, we came right back to the barracks and packed our service dress and all that stuff in boxes. We didn't know when we were going to see that again. At about two or three in the morning we were driven out to the tanks – and the tanks headed off to the concentration area at Gosport.[9]

Second Lieutenant Charlie Workman, 1 Troop, 'C' Squadron, 2nd F&FY

On 11 June, the main body of the regiment set off for Gosport. They had quite a send-off as they passed through various towns and villages on the way.

> We drove the tanks down there on the Portsmouth road to Waterlooville. All the ladies and the kids were all out on the pavements waving! We were all waving and smiling! The blokes were all chucking their money out of the tanks to the kids. The kids were running round picking it up – those kids must have been as rich as Croesus by the time we'd gone. There wasn't going to be any need for money where we were going![10]
>
> Trooper John Gray, Recce Troop, HQ Squadron, 2nd F&FY

Ron Forbes was confident in himself and his friends in the regiment. But he found a real immediate problem with the copious amounts of dust thrown up by the columns of vehicles of all shapes and sizes during that long journey.

> I don't think I was actually nervous. You just had your mates beside you and you just went on as usual. There was a sort of feeling, 'Ah well, nothing's going to happen to me!' The convoy down wasn't very pleasant, because of the dust. The weather was dry, and the roads were dusty. Of course, tanks are notorious for kicking up dust. It probably would have been worse if the exhaust wasn't diverted – but it was bad enough. Tracks kick up the dust. You had goggles. The worst part was a section of the south of England that seemed to be red soil – and the dust was red. It seemed to go for our eyes. One place there was a family at the roadside with basins and buckets of hot water – as we came along, we all stopped, got down and bathed our eyes.[11]
>
> Trooper Ron Forbes, 4 Troop, 'B' Squadron, 2nd F&FY

As they drove in their endless convoys, they gained a feeling of the massed power of the Allies that was about to descend on the Germans struggling to hold back the invasion forces in Normandy. Once they got to the Gosport, they went into a sealed-off concentration area, where the final stages of waterproofing were completed. Officers, NCOs and clerks were busy with a thousand and one administrative tasks. But at night the men had plenty of time to think. Most had never had any experience of combat – how would they cope?

I think one's great thought was, 'How will I make out on this? Will I be afraid?' One was very conscious that, 'I've had all this training and I reckon I know my job, but when it comes to it and the chips were down, how will I face up to death? How will I face up to being wounded?' Eisenhower once said that the only thing to fear is fear itself! You're afraid that you'll be afraid! It was a difficult period in a way. One wasn't sort of saying, 'Oh, I don't want to go!' One accepted we were going, but you thought, 'How will I make out?' Not as a tank man, but as an individual? Will I be afraid, or would I be one of these guys that's led gibbering away? The married bloke was much more aware of what was happening than us! We weren't married, and none of us as far as I was aware had even a steady girlfriend![12]

Second Lieutenant Charlie Workman, 1 Troop, 'C' Squadron, 2nd F&FY

The relevance of Workman's comments about the additional stress that married men were under is brought into sharp relief by the case of Trooper David Sutherland.

Dave Sutherland's baby was born just when we were going down to prepare to go on the landing craft. He had a letter from home and he did remark, 'Isn't it a funny thing that in the letter my parents say, "Oh you don't have to worry, we'll look after the baby and your wife!" They say that as if they don't expect me to come back!' Which unfortunately he did not – David got killed.[13] He never ever saw his baby.[14]

Trooper James Donovan, 'B' Squadron, 2nd F&FY

They expected to leave for France at any moment, but the

situation in Normandy was not going quite to plan, and there were more frustrating delays. For two more days, they were stuck in the sealed-off camps, with little to do but listen to irritating tannoy messages blaring out that there would be no move yet. They were all confined to camp, but the free-spirited Brigadier Roscoe Harvey was having none of it.

> We went into one of those camps where – not that I was ever starved – we had the most appalling filthy stew which we just couldn't eat. I said that there should be a notice placed up on the door 'Abandon Hope All Ye Who Enter Here' and I told my brigade major that I had no intention of stopping in the camp. He told me that they would not allow me out. I said, 'They bloody well will!' We were very close to Bosham where there was a very nice little restaurant, rather like a club, run by a fellow who used to be in my regiment. The officer of the gate asked me where I was going and I said, 'Don't worry, I'll be back!' I went out and had a bloody good dinner and came back again. The next day we embarked for France![15]
>
> Brigadier Roscoe Harvey, HQ, 29th Armoured Brigade

As his men would have said, 'It's all right for some!'

*

EMBARKATION BEGAN from the Gosport Hard on the night of 14 June and parties left in various batches over the next twenty-four hours. They were to travel on a mixture of landing ship tank (LST) and landing craft tank (LCT). Although the Allies had secured control over both air and sea, 'accidents' could still happen, and they did not want all their 2nd F&FY eggs in one basket. As they moved down from the camp into Gosport itself, they parked up in long lines along the residential streets, patiently waiting for their turn to board ship.

There'd been a lot of army people stopped before going on
board ship in Gosport. We were parked in side streets with a lot
of gardens and bungalows. I think the people were a wee bit fed
up of tanks being parked outside their door and men sleeping
in their garden – that was the only place you could sleep, unless
you were hardy enough to sleep on the pavement![16]

Trooper Ron Forbes, 4 Troop, 'B' Squadron, 2nd F&FY

Then, at last, it was their turn. It must have been an amazing
sight as the armoured regiments loaded up.

It was all dark except the inside of the landing craft was lit up,
so you could see where to drive into. I think we got either ten or
a dozen tanks in. They were put in position and then fastened
down with chains, so they were all firmly clamped down to the
deck. Then we had to go into a large cabin, just bare steel with
a few wire bunks. We had to stay there, we weren't allowed out
until we were out to sea – and it took a long time to get out
to sea! The diesel fumes were shocking, you were suffocating!
Once out to sea they let us get out on deck – and it was a fine
sunny day. [17]

Trooper Jack Edwards, 4 Troop, 'B' Squadron, 2nd F&FY

As the lines of tanks and lorries rumbled slowly down to the
slipway, Doug Hayes watched one touching tribute from a Great
War veteran.

As we dropped down into Gosport harbour, there was an old
man came out. He'd obviously served in the 1914 war. He came
out to brush his front path. When he saw us coming down, he
did all the correct moves, as if he had a rifle, presenting arms to
every truck that went past – as if we were officers! It touched
me! That brought it home to me a bit.[18]

Trooper Doug Hayes, MT Section, 'A' Squadron, 2nd F&FY

The old veteran had done his bit in 1914–18; now it was their
turn.

7

CALM BEFORE THE STORM

It was a rotten night; no cover from the rain and spray, and a collision with another LCT about three in the morning. At five, we loaded guns, primed grenades, ate biscuits and self-heating soup. At eight, France appeared as a misty black line, with a few houses and copses. At nine, 16 June, we 'waded' ashore in only 3 feet of water. After all that waterproofing, designed for 6 feet![1]

Lieutenant William Steel Brownlie, 4 Troop, 'A' Squadron, 2nd F&FY

IN NORMANDY, THE BATTLE FOR EUROPE WAS STILL RAGING. The landings on 6 June had caught the Germans by surprise and forced Field Marshal Erwin Rommel (Army Group B, responsible for the defence of the Atlantic Wall: Seventh Army, Fifteenth Army, Wehrmacht commander in the Netherlands and Panzer Group West) to commit all his local armoured reserves in a series of desperate but unfocused counter-attacks, which failed to throw back the invaders. Rommel sought then to hem in the Allies, while gathering a massed armoured force to launch a powerful counter-attack of some six armoured divisions intended to drive between the British and American armies and then move either left or right, depending on the situation, to smash the bridgehead once and for all. Rommel estimated he would be ready to start some time in early July. Throughout the campaign, Rommel and all the German High Command in Normandy were fatally hampered in their operational planning by the constant interference of Hitler, with his scathing distrust of his own generals and absolute refusal to consider *any* withdrawal – even for the very best tactical reasons. They must *all* stand and fight to the last. In these circumstances, Rommel must sometimes have felt that the Allied generals opposing him were the least of his worries. Chief of these was the Supreme Allied Commander, General Dwight Eisenhower. Then there was Rommel's old adversary from the Western Desert, General Bernard Montgomery, who was now in command of the Twenty-First Army Group in Normandy, which consisted of the British Second Army (Lieutenant General Miles Dempsey) and the American First Army (Lieutenant General Omar Bradley). Montgomery guessed what Rommel was doing, and consequently he launched a series of attritional limited attacks intended to erode the strength of Rommel's panzer divisions by dragging them into piecemeal actions to maul them before they were ready for a single coordinated blow. The main Allied attack would only be launched when the American First Army was ready to smash through on the right flank of the Allied bridgehead. At this point, the British Second Army was to take Caen and, in doing so, attract the attention of as many of the German armoured reserves as they could. Then the Americans would attack. Montgomery's overall strategy was designed to minimise casualties, seeking a low-risk approach of carefully planned set-piece battles on the firm foundations of the Twenty-First Army Group's overwhelming firepower superiority in artillery and airpower. The role of his armoured divisions was to assist the infantry to break through and then exploit any breach in the German lines.

Few of the men of the 2nd F&FY had any idea of what was going on in the battles that were raging across Normandy. Indeed, some were more concerned, or indeed excited, by some intriguing last-minute additions to their kitbags before they crossed the Channel.

We were issued with some odd things: an escape pack that
contained a silk handkerchief which had a map of Normandy
printed on it, a button with a compass in it, concentrated
chocolate, which was dreadful stuff, and some tablets to keep
you awake if you felt tired! Much more welcome we were issued
with tins of cigarettes – fifty Gold Flake in a tin! And some self-
heating cans of soup that you pulled the stopper off and struck
with a match – it fizzed and was boiling in a second or two![2]

Trooper Roy Vallance, HQ Troop, 'A' Squadron, 2nd F&FY

Once the assembled LCTs and LSTs had been loaded on board,
so the Channel crossing began. It was 19 June. They soon ran into
deteriorating weather conditions that would culminate in one
of the worst summer storms for decades. As the waves became
first choppy and then rough, seasickness became endemic, exacerbated by the all-pervading smell of diesel. But there were other
dangers ahead.

We loaded into a landing craft tank, we had three 75mm
[Shermans] and the squadron bulldozer. Off we go at night.
We hadn't got out all that far when it got very, very rough!
We hit another landing craft and all the bridge structure was
damaged. We were down below, down where the tanks were.
We tried to get up on deck, but we were told to stop where we
were! Because it was getting so rough, the tanks started to move
against the 'holding down' chains. We had to go all round the
chains, tightening them to stop the tanks from moving.[3]

Trooper Gordon Fidler, 4 Troop, 'A' Squadron, 2nd F&FY

Not all of the tanks had been properly chained down, as the skip-
pers were caught by surprise by the severity of the bad weather.

I said to the captain of this landing barge, 'Would we be better
to chain them down?' 'Oh, no!' he says, 'I've been across here a
few times, you don't need to chain the down!' But, by Jove, the
next morning he wouldn't give us our breakfast until we did

chain them down! We had a terrible crossing, there was a hell of a heavy seas – the tanks in the hold were sliding around all over the place. It is a bit of a thought when you think you're lying in a hammock and there's three tanks abreast banging against the side of the ship that you're on! You just think, 'Well, any time, they're going right through there!' He made us chain these things down – but getting sandwiched with 90 tons of armour isn't much of a thought![4]

Trooper Andrew Dewar, 'A' Squadron, 2nd F&FY

As they approached the French coast, their first impression was of astonishment. The sea seemed to be covered with vessels: indeed, many joked that they could barely see the sea for ships. There was also a naked demonstration of old-fashioned naval power as the 15-inch guns of a pair of mighty old superdreadnoughts pounded away at the German defensive positions and identified targets up to 20 miles inland.

As we approached the beaches, there was the *Warspite* and the *Rodney*, battleships, pounding away into Caen. It was a heroic sight to see them – it was the first time ever that I'd seen a battleship barking out in anger.[5]

Lance Corporal Bill Knights, Recce Troop, HQ Squadron, 2nd F&FY

The regiment landed over a period of two or three days and for all of them it proved far easier than they had expected as they were put ashore in very shallow water. The waterproofing had been a justified precaution in case it was necessary to fling them ashore in deeper water, but that was no consolation to the men, who were outraged at the waste of all their efforts.

All that waterproofing and we landed in about 2 feet of water! We complained bitterly about all that work we'd put in for weeks. We could have gone in with nothing! The beach wasn't all that busy – we saw one or two bulldozer Shermans and the usual beach assault vehicles. The only activity was there was a

Junker 88 flying about 'upstairs' and the sky was littered with red tracer shells. You were so busy occupied in getting off the beach inland that you didn't have much time to see what was going on on the beach! There was nothing exciting about it! We just drove on through some sand dunes and onto a road.[6]

Trooper Ron Forbes, 4 Troop, 'B' Squadron, 2nd F&FY

After landing, of course they then had to remove the water-proofing. There were two methods, the approved slow and steady method, and the easy quick method. There are no prizes for guessing which methods most of the tank crews employed before leaving the beach area.

We stopped at the heads of the beach and we were told to remove by hand the explosive charges and then to remove the waterproofing. But most of us accidentally fired them off! It was much cleaner and easier! Then we were told to follow little tin signs, arrows that had been stuck into the ground. Ours had '53' on it, which was our serial number. We followed them and eventually caught up with the rest of the squadron in a field.[7]

Trooper Roy Vallance, HQ Troop, 'A' Squadron, 2nd F&FY

Thus the various elements of the 2nd F&FY moved in small convoys about seven miles inland to concentrate just outside the small village of Cully. The regiment was gathered round the edges of a large field, with the headquarters and rear echelons of lorries and support vehicles in another field close by. The journey was not without incident.

In the dark. Flares everywhere, tracer bullets everywhere. Moving in under the second in command [Major George Trotter]. Our RSM was with us, he had been up the front and he came back to the 2iC and said, 'Sir, Jerry's 100 yards up the road! Reverse!' I think we could have got wiped out – we were going on and on with no idea where our regiment was! We turned in the dark and move back a mile.'[8]

Sergeant George Cozens, HQ Squadron, 2nd F&FY

The squadrons made the most of the natural camouflage that was all around them. Although the Allies had air supremacy, the threat of the Luftwaffe had not yet entirely evaporated. Sudden hit and run raids were still a possibility – and an entire armoured regiment would have been a tempting target.

'A' Squadron was in a sunken lane, which was overgrown with trees and high hedges. We were pretty well camouflaged naturally. We put our own camouflage nets up over the tanks and bivouacs. Just a net with coloured strips of material. Nobody was allowed to cross a field diagonally, we had to walk around the hedgerows so that there would be no tracks showing from the air. [Our bulldozer] went along this sunken lane and smoothed a patch where each tank would be, so they had a level 'playing field' to sleep on, which was quite good! Once we were in, all the vehicle marks had to be covered up. In the daylight hours we just kept under the camouflage.[9]

Trooper Roy Vallance, HQ Troop, 'A' Squadron, 2nd F&FY

From exercise in the UK, they already knew better than to sleep under their Sherman, as on soft ground the tanks could sink into the mud, with fatal consequences for anyone trapped underneath. If they were nervous, they could sleep in great discomfort inside the tank at their stations, but for the most part they got out the bivouac tents that were carried in the storage bins on the back of their tanks.

We had two tank sheets covering the tank when you were in a camp. One was a flat one which we could use as a groundsheet, and the other sheet was shaped so that it made a tent. You could fasten one end to the tank and the two flaps came down. After we'd been there a day or two, we dug a hole and put the tent over the hole.[10]

Trooper Jack Edwards, 4 Troop, 'B' Squadron, 2nd F&FY

Using the sheets they could create a small tent, about 10 feet by

8 feet and about 4–5 feet high! Under this cover they would roll out their sleeping bags. In the daytime, they could sit inside and play cards or chat if it was raining.

In the fields all around them were the rest of the 29th Armoured Brigade, including the gunner regiments who were certainly not keeping quiet – as the 2nd F&FY soon discovered.

> We were in a sort of field, below a raised bit – on this raised bit was the Ayrshire Yeomanry with their 25-pounders all lined up behind us. The first night we were there the artillery got a night target. They had to fire a complete barrage for half an hour to soften a particular area that the infantry was going to advance over the next day to try and clear a passage. We were all just about deafened, lying there! But funnily enough we went to sleep – sometimes you can sleep in a noise – and when the noise stops you wake up. This is what happened to us – when the barrage was over nobody could get to sleep after that – even when it was quiet.[11]

Trooper Ron Forbes, 4 Troop, 'B' Squadron, 2nd F&FY

Robert Nurse had been an office clerk in Bristol before his call-up. Now in this strange new world at war he was a Sherman driver. At Cully he recalled a most unfortunate accident as he climbed in his turret.

> The 3rd Royal Tanks were across a road in a similar field. I made the mistake of accidentally firing the smoke bomb! It was electrically fired from the turret ring and I accidentally pressed the button. It landed in the 3rd Royal Tanks adjutant's tent. I thought, 'Oh God! Court martial!' I rushed across and apologised, and he was ever such a nice character, a captain, he said, 'Oh, forget it!' We were still within range of German guns and there were signs 'Dust Means Death!' And there was this huge pall of smoke rising over the adjutant's tent. He wasn't best pleased, but he was very nice about it![12]

Trooper Robert Nurse, 2 Troop, 'C' Squadron, 2nd F&FY

To Nurse's great relief, there were no subsequent splatter of German shells crashing down on the adjutant's tent.

The regiment had practised living on hard rations, but now they were doing it for real. They were introduced to the composition ration system – or 'compo' as it was known to the men. This is what would sustain them for the most part for the rest of the war.

> We got compo rations; they came in a fourteen-man pack. It lasted a tank crew three days. Any of us cooked it because it was just a matter of warming up tins. Some of it was Maconochies stew, stewed steak, the potatoes were diced in a tin – you just warm them up. There was cheese in a tin, hard tack biscuits. Bars of chocolate in a tin. The tea was 'compo tea': tea, sugar and milk mixed as a powder and you just stirred it up with hot water and you got a reasonable cup of tea out of it! Breakfast was a bit of – sometimes it was tinned sausage. Just sausage meat marked so that you could cut it into sections. You didn't get a lot out of it! Some packs had tinned bacon. You opened it up and it came out like a tin of worms. All greasy rinds – the bacon was horrible! We once had a tin of American bacon and it was just like proper bacon – it was great![13]
>
> Trooper Jack Edwards, 4 Troop, 'B' Squadron, 2nd F&FY

The food was basic, but the system was designed to ensure that regular rations were delivered to the hundreds of thousands of frontline soldiers, rather than to provide any kind of a gourmet experience. This was plain, unimaginative food that was easy to move around, stack in huge piles and most importantly of all it would not go 'off'. They may not have liked it much, but it kept body and soul together – and enabled them to fight on a full stomach. Bulk feeding was the intention, and this was achieved.

> Breakfast would be some cans of beans, or a cooked bacon – horrible stuff! Tin of jam, tin of margarine, butter, little packs of coffee or tea, boiled sweets, bars of chocolate to munch if you

couldn't cook a meal. There would even be loo paper. For the
main meal in one pack you'd get stewed steak, Machonochies
or corned beef, which was very popular because you could do a
lot of things with that. You could also eat it uncooked. Cooked
tinned vegetables and a tinned pudding of some sort – spotted
dick or rice pudding! It was all tinned. Separate from the pack
we would get a tin of biscuits which would last you probably
fourteen days – very hard biscuits. The co-driver had a little
petrol stove and a dixie can about 6 × 6 × 4 inches deep. He'd
empty the cans into that and stew them up. Later on, when we
were moving, we used to jam the cans in the exhaust, and they
would be hot when you took them out – and ready to eat![14]

Trooper Roy Vallance, HQ Troop, 'A' Squadron, 2nd F&FY

Some of the men would have access to the simple food provided
by the regimental cooks, but most were thrown back on their
own resources and had to cook for themselves on primus stoves,
especially once the campaign became more mobile.

The cooks would be in action with their burners. They'd make
a shallow trench first in the field and put these iron grid irons
on which were shaped to take individual enormous dixies – the
size of three buckets, so you could get a lot of food in those
dixies. Then one of these special burners was placed at each end.
They roared away – almost like flame-throwers! To stop the
hot air escaping along the sides of these grids, they would put
turves of grass all along, and keep the air moving along in this
channel underneath the dixies. It would heat these dixies up
very efficiently. They produced a very satisfactory meal. We had
our primus stoves. A rectangular box and you could open the
lid up, which formed the back to the cooker. There was only one
burner, so you had to do things one by one. They were mainly
used for brewing up tea and soups! To cook up a couple of tins
of stewed meats with veg, you'd really have to be sure that you
weren't going to be called into action – sure you had time to do

it! The primus stoves often gave trouble because the jets on them got quickly clogged up with black stuff – soot – and you were constantly cleaning them with this little tool! They were difficult to get started and get up to the right heat! They weren't the ideal means of cooking, but we had to use them. Another method of cooking was to find one of these old type petrol tins, saw it in half, you could fill it with sand or earth, then pour petrol in it and set light to it. There you'd got another means of cooking. A couple of tins would do for the crew, they were sizeable tins! With anything else that was going – like a rice pudding![15]

Trooper Geoff Hayward, 'B' Squadron, 2nd F&FY

To the men, a regular cigarette supply seemed almost as important as food. Smoking was endemic in the British Army in the war years – perhaps it was the additional stress, but men seemed to crave them.

Each man got a tin of fifty cigarettes a week. But we had stacks of them in the tank! I don't know whether some didn't smoke – we always had plenty of cigarettes. I smoked all day – the days were very long days once we were in action, you'd smoke forty a day.[16]

Trooper Roy Vallance, HQ Troop, 'A' Squadron, 2nd F&FY

It seems a generous weekly ration, but it should be remembered that some men chain-smoked up to eighty cigarettes a day. A minor black market developed in cigarettes, with the few non-smokers well placed to cash in – or be generous to their pals – depending on inclination. There was also – occasionally – a rum ration.

The rum came in 1-gallon stone jars. The ration was a pint between twenty men. One chap would go from the troop with a mug which would hold a pint. He would bring it back and that would be divided in four mugs for the four tank crews. We'd just pass it round and have a sip each.[17]

Trooper Roy Vallance, HQ Troop, 'A' Squadron, 2nd F&FY

One essential part of life was latrine provision. When they were all closely packed in one locality, as at Cully, there would be properly dug latrines that everyone was expected to use without fail.

> There was always 'A' Squadron latrine. Well, when I say a latrine it was a big slit trench, a couple of poles sticking out, pole across the top and you hang your arse out of there! That was the latrine! Everything was there for you – and if you didn't use it you were a bit of a fool. Before there was any movement from the area that would be closed up. Somebody would have to go out with a couple of shovels and fill the whole latrine in.[18]

Trooper Gordon Fidler, 4 Troop, 'A' Squadron, 2nd F&FY

One other strictly unofficial facility was supplied for the men by some enterprising French women.

> A funny thing happened there with the French civilians. We suddenly woke up one morning and in the far corner of the field opposite a tent appeared. Everybody was saying, 'Cor, what's that?' When the military police went to investigate it was a couple of French ladies had set up a brothel!' Looking for business! They didn't stop for the war. They were definitely moved on![19]

Trooper James Donovan, 'B' Squadron, 2nd F&FY

Like most of the rest of Normandy in 1944, Cully had been a battleground and there was plenty of evidence still dotted around the local countryside. In their twos and threes, the men were drawn to the burnt-out carcasses of tanks like moths to a flame.

> What did frighten us was about a hundred yards from where we were camped, there was a black Sherman and an armoured car. We went over to these. Twenty yards away from the armoured car, there was a shell hole through the turret, and we could smell this turret. Clambered up onto the wheel, looked in the

turret and the driver and commander were splattered all round
the turret. Bits of 'meat' all over the place. You could see where
the shell had gone through and come out the other side. The
smell was horrendous. It was a hot day – and this didn't help.
Then there was the Sherman. That was absolutely brewed up,
just nothing left of anything really. They'll burn – or smoulder
– for days and days. We weren't too happy! Oh dear, why did
we join the Tank Corps! We didn't think it could be like this.[20]

Trooper Gordon Fidler, 4 Troop, 'A' Squadron, 2nd F&FY

Even worse, they could see that the extra armour fitted to the
Sherman had been of no help at all.

We'd had extra plates welded on the side to cover ammunition
bins – and there was a hole through one of the extra plates. The
tank was just a shell – it had completely burnt out. There was a
grave at the side with a piece of wood stuck in. Somebody had
pencilled a note on the wood, 'Four, possibly five'. So I thought,
'Well, the crew must have been all in bits!' It wasn't very
encouraging, we thought, 'Ooh, good God! Things are worse
than we thought!'[21]

Trooper Jack Edwards, 4 Troop, 'B' Squadron, 2nd F&FY

However, most still consoled themselves with the classic young
soldier's 'motto': 'Oh, well it couldn't happen to me!'

Meanwhile, some of the officers were going forward to
explore their surroundings in preparation for their role in the
offensive operations that were surely looming, as the reinforcements gradually built up in Normandy.

As squadron leaders we were able to do reconnaissance round
the area to get accustomed to the Normandy countryside. One
went to vantage points where you could have pointed out to
you where the German line was. We used a scout car and I also
used a motorcycle. One of the things was we had never had
anything like the banks [with hedges] which existed between

Normandy fields. That's a thing that didn't exist in the English countryside. It was bad for tanks in that when you were going over a bank and coming out the other side it put the belly of your tank, which was unarmoured, open to fire.[22]

Major Sir John Gilmour, 'B' Squadron, 2nd F&FY

Officers, NCOs and men all still had a lot to learn about the reality of tank fighting in the Bocage. They would find out soon enough. On 26 June 1944, the 2nd F&FY went into action for the first time.

8

OPERATION EPSOM

It was awfully difficult to see because of this enclosed country –
hedges and banks. You could glimpse a German tank from time
to time, crossing a little open bit – then it would disappear. We
knocked out some of them. We didn't make much progress at
all that day – and we came back to 'A' Squadron laager after
dark not very far outside Cheux. Not at all satisfactory.[1]

Captain Douglas Hutchison, HQ Troop, 'A' Squadron, 2nd F&FY

MONTGOMERY planned a major series of offensives to be
carried out by his Second Army, under the command of General
Miles Dempsey, with the purpose of drawing in newly arrived
German armoured divisions, thereby maintaining the tactical initiative, forcing the Germans to respond rather than give
them the chance to initiate their own plans. As with most large
offensives committing huge amounts of military resources, there
was also the additional hope that a significant breakout could be
achieved. Elements of three British corps would take part, but
the main role was assigned to General Richard O'Connor's VIII
Corps (Guards Armoured Division, 11th Armoured Division
and 15th Division, 6th Guards Armoured Brigade and the 8th
Army Group Royal Artillery). Under the plans for Operation
Epsom they would burst through the German line between the
city of Caen and the village of Tilly some 10 miles to the west. The
15th (Scottish) Division (Major-General Gordon MacMillan)

was to push past Cheux, cross the Odon river and establish a strong bridgehead. The 11th Armoured Division, augmented by the temporarily attached 4th Armoured Brigade, would then take up the charge, pushing further to cross the Orne river, pass the high ground of Hill 112 and sever the Caen–Falaise road, thus virtually surrounding Caen. Meanwhile on their left, the 51st (Highland) Division of I Corps would move east of Caen in a pincer movement to overrun the Carpiquet airfield. But a vital first move would be made by the 49th (West Riding) Division of the XXX Corps, which would make a preliminary attack under Operation Martlet a day earlier to seize the tactically significant Rauray high ground, thereby covering the VIII Corps' right flank during the main thrust. The original start date was set for 22 June, but that had been stymied by a storm that vented its fury over Normandy from 19 to 22 June. The disruption can be judged by the fact that the Guards Armoured Division had not yet even reached the beach areas.

The 15th (Scottish) Division had arrived in France on 12–13 June, landing on the eastern sector of Sword Beach. Their attack was now scheduled to commence at 07.30 on 26 June, following a creeping barrage starting a minute earlier from some 640 guns, a battleship and two cruisers. They would advance on a two-brigade front with the start line stretching from near Norrey-en-Bessin to Le Mesnil Patry, with the 44th (Lowland) Brigade on the left and the 46th (Highland) Brigade on its right. They were to be supported initially by the Churchill tanks of the 31st Tank Brigade, with the 9th Royal Tank Regiment accompanying the 44th Brigade, while the 7th Royal Tank Regiment supported the 46th Brigade. In addition, they could call on some of the flail tanks and Assault Vehicles Royal Engineers (AVRE), the 'Funnies', provided by General Hobart's 79th Armoured Division to assist in clearing minefields and other obstructions. Together they were to advance over the small Mue stream, then go past Cheux to the 100-foot contour ridge which ran just to the south-east of the village. Although low, this ridge offered a good viewpoint and artillery observation over the next phase of the advance to be carried out by the 227th (Highland) Brigade pushing forward to the line of the Odon river. Only then were the 11th Armoured Division intended to move forward. It was an ambitious programme made more difficult by the failure of the 49th (West Riding) Division attack on Rauray on 25 June, which left their right flank badly exposed. Heavy rainfall and low cloud also lost them much of the support they had been promised from the RAF. The ground they faced was typical of much of Normandy; an intensively farmed countryside with small villages and farms dotted around, plenty of sunken lanes and fields full of standing corn, usually delineated by thick tall hedges, with hidden ditches lurking at their feet. It was an ideal terrain for determined defenders, and not many could be as determined as the 12th SS (Hitler Youth) Panzer Division.

The exact nature of the 2nd F&FY role in the attack was revealed to them in a series of Order Groups, or 'O' Groups. Charlie Workman explained how they worked.

> An 'O' Group would consist of the CO saying what our next task was to be. He would explain briefly the aim of the brigade to advance towards Caen, 'Here is how I intend to do it!' You would hardly ever take notes; you would just get it in your head. You'd have maps, we would mark our boundaries, all the information you would put on your map plastic covering. You lived on maps – they were bread and butter, absolutely essential. The idea normally was one squadron would go forward and 'bump' the enemy and the regimental headquarters would be in the middle, so they could control what was going on. It would always end up with everyone comparing watches and making sure their watches were the same. Because a lot of attacks would take place behind an artillery barrage, so you had to be sure you weren't going to be caught.[2]

Lieutenant Charlie Workman, 1 Troop, 'C' Squadron, 2nd F&FY

Once the officers had been briefed, they held their own 'O' Groups to disseminate the plans to their NCOs and men.

When the attack started at 07.30, it was soon apparent that the 15th (Scottish) Division and 31st Tank Brigade were making slow progress. To speed things along, Lieutenant General Richard O'Connor decided to bring forward the involvement of the 11th Armoured Division. Somewhat amusingly, their esteemed divisional commander, Major General 'Pip' Roberts had already managed to gain himself an embarrassing distinction.

> By 09.00 hours, I felt I had better get a bit nearer the scene of operations, so I got myself into my tank, my ADC in a spare tank and my CRA[3] in another and set off towards Cheux. We had been going about twenty minutes when, 'Whoomph!' We had come to a grinding halt. We were in a very harmless-looking field, no signs of any kind around and well clear of any battle. We had gone over a mine, part of an unmarked minefield laid by the Canadians, so the Divisional Commander succeeded in becoming the first tank casualty of 11th Armoured Division in the war! No one got hurt, but then a lot of 'prodding' took place. We eventually got ourselves out of the minefield without further casualties, and finally came to rest about 1,000 yards north-west of Cheux, which had just been cleared by the Scotsmen.[4]

Major General 'Pip' Roberts, Headquarters, 11th Armoured Division

At 12.30, the 2nd Northamptonshire Yeomanry (the divisional reconnaissance regiment) was ordered to 'dash' for the bridges, but this rash move was soon thwarted, and in the afternoon the 29th Armoured Brigade was ordered forwards. The 2nd F&FY were to follow up the advance of the 227th Brigade (2nd Gordon Highlanders, 10th Highland Light Infantry and 2nd Argyll and Sutherland Highlanders) from Cheux to the 100-foot contour ridge and then on to the villages of Tourville and Grainville sur Odon, before assisting the 31st Tank Brigade in securing the Odon bridges at Tourmauville and Gavrus. The men of the 2nd F&FY were finally facing up to their first battle. Alf Courtneidge had been training as a bricklayer before he was called up in 1942. Now he was a wireless operator in a Sherman, but he remained philosophical over his immediate prospects.

> You know you're going to go into battle – and you know there's a certain number of people – it might be a large number – would get knocked out. It all comes down to the training and the discipline. You do things automatically; I don't think nerves or fear came into it. I think we had reached quite a good peak and if you were told to do something – you did your best to carry out what orders you had. I never knew anybody who would say, 'Ooh, I'm not going to go in the Sherman!' For one thing when you got in you didn't have to bother about the rain![5]
>
> Trooper Alf Courtneidge, HQ Squadron, 2nd F&FY

Just before going into battle the tank crews were given a final talk by Lieutenant Colonel Alec Scott. Tommy Willmott managed to overhear what was said.

> I remember him telling them they were going to have a battle inoculation – an experience of going into battle. He was a quiet kind of a person, but he made sure that nobody went forward into this action without the knowledge that things were going to be hard, people were going to die, and it was going to be tough. He didn't give them, 'England and Saint George' kind of stuff! He wasn't that kind of a man.[6]
>
> Squadron Quartermaster Sergeant Tommy Willmott, HQ Squadron, 2nd F&FY

Then 'B' Squadron and the Recce Troop moved off in front. The men were facing their first ever action and however determined they were to 'put up a good show', there were bound to be some anxieties in the pits of their stomachs.

The 2nd F&FY were following up behind the advancing Scottish infantry and the Churchill tanks of the 31st Brigade. At first all went well. After crossing the Mue stream, they began the gentle climb towards what was left of Cheux. Here they came under German fire for the first time.

> Nothing was visible, just a gently sloping field with a wood or thick hedge on our left, a distant hedge and trees over on our right. And that I gather was the approach to the village itself. A lot of shelling going on. Under shrapnel fire – once I'd heard the shrapnel hitting the tank and not apparently doing any damage – I didn't feel too fearful of what could happen from that point of view. A bit like the sound of hail on a shed roof. But I also thought, 'Well, if they can fire shrapnel at us, they can also fire armour-piercing shells at us!' We were moving very slowly.[7]
>
> Trooper Geoff Hayward, 'B' Squadron, 2nd F&FY

Then came an incident that Hayward never forgot and which left him with an enduring insecurity as to whether he had – or had not – done the right thing. He could never really make his mind up and it worried him.

> We'd been shelled for ten minutes or so, when the officer spotted that some of our gear on the back of the tank was smouldering and had obviously been hit by some hot metal. He said, 'Hayward, get out and stamp it out!' But as this shelling was still going on – and the tank was being peppered, I didn't really want to! I thought I was going to inevitably get wounded – I wouldn't be much good to anybody; I might even get killed! I was frightened to death at the idea of getting out of the tank while the shrapnel was still hitting it! I just sat there, frozen in horror and not knowing what to say. In effect I was disobeying an order! Even though I didn't say anything; I didn't do anything! After this silence, there was also a silence from outside, the shrapnel had ceased. At that point, the officer asked the driver to get out. I thought, 'Well that should really be me!'

But I was still in a state of shock. Penman got out and stamped it out and was quickly back in again uninjured – he was fine. I did feel very bad about it. Nothing was ever said to me. It may be that the crew sympathised with me. Any crew would have been horrified at the idea of being ordered to get out under shrapnel fire if it wasn't absolutely necessary. If it wasn't vital. And I don't think the fire on the back of the tank was serious enough to warrant getting out – just smouldering.[8]

Trooper Geoff Hayward, 'B' Squadron, 2nd F&FY

As 'B' Squadron pushed forward in front, 'A' Squadron was coming up behind on the right flank. Steel Brownlie was soon made aware that the 49th (West Riding) Division had still failed in their mission to seize the high ground around Rauray.

We had gone about 300 yards when two armour-piercing shots came from the high ground on the right, sending up showers of earth and killing two infantrymen. I wheeled the troop right and saw the turrets of three German tanks nicely positioned hull-down, about 1,800 yards. AP was no use at that range, so I did an HE shoot on them. They brewed up a halftrack nearby (you could see their solid shot whirling down in our general direction), but after a few minutes they withdrew. Encouraging! They had a whole squadron to fire at, sitting in the open fields, and hit none of them.[9]

Lieutenant William Steel Brownlie, 4 Troop, 'A' Squadron, 2nd F&FY

As 'B' Squadron pushed on, Sir John Gilmour was trying to find out what exactly was happening in front of them. In the closed-in countryside, it was difficult business. Every hedge, every wall, every orchard or wood could conceal German troops, tanks or anti-tank guns. The very ground ahead of them concealed mines which had already caused several losses to the 31st Tank Brigade. However, initially, the 2nd F&FY were advancing behind the frontline and perhaps had a false sense of security. It wouldn't last.

It seemed easier than one expected to a certain extent. There didn't seem to be as much opposition as one had thought there would be. One of the troubles about being in a tank is that you're tremendously isolated. Having to have earphones on in order to hear what messages were coming in, and also to speak yourself to give orders to your other tanks, you got a rather detached sort of situation. Cheux had been pretty devastated. There was a lot of rubble and mess. We were supporting the 15th (Scottish) Division. You had no radio link with them, one had to do it verbally. The fact that you were in a vehicle detached you, to a certain extent, from the action going on as far as the infantry were concerned. You were glad to be inside, rather than running about outside which the infantry had to do![10]

Major Sir John Gilmour, 'B' Squadron, 2nd F&FY

Jack Edwards was the wireless operator and loader in the Sherman commanded by Lance Sergeant Alastair McHattie as 'B' Squadron advanced towards Cheux.

The squadron moved up a track and the infantry were doing the main attack with tank support. One of their men came back down this track with a prisoner of war, he had his hands in the air. He was a real fanatic-looking type! I looked at him through the periscope and his eyes – the look in his eyes – I felt it was just as if he was coming straight through the tank at me. I thought, 'Good God, I hope they're not all like him up there!' We moved up this track and wound up on what was supposed to be our start line. We were the right-hand tank of the line – and just to the right of us there was an anti-tank gun, an M10 17-pounder, banging away way over to our right at one of two German tanks that we could see moving across in front of a wood. McHattie traversed round and had Pat fire at the other. He fired about three rounds to get the range, and then he hit it with the fourth one. It didn't 'brew' but he says, 'Oh, it's stopped!' I reckon they were Mark IV, but they were a long way off, three-quarters of a mile. We got the order from the 2 Troop commander to cease fire and get moving. Because everyone was moving off.[11]

Trooper Jack Edwards, 4 Troop, 'B' Squadron, 2nd F&FY

It is often forgotten just how limited visibility was for the driver when he was driving 'battened down', it was difficult to see shell holes or other obstructions in their path. Their driver, Ron Forbes, was trying the best he could.

I couldn't see much. Closed up, all I would see was angle of sight through the periscope. You kept twisting it, looking around all the time. When you're actually driving along, it's not like a car, where your hands are on the wheel, you could sit with your arms folding and go along quite well – you weren't steering until you pulled a lever. So, you had two hands to work the periscope – swivel it about![12]

Trooper Ron Forbes, 4 Troop, 'B' Squadron, 2nd F&FY

Peering through his periscope, Forbes missed a large craterous hole – and in they went with a huge crash.

We were driving with the driver's hatch down; he was closed down and he couldn't see very well. We ran into a big hole. Then we couldn't get out. McHattie had to get out and he wandered over, and there were two Churchill tanks nearby; they must have been the HQ of one of the Churchill tank regiments supporting the infantry. He got one of them to back up and give us a tow out. When we got out, the squadron had all disappeared, the other side of Cheux. While we were waiting, we got reports then from 'A' Squadron, they'd got two tanks knocked out, two [crew] have got out of one and three out of the other. That's when you know you're in the war – when the tanks start getting knocked out and blokes are getting killed.[13]

Trooper Jack Edwards, 4 Troop, 'B' Squadron, 2nd F&FY

Having emerged from the crater, Lance Sergeant McHattie now had to track down the rest of 'B' Squadron. Edwards got wireless messages that they were in an orchard just to the south of Cheux.

It was like half a mile of open ground to Cheux. We were toddling across it on our own, nobody else in sight. We passed a lot of our dead infantry lying about just in front of Cheux, we thought, 'Ooh, that looks great!' We went along the main street of Cheux. There was a church. McHattie said, 'Machine gun the church!' So, Pat fired a lot of Browning at the top of the church, in case there was a sniper up there. Then we turned left and made our way towards this orchard where the squadron was. We got in among the squadron. The infantry had dug in somewhere in front of us. We'd just arrived, trying to find our troop, and there was an explosion in a tree above us. It was a hell of a bang! Whether it was a mortar, or – at the time – we thought it was an 'S' mine, they put these 'S' mines in trees, with a trip wire so that a tank would hit it and explode it. We didn't know! Mac dropped right through to the bottom of the turret. He was a heavy man, 'Oh my head!' His tin hat had fallen off, he'd got a hole in his tin hat I could put my fist through! He had a nasty wound on his head. Pat got his dressing out, I had to wriggle under the gun, and I helped Pat to bandage his head up with this dressing. When we'd got him bandaged up, he'd got blood all over his face and hands. All I had was cotton waste – so I sort of rubbed him down a bit. We helped him out of the tank; he could just about walk. Pat pointed him towards the village and said, 'Best of luck – keep going!' We got back in the tank and Pat became the commander, I became the gunner and Cliff Pember, the co-driver, came in to be the loader.[14]

Trooper Jack Edwards, 4 Troop, 'B' Squadron, 2nd F&FY

During this advance on Cheux, the Shermans of 'B' Squadron

were accompanied by the Honey tanks of the Recce Troop. John Gray was acting as a gunner in a Honey. With their thin armour they were very vulnerable, but his Honey was put out of action in an unusual fashion.

> We just charged forward and hoped for the best. I don't know whether it was a mine, or we got hit with a shell or bazooka. But we had on the front of the tank a 5-gallon oil drum and a wooden box. It was the only place we could think of putting it. Something happened – we got hit. The oil drum disintegrated; the oil leaked in on us through the hatch. We wondered what it was – and when we opened it, of course it all came in on us! We didn't have any fire or anything – oil doesn't burn like petrol; you've got to heat it up first! Both Jimmy Byers, the co-driver, and I were sitting there, like a pair of jellies – I'm not kidding, we were shaking the pair of us! Jimmy got his fags out! He got this fag in his mouth, he lit it up and within three puffs he was as calm as anything. The man went from a jelly to a bar of steel if you like! That was the difference! He stopped shaking; he became rational. I said to him, 'Give us one of those, Jimmy!' I coughed a bit – heaved a bit – and I started to smoke! It was the fact that I had something to do – smoke the fag – I'd never smoked before. I virtually chain-smoked after that![15]

Trooper John Gray, Recce Troop, HQ Squadron, 2nd F&FY

After reaching Cheux, 'C' Squadron, under Major Chris Nicholls, moved up to take the lead, while 'A' Squadron, commanded by Major Joe Powell, manoeuvred in tandem just to their right, with both squadrons pushing towards Haut du Bosq. By this time, rain was pouring down and visibility was poor.

> 'C' Squadron was the lead squadron advancing down the road – I was No 1 Troop, I think I was in the middle. The general tactic was you moved down a road if you could and if the leading tank was fired on, you then moved off the road. You had to keep taking account of what the ground was like on either

side. We were going into Cheux. Suddenly, on the wireless I
heard somebody come up and say his officer's tank had been
hit. 'Lieutenant Pritchard is gone!' He was killed.[16] We saw the
column of smoke. That was them opening up on us.[17]

Lieutenant Charlie Workman, 1 Troop, 'C' Squadron, 2nd F&FY

After all their training they knew what they had to do: get off
the road into the fields on either side, but it wasn't always that
easy when driving up a typical Normandy sunken road.

Hemmed in between steep banks we could see nothing. There
was no room to turn round, and we couldn't reverse because
of the tanks lined up nose to tail behind us. We heard the
commanding officer, Lieutenant Colonel Scott, frequently
coming on the air urging the squadron leader to advance. But
Major Nicholls had had considerable experience and retorted
that he would advance only when the gain justified the losses.
That was a great morale booster to us![18]

Trooper Ron Cox, 'C' Squadron, 2nd F&FY

Just to the right of them 'A' Squadron was also coming under
fire. Steel Brownlie was soon in the thick of the action.

Don Hall took his troop round the edge of a wood, myself
following. Two of his tanks went up in flames, and he came
roaring back, laying smoke. I took cover, but could not see
anything to fire at, because of the trees and smoke from the
burning tanks. Two APs came just over my head, so I too laid
smoke and got out. As I was turning, two survivors from Don's
tanks came running back, burnt and their clothes smouldering.
For an hour, I shot at long-range targets, and was shot at, but
could see no certain hits and sustained none.[19]

Lieutenant William Steel Brownlie, 4 Troop, 'A' Squadron, 2nd F&FY

His co-driver, Gordon Fidler, was aghast at the brief glimpses he
caught of the fighting.

The troop in front of us, that had already lost three tanks. There was a tank 100 yards to our left, he was right on top of this German gun, probably about 50 yards from this anti-tank gun. It just erupted. It was engulfed in flames. I saw two coming out through the turret, their clothes were alight, aflame. Both jumped down off the tank and lay on the grass – burning. We didn't go over to them; we were still moving forward. Then the one on the right – that one brewed up. You can see this with your periscope. You're drawn to what's happening. We had two armour-piercing shots over the top of us. You can hear these. We don't really know what's going on. Steel Brownlie told us we were being fired at from a gun to our front. He told Jock Mackinnon to, 'Reverse, bloody quick!' We didn't get hit.[20]

Trooper Gordon Fidler, 4 Troop, 'A' Squadron, 2nd F&FY

Their gunner was John Buchanan. He remembered that Steel Brownlie spotted three hull-down German tanks in a wood about 1,800 yards away and ordered him to fire a HE shell.

To fire there was two studs on the floor. And your foot – if it was the big gun you were firing you used the left-hand one, and if it was the machine gun you used the right-hand one. The only thing wrong was the buttons were too close together. If you've got big feet and you pressed the wrong button – you'd find you were expecting to see a shell and all of a sudden the machine gun would go; or if you were only wanting the machine gun, then a great big flipping big shell would come screaming out.[21]

Trooper John Buchanan, 4 Troop, 'A' Squadron, 2nd F&FY

Steel Brownlie may have recorded in his memoir (now preserved at the Imperial War Museum), that there were no certain hits, but he was not averse to 'gilding the lily' for his gunner.

Steel Brownlie told me the shell had landed on the top of the turret! My good gunnery you see! I believed him, I could see the wood, but they were camouflaged in that wood. I saw the flash of the shell exploding. I thought I must have hit a tree and exploded, but he said, 'No, it hit the turret!' It wouldn't have knocked the tank out – not really! It depends on how it hit the turret. If it hits it on the top and went down into the tank it may have wounded the gunner – and they would bail out. If you could hit the tracks it would blow the track off, break the track, then the tank is useless. Hitting the turret ring would probably jam the turret. Or if you could get an HE shell where the gun comes out of the turret, take big chunks of metal out which would damage the gun.[22]

Trooper John Buchanan, 4 Troop, 'A' Squadron, 2nd F&FY

Held towards the back of the 'A' Squadron advance was the Sherman Firefly commanded by Lance Corporal Stan Bush, with Terry Boyne acting as his wireless operator/loader. In action each troop's Firefly would prove a much-prized asset, as the 17-pounder gun had the ability to actually 'knock out' opposing Mark IV and Panther tanks. Boyne's memories conjure up the chaos and confusion that day.

It all started: guns firing, targets popping up. It all bubbled up – and all exploded around you! All the chatter over the radio. In the Firefly you were moving to targets that were often spotted by the others. Because their gun wasn't that effective on range, they would select the targets for you most of the time. As a loader you were occupied just loading! On the Firefly you had your own hatch. Because on the 75mm, the wireless operator could get under the gun to get out, but on the Firefly, being bigger, they'd cut an extra hatch overhead, alongside the commander's hatch. To see anything, you either looked through the periscope in front of you, or you put your head up. You can't see a lot, you've only got your periscope: smoke, movement around you, a lot of dust. It was like mayhem. Orders coming over the air for this, that, everything else. A lot of firing – at what I wouldn't know, wouldn't see! It was only through the gunner's sight that you would actually see a target once you started firing, as you had the ammunition all round the turret ring. The commander's order would be, 'Load with HE!' You'd open the breech and just slam it in! You had to 'punch' the shell in because as the shell went in it hit two little [things] that tripped the breech to shut. You didn't want your fingers in the way of that – it was quite a sizeable chunk! The breech snapped shut and that was it! The gunner would fire it with the trigger. As soon as it fired the shell was ejected. It would come back, hit a deflecting plate behind it and then drop. You'd have one of each ready to pick up! If it was armour-piercing, 'Bang!' that one went in and could go off in a matter of seconds. You could get a rhythm going. Then when there was a lull when it wasn't firing you busied yourself to fill in the empty spaces near to you. You wanted everything near to you to lay your hands on. Get rid of the empty shell cases that are rolling round your feet! You might be firing the machine gun, then you'd have to stick another belt in that when it got down low or ran out. The gunner would be firing that, but he relied on you to reload it. You had boxes of the ammunition at your feet ready. Just a matter of flipping up the top cover, laying it in and then cocking it.[23]

Trooper Terry Boyne, 3 Troop, 'A' Squadron, 2nd F&FY

The ammunition stacked around the turret was one of the reasons that Shermans were so quick to 'brew up'. When they were hit, the metal shell fragments flashed to white hot temperatures which set off the ammunition.

How was the battle going? Few of the men involved could have given any kind of coherent statement, nor indeed could their higher command. A battlefield is always difficult to 'read' but especially when things are going wrong. Overall, the infantry of the 15th (Scottish) Division had suffered terrible casualties, the 31st Tank Brigade had also suffered heavily, while the 2nd F&FY, which had only joined the battle later in the day, had lost nine tanks. Of these, 'C' Squadron had lost seven and 'A' Squadron the other two. One consolation was that many of the crews had escaped and been able to rejoin their unit. During the fighting, there had been an evident lack of smooth cooperation between the larger formations in the battle: by and large the 15th (Scottish) Division, the 31st Tank Brigade and the 11th Armoured Division had fought their own battles, that is when they were not actively getting in each other's way. At the end of the day, only the preliminary objectives had been achieved, with a fragile salient stretching out through Cheux, reaching towards the low rise of the 100-foot contour. They had been stopped well short of the Odon river. Worse still was the situation on the flanks, where on the left the Germans still occupied Marcelet and Carpiquet, while the 'heights' of Rauray and the village of Le Haut du Bosq still bristled with German menace on the right.

Amid all the tragedy and real suffering, it would not be the British Army without elements of macabre, black humour, as 'Pinkie' Hutchison recalled.

> It came on to very heavy rain; it was a thoroughly unpleasant evening. Cheux was in a hell of a mess: burning tanks and houses. One thing I can remember particularly, was going over a nasty bump. I had a bottle of whisky which I'd stowed for emergency purposes at the back of the radio. This bloody thing went crash on to the floor – and I knew only too well what had happened – I'd lost my bottle of whisky. That was disastrous![24]
>
> Captain Douglas Hutchison, HQ Troop, 'A' Squadron, 2nd F&FY

It sounds cold-hearted, but this kind of humour was their defence mechanism, part of what enabled them to keep going.

*

THAT NIGHT, IN THE POURING RAIN, the 2nd F&FY fell back a short distance to laager for the night. In the pitch dark finding the rendezvous was not always easy, indeed Steel Brownlie claimed he only found it by the illumination of the burning tanks scattered about the battlefield. It was an even more difficult task for the rear echelon re-supply lorries, which had a lot farther to travel, across the debris-riddled battlefield that was by no means a safe environment. Tommy Willmott was one of those driving in a convoy of trucks.

> We were waiting for the regiment to laager at night. They told us where they were and they got word back to say that they would be needing – say three ammunition trucks, two fuel trucks – and send up four tanks with crews. I did the first one. We went down with this load of supply trucks to find the regiment. The most important thing was to find the bloody laager in the first place! I never thought we were ever going to get them the first time. Cheux was a real shambles – there was fires, there was burning tanks, there was dead cattle. We just couldn't find them in the dark. It was total darkness except for the lights from the fires. No lights on the vehicles. Well, we [eventually] found them.[25]
>
> Squadron Quartermaster Sergeant Tommy Willmott, HQ Squadron, 2nd F&FY

John Hunter, a French polisher from Kirkcaldy in his civilian life, was now experiencing a very different set of challenges.

> I had a Ford ammunition truck. It carried 75mm and 17-pounder shells – all the big stuff for the tanks. They were in wooden boxes – I'd say about four to a box. I'll tell you if it got hit – that was it – you had had it! There was quite a few that were hit. It made you a wee bit scared. We had to go up at night and supply the ammunition and petrol to the tanks. You were driving with practically no lights! You followed the lorry in front of you – it had a small light on the differential. It was sore on the eyes – no sleep like! We'd meet them at a certain map reading. The tanks were just like the red Indians, round

in a circle! You went into the middle round all the tanks and supplied them with the 17-pounder or 75mm. The guys would get the shells out of the boxes and put them into the tank turret. Then they got filled up with petrol – these jerry cans.[26]

Trooper John Hunter, 'C' Squadron, 2nd F&FY

The term 'laager' originated in the Boer War, coming from the Afrikaans laager, or defended camp. It summed up the tanks' night-time arrangements.

A laager was a grouping together, just for safety and for somewhere where you could replenish. Orders would be given over the air of the laager location, which would be an open space – a field, 'A' Squadron left, 'B' Squadron right, 'C' Squadron second left, RHQ in the middle!' You would drive in, the second in command would have gone back and he would guide you. You parked nose to tail, with a gap between the lines big enough for the lorries to come along with petrol and ammunition. The first thing you did was get something to eat, because the lorries wouldn't come up until it was well and truly dark. We'd got to wait for that. Clean the guns and sort out the ammunition if you'd fired a lot: what was left, throw out the empties and count how many you needed of each type. The driver would check his petrol, see how much of that he needed. If the petrol lorry came first, he would say, 'How much you want?' He would say, ten cans, twenty cans! Or whatever! He would get it off the lorry and hand it up to the driver on the tank. He's got a funnel and he'd pour it in. He'd stack the empty cans down the side of the tank and the lorry would come round again and pick them up to take away. The water truck would come, you'd fill your water cans. The ammunition lorries would come, I'd say, 'We want so many AP, so many HE!' We'd uncase them, each round was in an individual pressed cardboard case, or in some cases in a wooden container with perhaps four shells in – and you'd have to open them up and 'bomb up'. Once you'd done all that, you might put the bivvy up, but it probably wouldn't be worth it, you would sleep in the tank or just on the ground.[27]

Trooper Roy Vallance, HQ Troop, 'A' Squadron, 2nd F&FY

When the guns had been firing during the day, the gunner and his friends in the crew had a lot of work to do before they could relax. The guns would be needed next morning, and they had to be in perfect condition.

The first thing you do is to get some hot water on the go and get the gun sorted out. We stripped the gun. The big gun first of all, we unloaded the shell, there was always a shell up the breech – we gave it a wipe with a cloth at that end. Then we got the big ramrod, with a big pad on the end, and you stuck that down with hot water and you gave it a good scrub. Norman, the wireless operator, myself, and sometimes the co-driver, gives you a hand to push this thing up and down. If you can get a good tight fit, it cleans it better – it has to be tight or it's no use. That's if you'd fired the gun! After doing that several times you got onto the machine gun – well, I could do that on my own, you see.[28]

Trooper John Buchanan, 4 Troop, 'A' Squadron, 2nd F&FY

Even then Buchanan wasn't finished.

Then I had to get the meal ready – I was the unofficial cook. I'd just open a couple of cans and put them in hot water – pierce them. You got cans of meat and veg, pork, canned steam puddings.[29]

Trooper John Buchanan, 4 Troop, 'A' Squadron, 2nd F&FY

While the crews had plenty to do replenishing their tank, their officers were also busy, supervising the overall activities and planning for the next day.

There was the business of reorganising the troop, taking on fuel, ammunition, rations from echelon trucks, reporting mechanical defects and seeing them dealt with by the fitters, attending an 'O' Group to get orders for next day, folding and marking maps, ensuring that a member of the crew was cooking and another arranging the bedding, sometimes fitting in a wash or a visit to a hedge outside the harbour, with a shovel and a supply of Army Form Blank, which was issued on the scale of two-and-a-half sheets per man per day. What time would it be, after all that lot? Depending on snags, it might be one, two or three in the morning, and orders were to be ready to move at when? Dawn? But that meant getting started early enough to stow the bedding, have some kind of breakfast, maybe have a shave, sometimes net the wireless sets, start up the engines. Then you were ready to move. Here was the big snag – how long had you slept? In the mobile fighting of World War Two, especially in the summer months, tiredness was the daily ration. The chance of a good sleep was at least as attractive as that of a sit-down meal or a bath. That night, after our first day in action, I don't think that anyone slept. The petrol and ammo took three hours to reach us, the enemy were only a few hundred yards away, and everybody was shattered by the day's events. Long afterwards you thought about Cheux as just about the worst, and anything else seemed an improvement. You also thought about Cully, a tiny hamlet, as a sort of haven of peace.[30]

Lieutenant William Steel Brownlie, 4 Troop, 'A' Squadron, 2nd F&FY

When at last their work was done, they could think about getting some sleep. Some erected their bivouacs by the side of their tanks.

You slept like a log! Your head just touched the pillow – your kitbag stuck at the back of your head – and you were gone. You just flopped. You were tense all day – you were in action – you were all tensed up. I think that made you deadbeat at night – in fact, you could hardly keep your eyes open. To get you up in the morning was a heck of a thing! If you were last man on guard duty you used to shake hard, shake them like mad to get them up![31]

Trooper John Buchanan, 4 Troop, 'A' Squadron, 2nd F&FY

As they were still within artillery range and as it was also soaking wet, many stayed in their tank, sleeping as best they could, although there was often a distinct element of the contortionist about the whole procedure.

Tom Dines and Alec Perry used to sit on their respective seats and just sort of lean forward over the guns. The drivers would be in their compartment. But I had an old cushion which came with me all the way through the war. We traversed the gun so I could get my cushion into one of the ammunition bins, I curled up in the bottom of the turret with my head on the shells. I slept quite reasonably well![32]

Captain Douglas Hutchison, HQ Troop, 'A' Squadron, 2nd F&FY

Far more unfortunate were a few tank crews who were still stuck marooned on the battlefield with their tanks having been immobilised by German fire. Robert Nurse recalled a truly hellish night trapped in his crippled hulk.

This lieutenant's tank was blazing, another tank was blazing. Tibbet was even more frightened than I was, he was absolutely rigid with fear, he didn't say a word. We were sat there all night; we didn't have any sleep. We had to stay in the bloody tank because there were all sorts of things whizzing around. We were illuminated by at least two, if not three blazing tanks, in which several of my friends were killed – Tommy Morgan[33] and Ed Crowley.[34] Very shocked, I knew that at least two of my friends burnt to death, they didn't get out. Next morning, we wondered what the hell had happened! Why had we survived? We got out of the tank – obviously the German vehicles had withdrawn. There was a 75mm hole right through the metal casing on the back of the turret, about 18–24 inches from my head! Gone in one side and out of the other – through all the greatcoats and things. I think the German gunner, seeing the flash when his shell hit, presumed he'd knocked us out – and we survived! Simple as that![35]

Trooper Robert Nurse, 2 Troop, 'C' Squadron, 2nd F&FY

It was a long night.

Wherever the men were on the battlefield, their vulnerability to the horrors of war was apparent. Looking out for their pals, it was evident that some were missing. The loss of close friends was a big challenge for any soldier – and it soon became clear that not all of them could cope with the stress of combat.

One wasn't aware of the full picture, but gradually it seeped through in the night. I was pretty frightened and horrified to think that these tanks that we'd thought were impregnable were just brewing up and had already got the nickname of 'Ronsons' because invariably when they were hit they brewed up in a flash. I was young and it was exciting, and one just thought, 'Well it's not going to happen to me!' The commander [Corporal Jim Lister] became a nervous case, he was an excellent chap, but as soon as we got into action he just went completely to pieces. He couldn't do his job, he got down in the turret to hide, he wouldn't answer the 'A' set. It was obvious he couldn't go on – he was obviously ill. It was very sad. He was sent to the doctor and he never came back.[36]

Trooper Roy Vallance, HQ Troop, 'A' Squadron, 2nd F&FY

*

CHEUX HAD BEEN CAPTURED but it was evident that there would be a great deal more fighting before they could force a crossing of the Odon, particularly with the fire still pouring in from Rauray on their right flank. At 07.15 on 27 June, another miserable wet morning, the 10th Highland Light Infantry were ordered forward from Cheux and Le Haut du Bosq, along with the 2nd Argyll and Sutherland Highlanders (2nd A&SH). The two battalions got tangled up in the narrow streets and lanes, something sometimes exacerbated by the presence of tanks – whether they were abandoned hulks or still occupied. To add to the overall turmoil, the Germans also counter-attacked.

> At dawn we moved again to the east of the village, where the infantry had made progress during the night, and some of the anti-tank ditches bridged. Churchill tanks were to take the woods south-east of Cheux, then we would pass through and take the ground beyond. There was great confusion while their attack went in, and four Panthers came into the village, scattering the infantry and getting to within 200 yards of us before being knocked out. I saw the commander of one of them blown out of his turret, 20 feet in the air, in the middle of a huge smoke ring.[37]
>
> Lieutenant William Steel Brownlie, 4 Troop, 'A' Squadron, 2nd F&FY

Before the 10th HLI could reach their start line prior to attacking towards Grainville sur Odon, they were hit hard by fire from German Panzer IVs of the recently arrived 8th Company (commanded by Obersturmführer Hans Siegel) of the 2/12th SS Panzer Regiment. The experienced Siegel had taken up concealed positions along a hedge, with his own tank blocking a sunken road. Their turret machine guns tore tremendous gaps in the ranks of the Scots as they struggled across the open field in front of them. Siegel's subsequent reports were written in the third person.

> They let the attack approach them frontally. Fire only from machine guns, not from the Panzer guns, so as not to betray the presence of Panzers prematurely. Open fire only at the commander's orders. We let them come close and then hammer

at short distance, concentrated fire from four machine guns at the massed attackers who are anxiously firing bullets into the terrain, with no aiming. Experience has shown that our tactic works, and the consequence here is, too, that they run back in panic.[38]

Obersturmführer Hans Siegel, 8th Company, 12th SS Panzer Regiment

When the Churchills of 7th Royal Tank Regiment arrived, they were knocked out one by one by the virtually invisible German panzers.

We open fire from our panzer guns only on the tanks attacking with the second wave. Again, we achieve full success, without losses of our own. The crews bail out in panic from burning and exploding tanks. The rest of them turn away and, with them, the infantry disappears behind the hills. In the meantime, the sun is climbing higher.[39]

Obersturmführer Hans Siegel, 8th Company, 12th SS Panzer Regiment

The 2nd F&FY took up the attack on Grainville sur Odon. 'A' Squadron would lead, with 'B' and 'C' Squadrons coming up behind them. It is interesting to note that they had already learnt some lessons from their experiences the day before. When on exercises in the UK, the troop officer had usually led the way, but now they were actually in action, that job was more often undertaken by the troop sergeant. It was evident that if the troop officer led and his tank was put out of action in a sudden ambush, it would leave the troop temporarily leaderless just when they most required direction. Steel Brownlie describes what happened as the Shermans took over the advance.

The Churchill attack got nowhere, and we took over. We were to advance up a slope, over the skyline, and then down into the woods beyond, where the enemy positions were. We had two troops up, Freddie Craig on the right, and myself behind him. As he topped the ridge, three of his tanks were brewed, and his took cover in a slight hollow. I had to take his place, so kept going. We advanced in the prescribed manner, troop sergeant leading, and the Firefly in rear. The latter had the only effective anti-tank gun in our troops, the 17-pounder, while the rest of us had the 75mm, which was great for firing HE shells, but not sufficient muzzle velocity for AP shot. Now it was in action, ready to take on 'hard' targets, when summoned. The trouble was that the corporal commanding [the Firefly] did not intend to be summoned, and would not even keep up, but lagged behind – in spite of my orders over the air.[40]

Lieutenant William Steel Brownlie, 4 Troop, 'A' Squadron, 2nd F&FY

We should perhaps remember that criticism of individuals made in the press of battle is not always justified.

It must have been Corporal Croney, he had the 17-pounder. The trouble was getting them up. If you met a Panther or Tiger tank, the only person that could go against it was the 17-pounder. We could never get it in the right area at the right time. Steel Brownlie used to swear a bit, 'Where's that fucking tank! The 17-pounder was no use as a high explosive cannon – it was all right for AP but HE it was no use. The 75mm was a great gun for HE. That's what we used most.[41]

Trooper John Buchanan, 4 Troop, 'A' Squadron, 2nd F&FY

Then Steel Brownlie and his crew had a lucky escape, although their luck was another crew's misfortune.

Sergeant Greenfield topped the ridge safely, and was going flat out down the slope, when I saw a Panther emerging from the woods on his left and firing at him. On top of the ridge, I was ranging on the Panther, and trying to get Sergeant Greenfield on the air to warn him, when everything went wrong. A shell jammed in my breech, and all my electrics went dead. There was no radio, intercom, engine, and power traverse. Immobile on the skyline, all I could do was to fire machine gun, manually, at the Panther. Its gun traversed towards me, my .3-inch bullets bouncing off it, when suddenly it turned and disappeared into the wood. It was an incredible let-off. Dick Greenfield was not so lucky. He had gone on, alone and unsupported, and was brewed up. Thomson[42] and Sykes[43] were killed, Harper[44] died in hospital, he [Greenfield] and Ian Martin were burned and never rejoined. The squadron passed on, and I had some clearing up to do.[45]

Lieutenant William Steel Brownlie, 4 Troop, 'A' Squadron, 2nd F&FY

These losses may well have been the responsibility of Hans Siegel's 8th Company of Mark IVs. By this time 'B' and 'C' Squadrons were coming up on the flanks. Suddenly Siegel himself was hit.

An anti-tank shell coming from the right suddenly rips open the floor of the chief's panzer. The lone tank had sneaked close, and while our turret is still moving to the 3 o'clock position, a shell hits the front right and, like a flash, the chief's panzer is engulfed in flames. Hatch covers fly open, the gunner bails out to the left, in flames, the loader dives out to the right. The chief wants to get out through the top turret hatch but is caught by the throat microphone wire. He then tries to make it through the loader's hatch to the right, but bumps head violently with the radio operator who could not open his own hatch. The barrel, having been turned half right, is blocking it. The chief has to move backward. He pushes the radio operator through the hatch, is engulfed in flames for some seconds, in danger of fainting. Still he manages the jump to safety. But he still has the steel boom of the throat microphone at his neck, he cannot pull it over his steel helmet. So he is hanging at the panzer skirt, almost strangling himself while machine-gun salvos are slapping against the panzer. With a desperate jerk, he rips loose. The wire, almost finger-thick, dangles in front of his chest. In the hollow, scene of the attack at night, the crew assembles, except for the driver, Sturmmann Schleweis, who remained in the burning panzer. He was probably wounded, or killed by the impact. His hatch was free, he would have made it out otherwise. The gunner lies on the ground, still in flames. The crew covers him with their own, partly burned, bodies, trying to smother the flames. He was not wearing leather gear, but only fatigues, since he was taking the place of the regular gunner only for the night. The gunner died of his burns later in hospital. Initially, the chief as well as the others do not notice their own burns on their faces and their hands. The tank attack is still rolling ahead; it has not been stopped. However, this is soon looked after by the other three panzers. They seem not to have noticed the drama which just ended. The excitement of combat holds everyone in its grip.[46]

Obersturmführer Hans Siegel, 8th Company, 12th SS Panzer Regiment

Although he suffered bad burns on his face and hands, Siegel would soon return to the fray after only a brief hospitalisation.

By this time Steel Brownlie was also out of action with his Sherman immobile and helpless. Ever proactive, he got out of the tank to see what he could do.

Jumping down on to the grass, the first thing I saw was a complete leg, in a boot and a gaiter, and a bit of battledress trouser with quite a good crease in it. Nearby was one of Freddie Craig's tanks, not fully burnt out, and Corporal Sangster crouching underneath it. He and I got his tank moving, and arranged for it to tow mine back off the ridge. While the towrope was being shackled, I crawled around looking for Sergeant Hepburn,[47] whom I had seen struggling out of his burning tank, with both legs blown off. I found no trace of him. Corporal Sangster's tank towed mine back to the village, with numerous halts as we picked up wounded infantrymen who were lying in the fields.[48]

Lieutenant William Steel Brownlie, 4 Troop, 'A' Squadron, 2nd F&FY

As he fell back, they encountered a most unexpected visitor to the battlefield.

> We stopped near the village and set to work trying to repair the fault in my tank. It turned out to be a damaged master switch. We were heavily mortared, and at one point dived under the tank for shelter. We were astonished to see Padre Oswald Welsh walking towards us, in the open, and my driver, Jock McKinnon, poked his head out and shouted, 'For fuck's sake, Padre, come in oot o' there!' Oswald replied, 'Now, McKinnon, watch your language!' And, pointing to his dog-collar, 'I'm a non-combatant!' He walked on. I recounted this to him many years later, not long before he died, and his response was that he never really knew what was going on. The truth was, I believe, that he simply did not care what was going on (mortars or anything else), but just went about doing his job.[49]
>
> Lieutenant William Steel Brownlie, 4 Troop, 'A' Squadron, 2nd F&FY

With power restored to his Sherman, Steel Brownlie moved into cover and awaited the return of the rest of 'A' Squadron, which he was informed by radio would soon be falling back to replenish fuel and ammunition, while 'C' Squadron took over the push on Grainville sur Odon. Behind the 2nd F&FY both Cheux and Le Haut du Bosq were vulnerable to attack from the Germans from around Rauray and Noyers, with various threatening incursions of infantry and tanks during the day. Most serious was the arrival of some seventeen Panther tanks of the 3rd Panzer Division driving in from Fontenay in the west – and aiming straight for the 5th Duke of Cornwall's Light Infantry (DCLI) of the 43rd (Wessex) Division, who had moved forward to relieve the 46th Brigade. It will be noted that this is well behind the 2nd F&FY and driving into the side of the salient. Fortunately for the 5th DCLI, the Panthers had no infantry support and the infantry was able to deploy PIATs and 6-pounder anti-tank guns to considerable effect, knocking out several Panthers and forcing them to withdraw, although not before they had created a substantial amount of mayhem.

Once the surviving tanks from 'A' Squadron had made their way back and been replenished, they set off once again, back towards Grainville sur Odon. This might have been a thankless task, but luckily the surviving three Mark IVs of Siegel's detachment had by this time withdrawn to re-stock their ammunition. The way was open.

> I reassembled what was left of my troop and was told to lead the way up to the railway by Grainville. We crossed it unopposed 300 yards from the village. This was a commanding position, and I did an HE shoot on some camouflaged vehicles 3,500 yards ahead. Don Hall and I sat in the shelter of smoke from a burning house, and watched Kenneth Matheson's Recce Troop go into the village to see if it was clear.[50]
>
> Lieutenant William Steel Brownlie, 4 Troop, 'A' Squadron, 2nd F&FY

Steel Brownlie watched Matheson and the Recce Troop edge forward into Grainville sur Odon. Would the village be occupied? Or empty? It was occupied all right!

> He lost a tank, but no men, to a Panther sitting in or beside the church. As he was belting back past us, having done his job, Colonel Scott came on the air and asked him for his exact position. He replied: 'Position be buggered! Wait! Out.' The Churchills appeared again, and with infantry went into Grainville, while we supported by fire. They met strong opposition and were repulsed. Dozens of wounded were dragged back to where we were sitting, and some lay in the shelter of my tank until jeeps took them back. I still see one infantryman, both legs blown off, lying with his head pillowed on a groundsheet and puffing at a cigarette. I doubt if he made it. At dusk, the infantry dug in, and we withdrew to harbour, finding our way through woods and little fields bounded by

deep ditches and high banks. This was the Bocage. That was 27 June.[51]

Lieutenant William Steel Brownlie, 4 Troop, 'A' Squadron, 2nd F&FY

It had been a deeply depressing day for the 2nd F&FY.

Overall, when listening to the 2nd F&FY veterans or reading the regimental history, it seems that every German tank they faced that day was a Panther or Tiger, although we now know that there were more Mark IVs than anything else in the thick of the fighting. However, I find it difficult to fault men for poor AFV identification from mere glimpses of German tanks in battle conditions of dire visibility, with billowing smoke and masses of hedges or woods creating an environment ideal for concealment. But whatever the number of Panthers, it is undeniable that they did make a big impression on the men – Captain 'Pinkie' Hutchison was certainly not alone in his envious thoughts.

> I think we had a growing respect for Panthers – they were a very well-designed battle tank. They had a damn good gun – a long barrel 75mm with very good armour-piercing shot. We were money for old rope in our Shermans, which they could penetrate from any angle. When they were head on, they had a very sloped glacis plate and it was quite thick too. Even with a Firefly, 17-pounder, if the shot hit the glacis plate it would bounce off and not penetrate. It wasn't so well protected from the sides and the rear. So, if you got it sideways on, it was easier to knock out.[52]

Captain Douglas Hutchison, HQ Troop, 'A' Squadron, 2nd F&FY

In sharp contrast, his two days on the battlefield had opened his eyes as to the endemic weakness of the Sherman.

> It was rather horrifying to see how readily – sometimes almost instantaneously – the Sherman when it was struck and knocked out would explode. You would see a tank struck, a 'WHOOOSH!' out of the turret. There wasn't a hope in hell

of any of the crew getting out in those circumstances. One
of the reasons was we were carrying too much ammunition,
overloading with ammunition, and the ammunition bins were
not armour protected and therefore very vulnerable to any
penetration of the turret.[53]

Captain Douglas Hutchison, HQ Troop, 'A' Squadron, 2nd F&FY

The Shermans were exposed, but there was nothing they could
do. Adding extra armour to the sides didn't seem to help – they
would just have to put up with it.

However, amidst the dismay, there was one piece of good
news for the 2nd F&FY and the rest of the 11th Armoured Division on 27 June. On their right flank the 49th (West Riding)
Division had at last managed to wrest control of the dominant
heights around Rauray, although Le Manoir alongside it was still
held by the Germans. But the really startling development was
on the immediate left flank, where the 2nd A&SH had made an
amazing breakthrough, advancing along the road from Cheux,
and clearing successively the villages of Colleville, Mondrainville and Tourville. They then pushed on even further and by
17.15 they succeeded in capturing the 13-foot-wide bridge over
the Odon on the road that led into the village of Tourmauville.
A 200-yard diameter bridgehead was established on the other
side with dug-in PIAT teams. This was a precarious position – a
narrow 'Scottish corridor' based on just one country lane passing
through the Cheux salient. The question was, could they be
reinforced before the Germans swept them away in a counter-
attack? First to arrive was a company of the motorised 8th Rifle
Brigade followed up by the 23rd Hussars. The Scottish infantry
had done well, but it was largely achieved by their own efforts,
with little effective cooperation with supporting armour. That is
not to say the tanks were not busy, they were just fighting separate battles. General 'Pip' Roberts was determined to seize the
opportunity the bridge represented and ordered forward the
motorised infantry of his 159th Brigade. They drove down the

road to Colleville and then shook out to advance from the Villers Bocage–Caen highway to the Odon, with a theoretical zero hour of 21.30. Urgency was paramount, and although there were the inevitable delays, they managed to take up defensive positions around Baron sur Odon and Tourmauville, thereby expanding the Argyll's original bridgehead. Next day, it was planned that the whole 11th Armoured Division would drive across the Odon and on across the high ground dominated by Hill 112 towards the Orne river. This would be their next challenge.

9

HILL 112

I was just excited the first time. But within three days I was scared. We were all scared. We got shaken up a bit, we didn't expect this is what it was going to be like. Shells coming over, mortar shells, these 'Moaning Minnies'. All you could see was these tracers coming flying at you! The dirty crack of these shells as they passed over your tank. I got a shake-up. We suddenly realised, 'This is war! They're trying to kill you!' This is what got into your mind![1]

Trooper John Buchanan, 4 Troop, 'A' Squadron, 2nd F&FY

AFTER THEIR FRUSTRATING DAY on 27 June, the 2nd F&FY laagered for the night near Cheux. The battle was in the balance, for although the 15th (Scottish) Division and the 11th Armoured Division had made some progress, German reinforcements were beginning to arrive. Yet the pressures imposed on the German High Command were such that instead of concentrating their forces for a decisive counter-attack, infantry and tank units were hurled into battle as soon as possible, attacking unsupported and hence open to serious losses. German successes had been founded on their tanks, motorised infantry, air power and artillery being all meshed together to achieve their objectives. Air power had already been wrested from them, but now the other elements were beginning to have to fight separate battles due to the Allied pressure.

On 28 June, the Germans counter-attacked, pushing forward on either side of the 'Scottish Corridor'. On the eastern side, they struck along the Caen–Villers Bocage road, through the village of Mouen and thereby crashing into the rather flimsy left flank of the 'Scottish corridor'. They achieved some initial success, but were pounded mercilessly by the massed guns of the Royal Artillery and the attack was thwarted. Meanwhile, an attack was launched on the right flank of the salient, driving in on Grainville sur Odon, which had been finally captured by the 9th Cameronians (Scottish Rifles) at just after 12.00. They had scant chance to consolidate their position before the German attack hit them hard. Here too, fighting would rage all day long.

None of these tactical matters was foremost in the minds of the men of the 2nd F&FY. After the recent hard fighting, they were focused on getting as much sleep as possible, eating their rations and attending to other necessities of life. On the morning of 28 June, the 2nd F&FY were ordered forward, not to Mouen. or Grainville, but across the Odon into the very tip of the 'Scottish Corridor' salient. They were to use the Tourmauville bridge and push across the high ground and secure the Orne river bridges. This bold undertaking reflected 'Pip' Roberts's optimism that they had now broken through the German defence lines, and that the way ahead would be relatively clear. Ahead of them, the 23rd Hussars had been ordered to move up on to Hill 112, a whaleback hill, which was barely noticeable in itself, but which by a fluke of geography offered excellent views over much of the contested battlefield, looking towards Caen itself across the Carpiquet airfield and over to the Orne river. The Hussars were supplemented up there by the 8th Rifle Brigade who took up defensive positions in an orchard at the summit. Unfortunately, the Germans were also beginning to climb the hill, pushing up from Esquay on the southern slopes.

Although the Tourmauville bridge was inherently sound, it was narrow, and this, combined with the steep, sharply curving approach on the northern bank, made the crossing a difficult and slow business for armoured vehicles. Step forward the Royal Engineers, who cheerfully bulldozed a straight track down to the river through the trees, where they made an improvised fascine bridge just downstream from the original bridge. Here Norman Bradley, in his pre-war life a butcher's boy in Northamptonshire, but now a Sherman driver, came to grief.

> We got hit in the back end of the tank just by the River Orne. It hit the engine compartment and we lost control of the thing. It rolled down the embankment. We all got out. That's when I first came across the colonel of the regiment, Colonel Scott. He came along with his aides. He got the five of us lined up in front of him on the roadside and we were given a real dressing down for being in the wrong place at the wrong time! We'd done nothing wrong as far as I could see – it was just unfortunate. They moved on and left us.[2]
>
> Trooper Norman Bradley, 1 Troop, 'B' Squadron, 2nd F&FY

By 10.30, the 2nd F&FY were across the Odon, after which they moved forward to protect the right flank of the 23rd Hussars, while the 3rd Royal Tank Regiment moved through Baron and on to the northern slopes of Hill 112. As they moved towards Esquay, 'A' Squadron came in contact with panzers – as ever they were identified as Tigers.

> The whole brigade went across and spread out on the slopes of Hill 112, the summit of which remained in dispute – the Germans were very reluctant to yield the summit. We were astride a road going over one side of it, there was a ridge in front, and I got hull down. I remember seeing, quite a long way ahead, I wasn't sure whether it was a self-propelled gun or a Tiger, dug in on the far side. I bracketed the thing – and I hit it – it seemed to go up in smoke. It was at long range! What you could do with a deliberate shoot like that was you corrected for line after your first shot, pretty accurately, and then you simply bracketed and generally within three rounds you would

be on the target. With HE you could use it in two ways: either explosion on hitting, or you could do an airburst – when there was a delayed action, the shell came down and hit the ground in front, bounced up – and then burst![3]

Captain Douglas Hutchison, HQ Troop, 'A' Squadron, 2nd F&FY

When the 23rd Hussars were pulled back to replenish their ammunition, 3rd Royal Tank Regiment moved up on to Hill 112, while the 2nd F&FY shuffled round to take their place. Here they found themselves within easy range of the artillery based at Carpiquet airfield. Up on the wide-open summit it was becoming apparent that tanks could not survive. They were excruciatingly visible and hence vulnerable to fire from 88mm and other anti-tank guns that the Germans had deployed well back on the reverse slopes. However, the same applied to German tanks who were also unable to get a grip on the summit, as Willy Kretzschmar recalled.

We started the attack in a broad wedge formation on that wooded area at 09.30 or 10.00 hours. We worked our way forward, each panzer giving the other covering fire. Without firm targets, we fired anti-tank and explosive shells into the wood. The attack moved forward briskly. When we had approached to within 300 to 400 metres, we spotted retreating English soldiers between the trees. We fired the turret and forward machine guns into the wooded terrain. At approximately 100 metres from the woods, we changed from the wedge into a staggered line since the opening in the forest was only 80 to 100 metres wide. The incline on our left was covered with bushes and trees. I was now driving as the point panzer. Our direction was approximately north-west. The gun was pointing at 12 o'clock, an anti-tank shell was ready in the barrel. We cautiously made our way forward along the small forest which was 150 to 200 metres wide. At the end of the forest, I ordered an observation stop. I searched the terrain to the right in front of us with my binoculars for tanks and Pak [anti-tank guns]. Since I did not spot anything suspicious, I ordered, 'Panzer, march!' After a drive of only 10 to 15 metres there was a sudden bang, sparks were flying and we noticed a hit from the right, 3 o'clock direction. I shouted at the driver, Sturmmann Schneider, 'Backward, march!' He reacted at lightning speed, threw the panzer into reverse, and backed into the cover of the forest at full throttle. Not one second too soon, otherwise the British would have nailed us directly. Immediately in front of our bow, anti-tank shells ripped ugly black furrows into the green grass. Now, the forest came back to life. Fire from rifles and machine guns was pinging against the armour. We were covered by mortar and artillery fire. We did not hold back either and briskly returned the fire as we were backing away. We returned to our assembly area without any losses. There, we inspected our damages – a clean hit, gone through between the engine and fighting compartments approximately 25 centimetres below the turret. Except for a small shrapnel stuck in my right thigh, we all escaped with just a scare.[4]

Oberscharführer Willy Kretzschmar, 5th Company, 12th SS Panzer Regiment

Through it all the men of the 8th Rifle Brigade stayed in their trenches in the orchard, although they suffered terrible casualties. That night, the 2nd F&FY laagered on the backward slopes of Hill 112, dispersing camp just before dawn to return to their forward positions.

On 29 June, the Germans struck back hard. By this time, the II Panzer Corps (9th and 10th SS Panzer Divisions) had arrived, after a long and increasing laborious journey from the Eastern Front, harassed throughout by Allied air power and the consequent damage to transport infrastructure. Once again, these German reinforcements, irreplaceable military assets, would be flung into action with scant chance to rest, reorganise, recce, or coordinate with the intended supporting arms. Two thrusts were hastily planned: the 9th SS Panzer Division would attack the western flank of the 'Scottish Corridor' driving towards Cheux; while the 10th SS Panzer Division would hit the 11th Armoured Division clustered around Hill 112. Although the British had some inkling of this from 'Ultra' Intelligence, tight secrecy meant that this knowledge was restricted to the higher echelons of command, down only as far as General Miles Dempsey (Second Army). Although Dempsey warned Lieutenant General Richard O'Connor (VIII Corps) that German forces were building up, he could not – or did not – press home the true nature of the threat and it was only late on 28 June that he issued a direct order to withdraw from the Odon bridgehead. O'Connor did not immediately respond, perhaps still hoping to secure a significant breakthrough. In consequence, he failed to pass on Dempsey's orders to his divisional commanders and instead, merely moved up more of the 43rd (Wessex) Division to take over the defence of the eastern flank of the 'Scottish Corridor', while the 15th (Scottish) Division guarded the western flank. Roberts was told to temporarily suspend the advance on the Orne river and – for the moment – to hold his ground.

As the German counter-attacks crunched home, the 44th Royal Tank Regiment was heavily engaged, fighting off the attacks of the 10th SS Panzer Division on Hill 113, just to the east of Hill 112. The Germans also hit the 2nd Argylls defending the Gavrus bridge crossing and the surrounding wooded area. Meanwhile the 9th SS Panzer Division smashed into the 7th Seaforth Highlanders in Valtru and the 9th Cameronians in Grainville sur Odon. These attacks were, broadly speaking, withstood, thanks in part to the efforts of the massed batteries of the Royal Artillery, whose concentrated fire helped break up the German assaults and 'chewed up' newly arrived units before they even got into battle. The RAF also played a useful role as the weather improved.

These flanking attacks might well have doomed the 2nd

F&FY, isolated as they were five miles deep into German territory in the bridgehead over the Odon, but its focus was concentrated for the most part on Hill 112. In that fluctuating battle, a lot of the credit for maintaining any sort of a perch near the summit rested with the men of the 8th Rifle Brigade who held on to the positions with grim determination. In the morning, 'C' Squadron began to climb the hill, with 'A' Squadron on their left, while 'B' Squadron continued to watch over the safety of the village of Baron. When Charlie Workman approached the hill, he had a disconcerting warning that things might be going to get considerably tougher.

> I met a bunch of infantrymen running down like mad, headed by a major! I said to him, 'What's going on?' 'Oh,' he said, 'It's hell up there!' and he dashed away past me and disappeared. Hill 112 wasn't a massive hill, but it was big enough so that when we were on top, we could see what was going on on the other side. When I got up on top of Hill 112, down there was a road full of Germans. 'Right, let's have a crack!' We were banging away at them, there was no tanks, but we brewed up one or two lorries about half a mile from us – not all that far from us. There was a lot of mortar fire and nebelwerfers fired from a lorry. No tactical skill could avoid that if a mortar shell came down – you didn't know where the mortar was. You knew roughly where they were coming from. You could hear a shell coming, but with the mortar you had no indication at all – just 'WHOOF!' And usually somebody would 'buy it'! We saw one or two nebelwerfers down on that road. We fired at them and they shoved off. It was a rocket that made an awful scream – and then, 'Bang! Bang! Bang!'[5]
>
> Lieutenant Charlie Workman, 1 Troop, 'C' Squadron, 2nd F&FY

Given the vulnerability of tanks on the bare slopes of Hill 112, Roy Vallance's bulldozer tank was soon called into use.

We had to go forward to where the Rifle Brigade were on
Hill 112, to dig positions with the bulldozer. You'd pick the
positions where the tanks would want to be, with the aid of
the squadron leader, you lower your blade and push forwards
and then sideways, until you've dug a giant pit a tank would
be 'hull down in'. You could lift your blade right up high and
smooth the top down. This was under terrific opposition.
A Panther – probably – was firing at us from a wood. We
spotted it after a bit and fired back and it disappeared. I don't
think we hit it, but it went! There was also a terrific amount of
'Moaning Minnies' – nebelwerfers – just plastering the hilltop.
Very frightening, they made a terrible screeching noise, so you
knew they were coming in your direction. I don't think they
would hurt the tank – but [they would] if you had your head
out or were outside, which we were quite a lot, guiding the
driver in his bulldozing, because he couldn't see much except
the back of his blade. I was concentrating on digging these
holes![6]

Trooper Roy Vallance, HQ Troop, 'A' Squadron, 2nd F&FY

Robert Nurse was the gunner in the crew of Lieutenant Eric
Lamont on the slopes of Hill 112 when they thought they had an
opportunity to knock out one of the German tanks.

We were overlooking Carpiquet aerodrome on a forward slope.
There was a big wood across the other side of the valley – and
suddenly four – I think they might have been Tigers – started
crossing our bows from right to left! Lamont directed me on
the leading one with the 75mm – and I fired. I watched the
trace – and it hit the bloody thing! The turret. It went 'Boom'
and bounced off. We saw these four barrels coming round!
'Driver, reverse!' And we went back over the hill. They fired at
us, but all four missed. We were back on the other side of the
hill before you could say, 'Knife!'[7]

Trooper Robert Nurse, 2 Troop, 'C' Squadron, 2nd F&FY

This was the dispiriting truth about the 75mm armament of the Sherman. Even a direct hit with an armour-piercing shell would often achieve nothing against the armour of the latest German tanks – even from the side. Their best chance was to disable their tracks, or hit them from the rear. It could take three or four Shermans operating together to 'take out' a Panther, while many considered that the Tiger was best dealt with by the Typhoons of the RAF. In contrast the Sherman Firefly was proving more effective. The regimental history proudly boasted that Sergeant William Heard knocked out a 'Tiger' in his Firefly. His gunner was John Scott, but the driver, Harold Wilson, offered a more pragmatic version of their success.

> We shot up a tank. With the 17-pounder. We were anything from 1,000–1,200 yards from this tank. It certainly wasn't a Tiger or anything like that – it would be one of the Mark IVs.[8]
>
> Trooper Harold Wilson, 4 Troop, 'C' Squadron, 2nd F&FY

At some point in the fighting, the more powerful 17-pounder Firefly in which Terry Boyne was temporarily acting as gunner also claimed a success firing at a Mark IV, probably somewhat lower down the hill.

> We had a report on our radio from one of the dug-in tanks on our left that something was moving behind a hedge – and it was moving in our direction. This had happened frequently; you'd fire at something you thought was there and if you checked you'd find it was a cow – no doubt a lot of cows used to get killed like that! So we fired a couple of HE to punch a little hole in the hedge; we were scanning this area, I held the gun near enough where I thought it might be if it was moving – it was only a guestimate. With the gun sitting as it was, through the hedge came the nose of a tank! Edge on, oblique, with the tank climbing up to get over the bank. It just popped up in my sights – we're only talking about 80 yards – not far! I didn't have to do anything other than hit the button! I banged the

shot off which was armour-piercing – it hit it right behind the sprocket. It was a Mark IV, it had small cupola on the top and it was actually moving – the commander must have been moving it around as I fired. He must have looked straight down the barrel of the Firefly – that must have been his vision. A load of dust went up from around it from the impact of it! It rolled back and we punched another shot right in. [9]

Trooper Terry Boyne, 4 Troop, 'A' Squadron, 2nd F&FY

As the long day wore on, 'A' Squadron relieved 'C' Squadron up on top of Hill 112. As night fell, they remained *in situ* rather than falling back to laager.

It came on the air that they couldn't get the supplies through, because the Germans had cut the bridge again on the path back. So we were left up there! At night, the weird thing was the fact that the Germans were down the slope and you could hear them refuelling their vehicles – throwing cans about! Hear them actually talking! I suppose the wind was in the right direction. The bit that really got you worried was when you heard the engines start, and the old tracks start rolling – you're not sure whether it's coming up, going down, or whatever! And then after a minute or so they'd stop and switch off – it's a war of nerves. [10]

Trooper Terry Boyne, 4 Troop, 'A' Squadron, 2nd F&FY

Little did Terry Boyne know that in the game of 'poker' between the British and German high command, the British had already folded.

As night fell on 29 June, the situation was once again delicately balanced. The 8th Rifle Brigade were still clinging on to the top of Hill 112, the 29th Armoured Brigade was supporting them and so far was withstanding panzer attacks. The flanks of the 'Scottish Corridor', now defended by both the 15th and 43rd Divisions, were just about holding, despite serious pressure. Then at 22.00 on 29 June came the bombshell: Major General 'Pip' Roberts was ordered to pull back the 29th Armoured

Brigade with immediate effect. This decision was controversial at the time and remains so to some. From one perspective it seemed that the bridgehead over the Odon and Hill 112, which had been paid for with blood and guts, was now to be given up without a fight.

> Whether the enemy's thrust could ever have made a decisive penetration must remain doubtful. In fact, he broke it off that night and did not resume it. With the results of this its first battle, the division as a whole was by no means displeased. Epsom had proved abortive, but the abortion had been in the last resort the outcome of higher command decisions which caused considerable surprise at the time. The wisdom of these decisions is not here questioned; but the general feeling – that in spite of tank losses, a further sweep southwards from Hill 112, coupled with the continued repulse of enemy attacks on the flanks, was well within its powers – was indicative of the high state of the division's morale.[11]
>
> Lieutenant Edgar Palamountain, HQ, 11th Armoured Division

But the corridor was perilously thin – only 2,500 yards at best – so it would take only a small penetration by the German counter-attacks to 'pinch it out', leaving the units in the Odon bridgehead, high and dry. The ground taken may have cost much blood, but a lot more could have been lost if anything had gone wrong. Attracting the attention of the German panzer divisions was surely only a valid policy if their attacks were held without calamitous setbacks. And there is no doubt that the 29th Armoured Brigade was in a very vulnerable position. On balance, General Miles Dempsey probably took the sensible decision. Certainly 'Pinkie' Hutchison agreed.

> They were nervous about the corridor behind us being cut – and to have a whole brigade of tanks [marooned] over on the far side of the Odon. They had a lot of 88mm anti-aircraft guns on Carpiquet aerodrome. It could have developed in quite a

nasty way if the corridor was cut. That's what the Germans tried very hard to do! They weren't successful – happily! We were withdrawn during the night over a captured bridge.[12]

Captain Douglas Hutchison, HQ Troop, 'A' Squadron, 2nd F&FY

By picking their time under the cover of night they were able to retire in good order, crossing the Odon and pulling all the way back to Norrey-en-Bessin, which they reached at first light on 30 June.

By this time, everyone was completely and utterly exhausted. Charlie Workman remembered the awful state he was in. These were young, fit men, but sleep deprivation and prolonged combat had driven them to the very edge.

We never put hatches over, we always kept our head and shoulders out, map round neck, and used our binoculars. In fact, at first, we wore our cheesecutter, our ordinary cap, until we began to realise with the heavy mortaring and the nebelwerfer, 'We'd better wear these steel helmets'. One was on the constant lookout. We had had a rough time of it. These guys weren't that far away – so we never left the tank at all, we stayed put. I was in the tank for five days. Everyone else in the tank is seated: the driver and his co-driver, the wireless operator, your gunner. The tank commander has got a small seat he pulls down, just a little thing. In the nature of things, you don't really sit on a seat when you're in action – you're standing. I was in the tank for five days – I couldn't get out – I had to be pulled out and my ankles had swollen right up.[13]

Lieutenant Charlie Workman, 1 Troop, 'C' Squadron, 2nd F&FY

'Pinkie' Hutchison was also at the end of his tether. Extreme fatigue took many forms.

I was so damned tired that I was beginning to see things and my illusion was that everything I saw was a dead cow! There were a lot of dead cows about the place. In that sort of weather

their corpses were swelling up, the legs sticking up! Anything I
saw moving turned into a dead cow! This was pure fatigue – I'd
have no – very little – sleep for four days.[14]

Captain Douglas Hutchison, HQ Troop, 'A' Squadron, 2nd F&FY

There was something else other than fatigue preying on their
minds. They now knew what they were up against and they
knew that there were many such trials ahead of them.

I reorganised the troop slightly, trying to get the most efficient
team, and gave my Firefly commander a bollocking for not
keeping up. He exploded that no one had ever called him a
coward before, but I ignored that and walked away. Hearing
a scuffle, I turned to see Trooper Cross grappling with him.
He had his loaded pistol in his hand, and evidently intended
to shoot me in the back. I decided to take no action, on the
grounds that he had been feeling the strain, and that he had
been in action in North Africa, so had maybe a different view
from novices like us. In fact, he performed very well thereafter.[15]

Lieutenant William Steel Brownlie, 4 Troop, 'A' Squadron, 2nd F&FY

The regiment stayed on rest at Norrey-en-Bessin for a couple
of days, resting and recuperating in wheatfields. They were out
of the line, but not out of range of the German mortars based
around the Carpiquet airfield, and they suffered a steady drip,
drip of casualties.

We got mortared. One night we got a terrible deluge of mortars
coming down on us. In the tank it was all right – the tank
swayed a bit with the blast – I didn't worry about it. I used to
think, 'If one comes through the hatch, I won't know anything
about it, but otherwise I'll be all right!' When I was outside,
I used to dive into a trench, a ditch or under the tank – it was
frightening if you were out of the tank. They sounded as if they
were coming right down on top of you. I used to be sorry for
the infantry who were outside and might have been in among

it! Terrific bangs these mortars. You can't imagine what they're like until they drop around you![16]

Trooper Jack Edwards, 4 Troop, 'B' Squadron, 2nd F&FY

They knew better than to take cover under the tank itself, but they soon found a way to use its imposing bulk to protect them from the tumbling shells.

While we were in reserve in this wheatfield, we used to dig a big hole about 2 feet deep and run the tank over the top of it. Then we used to sleep in the hole, which was a bit safer than anywhere else. If there was any mortar or shellfire it was somewhere to dive into in the daytime. On this occasion, I unrolled my bedding roll, to try and get it sorted out a bit, because it had got in a mess. I got it nicely folded up and while I'm doing that, we heard this shower of mortars screaming down on us. Everybody all dived in the hole. When we came out my bedding roll was just covered in rocks and bits of steel and God knows what. One had landed 4 or 5 yards away! Good job I moved![17]

Trooper Jack Edwards, 4 Troop, 'B' Squadron, 2nd F&FY

While seeking solitude for a latrine break, Jack Rex discovered an unpleasant memento of the past fighting.

If you wanted to go to the toilet, you took a shovel, dug a hole and covered everything up so there wasn't diseases. I went out to this orchard, into a cornfield. As I went in there was a big corn ring. I thought, 'Well that's funny!' Being a farmer's son, I'd seen these rings in grass fields, which are caused by a fungi that grows in a circle. But I'd never seen it in a cornfield – and it was a perfect circle. The corn was trampled down about a yard wide. When I'd finished, I walked over and I was more surprised to see the inside of the circle sprayed pink! I thought, 'That's funny!' So I walked round – and when I got to the other side there was a young German laid dead. He had his hands round his neck – something had hit his jugular vein a little bit of shrapnel or a bullet – he'd tried to put a tourniquet on and all he had was a German newspaper. He'd run round in circles half a dozen times, the paper had got soaked, then it had broke – but he was still holding it when I found him. The seams of his trousers had split with his body swelling up. Because I found him, they made me in charge of the burial party. We buried him more or less where he was laid. I've often thought about it, nobody put anything on his grave to say who he was, never took his discs off – just buried him like a dog. He had a photo of him standing with what looked like his sister, dad and mother outside of a log cabin in among the pine trees. You could see mountains in the background. Even though he was the enemy I still think about him – he was only a bit of a lad.[18]

Trooper Jack Rex, HQ Squadron, 2nd F&FY

Another family that would never know what had happened to their son, not even where he was buried.

The withdrawal of 29th Armoured Brigade marked the end of the attempt made during Operation Epsom to advance to the Orne river. Now the focus shifted to defending what they had, sucking in and destroying as much German armour as possible. In this, the role of the massed medium and heavy batteries of the Royal Artillery continued to be vital. Rapidly deployed and superbly concentrated barrages of shells broke up German counter-attacks, inflicting serious casualties. As the weather brightened, the RAF were able to harass any concentration of German fighting strength, sometimes to devastating effect. The German reserves were swiftly eroded away and the attacks from 29 June to 1 July proved to be their most focused effort, after which the fighting ebbed away.

During Operation Epsom the British lost around 150 tanks knocked out or badly damaged; losses more than compensated for by new units arriving and tank/crew replacements, whereas the Germans are estimated to have lost around 120 tanks, which they could not easily replace. Montgomery would later claim that he had never intended a breakthrough, merely desiring only to suck in and destroy German armour, thereby allowing the Americans a free reign to attack. Much of this is an irrelevance: it is legitimate for there to be more than one objective in an offensive, and of course there were perfectly valid contingency plans for a breakthrough. Yet the British had much to learn from their experiences in Operation Epsom. The strength and resilience of the German defences had been badly underestimated. Serious problems had also been exposed in the coordination of the tanks with the infantry and artillery units, problems only masked by the overarching ability of the Royal Artillery to dominate the battlefield. For the Germans, too, the Epsom fighting had mixed results. In one sense they had succeeded, throwing back the attempt to reach the Orne river. But they had also abandoned their overall plan to gather together their panzer divisions, ready for the decisive blow to hurl the Allies back into the English Channel. Instead, the II Panzer Corps had been frittered away to no real purpose, as all their attacks had been blunted. For both sides, Operation Epsom was a disappointment.

*

THIS WAS ALL ABOVE THE HEADS of the 2nd F&FY. However, they too could sense that the pace of operations had slackened. On 3 July, they moved forward to take up a counter-attack role based around Colleville sector. Here they were still pestered, and suffered from the infernal mortars and shellfire. On 13 July, Scott-Brownlie's gunner, John Buchanan, was hit.

> We dug trenches. The driver and his co-driver had dug their trench next to the tank. And I had dug my trench at the bottom of a hedge. We were sitting having a cup of tea – brewing up! These 'Moaning Minnies', six-barrelled mortars, were firing regularly, but they were landing in a wood to our left – and we

didn't bother. We were sitting blethering away and this mortar battery opened up again. It came screaming over our heads, one landing in my trench in the hedge. I was having a cup of tea. One hit the ground next to the tank – the shrapnel hit the tank and ricocheted on to us lying in this trench. I got wounded, a bit of shrapnel in the back, my leg, the fleshy part of my hand, and my boot got hit. Immediately, we all scrambled to get under the tank. The Padre was there – his belt got caught on one of the hooks on the tank and he was left, literally, swinging. I can assure you the words he said weren't really religious words! My back was as sore as anything, but it was only a small piece of metal. It didn't go far in, but it's hot metal – it burns. Steel Brownlie had his cap on the aerial up on the top of the tank and that got riddled. He was quite chuffed! He'd seen action and his cap was all riddled with holes.[19]

Trooper John Buchanan, 4 Troop, 'A' Squadron, 2nd F&FY

Buchanan was evacuated in a scout car back to a field hospital where he was treated for his superficial wounds. He was determined to get back to his comrades as quickly as possible.

We went into this marquee and there was a chap looked at you. I says, 'I've got a piece of shrapnel in my back but as far as I'm concerned it's OK! The officer says I had to go back!' He says, 'Oh well, if it festers it'll come out, if it doesn't fester, you'll be all right!' And he put a bit of sticking plaster on it! I got a wee red stripe – wounded, you know. The worst thing was my mother got a telegram and she was really [upset]. Once you get your name in the book it's automatically sent.[20]

Trooper John Buchanan, 4 Troop, 'A' Squadron, 2nd F&FY

Robert Nurse suffered from a far more prosaic health problem during this period. It may seem amusing, but haemorrhoids could be a serious complaint.

I was suffering from intense constipation at that time. I thought to hell with this. The tank had stopped, so I got out of the tank and defecated under the rear of the engine – with great difficulty! In fact, I still suffer from internal piles now as a result of that – that didn't go on your record! You can imagine what internal piles were like when you were on a little metal seat, about this big! I went to the medical officer, Captain Beamish, and reported sick. Because I was in quite a lot of pain, believe you me! He virtually told me to go forth and multiply! Because he had far more serious things to deal with than my piles![21]

Trooper Robert Nurse, 2 Troop, 'C' Squadron, 2nd F&FY

While near Colleville, two squadrons sent forwards to support the forward infantry but they were largely undisturbed. The battle was slowly fizzling out, although the Recce Troop seem to have been fairly busy, as Geoff Hayward found when he was replaced by an experienced Sherman driver and posted as co-driver into the Honey tank commanded by Sergeant Bill Scott. He found Scott to be an impulsive and enthusiastic chap!

Scott always wanted to be in the forefront; always wanted to be in the thick of anything that was going on. Consequently, he made us crew members quite uneasy at times – as to what trouble he was going to get us into![22]

Trooper Geoff Hayward, Recce Troop, HQ Squadron, 2nd F&FY

During this period the Recce Troop were busy on a variety of patrols and when reports came in of a Tiger tank somewhere near, volunteers were called for to go and locate the threat. Scott at once volunteered – Hayward was appalled at the idea.

The idea of a Tiger – I think it was its firing power we were scared of – that it could shoot us up at a tremendous distance. And a shot from an 88mm gun would have blown us to smithereens in such a lightly armoured tank. This horrified the crew – the thought that we could be shot at from a great distance before we even saw it if it was well concealed. We were sitting in a rest position and this message came over from the commanding officer to the whole of the Recce Troop, asking for volunteers. We heard Bill Scott mutter, 'I'm going to do this!' The rest of the crew said, 'Oh, no you're not!' Anyway he got his way! He ignored us and said he would volunteer. He got his instructions as to where he was to go. We went on our own. We crossed several fields, perhaps a mile or two away and we entered a wood. We were feeling our way very cautiously. After a little while we could see a cottage almost surrounded by trees. There was nothing visible as we approached – all seemed quiet – no sign of any enemy, abandoned vehicles or any sign of war at all. We got right up to this cottage, by this time we were all quaking, because with the aid of the cottage anything could have been hidden. But nothing loath, Bill Scott told the driver to edge up on the right-hand side of this cottage. The driver was on the left, the co-driver out on the right. With the periscope the co-driver would be the first one to see round that corner. As soon as the periscope was in a position to see round the corner – I immediately saw a huge tank with an enormous gun pointing towards our side of the building. Straight away – I didn't wait to give a message to Bill Scott, I said, 'Driver, reverse!' Which he did, fortunately. I described what I'd seen to Bill Scott – I'm not sure to this day whether it was a Tiger, it was certainly a very big German tank, but it could have been a Panther. Bill Scott wasn't having any of that. I thought he would immediately fly like mad away from the area, but instead of that he said, 'We'll go round the other side of the cottage and have a look!' So off we went round the other side! Much to my relief when we got on the corner, there was the back of this tank with a huge hole blown out of it – so it had obviously been hit either by rocket-firing Typhoons or a very heavy gun.[23]

Trooper Geoff Hayward, Recce Troop, HQ Squadron, 2nd F&FY

After reporting this in they were told to report back. By this

time, it was evident to all that the pathetic armament of the
Honey would have been irrelevant in any encounter with a
German tank.

> The turrets had been removed. The object, I'm told, was to
> make the Honey more useful as a reconnaissance vehicle,
> because the 37mm gun was fairly useless and it could be less
> visible, more like a Bren gun carrier, if the turret was off.[24]

Trooper Geoff Hayward, Recce Troop, HQ Squadron, 2nd F&FY

The only problem was that although it made the Honeys slightly
faster, it also left a large hole to allow the rain to get in. Certainly, John Gray was not overly impressed by the change.

> It had the turret taken off. They said it would make them less
> conspicuous. It did lower the thing by 2 feet, so all you got was
> the hull, no turret on the top. So you could run along the side
> of a hedge and anything on the other side wouldn't see you.
> But you were pretty vulnerable because the turret ring hole
> was quite large. You had a crew commander, a radio operator, a
> co-driver and a driver. You had a Browning machine gun for the
> co-driver.[25]

Trooper John Gray, Recce Troop, HQ Squadron, 2nd F&FY

In essence, the Honeys were almost useless.

Meanwhile, John Thorpe had joined the unit. The son of a
fish and game shop proprietor in Worcester, he had trained as
a road surveyor in local government and served in the Home
Guard, but was called up for the RAC in November 1940. After
training as a driver, he was posted to the 1st F&FY before being
transferred to the 2nd F&FY in October 1942, then promptly
attached to the Forward Delivery Squadron for 'spare personnel'.
He was finally posted into 2nd F&FY as a casualty replacement
co-driver to the Sherman commanded by Sergeant Clifford
Jones with 4 Troop in 'C' Squadron. He soon settled in, and
despite the dangers he found the company congenial.

Colonel calls a parade! 'Paddy' Usher strolls up carrying his steel helmet in front of himself, 'What's up Paddy?' Paddy replies, 'I'd sooner lose me bloody head than me wedding tackle!' Hoots of laughter. It's great to have someone like this with us.[26]

Trooper John Thorpe, 4 Troop, 'C' Squadron, 2nd F&FY

*

ON 15 JULY, THE REGIMENT WAS greatly relieved when they at last moved out of artillery range back to the relative peace and tranquillity of Camilly, a couple of miles from their old haven of Cully. There was an issue of beer, which further improved the overall mood, but this was, after all, the army and they had to clean up both themselves and their Shermans. Neglected maintenance had to be carried out, to ensure they were ready for the next battle. Crews were also being juggled to blend new replacements and the 'old hands'. Terry Boyne was posted to the crew of Corporal Evans in 4 Troop.

We had replacement crews coming up and joining us to pump the numbers back up. I was asked to see Major Powell and he asked me to change crews to a corporal's crew with Steel Brownlie. I swapped with their radio operator, just a question of taking your bed roll and hoisting it aboard. Just rechecking that everything was there on this new vehicle – it was an ordinary Sherman that had just come up from the holding unit.[27]

Trooper Terry Boyne, 4 Troop, 'A' Squadron, 2nd F&FY

Late at night on 16 July, the regiment moved to a concentration area near Gasche.

They provided us with false moonlight – put searchlights up on the clouds which reflected down onto the ground. It must have been obvious to the Germans what was afoot, because they would hear this weight of traffic moving from west to east. The tracks we used across country were dust – the trouble was we were throwing up this dust, then it was settling on us. The inside of the tanks and the guns were covered in dust by the time we reached our destination.[28]

Captain Douglas Hutchison, HQ Troop, 'A' Squadron, 2nd F&FY

This dust lived long in their memory. Which is strange when one considers what was to happen to them within a few hours.

It was lousy. The dust from the tank in front of you – you were eating, breathing it and smoking it – whatever! I got it in my eyes. The next day I couldn't see – I had a lot of pain – my eyes were full of grit. I went to the old medic and he put this thick brown gungy stuff in my eyes. Whatever it was it worked! The pain went almost at once. But it was decided that I wasn't going to drive the next day; when the action started again, I was in the co-driver's seat, Jimmy Byers was driving.[29]

Trooper John Gray, Recce Troop, HQ Squadron, 2nd F&FY

At last the 2nd F&FY were laagered up, under camouflage in an orchard. While the men checked their tanks, the officers were briefed, ready for the next chapter of their story. They were 'off to the races again': Operation Goodwood lay ahead of them.

10

OPERATION GOODWOOD

> People say, 'How can something made out of steel burn?' It was frightening really because they just glow red hot. You've got so much petrol, oil, hydraulics in there – it's amazing how they do burn![1]

Trooper James Donovan, 'B' Squadron, 2nd F&FY

THE GOODWOOD PLAN ORIGINATED with General Miles Dempsey of Second Army. After initial reservations, Montgomery adopted the scheme for a battering-ram assault by his massed armoured divisions east of Caen on 18 July 1944. His intended tactical objective was to draw the main German armoured formation into a vicious dogfight in the eastern flank of the bridgehead, thereby allowing the Americans the opportunity to secure a breakout to the west. Dempsey and Second Army had three relatively fresh armoured divisions (7th, 11th and the Guards) which Montgomery wanted to deploy as a corps in the open country south-east of Caen, which itself had recently been captured during Operation Charnwood from 7 to 9 July. It was to be made in conjunction with Operation Cobra, the breakout offensive to be led by the US First Army (Lieutenant General Omar Bradley), which ended up being delayed until 25 July. By the time Operation Goodwood was launched it had become a secondary and limited offensive, designed to destroy German armour, and not primarily designed to secure a decisive breakthrough. It would be backed by an enormous, concentrated bombing raid to smash the German defences, followed by a stupendous artillery barrage.

In the planning process there were misunderstandings between Montgomery, the Supreme Allied Commander Dwight Eisenhower and Bradley as to which army was to launch the breakout and which the diversionary operation; this confusion was undoubtedly triggered and exacerbated by Montgomery's tactless behaviour. Whisper it, but this also reflected some slight confusion in the planning process, which originally included Falaise as an objective and hence betrayed some early aspirations for a breakout. However, such higher grand tactical concerns were far above the mental horizons of the men of the 2nd F&FY. What mattered to them was that the planned assault would feature a hidden rapid move of the armoured divisions and the supporting massed gun batteries to the small bridgehead area east of the Orne river. This was the reason the 2nd F&FY had endured their dusty ride on the night of 16 July, and why they had been so well camouflaged and 'in hiding' all the next day. They were delighted to hear of the massed bombing raid, which it was said would break all existing records in direct ground support. But more worryingly, the area they were moving into was ideal for defensive operations, and they faced well dug-in German tanks and anti-tank guns, fortified villages, the threat of minefields, and with batteries of hidden artillery scattered along the wooded ridges that overlooked their path of advance. Then there was the worry of German reserve panzer divisions – the operation may have been designed to attract them, but that was no consolation to the men having to face them in battle. Overall, the planned use of the armoured divisions as a 'battering ram' to smash through German defences was fundamentally misguided; armour was better used to exploit an opportunity that had already been created. This misuse of armoured divisions reflects Montgomery's preoccupation to use artillery, airpower and armour where possible to win his battles, to use technology and 'materiel' rather than risk severe infantry casualties against the backdrop of his severe manpower shortage.

Following the air raid, the 11th Armoured Division would lead the attack from the concentration area around the Ranville glider airfield, moving behind a massive creeping barrage, pushing across open wheatfields with the outskirts of Caen to their right and the Breville Ridge, the Bois de Bavent woods and the village of Cagny to their left. After crossing two railway embankments, (the Caen–Troarn and the Caen–Vimont lines), they would swing slightly right, where the ground gradually rose upwards towards the wooded Bourguébus Ridge. Here the division was to take the villages of Bourguébus, Hubert-Folie and Bras. Behind them, the Guards Armoured Division would swing to the left to take Vimont. Finally, the 7th Armoured Division would move up, pushing between the other two divisions to take the villages of La Hogue and Secqueville. It was believed that this would break through the main German lines of defence and expose them to vigorous exploitation operations by armoured car units. However, Lieutenant General 'Pip' Roberts had grave doubts about the intended role for his division – doubts that he did not hesitate to express.

> Our final objectives were on the right of the corps: Bras, Hubert-Folie, Fontenay. Our infantry brigade had to clear Cuverville and Demouville, two villages immediately in front of the start line, but also, we were ordered to take Cagny, which was on the left flank of our advance. I thought this was all too much. Why could not the infantry (51st Highland Division), now holding the front line, get up out of their trenches and attack Cuverville and Demouville? Our objectives were on the right, but we had to take Cagny on the left and clear the villages in the centre before we could get to our objectives on the right, and in doing this I would have no infantry brigade to clear the way as they were tied up in Cuverville and Demouville. I made these points verbally to the corps commander (Dick

O'Connor) but I got no change. Feeling rather strongly about it, I put it all on paper and sent it to the corps commander. I got a reply that the present plans could not be changed and if I felt they were unsound, then he would get one of the other divisions to lead. But he would ask me only to 'mask' Cagny, not to take it. I really had no alternative but to accept that situation and replied accordingly, but still think it was a stupid arrangement.[2]

Major General 'Pip' Roberts, Headquarters, 11th Armoured Division

Supporting operations were to be launched by I Corps on the left, and Canadian II Corps around Caen itself. All in all, VIII Corps would deploy some 750 tanks, while a further 460 would support the flanking attacks.

From their observation posts up on the ridges and night aerial reconnaissance flights using flares, the Germans had been able to identify the concentration of armour at Ranville. Their defences were ready: indeed, Rommel had already enacted a thorough programme of defensive improvements throughout the intended battle zone. In the front line was the 16th Luftwaffe Field Division, supported in the first instance by the 21st Panzer Division, although that had been affected adversely by the continuous fighting endured since the invasion. By this time, they could deploy only fifty operational panzer Mark IVs, but were boosted by the five batteries of the 200th Assault Gun Battalion under the overall command of the resourceful Major Alfred Becker. This gave them some fifty self-propelled guns (thirty 75mm PAK anti-tank guns and twenty 105mm howitzers) deployed in the key villages. A further addition was the thirty-nine Tiger and King Tiger tanks of the 103rd Tank Battalion. There was also the threat of the 1st SS Panzer Corps which was not too far away and ready to move up in support. In total, it was estimated that the Germans could deploy 324 tanks and self-propelled guns.[3] This was not going to be easy, particularly as in the planning process Dempsey had allowed for German defensive lines only 4 miles thick, rather than the rather more intimidating 10-mile breadth that the Germans had established. One last minute boost for the Allies, although they were unaware of it, was that a Spitfire attack on Rommel's staff car had wounded him badly enough to remove him from the front on 17 July. He would never return.

*

THE SENIOR OFFICERS OF 29th Armoured Brigade and 2nd F&FY were briefed as to their role in the coming offensive. They found that the 29th Armoured Brigade would be on the left of the advance and they were to pass to the left of the Le Mesnil-Frémentel hamlet, then to advance on Verrières and Rocquancourt. The motorised infantry of the 159th Brigade would advance to their right, clearing the villages of Cuverville and Demouville some 2 miles from the start line, before joining the 29th Armoured Brigade in the final assault.

> The briefing was quite explicit. This was to be an operation involving three armoured divisions, of which we were to be the leading one, then the Guards and the 7th Armoured Division. We were going to have tremendous support: a 1,000-bomber raid putting down a carpet of bombs in the area in front of us; the artillery – every gun in Normandy was going to be involved in this! We were then to advance in formation, behind a creeping barrage. We were not to attempt any tactical driving or operations until we'd got beyond the second railway line, which we were to cross a few thousand yards from the start point. But I think from the word go we were a bit sceptical![4]
>
> Captain Douglas Hutchison, HQ Troop, 'A' Squadron, 2nd F&FY

Major Sir John Gilmour, commanding 'B' Squadron, was certainly not enamoured with what he had heard at the briefing.

I think that it was a bad plan, because if you fought in closed
country, the enemy needed an anti-tank gun every 100 yards
or so if they were to stop you. Whereas if you went to open
country, a few anti-tank guns at long range could do a great deal
of damage. The North African concept which Montgomery
brought in was disastrous.[5]

Major Sir John Gilmour, 'B' Squadron, 2nd F&FY

Gilmour had hit the nail on the head: ideal tank country of
open rolling fields was also ideal for hidden defenders lurking
in woods and villages with a clear line of sight over the fields.
They would be advancing into a trap. The officers then trick-
led down the briefings to their own squadron and troop 'O'
Groups: Major Sir John Gilmour's 'B' Squadron would be on
the left; Major Joe Powell's 'A' Squadron on the right; behind
them the Recce Troop and Regimental Headquarters; and then
in the third wave, Major Chris Nicholl's 'C' Squadron.

The day began early for the men of the 2nd F&FY, as they
moved off just after midnight, but crossing the Orne bridge was
a slow business and it took some four hours to reach the concentration area in the field just north of Ranville, where the gliders
had put down on 6 June. The gliders were still there, somewhat
worn by this time through their exposure to the recent bad
weather. Some of the men could not resist scrambling up to
explore inside the fuselages. Others attended to their stomachs
in more ways than one. Most had their breakfast, but many of
the men had 'tummy troubles', later attributed to some nameless
pollutant that had got into their water supply.

We were sat there having breakfast. We had fried onions – and
just as we were moving out, I had the diarrhoea – I had to jump
out in the ditch! I think it was the fried onions! I got back in
and we moved off. That was my first experience.[6]

Trooper Len Hutchings, 3 Troop, 'A' Squadron, 2nd F&FY

At 05.45 on 18 July, the promised massive bomber air raid

began; this was the magic ingredient that was designed to clear the 8-mile path all the way to the Bourguébus Ridge. Some 1,056 RAF bombers would bomb all along the flanks, 482 American medium bombers would bomb along the line of advance using fragmentation bombs to reduce any cratering, while a further 539 American bombers were meant to eradicate the identified German artillery positions that lay beyond the range of the British medium artillery around the villages of Four, Soliers, Bras and Frénouville. These raids were at the centre of the British plans; if bad weather prevented air support then the operations would be cancelled. Fortified villages and farm buildings on the flanks and directly ahead of the tanks were to be pounded to oblivion. Sadly, not all the wooded ridges were included in the target areas, which was unfortunate as many harboured German artillery batteries. Nevertheless, the massed bombers streaming overhead was an impressive sight, which did a little to calm frayed nerves. The very ground seemed to quiver beneath their feet as thousands of bombs detonated in the target areas. As the frenzy of the carpet bombing subsided, the preparatory artillery barrage commenced: huge naval guns augmenting the massed guns of three army corps, all blasting away at identified German batteries. Then, slowly at first, the tanks began to edge forwards. As they attempted to move off, Steel Brownlie's Sherman crew suffered a humiliating engine failure, as recalled by Gordon Fidler, the driver.

> This was the big day! There was going to be a thousand bomber raid and a creeping barrage. This is marvellous. This is a piece of cake. This is what we'd come over here for! This is what we all thought! We couldn't lose. We were told that the Germans can't survive. We couldn't wait; couldn't get away quick enough – we all wanted to go. We tried to start up and couldn't start. Steel Brownlie has to get into another tank, because he can't stay back. The fitters come up – somebody's put water in the petrol! Our petrol cans are these square cans,

just an ordinary tin can, and we used to use one for our own water. Anyway, water in the tank: nobody got blamed, nobody was ever accused. I don't know how it got there, but it seemed as if it came from the crew. This wasn't [the case] as far as I'm concerned, because we were wanting to go. We wanted to be a part of it.[7]

Trooper Gordon Fidler, 4 Troop, 'A' Squadron, 2nd F&FY

The gunner, John Buchanan, was also mortified – although he was equally confident that whatever had happened, it was not deliberate and none of the crew was involved.

It was very dubious – when you got things like this happen, you always felt that people were saying, 'He didna want to go into that battle! Aye! Aye! Who put it in?' You know how the boys are – half serious and half kidding you on! You felt a wee bit guilty. We weren't really – I mean I had nothing to do with it! My gun was all right! It certainly wasn't any of the crew – we were confident of that.[8]

Trooper John Buchanan, 4 Troop, 'A' Squadron, 2nd F&FY

In the circumstances, Steel Brownlie took the news his tank was out of action relatively well.

It was almost light before we were all set, lack of sleep already a problem, and then we had to refuel. A jerry can of water was poured into my tank along with the petrol, so that it was a non-runner. I took Corporal Evans's tank, and left him with mine. This had disadvantages, because all our tanks were personalised in various ways, so that you could lay your hand on anything, without thinking. You also had established ways of working, with your own crew, not always 'by the book', so hopping into another vehicle at the last minute was disconcerting.[9]

Lieutenant William Steel Brownlie, 4 Troop, 'A' Squadron, 2nd F&FY

Meanwhile there were other problems ahead, as the bulk of

the tanks encountered a minefield laid by the 51st (Highland) Division which had not been properly lifted, rendering the massed tanks reliant on just four narrow cleared lanes. The 29th Armoured Brigade was the first to advance, with the 3rd Royal Tank Regiment feeding through the gaps, followed by the 2nd F&FY and finally the 23rd Hussars.

> There were minefields in front of us, with lanes taped, so we all went through the minefield in single file and formed up in formation on the other side. We didn't seem to hang about a lot; we just moved through these lanes.[10]

> Trooper Jack Edwards, 4 Troop, 'B' Squadron, 2nd F&FY

Once they got through, they began to shake out into their attack formation. Behind them the problems caused by the pinch-points at the bridges and minefields would proliferate, severely delaying the advance of the Guards Armoured Division and 7th Armoured Division.

> We got through the minefield all right. The trouble was that with 'return' shelling by the Germans, the marking of the minefield for the follow-up people got obliterated. The leading people got through the minefield all right. The following people had difficulties. The brigade attacked on a two-regiment front with the 3rd Tank Regiment on the right, the Fife and Forfar on the left, and the 23rd Hussars were in reserve behind us. The regiment moved off two squadrons abreast, with 'A' on the right and 'B' on the left. 'B' being on the left was on the outside 'open' flank. Where the start line was there was friendly people on the right but *everything* on the left was enemy.[11]

> Major Sir John Gilmour, 'B' Squadron, 2nd F&FY

At H-Hour, 07.45, the massed armour moved forward behind a creeping barrage sweeping the ground ahead of them with a line of bursting shells. It was an impressive sight.

To us in the lead, it was a solid grey wall of shell bursts, 200 yards ahead. It was hard to believe that anything could live in it, yet it left a big grey horse, tethered to a post, leaping about in fright, but unhurt. We drove on in formation for about a mile. We had never before driven in formation for more than a couple of hundred yards, except on exercises. Was it all over bar the shouting? No, it wasn't![12]

Lieutnant William Steel Brownlie, 4 Troop, 'A' Squadron, 2nd F&FY

It may not have been all over, but the combination of the massed bombing and the barrage had devastated not only the front-line troops of the 16th Luftwaffe Field Division, but also the more forward elements of the 21st Panzer Division. Tanks were destroyed, artillery put out of action, infantry defenders shredded, and communications to the rear areas disrupted.

When I tell you that the tanks weighed 58-tons and were tossed aside like playing cards, you will see just what a Hell we found ourselves in. It was next to impossible to see anything as so much dust had been thrown up by the explosions. It was like being in a very thick fog. As far as my company was concerned: two Tigers were completely neutralised; two others were so badly damaged that they couldn't be employed. All the tanks were completely covered with earth, and the gun turrets had been thrown completely out of adjustment by the shock effect. Fifteen men of the company were dead; two further had committed suicide during the bombardments; another had to be sent to a mental hospital for observation. The psychological shock of these terrible exchanges remained with us for a long time.[13]

Leutnant Richard Freiherr von Rosen, 3rd Company, 503rd Army Heavy Panzer Battalion

After a couple of miles, the infantry of the 159th Brigade moved off to the right to clear the villages of Cuverville and Demouville. The main body of the tanks drove onwards, heading straight for the embankment of the Caen–Troarn railway which they reached at around 08.30.

> We were going through quite a broad corridor of openish ground between a string of villages on the right and the left. They were being attacked by concentrations of medium artillery. That was separate from the creeping barrage: we were supposed to see the barrage and keep close up behind it. The difficulty was that when we got the first railway there was an embankment there. It was quite a business – you couldn't just sort of drive across it in line ahead because you had to select places where you could climb up the embankment and over. It wasn't all that difficult, but it just slowed things up a little bit. By the time we'd get across to the other side we'd lost the barrage.[14]
>
> Captain Douglas Hutchison, HQ Troop, 'A' Squadron, 2nd F&FY

There had been very little German return fire up to the time they reached this first embankment, but as it was about 6-foot high in places, it proved a more serious obstacle than anticipated, slowing progress, and impassable to the Bren gun carriers and halftracks of the accompanying 8th Rifle Brigade, who had to pass through the limited crossing places. After this embankment, the fields broadened out and the 2nd F&FY moved up to advance alongside the 3rd Royal Tank Regiment.

> One was intent on trying to keep in line! It was part of the drill for this operation. The idea was we would get sufficient weight of armour forward behind the barrage that it would have the power to manoeuvre tactically when it got beyond the second railway line. 'A' Squadron were the front rank on the extreme left, 'B' Squadron was to our right, and then the 3rd Royal Tanks to the right of that again. I was concentrating on keeping in line – as far as one was able to – with other members of the squadron.[15]
>
> Captain Douglas Hutchison, HQ Troop, 'A' Squadron, 2nd F&FY

Ahead of them lay the defended farmhouse of Le Mesnil Frémentel, occupied by a battery of Major Alfred Becker's self-propelled guns. The 3rd Royal Tank Regiment would pass to the right, suffering some tank losses as they did so, while the 2nd F&FY went to the left, between the farm and the shattered village of Cagny. Le Mesnil Frémentel would later be taken by the Support Company of the 8th Rifle Brigade. The embankment just behind, which carried the Caen–Vimont railway line, marked the rough limit of direct support from the massed field artillery. This left the 11th Armoured Division dependent on the 5.5-inch medium guns and the eighteen Sexton 25-pounder self-propelled guns of the 13th Regiment, Royal Horse Artillery, under the command of Major Robert Daniell (formerly of the 107 Regiment, RHA, the South Notts Hussars). At first, the 2nd F&FY seemed to be getting away with it, as 'A' and 'B' Squadrons approached the second railway line at about 09.30.

> All we saw on the way was German vehicles burning, we didn't see anything else – nothing to shoot at anyway! We came to this big railway embankment. We had to break formation to climb over it, because everybody was going up a diagonal track to get over this embankment, because it was quite a big steep one. Nothing happened while we were going over. We got down at the other side and formed up in formation again – got moving again.[16]

Trooper Jack Edwards, 4 Troop, 'B' Squadron, 2nd F&FY

Thus, the first two squadrons got past relatively unscathed. Then, suddenly, all hell broke loose. In the vicinity of the ruins of Cagny was either a battery of 88mm anti-aircraft guns swiftly repurposed for use in an anti-tank role on the peremptory orders of that legendary figure of post-war NATO staff rides, Major Hans-Ulrich von Luck, or more prosaically, another of Major Alfred Becker's self-propelled 75mm PAK anti-tank gun batteries. Or both. Whatever the truth of it, there was a storm of fire which took 'C' Squadron in enfilade as they were preparing to cross the railway embankment. The men of the 2nd F&FY were always convinced they were being fired on by 88mm guns, and that view has to be fully respected; but it is also undeniably true that British tank crews tended to imagine all German artillery fire was from 88mm guns, and they often underestimated the deadly penetrative firepower of the 75mm PAK guns. Amid the dust, smoke and confusion, it was difficult to pinpoint the source. The 'C' Squadron commander, Major Chris Nicholls, was one of the first to be hit.

> Suddenly, there were blazing tanks all round me: Nicholls' tank and sundry other tanks. Jack Keightley[17] was killed there. We knew our tanks were being hit by 88s, but we weren't sure where they were. If the petrol tank was hit there would be a 'WHOOF' of flame. If that then sent the ammunition up, it would almost blow the turret off. Most of the tanks were burning. It all happened so quickly, it's hard to feel anything. Obviously, you're saddened, depressed, but you're hardly aware of it. Everyone was in a bit of a panic quite honestly; we didn't expect this sort of opposition.[18]

Trooper Robert Nurse, 2 Troop, 'C' Squadron, 2nd F&FY

Charlie Workman had a horrific view of the demise of Chris Nicholls.[19] He saw him struggling to get out of his turret before falling back into the burning Sherman. The sheer unmitigated chaos of the battle was evident in the cacophony of voices gabbling in his headphones.

> As we started to get to the second railway line, I saw all the tanks blowing up, brewing up! Everyone was on the wireless, there was a regimental net. When a tank was brewed up, very often its wireless operator might come up and say, 'We've been hit!' Otherwise, all you would see was the smoke, the flames. It was a summer's day: there was blazing tanks, wounded men running around – people who had got out of a tank that had

been brewed up coming back towards us. It was an awful scene, people staggering past covered in blood, being burned. We were pretty sure it was 88mm guns, it wasn't dug-in tanks. It was the most feared thing – and the first thing ever reported on the wireless and they'd give a map reference – that went straight down on your map. Tank after tank after tank just going up! Blazing tanks. The Sherman was called the 'Ronson' because they went on fire so easily – like a lighter. We weren't hit, but the people to my right were all being hit – several were killed.[20]

Second Lieutenant Charlie Workman, 1 Troop, 'C' Squadron, 2nd F&FY

The sight of burning Shermans was terrible. Inside those steel furnaces were many of their friends. It could so easily have been them. The Sherman driven by Trooper Harold Wilson was hit, but he was very fortunate in that his tank did not immediately catch fire. The slight delay gave the crew enough time to make their escape.

All of a sudden, hell broke loose – there was everything firing. We dodged along – firing here and firing there. Moving along. You'd see a tank go up, but you keep going! We'd stopped and been firing and suddenly a command comes, 'We've been hit! Bail out!' I shouldn't feel it if it hit the turret. Not really. Besides, they went in so hard and so fast those shells you hardly felt them. It would only be a shudder. Well, a shudder could have been me hitting a hole or anything. I bailed out – I made a dive. When I got out there was the gunner and the crew commander out, but no operator. If it hit the turret and went in, it was usually bound to be fatal, one way or another. There wasn't that much room when one of them shells came through and buzzed round in it. We'd lost our operator, Dennis Stone,[21] from Bristol, 21 years old and 6 foot 4 inches [tall]. There were hayricks, we got behind some of them. Jerry started to set fire to them. We were creeping along in corn, 2 foot, 2 foot 6 inches high. The gunner, he had a bit of shrapnel straight through the front of his ankle, just at the top of his boot. Gone right through his boot, taken his sock and stuck out at the other side. We were helping him along, crawling along through the cornfields.[22]

Trooper Harold Wilson, 4 Troop, 'C' Squadron, 2nd F&FY

John Thorpe was also lucky to escape.

Very severe AP fire is met from a coppice on our left front, several tanks begin to go on fire. My orders are to fire into this coppice and keep firing while our 75mm is sending in some AP and HE. [The] Browning stops and I find the canvas bag for the empty cartridge cases is jammed full blocking my gun, I've never had to fire off so many rounds, I pull off the bag and sling the stupid thing aside and feed in another belt, belt after belt, my barrel warps and the tracer is leaving the gun in a cone of fire, I try to change the barrel but it is too hot to handle – no matter – keep the gun firing – my feet are buried in a thick carpet of empties all over the floor.[23]

Trooper John Thorpe, 4 Troop, 'C' Squadron, 2nd F&FY

Whatever damage their fire is inflicting on the Germans it was nothing compared to the hell that was surrounding them in the tanks.

Going on in front of me, brew up after brew up, some tank crews are on fire and rolling about on the ground trying to put their clothes out but this is a ripe cornfield and soon what with burning tanks, burning corn and smoke mortar shells, visibility is being shut out. Now all the tanks in front of us are burning fiercely and immediately in front 20 yards away I see a tank boy climbing out of a turret which is spurting flames but he does not make it, he gets as far as putting one leg up to step out of the turret and falls backwards inside. Explosions of ammunition are taking place in the burning tanks and in the almost still air of this hot sunny day huge smoke rings leave their turrets rising high into the windless sky.[24]

Trooper John Thorpe, 4 Troop, 'C' Squadron, 2nd F&FY

In desperation they reverse, retiring to the railway embankment. By then they had lost all touch with the regiment and attached themselves to the 23rd Hussars for the rest of the day.

Jack Edwards' tank had been held up before he got to the embankment, so he witnessed the destruction of 'C' Squadron from a far closer range than he would have liked.

> The troop leader, who I could see was slightly in front of us, moved half left and went through a hedge. We kept formation with him, turned left, and we went through the hedge. There's always a bit of an embankment at the bottom of the hedge, we went up over the embankment, and dropped down at the other side. Then the tank stopped and wouldn't go any further! We didn't know at the time, but there was a big log there and we'd bellied on top of the log so that the tracks weren't touching. Just at that moment, while we were messing about trying to get the tank free, gunfire came in from the left-hand side. The squadron leader told our troop to stop and face the gunfire. It was 88mm anti-tank guns. The troop leader never answered because he'd got 'brewed up' by it. As the fire came our corporal got Pat Ketteridge firing back where it was coming from. You could see the fire coming off the horizon in the region of Cagny. He didn't know any range and he couldn't spot it exactly – he was shooting more in hope than anything. We were firing lots of HE back. About twenty-odd HE and I was sweating cobs from doing rapid fire. I only had chance to look through the periscope once or twice, but the armour-piercing shots appeared to be coming straight at you – it's got a tracer. They were going past and there was a terrific 'WHOOOSH!' I thought, 'Good God, it sounds like Hitler's secret weapon!' They were only just missing the top of the tank I suppose! We were still stuck! They were going over the top of us and destroying 'C' Squadron who had got by then more or less level with us to the right of where we were.[25]

Trooper Jack Edwards, 4 Troop, 'B' Squadron, 2nd F&FY

With the almost complete destruction of 'C' Squadron, the German guns seem to have stopped firing for the moment.

The corporal had spotted some German activity a few hundred yards ahead, behind a hedge. He had us fire an HE through this hedge. We saw a flash or two – it had hit something. So, he called us off at that. Then he traversed right on to three haystacks – about 50 yards away. I could then see through my periscope, I only had a limited view, the troop leader's tank blazing away about 100 yards in front of us. Looking farther to the right, I could see all these other columns of black smoke going up from 'C' Squadron's tanks which were blazing away. I thought, 'Well things are pretty grim!' We put an HE into each of these three haystacks, which completely flattened each one. Lo and behold there were two anti-tank guns there hiding behind them – but nobody with them, whether they had just been abandoned I don't know! The co-driver, Clifford Pember, had dropped his escape hatch down and looked underneath to see what was wrong. He then told us we had bellied on this log. Having a look, he said to the driver, 'If you go forward on your right and brake on your left!' And eventually we wriggled off it! We went back over the hedge, back to the next hedge where the other two tanks of the troop were sheltering – and we joined them, still facing where this gunfire was coming from. The other two tanks had sergeants in charge – and one of them was Sergeant Truscott, so we were under his command then. We stayed there a long time, facing Cagny.[26]

Trooper Jack Edwards, 4 Troop, 'B' Squadron, 2nd F&FY

Roy Vallance had a piece of misfortune which – on balance – turned out to be lucky for him and the rest of the crew as his Sherman approached the railway embankment.

Tanks started brewing up all round. My own reaction was to tell the driver to, 'Speed up!' and go flat out. When the firing started, coming from the left flank, most people stopped to try and engage it. I always felt that to stop was fatal. I just kept going, I was saying, 'Faster! Faster!' The driver said, 'Where shall I go?' 'Just keep going!' I wasn't certain where the fire was coming from and I didn't know where I was going! Just going forward thinking, 'What can I do?' I daren't stop. It would be fatal. As luck would have it, there was a railway line going across our front, and where I was there was a deep cutting. We crashed down this cutting and everything cut out – the engine had stopped. We had a faulty battery and once we stopped, we couldn't start again, unless we charged up with the auxiliary generator. So, there we were stuck, we couldn't do anything – much to my relief! I said, 'Right! That'll do us – we'll stop here!' We were perfectly safe. I could see over the cutting top, but the tank was completely hidden in the cutting. It appeared to me that nearly everybody was brewing up in the squadron.[27]

Trooper Roy Vallance, HQ Troop, 'A' Squadron, 2nd F&FY

Eventually they managed to charge up from the auxiliary generator, but by then the battle had long 'moved on'. They remained in the railway cutting till nightfall, then moved back.

Just ahead of 'C' Squadron was the scout car containing the intelligence officer, Lieutenant Philip Noakes, accompanied by his driver Sergeant Hutcheson. They too had run into trouble.

Scout cars are not good over rough country, ditches and banks – and they're dreadful over railway lines. Sergeant Hutcheson had somehow bounced us over the first railway line, but now, on the second we came to a grinding halt, firmly stuck on the lines, totally exposed to fire from any direction. I jumped out to inspect the damage. The main shaft was broken and the rear axle bent. I went round to the front of the scout-car to speak to Sergeant Hutcheson, when, to my complete surprise, something hit me very hard in the face, fortunately at such an angle that the bullet went through my parted lips, across my lower jaw and out through my left cheek. I felt more affronted than anything else. By now the leading squadrons and regimental headquarters were out of sight, so I reported my vehicle and myself as casualties on the regimental net. There was an ominous silence. I doubt whether anyone heard. As we took stock of a thoroughly unpromising situation, just to our left another Sherman blew up. Hit amidships, there was a terrific explosion, with flames and smoke whooshing up from the turret. A few seconds later out popped the flaming torch of a man, Trooper Sedgebeer. Sergeant Hutcheson and I seized the fire-extinguisher from our scout car, rushed over to him and sprayed him from head to foot. Somehow, we managed to put him out. He was horribly burnt. It was impossible to get near the burning tank, which was already beginning to glow. There was no chance of any other survivors. This frenzied activity had rather taken my mind off my own problem, but I was bleeding copiously and beginning to feel rather light-headed. Then one of our tanks arrived heading north, crammed with wounded. It was still a runner, but I think it had a bent gun. We bundled Sedgebeer onto it and I clambered on too. I hung on to a side-rail with one hand and Sedgebeer with the other as we lurched our way north. We passed several smouldering Shermans. And there was the all-pervading, never-to-be-forgotten smell of the Normandy battlefield – the reek of hot metal, the stench of dead animals, acrid smoke and the sickly-sweet smell of growing corn.[28]

Lieutenant Philip Noakes, Headquarters, 2nd F&FY

Trooper Sedgebeer had been in the Sherman commanded by Corporal Truslove[29] with Trooper Haddock,[30] Trooper Belsham[31] and Trooper York.[32] Although Sedgebeer was severely burnt he survived his terrible experience to later write a letter of thanks to his rescuer.

After numerous skin and bone grafts I am now almost normal, although I have lost my right hand. However, my purpose in writing this is that at all the hospitals I have been told that I owe my life to the prompt action taken at the time of the accident. Perhaps you don't remember assisting me in any way because, after all, I was only one injured person among thousands, but during my stay in hospital I have had lots of time to think over the last few months, and I would like to take this opportunity to express my very sincere thanks for your assistance on that fatal day. It is possible that I may never see you again, and a letter of thanks does not compensate my debt to you, but in the future, I hope that you are always given that help which you so readily gave me. I am just learning to write with my left hand and I trust you are able to read it.[33]

Trooper J. Sedgebeer, 'A' Squadron, 2nd F&FY

The plight of his friends in that Sherman is beyond imagining. Three of the four had no bodies to bury and are commemorated on the Bayeux Memorial. A chastening thought.

Lieutenant Colonel Alec Scott believed that the fire from the left was emanating from Cagny, and he was determined to sort it out by sending in his attached company of the 8th Rifle Brigade. Then there was an untimely intervention from his divisional commander who had caught up with Scott and Brigadier Roscoe Harvey.

The Fife and Forfar squadron was burning in the field ahead and there was quite a lot of mortaring coming down in the area of the village in front. As I arrived, I heard Alec Scott of the Fife and Forfar tell the brigadier that he was ordering his motor company of 8th Rifle Brigade to attack Cagny. He was pretty certain that the fire had come from there. But you will remember that I had specifically asked to be relieved from having to take Cagny. We had 23rd Hussars in reserve looking after the left flank until the Guards Armoured arrived very shortly. So I told Harvey to cancel any attack by the motor company and to concentrate on getting forward onto the

Bourguébus ridge. Had I not told Harvey to cancel the attack, the company would have virtually walked straight into Cagny. In the event it was to take the Guards the rest of the day to capture the village after a considerable battle. How unfortunate it was that I arrived just in time to cancel Scott's attack, but that is the sort of thing that happens in war.[34]

Major General 'Pip' Roberts, Headquarters, 11th Armoured Division

It may not have been as easy as that, but the Cagny would remain a festering abscess in their left flank for most of the day.

The threat was not only from the left. As the line of 29th Armoured Brigade tanks moved over the railway embankment they presented clear targets to German anti-tank batteries ahead of them and on both flanks. As a renewed storm of fire burst upon them, the motorised infantry of the 8th Rifle Brigade were especially vulnerable, as they only had thin-skinned Bren gun carriers, or flimsy halftracks to protect them. Private Don Gillate was advancing just to the right of 2nd F&FY, located just behind the 3rd Royal Tank Regiment, but his account is both illuminating and chilling.

Things became very hairy indeed. They picked off our tanks like boxes of matches. They were brewing up all round us, it was absolutely terrible to see and it was equally terrifying to hear because they were using solid shot, armour-piercing shot. This made a sort of noise that high explosive shells did not make, it was like a clapping sound, perhaps why they call it a clap of thunder. It was not a bang, an explosive bang, it was a twanging sort of bang. The only way in which I could really describe it is that if you were to put your ear fast against a solid metal bath and somebody took a sledgehammer on the other side of the bath and hit the bath very hard, your ear would practically drop off. That is the kind of noise that this made, it was absolutely frightening. The most frightening aspect of course being: which is the one with your number on it?[35]

Private Don Gillate, 8th Rifle Brigade, 29th Armoured Brigade

Gillate was appalled as he watched the brigade's tanks brewing up all around him. They tried their best to help the surviving crew members suffering from burns, but what could they do?

> We became increasingly depressed by having to sit there absolutely helpless listening to this ghastly noise of the solid shot and then suddenly, unaccountably apparently, a tank of ours would burst into flames and the unfortunate crew would come out of the top or from wherever they could, often on fire and lie down in absolute agony, burning. Soon we also began to see these poor fellows, they were absolutely fried because very often it happened that the burning took place inside the tank and they came out with their hair burned right down to the scalp. Their faces were grey, red and yellow where they had been burned and their hands too and they could not sit down or rest or lie down. All they could do was to find whatever shelter they could, maybe standing in a slit trench or something of that kind and just stand there with their limbs apart so that they would not rub together and make their pain even worse. The poor chaps, we could do nothing for them, they just had to wait for medical attention.[36]

Private Don Gillate, 8th Rifle Brigade, 29th Armoured Brigade

On the left of the 29th Armoured Brigade, the 'A' and 'B' Squadrons of the 2nd F&FY were pushing on heading towards the well-defended villages of Soliers and Four. They were beginning to suffer severe casualties from strong fire emanating both directly ahead, and from Frénouville and Le Poirer on their left flank. By 11.15, the 2nd F&FY had come to a shuddering stop. Major Sir John Gilmour was struggling to keep control in an impossible situation as the problems multiplied around him. They were now beyond the range of most of the British artillery and so were effectively on their own – just when they most desperately needed help. Ahead of them were German infantry, multiple anti-tank batteries and, even more ominously, reinforcements from the 21st Panzer Division and 1st SS Panzer Division that were beginning to move forward to join the fray. Gilmour's tanks were all but helpless in the wide open fields, with the Germans on higher ground able to pound them at will. In all the chaos, Gilmour kept his head and called for aerial support.

> We were advancing two troops up. Smoke was quite a problem; you lost sense of direction because of the amount of smoke. Mainly [the British barrage] but also fires had started, particularly in the villages. Some of the tanks had trouble in crossing a small embankment, probably about 4–5 feet high. It was steeper in some parts than in others. Soon after we crossed the second [Caen–Vimont] railway line we ran out of the protection of the barrage, because we were then getting beyond the range of our guns. There was a village sort of half-left, which obviously was held by the Germans and which had anti-tank guns in it and up on the ridge beyond. We called in Typhoons through brigade to help try and knock out the anti-tank guns. We saw the Typhoon attack – I think they were quite effective. I don't think at the time that we realised some of the fire was coming from anti-tank guns even further back than we were actually seeing. We came to a halt just after the second railway line.[37]

Major Sir John Gilmour, 'B' Squadron, 2nd F&FY

The Typhoons intervention helped, but, as an account from Flight Lieutenant Jack Scott makes clear, they were not a precision weapon.

> The leader would put his nose down and dive at about 60 degrees. Behind him we would follow hot on his tail. Maximum revs – full speed – you must be below 5,000 feet for the shortest possible time. No time to search for the target. Throttle and stick well forward, concentrating like mad on the aircraft in front. The sudden dive from patrol height to attack took

just a few seconds – just time to flick up the cover of the firing button with the thumb of the right hand, while the left kept the throttle fully open. Peering ahead, almost mesmerised by the leader, you had no option but to follow and hope that at the last moment you could identify the target. Fire at about 4,000 feet – quite a judder as two of the eight 60-pound rockets took off. If you were a back number, you really had no chance of picking out the target. The whole area would be a maelstrom of earth and debris thrown up by earlier rockets. You just fired into the general area, hoping that the leader had got it right. He often used his four Hispano cannons to observe strike before firing his rockets. As soon as you had fired, pull up, climb to a safe height and reform. The dive had probably taken you down to about 1,500 feet, where the flak and the debris thrown up by your own attack caused most of the damage which we sustained.[38]

Flight Lieutenant Jack Frost, 175 Squadron, RAF

For Sir John Gilmour the situation remained dire, as one by one his squadron was being torn to pieces. Driver Norman Bradley remembered losing his crew mates when his Sherman was hit.

I used the machine gun in the hull of the tank. There were Germans in the growing corn. It wasn't long before we saw tanks afire – tanks burning – and it wasn't long before ours was burning. We were stationary, we'd been firing at something or other. We ended up with three 88mm shells one after the other. They hit the turret – I think the turret crew 'had it' first – they were killed – that was Ken Gillmore[39] and Claude Marchant.[40] I think Doug Bostwick[41] had got out of the tank and was standing alongside talking to someone, it may have been the commander of another tank. I don't know what happened to him. I looked for the escape hatch on the floor, but you could only really get at it if the turret was in the wrong position.

Then you had to get out through the top – that is what I did.
I don't think the back end, the engine compartment, was
burning all that rapidly when I got out – the front seemed all
right. John Murray I never heard. When I got out I was fired
at by a machine gun. I moved far away from it. I was in fairly
high growing corn, that was good camouflage, and I got into
a hedgerow ditch. I lay there for a number of hours. There was
so much happening. What went on was of little or no interest
other than preserving your own life! I was very lucky really.[42]

Trooper Norman Bradley, 1 Troop, 'B' Squadron, 2nd F&FY

Later, Bradley was picked up by one of the turretless Honey
tanks – presumably one of Recce Troop – and taken back to the
Ranville glider field.

The remnants of 'C' Squadron moved forwards across the
embankment behind 'A' and 'B' Squadrons. But it was hopeless.

We stopped about half a mile past the second railway line; we
couldn't go any further. Every time we advanced, we were just
knocked out. It was a very confused situation. We were looking
for targets, trying to identify who it was that was killing us,
'Where the hell are they?' We were firing all the time, 'brassing
up' the woods in the hopes we were hitting something, because
the 88mm is fairly easily concealed compared to a panzer.[43]

Second Lieutenant Charlie Workman, 1 Troop, 'C' Squadron, 2nd F&FY

Captain Hutchison and two of the troops from 'A' Squadron
were ordered to try and suppress the fire coming from Le Poirier
and Four.

Joe Powell and half the squadron continued on in front with
'B' Squadron – John Gilmour's squadron. I was told to protect
the left flank with our two remaining troops – 4 Troop (Steel
Brownlie's troop) and 2 Troop. Pretty soon, Powell and his
troops and the 'B' Squadron people came into trouble in front
and really got stopped. Powell had the tracks of his tank shot

off! Then the 23rd Hussars came up through us and they ran into the same sort of trouble. They were all mixed up. It was getting very confused. We had plenty to do – I saw a Panther. In Le Poirier village there was a nice old Norman wall in front of it round the orchard. I could see this Panther blow a hole in the wall with its gun, so it could poke its gun through. Then we got on to it before it did any damage to us – we blew it up with the 17-pounder, I think that fixed it! Guns were shooting at us and we were shooting at them. We lost some tanks. I think there were some Tigers there – or were they Panthers? They waddled out and started swatting us! We returned fire and our shells were bouncing off these bloody things! We had quite close liaison at regimental level with the RAF. If you wanted support, you asked for 'Lime Juice!' If you were sufficiently high priority you got it quite quick. And there were these rocket-firing Typhoon fighters. I was down to my tank and Brownlie's troop.[44]

Captain Douglas Hutchison, HQ Troop, 'A' Squadron, 2nd F&FY

Shortly afterwards, Major Joe Powell took over Hutchison's tank so he could continue to command the squadron. Hutchison in Powell's trackless Sherman was towed back to safety by a turretless AVRE Sherman. For him, the battle was over. Steel Brownlie's troop continued to defend the left flank and Terry Boyne left a vivid account of his perspective of the fighting as a loader operator. More and more German tanks and anti-tank guns seemed to be joining the fray.

It seemed that fire was coming from all places! The radio was full of voices coming up, picking out targets. The trees seemed to house the 88s and round the sides of them there were Panthers reported here, there, and everywhere! People were just firing at will on the move, which is not the most accurate way of doing it. We were firing at all sorts. The commander would be selecting the target. If you had a second you could look out – get the gist of what you were 'potting' at. Within the trees you could pump HE into it so that they got airbursts and if it was an 88mm crewed by seven or eight, that would at least keep their heads down – it would give them something to think about rather than giving them the pleasure of firing at you. When it came to Panthers, then HE was no use to you at all. You needed to be something like 600 yards range to really do damage – anything more than that the AP shots would just skate straight off. There is nothing worse than watching an accurate shot hit and then just fly up in the air! The rolling barrage that was running in front of us limited our speed to some degree. Infantry couldn't have caught up with the speed we did move across it. As the firing towards us intensified, you had to go faster to try and avoid it. You could hear shrapnel twanging on the outside – nothing major fortunately. You could see flashes from the guns. It was hectic, it was very hot, you were sweating because of the heat. A petrol and cordite smell pervaded everything. A burning sensation in your throat. The noise was fairly fierce. You'd got the engine noise and with headphones on you got the persistent crackle of the radio. When the gun fired you got this 'rock' as the thing went off, the recoil, the hot shell, the case would come flying out the back and land on the floor. You had another one ready – and as soon as the shell case ejected you 'wanged' another one in. As the operator you had a little port at the side of the turret – you could open that and throw the empty shells out. Otherwise, you were standing on them, they were rolling about all over the floor. You had to be aware of what was happening in as much as the radio told you, when there was a sudden lull and you looked round, you had 'butterflies'; I don't think you'd be human if you didn't. It felt at the time we were throwing ourselves at a very solid brick wall and there didn't appear to be any real 'give' in it. As soon as you cleared one bit then the firing started from another bit just alongside it. You don't get the overall picture; you only see the little fragment that you're really looking at.

And as a loader/operator you don't look at an awful lot, you hear it more than you see it.[45]

Trooper Terry Boyne, 4 Troop, 'A' Squadron, 2nd F&FY

Wherever they were, whatever they did, it seemed the 2nd F&FY tanks were being picked off one by one. James Donovan remembered an exchange of fire with two German tanks. It was a hair-raising business.

Looking through the periscope, I saw two tanks, moving up behind the hedge facing us. You could just see the tops of the turrets. I said on the intercom to the crew commander, 'There's tank on our left!' One of the crew commanders was actually combing his hair! He was so unconcerned – I don't think he'd seen us! I can picture him now, he had blonde hair! He picked a field hat up and put it on – and I realised they were German tanks and not ours! They were Panthers. We started to reverse, and the crew commander brought the gun around onto them. They'd seen us by then. The first one came crashing through the hedge in front of us, 40–50 yards away. As he came through the hedge our gunner fired and it hit him – we saw the tracer from our shell come off the front and just zoom off into the air! It bounced off! As our driver was reversing, you could see the gun of their tank come round and 'WHOOOFF!' It came through the front somewhere. There was a hell of a noise – you don't know what it is! It all happens within seconds! The next thing we heard was, 'BAIL OUT!' I was in the co-driver's seat; I turned round and kicked the release on the escape hatch in the floor behind me. My thoughts were, 'If we go out through the front, they'll just shoot us down!' I kicked the lever over, and the escape hatch dropped and 'The Crow' [Dave Sutherland's nickname] and myself went through and the others came out of the turret. As we crawled back, boiling water was coming down, it must have gone through the radiators. So we came out the front and ran round to the back. Other tanks were firing – what they were firing at I don't know – it's all going on! All five of us got out and got to the back of the tank.[46]

Trooper James Donovan, 'B' Squadron, 2nd F&FY

Amid the death and destruction Donovan fondly recalled a rare moment of humour.

Officers used to get issued with a bottle of whisky every now and again, and Lieutenant Black had a bottle he used to share with his crew. The radio operator got on to the back of the tank when he came out of the turret and he's leaning back into the tank as it started to catch fire, trying to retrieve the bottle of whisky![47]

Trooper James Donovan, 'B' Squadron, 2nd F&FY

Although they had bailed out successfully, they were by no means safe. German tanks and infantry were in the immediate vicinity. They decided to make a run for it on foot.

As we all gathered at the back of the tank, the crew commander said, 'Right, let's get away, get into the corn and get away from here!' We couldn't do no more – we'd lost our tank! He said, 'Right, we'll all make a dash for it!' And to be quite honest I was the fastest – I was way out in front! Just running trying to get to safety. Although we had army boots on, I sure could move – I would have won an Olympic medal that day![48]

Trooper James Donovan, 'B' Squadron, 2nd F&FY

Soon it was all over for the 2nd F&FY bar the shouting. The Headquarters Squadron had moved forward in the final stages to join the sabre squadrons in action. But it made no difference; it merely added to the number of tanks knocked out.

We went across the second railway line. About 100 yards the other side we found a small cottage with an orchard. We tucked ourselves in that for cover. In front of us there was this valley. We were accompanied by that time by a number of the various fighting squadron tanks – about six or seven of us. Then five or six Panthers drew up the other side of the valley – about 1,500 yards away. We began to engage them, but unfortunately, they outgunned us – and also their armour. You hit them and the shells just bounced off. With a short barrelled 75mm at that range you couldn't do much. A couple of the other tanks were 'brewed up'.[49]

Trooper Alf Courtneidge, HQ Squadron, 2nd F&FY

By around 12.30, there were just about twenty 2nd F&FY tanks left as the reserve regiment, the 23rd Hussars, began to arrive on the scene.

We found it impossible to advance any further – the number of tanks we had lost. We lost half the squadron – we had lost so many tanks that we really lost all impetus to advance. At this time, the 23rd Hussars, who were in reserve, came up and ran into the back of us – as you might say! In fact, the 23rd Hussars really took over from us in trying to push on. Because of the number of tanks we had lost, we concentrated as one squadron during the late afternoon. Major Trotter, who was the second in command of the regiment, was either wounded or his tank knocked out and I had to take over as second in command of the regiment, in order to do the link with brigade headquarters. I finished up alongside the colonel.[50]

Major Sir John Gilmour, 'B' Squadron, 2nd F&FY

Shortly afterwards, Lieutenant Colonel Alex Scott's Sherman was knocked out by a Panther in front of Four, which was in turn knocked out by a Firefly. Scott was fortunate enough to escape unscathed. The regimental signals officer, Lieutenant Robert Clark, was acting as radio operator in Major George Trotter's Sherman. He recalled the moment they were hit.

The round came into the side of the tank just below the turret, passed within a few inches of my back and went into the engine compartment. George Trotter immediately ordered, 'Bail out', which we all did. This was quite difficult for Lance Corporal Crichton, the driver, and the co-driver because of the gun barrel above their hatches. We all took cover in some nearby trees or shrubs. The tank did not burn immediately, but about five minutes later it just exploded, with flames and smoke whooshing up into the air. Orders were to make one's way back to the echelon near the start line if knocked out, so we set off.[51]

Lieutenant Robert Clark, Headquarters, 2nd F&FY

From around mid day, strong German reinforcements in the shape of the 1st SS Panzer Division had begun to make their presence felt, although the Panthers may have wasted some of the advantage they held over longer ranges by getting rather too close in their enthusiasm for the fray. The arrival of the 23rd Hussars made little difference to the deteriorating situation as they were advancing on the same objectives as the 2nd F&FY and met the same fate as they entered the killing ground in front of Bourguébus Ridge.

But where were the Guards Armoured Division and the 7th Armoured Division? They had been late starting and the delays multiplied as they struggled to cross the Orne bridges and pass through the limited minefield channels. Then, after around three hours, the first elements of the Guards Armoured Division began to arrive and moved to attack Cagny and Le Poirier before pushing on to Frénouville and theoretically on to Vimont. They were thwarted by the same potent combination of German panzers, self-propelled guns, anti-tank guns and infantry. Behind them the 7th Armoured Division were also severely held up by the substantial congestion, then further hampered by what some observers described as excessive caution in their approach to the front line with the unpleasant prospect of attacking Fours and Soliers.

I suddenly saw Brigadier 'Loony' Hinde, who was commanding 22nd Armoured Brigade in 7th Armoured Division. He had been making a little recce and I thought, 'This is good, we will soon have 7th Armoured Division to take over the area between us and Guards Armoured Division.' But not at all; when he reached me, he said, 'There are too many bloody tanks here already; I'm not going to bring my tanks down yet.' I was staggered, and before I could explain that a lot of the tanks he had seen were knocked out, he had disappeared. And I may say 7th Armoured Division did not put in an appearance before 5 p.m. I cursed both my old division and my old brigade![52]

Major General 'Pip' Roberts, Headquarters, 11th Armoured Division

The presence of smoking Shermans across the battlefield may well actually have partially excused Brigadier Robert Hinde's caution – as indeed did their long history of hard fighting in North Africa and Italy. The end result was clear: as a powerful blow by three armoured divisions, it had been a total failure. Collectively the advance lost all cohesion and impetus. It had degenerated into isolated squadrons bashing themselves against the deeply layered German defences.

Then the Guards Armoured Brigade came through us: they immediately lost two or three tanks as well. I got out and I ran up to the squadron leader – Bowes Lyon,[53] a Scots Guardsman – climbed up on his tank and said, 'Look, that's our tanks ahead of you, we've got no further than here – this is the 2nd Fife and Forfar you see brewed up in front of you!' I pointed out there were 88mm all over the place. I got down and went back to my tank. Then we were pulled back. To me it was a disaster. It was such a shambles; such a mess.[54]

Second Lieutenant Charlie Workman, 1 Troop, 'C' Squadron, 2nd F&FY

At about 15.00, the remnants of the 2nd F&FY were ordered to pull back across the railway embankment east of Grentheville. Their battle was over. They had lost thirty-seven tanks. Behind them the battle stumbled on. At the end of that long day, the I, VIII and II Canadian Corps had between them lost some 1,500 casualties and 200 tanks. But in the hard fighting the Germans too had suffered. There was no doubt the tremendous bombing and artillery barrage had taken their toll on the Germans. But then every yard had been contested as their counter-attacks rained down on the British advance, causing more serious losses, while the Allied aircraft harassed them at every opportunity. At the end of the day, it is estimated that the Germans lost some 109 tanks. They were also forced to bring up both the 12th SS Panzer Division and the 116th Panzer Division to stem the attacks. In that sense, Montgomery's plan was working.

*

THE RECCE TROOP HAD BEEN IRRELEVANT to the fighting in their Honey tanks, and Geoff Hayward was one of those who had watched the devastation unfolding in front of them with a mixture of disbelief and horror.

> We could see our Shermans going forward in this cornfield. We were very surprised when suddenly these tanks began to get picked off one by one by German gunfire. I could see the German guns firing – I could see the muzzle flash up in the woods on the top of the opposing hill. We were horrified at what we saw. These tanks were catching fire and we could see little dark figures jumping out here and there and coming back through the corn towards our position. I was so dejected, I said to somebody, 'We've lost the war!'[55]
>
> Trooper Geoff Hayward, Recce Troop, HQ Squadron, 2nd F&FY

Even the intrepid figure of Bill Scott was shaken by what he saw. The flames reduced men in a few moments to something that was barely recognisable as human.

There were tanks going on fire all around you and black smoke. It's a selfish attitude, 'Oh, God!' You've got a good idea which tank it was, but you're very glad it's not you! You wait to see if there's anybody bailing out. But you've still got to go forward. You've got to go forward all the time, you can't stop. Infantry came up to my tank and said, 'There are two of your men in that tank!' I went across to the tank and there were two troopers there, the driver and the co-driver, strapped in, they were black-red. They weren't dead, they were still moving, their lips were moving. I couldn't do anything for them. I was dead scared – I think everybody was. You've got to keep going.[56]

Sergeant Bill Scott, Recce Troop, HQ Squadron, 2nd F&FY

But as the tanks fell back, the Honeys were pressed into service to carry back any surviving bailed-out crew members. Many of the crews had escaped unharmed; after all, they had practised bailing out, and fear had lent them metaphorical wings. But if unprotected crew stayed on the battlefield they would soon have been hit in that maelstrom of fire. Scott encountered Major George Trotter making his way back from his burnt-out Sherman.

I got the order to take back the second in command, Major Trotter, because he was shot out of his tank. He was dazed and a wee bit incoherent – shock. He just didn't know where he was. I had to take him back through the minefield to the Ranville glider field.[57]

Sergeant Bill Scott, Recce Troop, HQ Squadron, 2nd F&FY

Of course, some of the men that they collected had been wounded. Gray had picked up a few, but then his own Honey was hit by a shell, with horrific results.

We had the instructions to turn around, pick up any crews and bring them back. We had Lance Sergeant 'Tubby' Watson; he was the drummer in the pipe band. We picked up several others – we put them in the hull – [with] no turret we had all the hull space. We had one in the co-driver's seat; I was lying across the back of the engine on the outside. Most of them were all right, except for 'Tubby'. He had half his head blown away; he was alive, moaning like hell, but he was alive still. Nothing we could do – we weren't medics – we needed to get him back. Suddenly I got covered in evaporated milk – somebody had fired a bullet at my head – missed me and it had gone into a compo pack, hit the can of milk. Seconds after, the tank went up. I went up in the air and landed down on the ground – it was on fire. I had burns to my face and my hands, part of my arms. Everybody who could get out, got out. I know the wireless operator got out. An officer and I tried to get 'Tubby' Watson out climbing up on the side, but the flames were such you couldn't get to him – we would have been putting our heads and faces and arms into flames. He wouldn't have been aware of anything that was going on. He died in there.[58] We did get Jimmy Byers out through the hatch. His leg had gone, it was a mess. He must have been unconscious – he wasn't bawling and shouting – and Jimmy was one for shouting if he wanted to! A Bren gun carrier came – and we got him onto it.[59]

Trooper John Gray, Recce Troop, HQ Squadron, 2nd F&FY

Jimmy Byers seems to have survived his terrible ordeal. Padre Oswald Welch arrived and leapt into action as best he could.

The padre arrived with what we called the 'Blood Waggon' which was a halftrack ambulance. They dropped the padre off and a couple of stretchers. A tank came and dropped of some wounded, off the back, near us, lay them out on the ground. Somebody came up with some prisoners. The padre got two of the prisoners, two older men, gave them a red cross armband and a stretcher. He sent them out looking for wounded. They started bringing more wounded in, lay out these wounded on the ground. By then, it was getting towards the afternoon and some infantry of the Guards Armoured arrived. They all marched off heading towards Cagny, towards where these guns had been. We then took it very easy! We broke open the new ration pack – got the tin of peaches out and ate it![60]

Trooper Jack Edwards, 4 Troop, 'B' Squadron, 2nd F&FY

The juxtaposition of the personal tragedies being played out all around him and the soldierlike preoccupation with food is noticeable. But there was a yet more terrible task awaiting prospective volunteers from the Recce Troop. Geoff Hayward and most of the others simply couldn't face it and declined. Who can blame them?

Somebody came round asking for volunteers to help get bodies out of tanks. We'd already been told what happens to you when the tank catches fire. How they got these bodies out? We were told how to attach a rope around what was left of them – and sometimes the horrifying thing happened – that the body would disintegrate when pulling. It was something that the average person couldn't face. There was only one volunteer, it wasn't me! It was a former grave digger in civilian life. I gather that some of the tanks that were serviceable were even put back into use – the thought horrifies me that some crew had to get into one of those tanks.[61]

Trooper Geoff Hayward, Recce Troop, HQ Squadron, 2nd F&FY

Gradually the wounded were gathered up and ferried back to the Royal Army Medical Corps dressing station.

We were sitting on the grass outside the big tent. People were being evaluated and then taken in and looked after. I saw Sergeant Bob Wann come in – he was as black as the night and rolling about in pain. He was asking for water – there was a German prisoner there with a water bottle – we said, 'Give him the water!' And he wouldn't, so I clumped him, took the bottle, and gave him the water. I don't know whether I was doing the right thing in giving Bob the water or not.[62]

Trooper John Gray, Recce Troop, HQ Squadron, 2nd F&FY

It had been an awful, terrible day, surely nothing else could go wrong?

*

THE SURVIVING BAILED-OUT CREW MEMBERS were taken back to join the 'A' and 'B' Echelons who were still back at the Ranville glider field. Many had suffered terrible experiences and were not unnaturally shaken to the core.

> Half of them were really 'bomb happy'. You couldn't talk to them; they didn't really want to tell you anything about it. They more or less wanted you out of the way. They were in a state of 'I don't know where I am!' It was really frightening. They couldn't speak of what happened.[63]
>
> Trooper Gordon Fidler, 4 Troop, 'A' Squadron, 2nd F&FY

Ranville was also where the knocked-out tanks that had not been damaged irreparably were towed back by the AVRE or other tanks. The area was still the epicentre of British rear echelons for the three armoured divisions and was thus absolutely jam-packed with vehicles and men. The men set about making themselves comfortable for the night as best they could, choosing to sleep either inside the tanks, in slit trenches, or inside the looming gliders.

> We decided we would stay in the glider for the night and sort ourselves out next morning. When a lot of them landed they used to break in half – and we were lying in one of these. All I had in personal gear was my black beret, my tank suit, a vest, a pair of football shorts, boots and socks. We said, 'Oh, at least we'll get a night's sleep tonight.' Off came the tank suit, because it was ever so warm. That was my pillow! All I'd got on was just my football shorts – I'd even taken me socks and boots off! We're lying there and the German aircraft started to come over and they were dropping flares. I said, 'Oh Christ, they're going

to cop it on the beachhead tonight!' We heard machine guns rattling and the planes diving! We still thought they were going for the beachhead! After the flares had dropped, 'Geordie' Wardrop, another member of our troop, he says, 'Oh, looks like Blackpool lights out there!' Everybody laughed![64]

Trooper James Donovan, 'B' Squadron, 2nd F&FY

They wouldn't laugh for long. Somehow the Germans had a knack for doing just what you wouldn't want them to do in any wartime situation. This time they sent across some bombers. First, they dropped flares to illuminate and mark the target – the Ranville glider field. From up in the air it must have looked like a disturbed ants' nest.

That night the Germans dropped what we called 'chandeliers', they were parachute things that lit up the whole battlefield. Then they started bombing us. I was near a recovery tank, I got under there and everybody that could possibly squeeze under a vehicle was under one. We were like sardines! It was a hellish raid. The bombs were landing all round the vehicles – they were anti-personnel-type things that spread their shrapnel about. There was a lot of casualties. A bomb landed fairly near and some of the shrapnel went through between the bogies – and anybody who had their bottom sticking up got a dose of it. Two of my mates got wounded there: Johnny Murray and Jimmy Fraser. When we got them out, we had to manhandle them across the rest of the field, getting them on this Bren gun carrier – it was difficult to get them on and settled because they were both wounded in the posterior.[65]

Trooper Ron Forbes, 4 Troop, 'B' Squadron, 2nd F&FY

Norman Bradley also dived under a nearby tank.

George Wooldridge was the driver in another tank, my best army mate, and he had survived it [Goodwood] – we were absolutely delighted about that with each other. The tanks had been driven under the wings of gliders so that they couldn't be seen from the air. But it was unfortunate, because a lot of the turrets were left open and when the Germans came over and bombed this area, the burning wings of the gliders dropped into the tanks and added to the pandemonium. George Wooldridge and myself got under a tank for protection from the bombs. We lay side by side under this Sherman. He was severely wounded, and I just got shrapnel in my leg – just below the left knee – and face. I was bleeding profusely round my neck. I got from under the tank when the thing died down. George was whipped away to a field hospital. I wandered around in a daze. My concern was the blood coming from my face – I thought I'd lost half of my face! There was a captain asked me if I was OK, I said, 'Apart from all the blood!' He looked at it and said, 'I've had worse than that in the boxing ring!' I then went off to a field hospital.[66]

Trooper Norman Bradley, 1 Troop, 'B' Squadron, 2nd F&FY

Sadly, George Wooldridge[67] died the next day. Bradley himself had a 'Blighty' wound. All around them men took shelter where they could; it was literally every man for himself.

Bombs started dropping. I was at the side of a wood and I jumped into a trench – that had been used as a latrine. It was the only place I could get. I wasn't by myself, there were three or four of us in there – we daren't move. This London lad was giving us a commentary of what was happening! 'Another bomb dropped there! He's set the hedge on fire!' I used to sit and be quiet, listening for every little noise. A few of them had gone into the gliders to sleep, they'd get a bit of cover. But they set the gliders on fire – one of my pals was burnt to a cinder – he was just like a piece of roast beef when we pulled him out.[68]

Trooper Jack Rex, HQ Squadron, 2nd F&FY

James Donovan was still lying in his glider when he finally grasped that this was not a raid on the beach area – that they were the target.

The next thing we know, lying there looking up at the top of the glider, and all of a sudden, I saw loads and loads of little holes! We could see the lights from the flares were shining through the holes! We realised then that they were machine gunning the glider field – and dropping their bombs. We jumped out of the end of the glider because that was the obvious target and ran! You can imagine, I'd got no shirt, boots or socks on – all I'd got was my football shorts on![69]

Trooper James Donovan, 'B' Squadron, 2nd F&FY

Peter Young was one of those that was badly wounded.

Alec Wallace was hit in the head, he was the driver from one of the other tanks. I got hit in the legs, wrist and back. The troop commander got hit in the stomach. I couldn't get into my own tank – I was running to get under the back of the tank. I tried to crawl underneath, but my legs were hanging out. With the blow in my back, I thought my legs were away. I couldna move. Folks say their life flashes in front of them – that did with me – like the pictures. I thought I was away; thought it was the end because I couldn't feel my legs. Wallace got me out. They managed to get one of the tanks running and they put me on the back of the tank. There was another chap there – a Corporal Eric Asher,[70] but they told me he was dead. He'd been sleeping in the glider. They took us to the dressing station, which didn't seem to be very far away. They cut my trousers up to the waist, ran the scissors up the back of my shirt and everything – they took everything off. I had no clothes on – I was lying in there with a blanket. I was shouting at them, 'For heaven's sake give me something to put me out of my misery!' I was in pain! They gave me morphine. I kept shouting. 'You've already had it!' They gave me a big bowl of tea.[71]

Lance Corporal Peter Young, 3 Troop. 'B' Squadron, 2nd F&FY

Young was evacuated by hospital ship to England where he

underwent hospital treatment for his serious thigh and back wounds, after which he had to learn to walk again.

The regimental signals officer, Lieutenant Robert Clark, was another that suffered severe wounds in the bombing.

> I crawled under a nearby vehicle, and that was when I was hit. A bomb must have landed just beside me, and a large piece of shrapnel hit me in the stomach. Realising that it was serious I thought that if I didn't do something quickly, I would die. Fortunately, I remembered where the medical tent was, so I set off to get there. I found an abandoned jeep and somehow managed to drive it. Flares still lit up the area, so I could see where I was going, although bombs were still dropping all around. Eventually I reached darkness, drove into a bomb crater and was thrown out of the jeep. When I had recovered a bit, I crawled on till I reached the medical tent. There was no one there – I suppose they had taken cover. I found a stretcher and just lay there until the bombing ended and someone came. He asked me what I was doing, so I told him that I'd been hit. He took a look and clearly didn't like what he saw. He patched me up a bit and then sent me quickly back by truck to the Field Hospital near Bayeux.[72]

Lieutenant Robert Clark, Headquarters, 2nd F&FY

Clark was operated on as soon as he got to the field hospital, which saved his life. He was then sent back to England, where he spent six months in Liverpool Royal Infirmary. Sometimes there could be a relatively happy ending.

*

THE REGIMENT HAD BEEN DEVASTATED on 18 July. The scale of their losses was difficult to process. Men could not help but ponder how they had survived unscathed, when so many of their friends had been killed or wounded. That night they went into laager just to the west of Le Mesnil Frémentel.

There must be an element of luck in this – where the one next to you goes down and you stay up. There is luck or a divine somebody up there! You're just thankful that you got through the day. But you then start this feeling, 'Will I see this tomorrow?' Because the casualties were so heavy that you wondered what will tomorrow bring. The thought was, 'You just can't carry on at this rate!' We just couldn't, it was not possible! The whole conversation was, 'Have you seen "Smudger" or so and so?' It was pretty traumatic![73]

Trooper Terry Boyne, 3 Troop, 'A' Squadron, 2nd F&FY

There were just twenty-five serviceable tanks left in the regiment which were organised ad hoc into two squadrons: 'A' Squadron commanded by Major Joe Powell and 'C' Squadron commanded by Captain J. E. F. Millar. On 19 July, the 2nd F&FY were meant to be left out of action in reserve, when the 11th Armoured Division mounted a renewed assault on the villages of Bras, Hubert-Folie, Soliers and Four. It would prove to be another miserable and depressing day, not helped when they suffered another significant loss.

I was a bit angry with Major Powell. He'd called us over to his tank to give out orders at an 'O' group – and there was a lot of shellfire going on! About half a dozen of us tank commanders tore over and dived under his tank. He gave us some very simple orders which he could have given us over the air – then we had to make our way back to our tanks! It wasn't necessary! I dashed back to my tank and a shell fell at the side, just as I was leaping up, and I went in my turret head first! I hurt my back – and I still suffer from that today! I was cursing him saying, 'That silly bastard, making us go over there for nothing, nearly got us all killed!' But I survived all right. He didn't: getting into his tank, Powell was killed.[74]

Trooper Roy Vallance, HQ Troop, 'A' Squadron, 2nd F&FY

Terry Boyne saw it happen at close range from the relative safety of his Sherman.

> We were getting stonked by these nebelwerfers. They didn't alarm us particularly much, but for infantry or anybody out on foot they were pretty horrendous. They were coming over in droves – like little dustbins – you could see them in the air. Major Powell and another were coming along the hedge in front. His tank was just behind us. They came trotting along the hedge and they parted. He turned to face my vehicle and he started running. He was bending, getting lower and lower, he was almost folded in half, he ran right alongside our vehicle. This cluster of nebelwerfers landed aside of us, at the back of us, in the front of us. The dust was still in the air, you get smothered in dust, the dirt. A radio called up for him: the answer was, 'I'm sorry, but the squadron leader is not available!' He'd copped the one that was almost alongside me. He heard it coming I'm sure.[75]

Trooper Terry Boyne, 3 Troop, 'A' Squadron, 2nd F&FY

Major Joe Powell[76] was not the only one who was hit. After being on wireless watch overnight, Alf Courtneidge was one of three men wounded by the shelling.

> Somebody was having a brew up and I went over to join them. Just having a cup of tea with some of the lads. Artillery opened up on our position – next minute I'm on the ground with a hole through my side! And I was alight – my hand caught fire! These things happen so quickly, the petrol cooker – the petrol sprayed over me and the other people in the vicinity. I was put out, the flames were extinguished – I think it was Frankie Ellison from the anti-aircraft tank. Corporal 'Chips' Eady – he also was burnt. This great big blister came up.[77]

Trooper Alf Courtneidge, HQ Squadron, 2nd F&FY

In addition to the burns, shrapnel had smashed his left hip bone, missing his femoral artery by about an eighth of an inch! He was soon whisked away on a stretcher in a halftrack back to the forward first aid post.

After a morning spent reorganising, the armoured assault recommenced. Some progress was made but the fighting was hard. Although Bras was captured by the 3rd Royal Tank Regiment, the 2nd Northamptonshire Yeomanry had been repulsed from Hubert-Folie. This meant that, late in the afternoon, the remnants of the 2nd F&FY were once more called into action. By this time, the artillery had been moved up and there would be a dense concentration of 5.5-inch guns and 25-pounders to help blast their way forward. Close behind this wall of shells, 'C' Squadron, followed by the 8th Rifle Brigade, were to dash in to take the village on the crest of the Bourguébus Ridge.

> Lamont was asked to volunteer to motor fast along the ridge, to take Hubert Folie. I don't know whether he was detailed, or he actually volunteered, quite honestly! He was promised support – they would put up a curtain of fire in front of us. We would advance at top speed behind this gunfire and take the village. And we did! The divisional artillery opened up with their 25-pounders and created a scene like Dante's *Inferno* about 200 yards in front of us. It was a beautifully executed operation – they moved this fire forward and we were racing along at top speed, 25–30 miles per hour behind it![78]
>
> Trooper Robert Nurse, 2 Troop, 'C' Squadron, 2nd F&FY

Behind them came 'A' Squadron, including the Sherman commanded by Roy Vallance.

> There was an *awful* lot of firing; there was enemy in the village. There was a sniper up in the church tower – we saw him, and my tank got him with a shell. We were firing the Browning, so much that the camouflage net we had over the turret caught fire round by the barrel of the gun. By this time, we had a spare co-driver. I said to him, 'Open your hatch and squirt the fire extinguisher onto the camouflage net!' I got no answer and said

it again on the intercom. The driver he came up and he said,
'He won't do it, he's had it!' He was a very young lad – even
younger than me – and he was in a funk! Nothing wrong with
him, he'd just got scared stiff! So, I got out, pulling this net off,
because we were in danger of blowing up. The driver in turn
got out. He saw somebody firing at me from a building and he
grabbed a Bren gun, which was lying on the top somewhere and
stood there firing that. I pulled this net off and everything was
OK. We saw German soft vehicles that were getting out of the
village at the last minute – most of them didn't.[79]

Trooper Roy Vallance, HQ Troop, 'A' Squadron, 2nd F&FY

Robert Nurse was one of those who hit the retiring German
vehicles hard.

Got into the village, obviously the gunfire stopped – and I got
to the other side of the village – and got my first hit! It was
dusk and there was one of these semi-tracked German vehicles,
wheels in front and tracks behind, I took a shot at it – and I hit
it![80]

Trooper Robert Nurse, 2 Troop, 'C' Squadron, 2nd F&FY

The ruins of Hubert-Folie had been captured and were then
secured by an additional company of the 4th King's Shropshire
Light Infantry. The remaining 2nd F&FY tanks then retired into
a laager. For them, the battle was over at last. For the next two
days the fighting died down but little more ground was taken,
and consolidation became the prime consideration. They were
on the Bourguébus Ridge. But at what cost?

Operation Goodwood has long been deeply controversial among military historians. The massed armour had been
employed in a very narrow front attack to try and take strong
German positions organised in considerable depth, beyond artillery range and without the proper immediate infantry support
that was essential to maintain momentum. Hence the armour
failed because it was being used *wrongly*. The armoured divisions

needed space to manoeuvre and close infantry support if they were to succeed. If – and indeed when – the German panzer divisions were employed in such a careless manner, they too were roughly handled. The result was terrible British tank losses which are somewhat difficult to accurately tabulate for the three armoured divisions involved – estimates range widely from 275 to 500 (destroyed or damaged to a varying degree) – while the Germans may have lost just over eighty tanks and self-propelled guns. Once again it should be noted that these losses were relatively more damaging for the Germans, in the sense that they could not be easily replaced, whereas British replacements were close at hand.

Whatever debatable merits the Goodwood plan had were also stymied at the outset by the congestion and resultant severe delays inflicted by the pinchpoints created by the river, canal and minefield that the tanks had to pass through to reach the start lines. Although useful ground had been taken to enlarge the Orne bridgehead, the Goodwood gains had not come up to expectations, and any fond hopes of a breakthrough advance to Falaise had been exposed as unrealistic. It was evident that the artillery fire plans and aerial bombing needed to be controlled with greater flexibility if they were to meet the needs of the men on the ground in a fast-developing battle situation. The main achievement of Operation Goodwood was in the attritional grinding down of the German panzer divisions, and for Montgomery this became the mantra he deployed in defending the battle. After all, he knew that in a few days the Americans would launch Operation Cobra to the south in an area that was relatively denuded of German armour. While some six and a half panzer divisions were facing the British Second Army around Caen, there were only one and a half panzer divisions facing the American First Army. Perhaps it was a necessary battle, but there was a terrible human cost, with over 5,500 casualties killed, missing and wounded across the British forces involved in the main and subsidiary operations. The horrors hidden behind these bland statistics were brought home in a brutal fashion to Lieutenant Graeme Hutchison.

> In the clammy light of dawn, a halftrack vehicle with a Red Cross flag on its aerial drew up, and our padre, Oswald Welsh, got out. In a gentle voice he said, 'Good morning, Graeme, I have permission to borrow you for a short time – I am told you are a brave man!' Tired and extremely damp, no one could feel less brave. I took off my pistol and got in. There were three of us besides the padre and we searched dead and broken tanks, where we might find a poor survivor, or there might be at least some personal possessions to identify. At first there was some mortaring and then a deathly silence. We gave some of the fallen a shallow grave and put up a small cross with a name on. Of Chris Nichols and his crew, we could find nothing, not even a pay book. It was eerie work, and it seemed an age before the padre called a halt, and we headed back.[81]
>
> Lieutenant Graeme Hutchison, 4 Troop, 'C' Squadron, 2nd F&FY

On 20 July, the 2nd F&FY pulled back, first to Demouville and then right back to Ardenne Abbey near the village of Cussy, just to the south, near Carpiquet.

> We moved back to the abbey. It was raining hard and we were driving through what seemed like a sea of mud for ages. It was one of these army roads that had been made cross-country. They just used to bulldoze a road and of course when it got wet it just got churned up into mud. Only tanks could go through it when it was wet. While we were churning through it, we were attacked – the Luftwaffe arrived. I could see explosions in the mud in front of us – they were attacking us with cannon fire – the shells were splattering all round us. As far as I know, no casualties.[82]
>
> Trooper Jack Edwards, 4 Troop, 'B' Squadron, 2nd F&FY

For once they had been lucky. At the Ardenne Abbey their

future as a regiment would be decided. In view of their losses there was a strong chance that it could be broken up to supply reinforcements for other regiments. Or would the 2nd F&FY survive to fight again?

11

OPERATION BLUECOAT

Everybody was pretty shattered. We thought we were going to
have this marvellous victory with all these tanks – invincible
– and in fact as far as we could see we'd lost three quarters of
our vehicles. By this time, we knew the Sherman was no good.
Personally, I felt, 'We're never going to survive this! So, one
might as well make the most of it!' I was young! I thought, 'If I
get brewed up, or whatever, at least I'll go down fighting!'[1]

Trooper Roy Vallance, HQ Troop, 'A' Squadron, 2nd F&FY

PEACE, PERFECT PEACE, it may have seemed in retrospect,
but the 2nd F&FY sojourn at Ardenne Abbey was at the time
a period of considerable tension within the regiment. For the
men, the focus was on whether the unit would continue to exist.
Their ranks were thinned with hardly any tanks left, meaning
the risk of being broken up to provide reinforcements for other
units was obvious.

Everybody was convinced that we were going to be broken up
– the Fife and Forfar were to be disintegrated – collapsed. We'd
had so many casualties. There was a distinct feeling at ground
level that we were not going to survive this at all. That a new
regiment would come up and we would 'fill it up'. That would
have been terrible, an absolute disaster for us. It could have

happened. Why it was decided to keep it I don't know, possibly because of Colonel Scott and Gilmour.[2]

Squadron Quartermaster Sergeant Tommy Willmott, HQ Squadron, 2nd F&FY

In the end the 2nd F&FY escaped intact, as the 24th Lancers was the regiment chosen for 'the chop'.

I went with Major Blacker of the 23rd Hussars to the 24th Lancers, which was the regiment that was broken up in order to get us brought back to something like regimental strength. Funnily enough, the 24th Lancers were commanded by a cousin of mine, Colonel Anderson, whose family came from Largo in Fife. If the 24th Lancers hadn't been broken up, I think we would have been disbanded. We didn't really have time to worry too much about that – it happened all so quickly! We saw their acting commanding officer as Colonel Anderson had been wounded and was invalided back. We agreed how many officers and men were available and we split them up between us! We got the equivalent of about two squadrons. We kept them together as tank crews, but mixed up among us. They fitted in very well – there were a whole lot of officers we knew quite well because they'd been serving with us ever since 1941. I don't think that they had an identity in the same way that our regiment had – of all coming from the same geographical area. It wasn't such a wrench as far as they were concerned.[3]

Major Sir John Gilmour, 'B' Squadron, 2nd F&FY

A new commander, Major Richard Leith, was appointed to replace Chris Nichols in command of 'C' Squadron. A member of the landed gentry, who was known to be fiercely anti-Communist, Leith was generally regarded as a competent officer. They also had a change in medical officers as Captain B. C. H. Luker was brought in to replace Captain Beamish, who had suffered a nervous breakdown.

Captain Beamish, he gave up – he went to bits and pieces. It must have been terrible for him. He was trained to save life and he couldn't do anything about half the things that were happening.[4]

Squadron Quartermaster Sergeant Tommy Willmott, HQ Squadron, 2nd F&FY

Any remaining gaps in the ranks of the officers and NCOs were filled by promotions, and Roy Vallance found himself given a well-deserved endorsement when he was raised to the dizzy heights of lance corporal, freed from the bulldozer Sherman and returned to 4 Troop.

There was no shortage of tanks – there were plenty of tanks held in the tank delivery squadron somewhere in the rear areas. We were pretty shattered to think of the casualties we'd had and the numbers of tanks we had lost. It didn't bode well for the future![5]

Lance Corporal Roy Vallance, 4 Troop, 'A' Squadron, 2nd F&FY

As part of the reorganisation, the Recce Troop was reduced in size to just three turretless Honey tanks and the personnel redeployed on to the Shermans. The qualities and enthusiasm of Sergeant Bill Scott were recognised, and he found himself placed in command of 2 Troop, 'C' Squadron. Gradually the regiment settled down, assimilated the new arrivals and the new command structure. They didn't have time to waste; within just ten days they were required to be ready for action. There had also been a change in the brigade structure, with the 2nd F&FY now temporarily assigned to the 159th Brigade Group, where they were to support the operations of the 1st Herefordshire Regiment. Newly promoted 'Pinkie' Hutchison explains the changes.

It had become evident that far closer cooperation with tanks and infantry was necessary. That applied particularly in the type of close country – the Bocage – that we were going to be

operating in in the foreseeable future. It was ideal defensive
country: small fields with great big hedges, road banks, dry
ditches if not wet ditches. It was really quite difficult country
for tanks to operate in from every point of view. You never had
any sort of field of view of more than a few yards. So, you can
imagine that it wasn't easy. Infantry could be of great help – and
were. Effectively the units of the division were divided up into
two identical mixed-brigade groups, each with two armoured
regiments, two infantry battalions, a gunner regiment and
anti-tank guns too. You'd have these two groups operating on
parallel routes of advance.[6]

Major Douglas Hutchison, 'A' Squadron, 2nd F&FY

Tanks were vital to the infantry, but it had now been fully
acknowledged that the infantry were equally essential to the
tanks. The organisational and tactical changes introduced
represented a considerable amount of increased flexibility in
response to the challenges unfolding before them in the Normandy campaign.

After Goodwood we were so much better integrated with
the infantry in all the attacks that we made. We never moved
unless we had close infantry support. It gave one confidence
that you had help to deal with being ambushed from behind.
If you didn't have infantry support, you always had the danger
that somebody would 'come to life' behind you! But having the
infantry there protected your 'behind'. The back of a tank was
very vulnerable to a bazooka – petrol engines exploded very
easily.[7]

Major Sir John Gilmour, 'B' Squadron, 2nd F&FY

The 159th Brigade Group consisted of the 2nd F&FY, Northamptonshire Yeomanry, 1st Herefordshire Regiment and 4th King's
Own Shropshire Light Infantry (KSLI). To assist them in
communicating with the infantry, always a problem for tanks,
additional wireless sets were fitted.

The wireless mechanics came and fitted No. 18 sets and an aerial for it. We could speak directly to the infantry – they had 18 sets – to the platoon commander of 13th Platoon, the Herefords.[8]

Trooper Jack Edwards, 4 Troop, 'B' Squadron, 2nd F&FY

It was clear that at least some of the painful lessons of Epsom and Goodwood had already been digested.

On 28 July, the 11th Armoured Division began the tortuous journey from Ardenne Abbey in the east sector of the British bridgehead, right across to Caumont in the west.

We moved at night to the west to the edge of the American zone. That was an extraordinary move. The Germans must have been aware that something was going on: the noise of a whole division moving and the huge clouds of dust. It was quite light, until probably midnight, it was mid summer, but it was so dry and there was so much dust! Each tank commander was told to have a cigarette burning on the top of the tank all of the way as a help to the one behind. It was close country, more dense than around the Caen area, more small fields. Bocage type country.[9]

Lance Corporal Roy Vallance, 4 Troop, 'A' Squadron, 2nd F&FY

The move to the western flank of the British Second Army was part of the preparations for the launch of Operation Bluecoat. Since 25 July, the American First Army had been engaged in a major thrust on their front, which stretched from St Lô in the east to Lessay on the coast. Supported by massive bomber raids they had smashed their way through the relatively weak German Seventh Army forward defence lines. By 27 July, the German Seventh Army was in a headlong retreat in the coastal sector as the strong American right hook swung round, capturing Coutances and then pushing on to take Avranches on 30 July. This was an American triumph. Here, then, was justification for the sacrifices of the British at Epsom and Goodwood, which had succeeded in attracting most of the German armoured reserves away from the American front. Indeed, the Germans still believed that the British intended a renewed assault towards Falaise and Mézidon, thanks to a diversionary operation carried out by the Canadian II Corps on 25 July.

The British role was to continue to maintain pressure all along their front, but the XXX Corps and VIII Corps were to strike hard in support of the Americans in the Caumont sector on the immediate left flank of the American First Army. They were to drive into the area between the Orne and Vire rivers, with a view of taking Mount Pinçon and thereby preventing the Germans from using it as a 'hinge' to assist in an orderly withdrawal from the advance of the American First Army. The 11th Armoured Division would be on the right flank, pushing forward towards St Martin des Besaces, covering the advance of the 15th (Scottish) Division to their left. The Guards Armoured Division and 7th Armoured Divisions were back in reserve; indeed, they were still in the process of moving across from the area of the recent operations east of Caen.

The shift to the west meant that the 2nd F&FY were now in the heart of the Bocage country, a complex, crowded landscape of small fields bounded by thick hedges. Little woods, hills and valleys abounded, while the sketchy road network had high banks, thick hedges and deep ditches on either side of most highways. Little villages were dotted about, although there were few major towns in the region. Overall, lines of sight were very restricted and thus it was ideal ground for a close-range ambush by anti-tank guns, panzers, self-propelled guns such as the Sturmgeschütz III (a 75mm mobile assault gun used for direct-fire support for infantry or in an anti-tank role – often known as the StuG III), or conventional artillery. In essence, the defenders would have the advantage of firing the first shot, using low-smoke propellant, from concealed positions, which meant the potential for further shots before they could be accurately located. There was also a new threat from the increasingly widespread deployment of the Panzerfaust (often known at the time as a bazooka after a similar American weapon), a short-range single-shot anti-tank weapon with a High Explosive Anti-Tank (HEAT) warhead that could be wielded and fired by a single German soldier. Panzerfausts could lurk anywhere in the Bocage and were well capable of knocking out a Sherman, penetrating the armour and causing terrible 'spalling' as fragments tore into the crew. All this was to the advantage of the defenders, but, on the other hand, the Allies had an overwhelming superiority of both air power and artillery, which they could call on whenever required.

At 06.55 on 30 July, the 2nd F&FY followed the 1st Herefords of 159th Brigade Group into the attack on the high ground west of Caumont, forming the right-hand columns, while the 29th Armoured Brigade Group advanced to their left. The sappers were supposed to have cleared three tracks to pass through the minefields, but the mines were laid deeper than usual, and this, coupled with time pressures, meant little or nothing had been achieved. The mines would take a severe toll. After a difficult journey to the start line, 'A' and 'B' Squadrons moved forward behind the Herefords as they advanced on the village of Cussy. The infantry suffered heavy machine gun and mortar fire, and Major Sir John Gilmour led his squadron round to their right, trying to outflank and destroy the opposition. Jack Edwards described what happened.

> We just moved up the field about a couple of hundred yards, turned through an orchard and we were in the fighting line. There was machine-gun fire going – and I could see two stretcher-bearers sitting on the farmhouse steps, bandaging their own legs. They'd been hit first, evidently. The squadron moved through this orchard and tanks started hitting mines. About half 'A' Squadron got stopped – knocked out – by mines. Our tank missed them all. The troop leader Mr Darke came to take over our tank. He'd only just climbed in when Sir John Gilmour, the squadron leader, said, 'I'm having this tank!' So, Mr Darke had to get out and Major Gilmour took

over – we were squadron leader's tank for the rest of that day.
It meant we didn't do any fighting, but we were zipping about,
all over the place. He kept jumping out to have a word with the
infantry, jumping out to have a word with tank commanders.
It was in the Bocage country, all these thick hedges and deep
ditches! It gave me a headache because we kept dropping into
these ditches and climbing out. Then bouncing flat onto the
field, climbing over these high banks at the bottom of all the
hedges. Very hard going. To me it was a bit strange having a
major on board. I'd never had an officer on the tank before – so
I didn't know what to do about it. But he said, 'Have you such a
thing as a bar of chocolate?' I found him a bar and a bit later he
saw somebody throwing hand grenades over a hedge, as we were
passing. He said, 'Have you such a thing as a hand grenade?'
I gave him a couple of hand grenades, which he lobbed over
the hedge! He was very polite! I was very impressed by his
maps – we just had the ordinary maps – like a cheap version of
Ordnance Survey maps. But he had these aerial photographic
maps, with all the details, you could see all the fields and
everything on them – marvellous maps. The day was spent
galloping about from one unit to another – organising the
advance.[10]

Trooper Jack Edwards, 4 Troop, 'B' Squadron, 2nd F&FY

The squadron lost some seven tanks to the mines.

To their left, Steel Brownlie was in the thick of the action as
the 'A' Squadron tanks edged forwards, only to be hit by a mass
of mortar fire.

Several tank commanders were killed or wounded by the
mortar fire. In theory, we should have had the hatches closed,
and looked through periscopes. In fact, these were useless, and
the only way to see where you were going, to spot targets and
to control your troop, was to put your head out. My corporal's
operator, Trooper Cross, went back with a splinter in the head.

Then Charlie Workman staggered past, with a hole in his helmet. Would my luck hold?[11]

Lieutenant William Steel Brownlie, 4 Troop, 'A' Squadron, 2nd F&FY

Even after his head wound, Workman had tried to stay on with his tank crew, but his wounds proved to be too disabling.

When I was hit by shrapnel – it was these 'Moaning Minnie' rockets – a nebelwerfer – there was a 'BANG!' As commander I was standing up, nobody else in the tank was hit – it was just me! First thing I knew was a pain in my arm and my leg – I disregarded that! We rang up and said we'd been hit, but we continued to move. Then apparently my voice was getting weaker and weaker, and the squadron leader said, 'Charlie, are you OK?' I said, 'Yes, I'm fine!' Then I was beginning to sort of slip and the wireless operator said, 'No, he's not! You'll have to take him away!' They stopped to take me out, brought up the ambulance, a halftrack, and it took me away. A very bumpy run back to the field dressing station.[12]

Second Lieutenant Charlie Workman, 1 Troop, 'C' Squadron, 2nd F&FY

He had suffered burns, had shrapnel in his leg and at his interview he showed me the considerable hole still clearly visible in his arm just below the shoulder along with a splendid photo of the hole ripped in his helmet by shrapnel. Workman's Normandy campaign was over, as he was evacuated and hospitalised back in the UK. But he would return to the regiment early in 1945. The Herefords had severe casualties, losing some 22 killed and 104 wounded – mainly from the German mortars and artillery.

Yet, despite it all, the brigade groups still pushed forwards, the pressure built up and suddenly the German resistance collapsed. 'A' Squadron, accompanied by the 4th KSLI, was sent forward to capitalise on the chance to make real progress. Steel Brownlie was determined not to waste a minute.

The crust of the German defences broke, and we were told to move, and move fast. We called it 'baffing'. No more creeping through hedges and grinding about in first gear, but doing what we had been trained to do – move! 'A' Squadron went first, and I was leading 4 Troop. It was a case of motoring flat out, on the straight, for the faster you went the harder you were to hit. There were Germans all over the place, running and scampering. We fired wildly at them, overtook them and left them far behind. There were targets at every turn of the road. It was exhilarating. Corporal Croney failed to take a bend and went off the road. Corporal Litster's power traverse jammed, and he fell out too. Corporal Newman's wireless packed in, so I told him to halt. I was now a one-tank troop, but that made no difference; only one tank could go along narrow country roads, and there was no chance of mutual support. Round a bend, there was a six-barrelled nebelwerfer sitting in the road. Buchanan hit it with an HE without even being given a fire order, and it went up in flames. We drove over the wreckage and went on a little more cautiously. Beyond the next bend was a camouflaged vehicle, so I halted. Buchanan brewed it first time. He was a splendid gunner.[13]

Lieutenant William Steel Brownlie, 4 Troop, 'A' Squadron, 2nd F&FY

While Buchanan did not remember the specifics of his targets on this wild drive, he did remember what it was like.

The gun was loaded with HE shells at all times and I was given carte blanche if I saw something, fire at it – and then tell the commander. Because he couldn't watch everything. So, when I saw these things – I just fired at them. Norman was ready to reload, I would say, 'Firing now, AP!' And he would get an AP next shell and shove it up! I had to clear the gun first! But I just fired on my 'own bat', if I saw something which was out of the ordinary I just 'let go'. If it was infantrymen, I would use machine guns; if they were going into a wood, I would spray the wood. [14]

Trooper John Buchanan, 4 Troop, 'A' Squadron, 2nd F&FY

Then they had a close escape.

We went very fast round a bend, firing at some twenty Germans in a field, and I saw a small, black object down the straight stretch in front. Something came flying from it and burst on the turret. I could not see or hear – and putting my hands to my face I could feel no features. I rolled out, down over the engine and into the ditch, really frightened. I lay wondering what had happened to me, and by the time I had recovered my senses the rest of the squadron were roaring past, my own tank half through the hedge at a crazy angle. I was surprised to find myself all in one piece, except for a few cuts on the forehead. Inspection revealed that a Panzerschreck (heavy bazooka) had hit the turret a foot in front of my head and blown the camouflage netting off my helmet. Metal splash had welded the turret to the hull, so that it was impossible to traverse. My German P38 pistol had disappeared in the confusion. All the crew were uninjured. While we were finding all this out, the tank was spattered with bullets. We hurriedly got inside, and spotted some trenches a hundred yards away, with helmets poking from them. With no turret traverse, it was necessary to manoeuvre the whole tank to get on to them, while staying out of panzerfaust range. A few HE on delay fuse brought them out with their hands up. We managed to free the turret and set off to rejoin the squadron. By following their tracks, we found them at nightfall as they were going into harbour, near La Foucquerie. There were fires all around. [15]

Lieutenant William Steel Brownlie, 4 Troop, 'A' Squadron, 2nd F&FY

The tanks kept right up with the infantry as they advanced and managed to get to La Fouquerie and La Morichèse, where the regiment harboured. By this time, the 4th KSLI were exhausted, but the corps commander, Lieutenant General Richard O'Connor, would accept no excuses, overruling both Brigadier Churcher and the battalion commander, Major Max Robinson, to order that the exhausted men be roused and sent forward another 5,000 yards to St Ouen des Besaces.

Next day, 31 July, the pressure was still on to increase the pace of the advance. Now the village of St Martin des Besaces had to be taken as soon as possible. The task was assigned to Major Hutchison and his 'A' Squadron, along with the long-suffering 4th KSLI.

> We got up to the east of a small village on the main road on the top of a hill, called St Martin des Besaces. We were told to go and clear that with the KSLI. I met Max Robinson, a delightful man who commanded the KSLI, and we made a plan of how we were going to do it: to take the village from the west, with tanks advancing in support of the infantry on both sides of the road. Trouble was, we discovered when we started that it was absolutely impossible going for tanks, with tiny little fields and orchards – banks everywhere. So, we weren't able to support the infantry forwards the way we'd hoped to be able to do. There was a German Mark IV seen in the village.[16]
>
> Major Douglas Hutchison, 'A' Squadron, 2nd F&FY

Gordon Fidler was all too aware of the Mark IV, as he believed it was this tank that knocked out his Sherman.

> We are told that there's a Mark IV firing up the road, firing from our left. We get across the road and we get hit. The tank rocks on the suspension – it really does rock! And it seems as if all the paintwork – bits and pieces – are falling down inside the tank. But you don't stay long enough – your immediate [aim] is to get out, even though it's not on fire. The tank doesn't catch fire, but we're knocked out, we can't move. We all bail out, out the top. On our earphones we've got a snatch plug, you snatch that when you get out. In a panic situation, you want to get out

as quick as you bloody can. I got halfway through, and I had a head harness on with my earphones attached – and I can't get out because I haven't pulled my snatch plug. So, I've got to go back down inside, pull the snatch plug and then out. We all clamber out to the tank, three out of the turret and two out of the front compartment. There is a ditch and also a lane that's leading from the road, by the side of the tank. We all make for this lane. The Herefords are in front of us. The Mark IV was in a house, apparently. In the meantime, the Mark IV dropped an HE shell on the road. We get up this lane, and there's only four of us. Tommy Smith, he's been wounded in the arm by shrapnel, but there's only the four men. We can't move back on to the road as yet, because we're strung up along this lane. Eventually, we do crawl back down the lane up to where the tank is – and there is our gunner stretched out. He came up with the echelon the night before. We only knew him as John,[17] and he'd only been over about a week when he joined us. And he was killed there. We knew he was dead when we got out there because we just felt him round the neck. We couldn't see any form of injury. We thought blast was the cause.[18]

Trooper Gordon Fidler, 4 Troop, 'A' Squadron, 2nd F&FY

In all, the combination of the Mark IV, anti-tank guns and panzerfaust knocked out two 'A' Squadron tanks. Lieutenant Don Bulley fired several shots at the Mark IV and claimed a hit. No one was really sure if it was still a threat, but they decided to push on regardless. Steel Brownlie subsequently enjoyed telling a story of his entry into St Martin des Besaces.

I cautiously turned right and saw two things. One was a naked female standing in the middle of the street: a tailor's dummy set up by a German with a sense of humour. The other was the broken track of a Mark IV, and skid marks showing that the tank itself had been towed away.[19]

Lieutenant William Steel Brownlie, 4 Troop, 'A' Squadron, 2nd F&FY

The village was secured, and the regiment moved a little way back to laager.

By 1 August, it was apparent that although the VIII Corps was doing well, on their left the XXX Corps was being held up, as indeed was the American V Corps to their right. Nevertheless, the 11th Armoured Division was still being ordered by Lieutenant General Richard O'Connor to push on with all speed. This bold concept caused some concern to Major General 'Pip' Roberts, who preferred to advance at a speed that allowed him to retain control of what was happening, rather than a pell-mell 'charge' into the unknown. Therefore Roberts to some extent ignored his orders and consolidated, ordering his units forward only as far as Bény-Bocage, waiting for a commensurate advance by the 15th (Scottish) Division. The 2nd F&FY spent a relatively quiet day, moving forward through Forêt l'Evêque, crossed the Souleuvre river and moved on to the high ground to the west of Le Bény-Bocage. On 2 August, they continued the advance, pushing on to first Le Reculey and then Burcy (which lay in the L'Allière valley with high ground rising up to Le Perrier Ridge), before the key objective, codenamed 'Rugby', which was the Vire–Vassy main road.

> We went to Burcy. We were doing a fast advance along the road, Mr Darke leading. We were second tank. We'd done a few miles. Then he went round a corner and disappeared in a big cloud of smoke and dust. We stopped and he backed out. He said he'd been fired on. He got some artillery on where he said he'd been fired from. He was quite satisfied, so after a while we carried on the advance. Our tank had to lead then, down a very exposed road into Burcy. The ground fell away over to the right and you could see the countryside for miles. Very exposed! We crawled down this road, but we didn't go into Burcy, because as we got to the bottom there was a junction and we turned right. A car came round the corner, with three Germans inside and one sitting on the wing! It came nearly right up to us – and the

bloke on the wing gave us a wave – thinking we were friendly. Anyway, our commander, [Corporal Edmund Whatmough], we called him Wilco, said, 'Bleeding Jerries, get shooting!' I thought, 'Give them chance to surrender!' Pat traversed across them and gave them a long burst of Browning, the Jerries, to one side and two went like lightning into the ditches at the side. Wilco said, 'One of the buggers is potting at me!' I gave him a hand grenade and he tossed one over the hedge, then I heard another one go off, so I think Mr Darke had thrown one over as well, because he was right behind us. We carried on, and just round the corner was a supply truck, stuck in the ditch, I think it had done an emergency reverse and got stuck! I suppose the car was leading the supply truck.[20]

Trooper Jack Edwards, 4 Troop, 'B' Squadron, 2nd F&FY

'B' Squadron moved across L'Allière river and up onto Le Perrier Ridge which they consolidated with the help of the 3rd Monmouths. Hutchison's 'A' Squadron was then ordered make the final advance to cut the Vire–Vassy road a mile further south running along the next ridge.

I went very cautiously up a narrow, sunken lane. In parts it was so narrow that one track was in a rut, the other halfway up the bank, so that the tank tilted to about 45 degrees. The tank behind mine stuck, blocking the path of all the others, so I went on even more cautiously. Short of the road, I put on a German helmet and took a German rifle that I kept on top of the turret and crawled the last 30 yards. The road was quite empty for 2 miles in both directions. I brought the tank, up, and backed it into a lane on the far side of the road, so as to look east. When my corporal came up, he parked on the near side, looking west. We waited, for the squadron was jammed again. Nothing happened for ten minutes, when a motor cyclist came fast along the road from Vire. He waved, not realising who we were. I hit him in the right leg with the

German rifle, and my corporal hit him in the left leg with his pistol. He fell off and lay in the road. When the squadron came up, I went to him, and he tried to draw his pistol, which I took from him. I gave him a shot of morphia and put him in the ditch out of harm's way, as I thought. I still have his cap and shoulder straps, which indicate that he was an Oberfeldwebel in 116 Panzer Division.[21]

Lieutenant William Steel Brownlie, 4 Troop, 'A' Squadron, 2nd F&FY

The 'Rugby' objective, unlike almost every other road in the area, was a significant carriageway. Shortly afterwards, they saw other vehicles approaching.

A small convoy of German trucks came down and we hit them – the impact of them being hit pushed them off the road virtually. A lot of smoke and fire. The Germans that came out of the trucks came towards us and gave themselves up. But one of them was very badly injured and he was laid out at the side of the hedge. We stayed there all night, but this lad that was wounded was crying for, 'Mama' at intervals. It was quite harrowing. He was literally dying at your feet. That was the only word he was saying, 'Mama!' I was thinking that somewhere there is a mother and father going about their life and there's their son, his life draining away. The volume got less and less as he just faded away – nothing we could do for him; nothing at all.[22]

Trooper Terry Boyne, 4 Troop, 'A' Squadron, 2nd F&FY

Among the trucks there appears to have been a couple of German ambulances and 4 Troop took some medical personnel prisoner. Then there was a more serious development as the Germans reacted to these unwelcome intruders on a vital communications route.

We hadn't been there very long, when several tanks came up on the road. My immediate assumption was it was the 23rd

Hussars, coming out on the road, parallel with us. But it turned out to be German tanks – Panthers! At about 2,000 yards, we started having a shooting match with them. If you got off the road you couldn't see them, so we had to stay on the road and felt slightly at a disadvantage with their gun power. I don't think they did too much damage to us. I called almost immediately for 'Lime Juice' and because we were so far forward, we got immediate priority. Really it wasn't very long, only a matter of minutes, before these Typhoons arrived. They were thoroughly effective – they dispersed them – and looking through my binoculars I thought they'd blown one into the ditch. These rockets were really quite powerful if they struck their targets. It gave us immediate relief.[23]

Major Douglas Hutchison, 'A' Squadron, 2nd F&FY

However, John Buchanan was soon reminded of an amusing adage that had gained some traction within the regiment.

There was an old saying in France, 'When the German planes came over, the British and Americans head for cover; when the British planes came over, the Germans went for cover; but when the American were over, every bugger went for cover!' We were bombed by the American planes – they hadn't been told the Vire–Vassy road had been cut.[24]

Trooper John Buchanan, 4 Troop, 'A' Squadron, 2nd F&FY

It all happened so very quickly.

Thunderbolts hit us. The American Air Force. They came swooping over the trees, you don't realise how big they were. They were quite frightening when these things come swinging in, firing machine guns. We must have been further advanced than they recognised. But when you think we had white stars on top of the turrets! We had an orange recognition mat we could put out, so we were all diving down the bins at the back to get these mats out to put down – and we had recognition smoke grenades – we were slinging them all over the place! It didn't make the slightest bit of difference – they still came in! I think they hit one of the scout cars – there was a couple of casualties from that. They talk about friendly fire, but there was nothing friendly about that![25]

Trooper Terry Boyne, 4 Troop, 'A' Squadron, 2nd F&FY

Major Hutchison was trying his best to give the correct recognition signals, to try and stop the attack, but it was all in vain. From the fast-moving Thunderbolts it was all presumably nothing more than a blur as they screamed overhead.

Happily, they only had cannons or machine guns – they weren't equipped with rockets, but they killed quite a lot of people – most of these German prisoners sheltering in the ditch. They wounded several of our people. It was a bit terrifying for a few minutes.[26]

Major Douglas Hutchison, 'A' Squadron, 2nd F&FY

Andrew Dewar was one of those who were wounded by the Thunderbolts.

Before we knew it, they were spraying us as if it was water. The bullets from the Thunderbolts were going through the ammunition in the tanks – with the turret open. We didn't think much of that idea either. We got below the tank for cover. Sergeant [Mathers] and myself were wounded – in the right side of the shoulder, above the knee and though the calf of the right leg. We got attended to by this German orderly on the German ambulance.[27]

Trooper Andrew Dewar, 'A' Squadron, 2nd F&FY

It turned out that Dewar had a 'Blighty' wound and he was evacuated back for hospitalisation in the Glasgow area.

As night fell, most of 'A' Squadron was withdrawn about a mile, but – one might have guessed – Steel Brownlie's troop was left behind to lie in ambush should any German traffic attempt to use the vital Vire–Vassy road. Supported by only a single platoon of the 3rd Monmouths, it proved a very tense and nervous night – even for the intrepid Steel Brownlie.

> Well, at dusk Colonel Alec called the two squadrons back for the night, but added that 'Code-Sign Steel' would stay, and see that the Germans could not use the road. I protested – and stayed. A platoon of 3rd Monmouths joined me, just a Canadian lieutenant and about fifteen men, while the rest of the squadron went back the way we had come. It was no comfort to us that their rear tank was brewed up. The Canadian and I arranged all-round defence of our little pocket. No smoking, and anyone found asleep would be shot. The infantry dug in with their hands, shovels too noisy. Barbed wire and Hawkins grenades were stretched across the road. Tank guns were pointed at possible approaches, and the plan was to fire everything full blast if there was an attack. We sat, pricking our hands with pins to keep awake, and listening to German tracked vehicles moving somewhere to the south; and wishing we were somewhere else. But the only intrusion was when Padre Oswald Welsh came up the track behind us in a Honey, as he had heard about the German wounded who had been put in the ditch. We had been so busy that we had forgotten them. He picked his way through the mines and barbed wire, and took away those still alive. He was a remarkable man.[28]

Lieutenant William Steel Brownlie, 4 Troop, 'A' Squadron, 2nd F&FY

Long afterwards, Steel Brownlie was awarded the Military Cross (MC) for this lonely night vigil isolated on the Vire road. The citation was impressive.

> Lieutenant Brownlie was leading the troop which first arrived on the road running east from Vire. When a troop was required to remain behind during the night to harass the road he volunteered for this task knowing that enemy were all around,

while the remainder of the squadron withdrew. The following day his troop was in reserve to the squadron when a counter-attack in force was put in by enemy tanks and infantry. Our leading troop was largely knocked out. Lieutenant Brownlie brought his troop up into action immediately and was directly responsible in breaking up the attack in this area destroying five enemy tanks and self-propelled guns, killing a large number of infantry. Throughout he displayed the greatest initiative and determination and no thought for personal safety. His prompt action was directly responsible for the successful breaking up of the enemy counter-attack.[29]

Steel Brownlie's version is far more down to earth.

For the record – I most certainly did not 'volunteer' to stay all night on the Vire–Vasey road. I may have been young and daft, but I wasn't as daft as all that. And where the figures for enemy vehicles destroyed came from, I don't know; they certainly weren't from me. So I've always been suspicious of citations, preferring personal versions of how one got a gong. Mine is that I stayed out all night.[30]

Lieutenant William Steel Brownlie, 4 Troop, 'A' Squadron, 2nd F&FY

Whatever the truth of it, few of the regiment would have begrudged him his MC.

Two very different external forces were beginning to impact on the 2nd F&FY. First, it had been decided that despite the opportunities for the 11th Armoured Division to take the – then – almost undefended town of Vire, they would instead respect the original boundaries between the Allies and leave the town to the American XIX Corps. Second, the 9th SS Panzer Division and the II SS Panzer Corps were in the process of moving up to cover the yawning gap in the German lines north-east of Vire, although on the way they suffered delays from the assiduous attentions of the British and American air forces. Nevertheless, it was apparent that the Germans had been reinforced, with several infiltrating forces beginning to push forward, threatening both the Burcy area and the British communication lines stretching back to Le Reculey. Soon it was evident that the advanced 'Rugby' objective on the Vire–Vassy road could no longer be safely defended. Major General 'Pip' Roberts was worried at being out on a limb due to the slower progress of the US First Army on their right, and the Guards Armoured Division to their left. As a result, he called a stop to any further advances by 11th Armoured Division. He ordered his units to take up defendable positions within the overarching protection of the massed guns of the VIII Corps artillery. The next morning, 3 August, the rest of 'A' Squadron moved back up onto the Vire–Vassy road, but as they did so they were hit hard by another concentration of German tanks, losing three of their own.

> The Germans made a really determined effort to see us off – using these tanks from the east. It was a bit awkward, because it was the early morning and it was sunny – and they had the sun behind them. It was quite difficult seeing them, whereas they could see us very clearly. They were coming round us from both sides and I could see that we weren't going to be able to stay there. We'd lost a tank – it brewed up, then another very unfortunate thing happened – Hotblack,[31] putting out a smoke grenade from his tank, dropped the thing into the turret and he got a nasty burn when it exploded – nobody was killed, but that put him out of action. I was given permission to withdraw the rest of the squadron. We had quite a lot of wounded people lying about from the tanks that were knocked out. We got everybody onto the tanks and we got out via a side road: we went down towards Vire, which was the only direction from which we were not being attacked.[32]
>
> Major Douglas Hutchison, 'A' Squadron, 2nd F&FY

That day, the Germans counter-attacked, moving down the ridge toward L'Allière river and Burcy. A considerable battle blew up, with the 3rd Monmouths and 2nd F&FY resisting, supported by long-distance fire from the 25-pounders of the Ayrshire Yeomanry. The overall 11th Armoured Division policy was to sit tight, hunt down any infiltrators and try to strengthen the overall position. While the 29th Armoured Brigade Group occupied the Perrier Ridge, the 159th Brigade Group were based around Forgues and Burcy. The 9th Panzer Division counter-attacked for the next couple of days, during which they managed to infiltrate Burcy itself, which meant that for a time the supply lines were severed for some of the 2nd F&FY. 'A' Squadron tried to recapture the village, but the situation remained obscure and the attached infantry only finally ejected the remaining Germans on 5 August. It was a difficult period, as no one seemed to know what was happening.

> We are isolated and this countryside is covered by sunken roads, narrow tracks, 6 feet and more below the level of the fields with hedges growing up on extra banks each side – they are excellent cover for the Jerries to sneak up on us! We are standing to again, very jittery, the weather is unbearably hot, the day drags on and my eyelids are as heavy as lead. We have to keep a careful watch and keep awake and alert to stave off any attack – God what would I give for a bit of shuteye.[33]

> Trooper John Thorpe, 4 Troop, 'C' Squadron, 2nd F&FY

On 6 August, a day marked elsewhere by the capture of the key height of Mont Pinçon, at first all seemed relatively quiet on the 2nd F&FY front around Burcy. 'A' and 'C' Squadrons had taken up positions guarding the approaches to the village. Meanwhile, Lieutenant Darke's Sherman had been dispatched back to assist the 4th KSLI further back on the ridge that lay behind Burcy. Then, at about 14.00, German artillery and mortars burst into life, marking the arrival of the 10th SS Panzer Division to take over the counter-attack. Soon their tanks were rumbling towards 'C' Squadron positions. During the fighting the Sherman commanded by Sergeant Cliff Jones was soon put out of action, as John Thorpe relates.

We move forward to support infantry when a mortar explodes on our engine hatch and the engine dies so we have to stop where we are. Jerry is attacking with everything: one unceasing barrage, a tornado of shells, an inferno which goes on and on, all around the pitch of noise rising in intensity, scream of shells, explosions. The echoes from the trees is like thunder and together with the scream builds up to sound like tramcars negotiating sharp curves – can we survive this lot? To add to the barrage is the crash of bombs as the American Air Force now bomb our positions! Cliff in our turret is keeping a sharp lookout and says Hutch [Lieutenant Graeme Hutchison], our Troop Leader, whose tank is some distance behind ours, has been injured and lying on the ground in the open. He says we shall have to do something about him as soon as there is a lull. Hutch's tank is under a tall tree and HE has hit the branches, sending shrapnel down into his tank. Cliff and I go to him and attend to his injuries; head and left leg, bad – through the knee with bone showing. Dress wounds with field dressings and give morphia. Try to get stretcher-bearers from the dug-in infantry, and I am sent from slit trench to slit trench. After two fields I find two – both on their knees praying and reading the Bible! They refuse to leave the shelter of their trench! You wouldn't hear what I shouted at them! Colonel Scott comes up, standing right up out of his turret, he wants to know what in hell are we doing here? Gives orders to move and come with him straight away. We explain our tank is disabled, but he says we are to be court martialled and takes our names – orders us to take Hutch's tank. We have a job to evict the remainder of Hutch's crew from their tank and eventually get them out and carry Hutch and place him under our tank to await medics to pick him up.[34]

Trooper John Thorpe, 4 Troop, 'C' Squadron, 2nd F&FY

Scott's acerbic threat was made because it was against Standing
Orders to attend to wounded crews during a battle, but in the
end as their tank was disabled the matter went no further. At
least Graeme Hutchison was grateful!

> I was wounded by an airburst in the early morning. Sergeant
> Clifford Jones and John [Thorpe] gave me first aid and
> administered morphine and, having placed me under a
> disabled tank, left me in the care of a less disabled member of
> my crew. I found out much later that the medical officer of
> the Monmouthshire Regiment picked me up and took me by
> carrier to their field dressing station, and that, in the afternoon,
> this FDS came under heavy German mortar fire and the MO,
> Captain Carrick,[35] was killed while attending the wounded.
> I have very brief and hazy memories, until being put into an
> ambulance after dark, which must have done extremely well to
> have got up to the Perrier Ridge from Burcy, even to have got
> there at all, and then being transferred again later that night,
> finally waking up to full consciousness in a large white marquee
> with the sun shining through the rolled-up sides and nurses
> scurrying all over the place. One arrived with a mug of tea –
> total bliss![36]

> Lieutenant Graeme Hutchison, 4 Troop, 'C' Squadron, 2nd F&FY

Back on the Le Perrier Ridge, the German counter-attack was
developing into a very real threat. Graeme's cousin, Major
'Pinkie' Hutchison and 'A' Squadron were coming under heavy
fire.

> About 6 o'clock in the evening they had quite a bit of artillery
> support and we were getting a real concentration of fire on us.
> Also, they'd raked up some aircraft – and they were bombing
> us a bit too. This was a prelude to an attack by both tanks and
> infantry, at the start of which we lost one or two tanks brewed
> up. Then we saw where these Germans had got into a sunken
> road and we started having a duel. I remember getting one, I

think it was a Mark IV. I got him about third shot, solid shot, and then I changed to HE after that – I saw it brew up. I was having a duel: he was shooting at me and I was shooting at him! I won, fortunately! It was the only tank I can remember positively knocking out myself. We didn't lose any more tanks – and we shot them up – Steel Brownlie certainly got one too there. We silenced the tank side of that attack. After that the infantry were easier to deal with. We had quite a good shoot at infantry trying to get in to where we were – they never did.[37]

Major Douglas Hutchison, 'A' Squadron, 2nd F&FY

Bill Scott's Sherman was called forward from reserve into action against two panzers that were threatening to break through.

I went up to the high ground and went forward on foot with a long lead on my wireless. I saw a couple of German tanks – I think they were Mark IVs – an anti-tank gun and infantry. I came back. Then I judged the distances, crawled up in my tank, and got a couple of shots off over the top of the hill. I hit one, I saw them depress their gun and they came out. I came back and went forward again in a different spot for the other one. You try to keep yourself hull down. To protect your 'soft belly'. If I could get two shots off, fire at them, then get back, get the protection, so that they'll not pick up the flash to fire back on you. I got one, drove the other one off. I thought I got the anti-tank gun, and I got a few infantry – I used my machine gun.[38]

Sergeant Bill Scott, 2 Troop, 'C' Squadron, 2nd F&FY

Scott was awarded the Distinguished Conduct Medal (DCM) for his actions. The fighting carried on until about 21.00 before the Germans gave up for the evening. The tired tank crews were pulled back, but there was little sleep for them that night.

We were pulled back a short way into laager. As we moved back there was all these burning vehicles all around. There were trucks and tanks and all sorts on fire. We laagered up, the

German artillery was coming over the top of us and dropping one side – and our artillery was dropping on the other side of us. When it went quiet, we could hear tanks moving. We used to think, 'Tigers on the move!'[39]

Trooper Jack Edwards, 4 Troop, 'B' Squadron, 2nd F&FY

Crew casualties had been surprisingly light, probably because in a defensive action they were able to adopt hull down and concealed positions awaiting their attacking 'prey'. But that night John Thorpe became aware of one tragic case.

I'm doing my stint of 'stag'. An infantry corporal begins to bellow at one of our chaps and I ask him what he wants, and he tells me that one of our knocked-out tanks has still got crew members alive in it and they can't get to them to get them out as the driver's hatch is covered by the gun turret and 'no bastard tankman' he has spoken to will go with him. I waken Cliff and ask if I can go, but as I'm on stag Cliff goes himself and when he returns, he says it is our third tank and McLaren[40] was still in the driving seat with both legs smashed and his back burnt black. They got him out, but he soon died – eight hours of solid torture! Johnny Smith,[41] Dutch Holland[42] and Harry Skelton[43] were all in the tank and burnt to cinders.[44]

Trooper John Thorpe, 4 Troop, 'C' Squadron, 2nd F&FY

The drip, drip of tank losses over the last week meant that next morning, 'A' and 'C' Squadrons were temporarily amalgamated under the command of Major Hutchison.

On 7 August, the Germans resumed their attacks from both flanks, and again there was some severe fighting. The Tigers had climbed the high ground to the east of Le Haut Perrier (Hill 242) and opened up a damaging fire on the 2nd F&FY; indeed in a matter of a few minutes they knocked out five Shermans. Unterscharführer Willi Fey left an account of a similar engagement on 7 or 8 August, which allows us a sense of what it was like on 'the other side' of No Man's Land in this fighting.

Trooper Geoff Hayward in his wartime uniform and in 2021 when I visited him last. Geoff is one of the last surviving Fife and Forfar Yeomanry veterans and it is an honour to know him.

William Steel Brownlie wearing the badge of his post-war regiment the Ayrshire Yeomanry. Rated by many as one of the finest tank commanders in 11th Armoured Division.

Bessbrook children on a Mark VI tank. The men of the 2nd Fife and Forfar Yeomanry proved a real hit with the local civilians.

Valentine tanks of 2nd Fife and Forfar Yeomanry on
the South Downs in Sussex, 27 June 1942.

A Sherman dozer tank of 2nd Fife and Forfar Yeomanry
during Operation 'Epsom', 29 June 1944.

Sherman tanks advancing along the highway towards Vire, 2 August 1944.

Major General 'Pip' Roberts and Brigadier Roscoe Harvey
alongside Harvey's Sherman command tank.

Infantry
of the 3rd
Monmouthshire
Regiment aboard
Sherman tanks of
the 2nd Fife and
Forfar Yeomanry
wait for the
order to advance,
near Argentan,
21 August 1944.

An investiture by Field-Marshal Montgomery at Ypres, 10 March 1945. *Standing (fourth from left)* Major R. L. Leith, *(seventh from left)* Captain W. Steel Brownlie, *(eighth from left)* Lieutenant J. W. Samson, *(ninth from left)* Padre Welsh, *(tenth from left)* Lieutenant E. A. Lamont. Sitting *(extreme left)* Major J. D. Hutchison.

A Comet tank of 2nd Fife and Forfar Yeomanry carrying infantry of the 1st Cheshire Regiment.

Bridging equipment was vital if the tanks were to maintain the speed of the advance.

Comet tanks of the 2nd Fife and Forfar Yeomanry crossing
the Weser at Petershagen, 7 April 1945.

'Saint Patrick' a Comet of 2nd Fife and Forfar Yeomanry
passing through a German town.

After the war is over: men of the 2nd Fife and Forfar Yeomanry relaxing by a
lake in Schleswig Holstein. Geoff Hayward's truck is in the background.

We manoeuvred our panzer into the desired direction for firing. The gunner had already had his first target in his sight for some time. It was the tank at the point, exactly in the centre of the attacking pack, probably its leader. The second and third targets were also determined, first its neighbour to the left, then the one to the right. After that it was to be the Shermans at the extreme left and right. They could have been dangerous if they were able to come around on our flanks; even a Tiger was vulnerable inside the 400-metre range. Finally, the relief-bringing order came, 'Anti-tank shell – 600 metres – fire!' The first shot was wide, realising this froze us only for a few seconds. 'Gun sight 400 metres – fire!' That was a hit. A second shell followed immediately, another hit. Then, the next target, 'Tank on the left – fire!' It too, took two shells. Within a short time, four Shermans stood in flames on the slope.[45]

Unterscharführer Willi Fey, 102nd Heavy SS Panzer Battalion, II SS Panzer Corps

The German positions were deluged with shells as the long-range medium 5.5-inch guns came up into effective range. However, something else needed to be done if they were to clear out the Tigers quickly, and Lieutenant Colonel Alec Scott asked Major Sir John Gilmour to try to resolve the situation. Gilmour was a determined officer, and he used a combination of his tank experience and pre-war game hunting to 'stalk' his quarry.

I had to change to a different tank, because on my own the wireless set had given out. So I had to go to another tank in order to get the use of a wireless set. Of course, there was still a chap inside the turret. There was a long enough lead to stand on the back of the tank. It was the practical thing to do! It was a question of trying to make certain that you kept your own vehicle in a sort of hull-down position to reduce their vulnerability to attack. You needed to be certain that you didn't advance too much into the open. You would have to direct the gunner. He, eventually, through his telescopic sight on his gun, he should be able to take over.[46]

Major Sir John Gilmour, 'B' Squadron, 2nd F&FY

Thus, the regimental history makes admiring mention of Gilmour, 'Standing up on his tank, microphone in hand giving out orders, even when there was a deal of lethal metal flying about'.[47] Gilmour got into the tank commanded by Sergeant Bert Shaw, and the driver, Ron Forbes, well remembered how they manoeuvred to gain the best possible position to 'get' the Tiger.

'A' Squadron were getting pretty badly hammered by this Tiger in the woods up on a promontory, or small hill. He was dug in reversed back into an emplacement. Every now and again he was coming out, choosing his time and target and knocking out 'A' Squadron tanks on the slope. Sir John came on my tank, which was a Firefly, and we did a wide detour round the back, along roads, crossed several open bits of ground, saw some German infantry. They were mostly running away! I think there were two other tanks behind me. We got up to this bank and Sir John chose his spot well – he knew what he was doing – he had obviously read the map quite well. I sort of stuck my 'nose' into this hedge and the gun was just above it sited on the Tiger up on the hill – we'd got right round on the side of it. Sir John said, 'Engage the reverse gear and keep your foot on the clutch!' My foot was on the clutch – and it's a fairly heavy clutch, you have to press it in hard. I got a twitch in my knee, I was scared in case I let the clutch out and foul the whole thing. All I saw was a flash when Bertie [Moir] fired – three rounds – quickly – one after the other. Andy [Mathers] must have been on his game too – he must have loaded quite fast! The shots went home – apparently, we knocked out the Tiger. Then it was a question of getting out as quickly as possible – my foot was right down on the board. We shot back quite violently.[48]

Trooper Ron Forbes, 4 Troop, 'B' Squadron, 2nd F&FY

Unterscharführer Willi Fey records what it was like to be hunted by a Sherman making a similar surreptitious approach to try and secure a shot straight into the vulnerable side armour of a Tiger.

> We heard the familiar rattle of tank tracks but not from one of our comrades. It came from half-right ahead of us, where the gully flattened into groups of trees and bushes. We slowly brought our gun around, almost unnoticeably. We aimed it, with the lowest possible elevation, at the cluster of bushes. We only had two anti-tank shells left, one of them already in the barrel. Our nerves were tensed to the breaking point. Was it one tank, or two? There were only 100 metres between us and the gully. The driver and radio operator sat in the open hatches ready to bail out. Paul was holding the second, and last, shell ready in his arms. If these two were fired and missed it would have meant bailing out as quickly as possible. The rattle of tracks and engine noise came ever closer. Seconds turned into eternity! Maybe, the others did not know that a German panzer, ready to fire, was sitting there. Our other Tigers had long since pulled back, and we had been giving off smoke all afternoon. But enough of these thoughts! Ahead of us the bushes parted. A long, smooth barrel without muzzle brake came into view; no doubt, a Sherman. Then the curved hull and the turret appeared. 'Fire!' Our first shell glanced off and we saw it rise steeply into the sky. Surprising, the details one noticed even during such a tense situation. 'Aim lower – fire!' We roared loudly as the shell disappeared precisely under the barrel, at the base of the turret. As if gripped by an iron fist, the tank stopped with a jerk. A fine column of smoke growing increasingly denser rose vertically into the sky.[49]

Unterscharführer Will Fey, 102nd Heavy SS Panzer Battalion, II SS Panzer Corps

With the exception of the reported result, this is almost the obverse of the story of Gilmour's stalking and destruction of a

Tiger. At this distance it is difficult to decide what really happened in such incidents – indeed often the participants did not really know the end result themselves. In all, Willi Fey claimed he had hit fifteen Shermans that day, as well as innumerable armoured cars, halftracks, and other vehicles. This may well have been an exaggeration, but he would not have been alone in this, as a glance at some of the more fanciful tallies claimed in the F&FY history would reveal.

What is certain is that it was a nerve-wracking business fighting in the Bocage. Although ideal for ambush, it was also equally ideal for a covert approach, and the men were always kept on tenterhooks.

> Anxiety was the main thing, because you were always so frightened of enemy sneaking up on you. I was forever searching through the periscope, although I hadn't got a very good view through the periscope. Forever searching, in case I could see anything creeping up on us. I used to look at the tank and imagine a shell coming straight through us or something like that. So many people got badly burnt in tanks. Next to me in the turret was a large fire extinguisher – and I used to practise grabbing it so I was really quick on the 'draw' with a fire extinguisher. I thought, 'If the thing goes up in flames, I'll have to try and fight my way out with that!' To get out I had to crawl under the gun shield – which would take a while. Anxiety and the worry that in an emergency would I do the right thing.[50]
>
> Trooper Jack Edwards, 4 Troop, 'B' Squadron, 2nd F&FY

There were several casualties that day, including Colonel Alec Scott, who was lightly wounded, but for the moment he was able to remain in command of his unit. The fighting resumed on 8 August, with the Germans confining their actions to prolonged shelling of the Perrier Ridge. However, to considerable rejoicing among the men, that afternoon the regiment were relieved by the Royal Scots Greys.

We got into our defensive positions – and we were mortared again. In the afternoon, the Scots Greys arrived to take over from us. The artillery put down a ten-minute smoke screen round the Burcy area, round that exposed road, so that the Scots Greys could come into us. Then, when we were ready to move, they put another ten-minute smoke screen down so that we could get out. We pulled back about 3–4 miles, well to the north of Burcy.[51]

Trooper Jack Edwards, 4 Troop, 'B' Squadron, 2nd F&FY

Bill Scott was one of the last Shermans to pull back from the ridge.

We were relieved by the Scots Greys. They dropped smoke and everybody was going back – and boy we are getting worried! I was going on the radio, 'When are we coming back?' 'Stay there! Stay there!' [Then] we got told, 'You can come back now!' They dropped smoke to let the Greys come in. I said, 'Conform to me!' The smoke was clearing – everything was visible. We had to go into the dip and up. They were shooting us. There was a tank in front of us – I think it was 'B' Squadron, it was limping along – and we were being held up by this. They asked me where I was, and I told them. They said, 'Get past that blinking tank, we've got to get back!'[52]

Sergeant Bill Scott, 2 Troop, 'C' Squadron, 2nd F&FY

This was to be Scott's final act with the regiment, as he was evacuated next day with a suspected stomach ulcer.

The regiment pulled back to La Queille where they would stay for four days. Again, there was a requirement to rebuild the regiment and this time they were the beneficiaries of two more full troops transferred from the 24th Lancers. With them came two young, but already experienced troop leaders: Lieutenant Peter Northern and Captain David Voller. There was also another troop transferred in from the 1st Lothian and Border Yeomanry.

The rest at La Queille was much appreciated – and at last a chance to get a proper wash. Fighting in tanks in high summer was a sweaty, dirty business with few chances for the normal ablutions.

We were there relaxing for a few days. I got a bath in a stream! There was a deep part of the stream where some artilleryman had put some steel ammunition boxes. He put one upside down to sit on, two the right way up that you put your feet in. You could sit on this ammunition box with your feet in the two empty boxes and give yourself a bath – it was very refreshing – especially in the hot weather. The first bath I'd had for a month or more! Somebody said, 'Oooh, the farmer's daughter will be peeping from behind the hedge!' But I think that was a bit of wishful thinking that![53]

Trooper Jack Edwards, 4 Troop, 'B' Squadron, 2nd F&FY

For the men it was also a chance for some hard-earned relaxation – and to experiment with the local calvados.

The farmer gave us a drop of calvados – this bottle of pure calvados, he made it himself; it's apples. He gave us wee glasses! I said, 'By God, that boy must have a bit of Scots about him!' Because all I was getting was just a wee tot! It went over in a 'oner' and Honest Christ, it must have been about 200 per cent proof! It went right down to your toes and came shooting back again! We got some of these bottles of calvados and we had a night. One of the boys went mad with it! He was screaming and shouting, we had to sit on him! It was calvados that set him off – twenty-four hours later he 'came to'. The hangover from calvados is something again![54]

Trooper John Buchanan, 4 Troop, 'A' Squadron, 2nd F&FY

Nothing much has changed on that front!

Operation Bluecoat, undertaken in conjunction with the American Operation Cobra, had been an undoubted success.

Bluecoat played its role in fixing and wearing down German armour on the British front and the sudden switch from the Caen area to Caumont had undoubtedly surprised the Germans. It forced the Germans to counter-attack and this had eroded much of the strength of the 9th and 10th SS Panzer Divisions (II Panzer Corps). Overall, the Americans had made fantastic progress, while the German strength had been so dissipated that the Mortain counter-offensive, demanded by Hitler against the Americans, was rendered stillborn a couple of days after it began on 7 August.

To make things far worse for the Germans, at 23.00 on 7 August, Operation Totalize was launched as the First Canadian Army (General Harry Crerar) had renewed their attack pressing towards Falaise. This was a more open terrain, and they were facing strong German defences. As a result, innovative methods were employed by the reinforced II Canadian Corps (General Guy Simonds), which was leading the attack. It commenced as night fell with mass bombing raids – guided by wireless-controlled Pathfinders – and heavy supporting artillery bombardments. When day broke, Typhoon squadrons haunted – and hunted – the German armour, while Spitfires and Mustangs roamed behind the lines smashing up German transport columns. The follow up armour formations then came forward to exploit any breakthroughs. The fighting was grim, but II Canadian Corps made good progress, breaking through the German defences and pushing some 6 miles down the line of the Caen–Falaise road before being stemmed by desperate German counter-attacks on 11 August. But the gap between the Canadians from the north and the Americans in the south was narrowing. The German Army teetering on the brink of disaster: could the German Seventh Army escape the trap?

12

WHAT'S IT LIKE?

> When one started up the tank, it's got these big fans in the Sherman to pull out the gun fumes. When you get sixty-odd tanks all starting up, there was the smell of the fumes and the smell from the wet grass that sometimes I still get today.[1]
>
> Second Lieutenant Charlie Workman, 1 Troop, 'C' Squadron, 2nd F&FY

NOT EVERY ANECDOTE OR EVERY EXPERIENCE fits into the smooth retelling of the history of a regiment. This is even more the case with oral history recorded sixty years after the events. Some stories can't be 'tied down', often because the soldier concerned never knew where he was, or indeed what the date was. They were, after all, 'busy'! It was just another part of the Bocage, another day in action, when events pressed hard and fast. Nor do details of the daily routine always fit into our narrative, without risk of us losing our focus. But collectively these stories and experiences still have a value in giving us a sense of what the Normandy campaign was like for the soldiers who fought there.

One thing had soon come to dominate their thoughts: the nature and capabilities of the Sherman tank. Yes, it had merits, it was fast, it had a better gun than the previous British tanks they had been equipped with in the UK, but it was simply not capable of standing up to the offensive weapons directed against it – with the unfortunate consequences which we have charted during Operations Epsom, Goodwood and Bluecoat.

One of the things that became apparent was that the tanks were under-armoured. The design of the Sherman was a very 'straight-sided' tank, so therefore there was very little chance of getting a ricochet off a sloping surface – it was very much vertical – it would penetrate it. They put extra armour welded on to the outside of the Sherman, in order to protect where the ammunition was stored. This turned out to be a mixed blessing because the Germans got to know of it. They found that to fire at this particular place was the best place to brew a Sherman tank up.[2]

Major Sir John Gilmour, 'B' Squadron, 2nd F&FY

The problem was that if a shell penetrated the Sherman then it would 'brew up', hence their reputation as 'Tommy cookers'. The shells were in bins and often on the floor all around the turret, which was an obvious risk, while the petrol engines were highly vulnerable.

The shells were inside the tank. They had to be because the gun was inside the tank. They always aimed at the side of the tank. The front of the tank was more heavily armoured, and we used to put track plates along the front. The shells normally came in at the side – and because the ammunition wasn't in a bomb-proof bin they blew up – there was no lid on it – you had to have quick access to the shells. At the end of the day, these were petrol vehicles not diesel. Once you hit petrol with a flash – burning was a problem.[3]

Second Lieutenant Charlie Workman, 1 Troop, 'C' Squadron, 2nd F&FY

After a few weeks in action the men could work out their chances in action with the various German tanks they had encountered.

The Mark IV was a tank comparable to the Sherman. If we met them, we were OK! A good gun, their gun was slightly better than us, but we could give a good account of ourselves if we

could get close enough, we could penetrate it. That was a fair
fight. The Panther, you just don't argue with it! You try and hit
on the side or the rear – the Germans always put their armour
on the front. If you shoved a few shells at it – two or three tanks
aimed at it – the Panther will disappear, or blow up, or you'll
damage the tracks. The [Firefly] 17-pounder, that could take
a Panther out, that could penetrate. The Tiger you could do
nothing really. You got the artillery on it, the big 6-inch guns
on to it, a stonk down on it. The weak point was its tail – you
could knock its engine out by getting behind it and shoving a
shell up the rear – or break its track. But you couldn't get close
enough – it had a big 88mm gun that could fire 5 miles away, hit
you and knock you out! They were usually hull down in their
position used as an anti-tank gun. You'd get out of the way and
think of ways and means of getting it out. The best way was to
get the air force on it – these Typhoons were great boys! We'd
put a red smoke shell over its head to mark the position, so that
aircraft would look at that red smoke and say, 'Right!'[4]

Trooper John Buchanan, 4 Troop, 'A' Squadron, 2nd F&FY

There is no doubt that 'Tiger mania' became rife among tank
crews. Early on, Montgomery had weighed in to try and prevent
a sense of defeatism creeping in. He had to stand up for the
quality of his tanks; he had no option if morale was not to crash
through the floor, but it is also important to note that despite
British occasional despair, the most numerous German tanks in
Normandy were Mark IVs. Although the Mark IV had a high
velocity 75mm gun which out-performed the Sherman gun, the
Sherman had better armour and a faster turning turret function,
which just about balanced it out. At normal Normandy battle
ranges, both types could knock each other out. The Sherman
also used less fuel, was more reliable and far easier to maintain/
repair than the German Panther or Tiger. And the Sherman had
one more very important thing in its favour – and that was sheer
weight of numbers. They were cheap and quick to produce and

were churning out of the factories in their thousands – so whenever one was knocked out, it was swiftly replaced. This was not the case with the German Panthers and Tigers, they were manufactured in far more limited numbers and were hence a precious resource. In the final analysis, the Sherman was available en masse and although flawed it was a useful weapon of war. And what else was there? The loss of so many tank crews killed in Shermans was unbearably painful for those who knew them, but replacements were also churning out of the training establishments.

In action, the Sherman commander was the most vulnerable member of the crew. Most tank commanders had their hatch open and their head and shoulders protruding out. It wasn't bravado, it was necessity if they were not to be surprised.

> Head out! I think we all found that there might be slightly more risk and occasionally people would be killed by having their heads out, but I think the danger of that was overweighed by the fact that if you keep inside and looked through periscopes, your vision was that much more limited; you couldn't really see what was going on.[5]
>
> Captain Douglas Hutchison, HQ Troop, 'A' Squadron, 2nd F&FY

The tank commanders were incredibly busy. This was particularly the case for those with extra responsibilities as troop or squadron commanders, who also had to tactically manoeuvre all the tanks in their formation via the wireless. When it came to action many found that all their frenetic activity threw a very welcome blanket over any underlying fears they may have harboured.

> In action one never had any fear: a tank commander was too busy. You were watching your map. Looking at your troop, talking to your own tank. Giving your driver, 'Go slow! Turn left! Stop!' You were telling your gunner, 'Traverse left Traverse right! Pick up the target!' The wireless operator would be giving you instructions! You were so busy. But the worst of it was

when you came out and you were looking round to see who was still there. Then you would be told so and so gone and that was the worst bit.[6]

Second Lieutenant Charlie Workman, 1 Troop, 'C' Squadron, 2nd F&FY

As they gained experience they learnt how to survive on a crowded, complex battlefield. It was obvious that speed was important if they suddenly sighted a German panzer or anti-tank gun – because if they didn't fire first – and accurately – then that might be the last thing they ever did. It was all about team-work between the tank commander, the gunner and his loader.

Depending on how proficient the commander and gunner were, they would be lined up on target quickly. The more they did it the quicker it was done! One could get as many as three or four HE shells in the air at the same time if you were really on the ball. It was a very easy gun to fire – and very accurate, extremely good with HE, but its penetration with AP was abysmal – just not powerful enough.[7]

Lance Corporal Roy Vallance, 4 Troop, 'A' Squadron, 2nd F&FY

Generally, the good tank commander learnt not to take chances and to react quickly to any threat. There was no benefit in hanging around; it was important to try and confuse their enemies.

Whenever I was fired at, I got moving, straight away, that was my philosophy, rightly or wrongly! And chuck out smoke until you could find some cover – get behind a hedge or something. It may not sound very warlike, but the first thing in my mind was preservation. Traverse your turret round and keep your gunner onto the target. Try to get him to hit it or put it off its aim! You would see a gun firing, probably a mile away, you fire at it, it stops firing! That's it – you don't actually go and look at it! You might see something through your binoculars, but you didn't hang around much – or at least I didn't if you were being fired at![8]

Lance Corporal Roy Vallance, 4 Troop, 'A' Squadron, 2nd F&FY

There was also the problem of how to deal with panzerfausts, which were almost invisible from the perspective of a tank. In the Bocage country they could hide almost anywhere and fire from point-blank range.

> Panzerfausts were highly mobile. It was a hand-held rocket. A chap with a panzerfaust could come creeping up a hedgerow. It was an anti-tank weapon that could blow your sprockets off the tracks – immobilise the tank or, more importantly, get at the commander! In the Bocage country as we were advancing, if you saw a wood or a house, you just pour HE shells into it and 'brassing off' with machine guns.[9]
>
> Second Lieutenant Charlie Workman, 1 Troop, 'C' Squadron, 2nd F&FY

It had been noticed that when they tried to run through a dense hedge on an earth bank the Sherman would rear up, thereby exposing its vulnerable, almost unarmoured belly to any lurking panzerfaust operator. A simple solution had been devised by an American serviceman (Sergeant Cullin); a plough-like metal projection welded to the front, which prevented the Sherman from 'climbing up' and instead pushed right through the hedge and earth bank together. A panzerfaust could still hit them, but at least it would be on the front armour.

By this time, most of the officers and NCO tank commanders had gained the respect of their men. Some had their eccentricities, but their abilities in action were generally appreciated. A good example of this is Sir John Gilmour. Not a typical soldier and clearly emanating from the Scottish landed gentry, his men knew he was 'different' from them, but he also had qualities that earned their admiration. Whatever 'leadership' was, he exuded it.

> Sir John Gilmour was a brilliant man. He was calm, he wasn't a bullshitter. He was a down-to-earth man – man you could trust. You'd think to yourself, 'Well, I could follow him!' We always used to say, 'He's the most "slummocky" soldier we've

ever met!' Untidy! He didn't have the carriage of a military man. Where we wore our berets slanted over nicely, you had your gaiters and trousers tucked over nicely in line, he never really looked smart. His hat used to be on, but not pulled down sharply and creased like we used to have it! But he was well respected.[10]

Trooper James Donovan, 'B' Squadron, 2nd F&FY

A more junior figure was William Steel Bownlie. His reputation had spread beyond his tank crew, throughout the troop and squadron, until in the end his thrusting approach was recognised and admired across the whole regiment. He wasn't always easy to get on with, possessed of strong opinions he was not afraid to express, but he knew what was needed in the presence of the enemy, and he had the skills to deliver time and time again. Roy Vallance had been posted as a tank commander to Steel Brownlie's troop and he was won over despite his initial reservations.

Steel Brownlie was just a young boy really! I was 23, I think he was 21 or 22! Very boyish in his manner, very much so. He was completely fearless, mad as a March hare. At the start, we weren't the best of friends, we had crossed swords in the past and I didn't do anything to improve it! When he put some water on to have a shave – and when it was hot, I took it and washed our mess tins in it – relations further deteriorated! I had great admiration for him as a troop leader – he knew what he was doing. He was competent *and* he was lucky – that is a very good combination! I hoped that I knew what I was doing! We had confidence in each other and the rest of the troop. From here on we became the best of friends![11]

Lance Corporal Roy Vallance, 4 Troop, 'A' Squadron, 2nd F&FY

High praise from a man who was not easily impressed. Vallance himself was carving out a reputation as a brilliant tank commander who did not 'kowtow' to officers.

Vallance was one of the best. He was cool, calm and collected. He knew what he was doing. The crew said that he was a great boy to work for! He showed his true worth in battle. He used to stand up for them, 'If I take my tank across that open ground, I'm going to lose it! There's going to be tanks there. You've got to put smoke down or make sure I'm getting [support]!' He wasn't backwards in telling the officers what to do! A great chap![12]

Trooper John Buchanan, 4 Troop, 'A' Squadron, 2nd F&FY

The next crew members to consider are the gunner and wireless operator/loader. They too had highly skilled trades to master. If the gunner missed a target, or was too slow, that could be 'curtains' for the whole crew. But the loader had to work in complete harmony with the gunner to achieve the fastest possible rate of fire, with the right shell fused and loaded depending on the nature of the target. Here again experience could give them an edge in a sudden encounter in the Bocage. John Buchanan was Steel Brownlie's gunner and made sure he was always ready to fire almost instantaneously. One of the main Sherman assets would prove to be the lightning speed with which the turret could be traversed – just ten seconds to make a complete revolution, which was more than twice as fast as that achieved by some of the German tanks – it could give a vital advantage in combat.

We always carried a shell up the breech in action. It was a high explosive shell, never an armoured piercing. The drill was the officer would designate a target and he would say, 'High explosive, delay!' Well, there was a shell up the breech, so we got rid of that first. If it was HE shell in the breech and he wanted an AP, well it is as quicker to fire it than to unload it – so you just fired it at the target. And then put an AP in right away. They were very fast loading. Then the next shell was ready; a good wireless operator had it ready in his hand to shove up the breech. The breech would automatically open, the shell would come out and clattered on the floor, so all he had to do then was throw in the next shell. You could bash off a few shells inside a minute – two or three a minute. The officer would put me onto the target, 'Target there, white house in the distance, left!' That's how we were taught, to pick something out which you could put your gun on, then you searched through your telescope and found which target he was after. Then he would give you the range, he could see it better from where he was. You would alter your range to that and get on the targets. Then he'd say, 'Ready to fire? Fire!'[13]

Trooper John Buchanan, 4 Troop, 'A' Squadron, 2nd F&FY

They had learnt another little wrinkle in gunnery technique that might mean the difference between life or death in a tank duel.

The high explosive shell had a wee screw on it, which you turned to 'delay' – that was the loader's job. You'd say, 'On delay!' And he would turn the screw onto delay. That gave you one second, the shell would land, and it would wait, and then blow up. We found that by firing the shell in front of your target, on delay, and it would skid off the ground – bounce – go up into the air and it blows up – so you had an airburst. And that we found was very effective. It would certainly knock the commander out if you got an airburst above his head.[14]

Trooper John Buchanan, 4 Troop, 'A' Squadron, 2nd F&FY

Success in action meant a combination of good basic skills and drills, but also to some extent, luck. Just which way your opponent happened to be looking in the vital seconds that defined the incident. John Buchanan remembered how he got his second German tank.

The Germans had counter-attacked us, and the infantry were falling back. They were pointing, but I couldn't see anything. A Mark IV tank came out of the sunken lane to turn into the field I was sitting in! It got sort of jammed. The commander couldn't see me, I could see him! He got his leg over the turret to get out to try and guide his driver. And then he saw me! His leg was hanging over the top of the tank – and I can still see the expression on his face today! 'Will I jump or go back into the tank?' Before he could make up his mind, I had pressed the trigger – an explosive shell had gone! It hit just below where his foot was. When the smoke cleared, he had gone, the tank was there but he'd disappeared. The crew had bailed out.[15]

Trooper John Buchanan, 4 Troop, 'A' Squadron, 2nd F&FY

The gunner also had control of the co-axial Browning machine gun in the turret. This was often used in a precautionary fashion, fired into hedges alongside the narrow Bocage country roads. But sometimes they caught German infantry in the open and could wreak havoc.

There was a German infantry attack – they came forward towards us. We had warning that they were coming. Up to then we hadn't seen a lot of them. We were formed up in front of the hedge, fairly well camouflaged. They came charging down and they got raked. This is where we burnt out the machine-gun barrel firing. They came down so far and then when we started opening fire they turned round and started running. I had to change the barrel. That was the .30 Browning – you'd have a belt of ammo that was in a little ammunition box. That would be threaded through, then the gun would be cocked and then you could fire that from your control. The loader would put in the new belt when required – every time the belt ran out, he'd stick a new one in! That moved with the turret; they worked in unison, you see – if you aimed one you aimed the pair! Unlike some, the Browning always left the next fresh round in the barrel. If you used it a lot, put a few belts through, the barrels got very hot, so the round in there would get hotter and hotter – and they would probably 'go' – used to fire on their own! For the co-driver that was a bit dodgy, because he used to hang onto that to pull himself out – and to look down a barrel of a Browning that's got a hot round in it wouldn't be particularly funny! The way to overcome that was to pull the belt back! If you fired a lot of ammo through quickly, it used to take all the rifling out – then the shots would be all over the place – you lost all accuracy. When you saw the tracers flying all over the shop you knew you were well out! You could change the barrel from the inside quite easy. You carried replacements as part of your normal spares. You took the breech out, and there was a locking device. Once you undid that, you could slide the barrel back out from its outer covering, put another one in! It had a sleeve over the outside full of holes for cooling. Lock it and put the breech back in – it didn't take long![16]

Trooper Terry Boyne, 4 Troop, 'A' Squadron, 2nd F&FY

The gunners also had a big responsibility to the driver and co-driver should they have to bail out. If the gun turret was in the wrong position, blocking the driver compartment hatches, then the driver and co-driver would have to escape through the floor hatch – if there was sufficient ground clearance, which was unlikely in soft ground conditions.

The driver was another skilled member of the Sherman crew, the man who put the tank where the commander wanted it to go. But he had to do that either with his head exposed out of the open driver's hatch or with extremely limited visibility.

If you had your seat and lid open you could see out then, but if you had the seat down and the lid shut couldn't see much at all through a bit of a slit. The tank commander told you what to do! You didn't drive just where you want in action. You were only doing what he said, 'Driver, right!' He always repeated himself, or 'Driver, left!' or 'Driver, reverse!' He always said, 'Driver' first, then you would listen! If he wanted it fast he would say, 'Driver, reverse fast!'[17]

Trooper Jack Rex, HQ Squadron, 2nd F&FY

The driver also had to bear in mind the capabilities of his tank. There was little use in taking up a good hull-down position, if they were then unable to quickly withdraw in an emergency.

> A commander had to make a quick assessment of the terrain he was in and look for a safe spot where he could probably get a good field of fire – and still have most of the tank protected. A hedge, a sunken lane – but you had to make sure you were able to withdraw. That was one of the important things. Once you found a place, you had to look to escape if you were fired on by something heavy like an 88mm – you wanted to get out quickly. For instance, across a sunken lane you might go hull down and get bogged in – stuck – and that was a bad thing![18]
>
> Trooper Ron Forbes, 4 Troop, 'B' Squadron, 2nd F&FY

If they were the leading tank of the troop, then the driver was driving almost blind into who knows what perils. Not surprisingly, they found it a tense business. When driving down a sunken road they would be constantly worrying as to what might be round the next corner.

> It's a funny thing, when you're leading tank, it's a lot more frightening. You could have ten times more German soldiers in front of you – so long as you could see somebody alongside you it wasn't so bad. Do you know, when you're a driver in the front compartment, you were that much in front of the turret crew! When you went into action you would swear you were twenty yards in front of the rest of them![19]
>
> Trooper Len Harkins, 3 Troop, 'A' Squadron, 2nd F&FY

The co-driver was basically a spare crewman, often charged with brewing up the tea, taking over occasional stints as the driver and using the hull Browning when necessary in action. James Donovan was very dissatisfied with his co-driver, considering him worse than useless.

The chap who became my co-driver, I found out that when we went into action, he always had bottles of wine from the various farmhouses. Quite often he would be three parts drunk. His attitude was, 'I'm not afraid to die!' I used to say to him, 'Well, I don't care what you're not afraid to do, but I don't want to die!' When I said to him when we were moving from one sector to another, 'You drive – and I'll have a break in the co-driver's seat!' he said, 'There's no point in me doing it, mate, because I can't drive!' That was my first indication he couldn't drive – which wasn't very helpful to me![20]

Trooper James Donovan, 'B' Squadron, 2nd F&FY

*

WHEN ALL IS SAID AND DONE the tank crews usually got on well together. The officers would 'muck in' as they were living cheek by jowl and it was mutually beneficial to relax many of the usual formalities. But officers were still officers.

I knew they called me, Charlie! They would say, 'Oh God, there's old Charlie at it again!' But never to my face – I was always, 'Sir!' There was still an inbuilt respect for position in those days. And a very healthy respect for each other. I didn't smoke. War is a lot of waiting and the chaps would all be smoking – and I would take these boiled sweets and we'd crack silly jokes with each other. I think it's a British habit! It's one of the things the army got absolutely right: the tank crew. You relied on them. We used to have great arguments about, 'Who is the most important member of this crew?' You had your driver, your front gunner, your wireless operator and your gunner and the tank commander. 'The purpose is to bring the tank somewhere where it can fire its gun – therefore I – the driver – am the most important!' The wireless operator would say, 'Nonsense, I'm the guy that tells you where you should take your gun!' Then the gunner would say, 'Well that's a load of balls, because I'm the guy that fires the gun!' I would say, 'Well I'm the chap that ensures all of you get there!' It was quite a healthy debate, quite good fun, there was great expertise – it was based on a mutual respect – and the fact that we relied on each other. It worked very well.[21]

Second Lieutenant Charlie Workman, 1 Troop, 'C' Squadron, 2nd F&FY

Every crew member knew that he was in a team and that the rest would look after him. Any outsider's attempts to undermine this bond were doomed to failure, as Workman recalled in a telling anecdote.

We had a brigadier – not Roscoe Harvey, he was a great chap – who turned up, and he said, 'When a man is wounded in your tank, you will put him out, you will leave him, put some sort of identification for him – and you will press on and leave him to the ambulance.' I got my troop and I said, 'This is what the brigadier has said. I want to make it clear to you nobody in my troop will ever be put out when he is wounded. You will be kept by the tank until an ambulance can take care of you!' I discovered that every other troop leader had done the same thing![22]

Second Lieutenant Charlie Workman, 1 Troop, 'C' Squadron, 2nd F&FY

The 'togetherness' of the tank crews, all mucking in, sharing routine task and dangers, whilst living in close contact, was a crucial factor in maintaining morale in the 2nd F&FY and other tank units. However, that very intimacy brought with it some unpleasant aspects. For the crew of five, the interior of a Sherman was a cramped, claustrophobic and unpleasant environment.

When the tank was on the move it was a noisy place! Noisy, smelly, an oily smell. And when the guns were firing, especially machine guns, it got very choked up with the smoke and fumes off the ammunition. You had to try and keep your turret open if it was at all possible. In the summertime it was very, very hot, with the heat of the engines coming through the tank – it was damn hot![23]

Trooper John Buchanan, 4 Troop, 'A' Squadron, 2nd F&FY

Crew members knew only too well what might happen if their Sherman was hit, and they were often – understandably – nervous.

Well let's say every time a Panther or a Tiger was mentioned, we began to use toilet paper! I mean that literally! We were scared stiff! But I will also say that every tank that was seen was a 'Panther' or a 'Tiger'. Everybody used these words: it was a Tiger that was facing me – and half the time it wasn't! There was a lot of Mark IVs about as well, and a lot of self-propelled guns as well. It was ingrained, I think, in the mind.[24]

Trooper Gordon Fidler, 4 Troop, 'A' Squadron, 2nd F&FY

When they were locked up in their Sherman, the crew's toilet 'needs' had to be managed as best they could.

If it was a 'pee' you did it in an empty shell case. If you had anything more 'serious' you had to nip out and just squat down, with somebody watching that nobody took a pot-shot at you! In those first few days nobody went for a crap at all. They were so 'tied up'.[25]

Lieutenant Charlie Workman, 1 Troop, 'C' Squadron, 2nd F&FY

Toilet humour is never far from the mind of the British soldier and James Donovan could not help but be amused when he saw a man racing to complete a 'mission' *in extremis*.

The driver of the tank in front of us, when we'd been stationary for a long time, he got out to go to the toilet. We were sitting behind them, just looking through the periscope! He came out, dashed round the back of the tank, dropped his trousers and before he'd finished doing nature's call, the nebelwerfers started coming over – the 'Moaning Minnies'. There was a panic then, to see the man trying to pull his trousers up and scramble back in the tank! [26]

Trooper James Donovan, 'B' Squadron, 2nd F&FY

But sometimes their need was great. John Buchanan remembered an incident which could have had tragic consequences.

I was desperate for the toilet – 'Shine' Grant was desperate too! The idea is to take your wee spade, go somewhere quiet and dig a hole. He said, 'I'm going down beside these trees!' I said, 'I'm going into the middle of that field!' There wasn't much grass on it and there was a big thick tree trunk lying there. I said, 'I'll get behind that tree trunk!' I could see the odd German moving around, but not realising that they could see me moving around! I go behind this tree and started. I couldn't dig a hole because the ground was hard and flinty. All of a sudden you could hear in the distance, the moan of the mortars coming – the 'Moaning Minnies'. Oh God! I went down and I hugged this tree. The shells all landed roundabout me. A shell landed about 8 to 10 feet away! But a mortar shell, because the ground is hard, it 'blows 'up' and the shrapnel went over my head. If it had been soft – I wouldn't have been here. When the barrage finished, I grabbed my shovel and hared it back to the tank! [27]

Trooper John Buchanan, 4 Troop, 'A' Squadron, 2nd F&FY

By this time, it was evident to all that the tanks needed the infantry – and vice versa. Both tank crews and infantry had come to respect each other, both appreciating the inherent risks their opposite numbers were taking on a daily basis.

When you got into trouble, if you can't get your own infantry up to surround the danger area, you asked the local infantrymen to do something. At the back of the tank was a telephone, which they could lift and speak to the commander up at the top. They would say, 'Look, there's "so and so" over there, some machine guns over there!' I admired them greatly.

I thought they had the roughest, toughest time because they were in the open – and minefields – you put your foot down and next thing you've blown yourself up! I thought they were great. They say, 'I wouldn't like to be a tank man! Imagine being in one of them!' Because they came across these tanks that had been brewed up. Being curious, they would look in and, 'Oh God!' They thought we had a tough job. They were OK, because they could dig a hole and get into it! We respected each other.[28]

Trooper John Buchanan, 4 Troop, 'A' Squadron, 2nd F&FY

Many of the infantry avoided being too close to the tanks in action, which they rightly considered would attract German shell and mortar fire. It also seemed that a foot soldier's fear of being enclosed, vulnerable to 'brewing up' and burning alive inside a tank, could be very real.

If we picked up wounded infantry, as bad as they were – and some were very bad – you'd say, 'Get 'em in the turret!' With the strength that they had left, they'd fight it all the way – they would never get in the turret. As bad as they were, they would sooner lay out on the engine covers at the back, being held on by their mates. There was no way they would get in – they just wouldn't.[29]

Trooper Terry Boyne, 4 Troop, 'A' Squadron, 2nd F&FY

*

THE FREQUENT CASUALTIES within the 2nd F&FY meant that their officers were kept busy writing letters to the bereaved families in their troop. Charlie Workman was happy to perjure himself rather than add even more pain to their grief. No one died screaming after hours of unbearable agony, suffering from horrendous burns. Everyone died cleanly in his letters.

It was an absolute tradition that you wrote to the parents or the wife of any of your crew who had been killed. Mostly it was parents; we were a fairly young lot. I wrote to this young chap's parents. It was almost a standard thing. You knew they were going to get the official notification. You just said, 'I'm awfully sorry, I can assure you he died bravely, and the end came quickly.' Whether he died bravely and quickly – or not.[30]

Second Lieutenant Charlie Workman, 1 Troop, 'C' Squadron, 2nd F&FY

The padre took his responsibilities to the dead extremely seriously. He hated leaving a man in an unmarked grave and tried to secure a supply of wooden crosses. This led to a dispute with the medical officer who did not want his wounded in the regimental aid post upset by the ominous sight of a supply of grave markers.

The padre came along and was having a conversation with the medical officer. His argument was, 'I can't always get up to the tanks where somebody is being buried and mark the grave – I don't like to leave an unmarked grave.' All I heard him say was, 'No! Certainly not, padre! I'm not going to allow that at all!' It was very unusual for somebody to go against the padre. The padre said, 'I don't know why?' The MO said, 'What would you think if you were put on an ambulance and saw half a dozen wooden crosses on a stretcher? No, I'm not doing it!' The conversation got a bit heated in the end.[31]

Trooper Doug Hayes, MT Section, 'A' Squadron, 2nd F&FY

The padre would call for volunteers to dig the graves. Many sought to evade this unpleasant task as some of the corpses had to be scraped out of the burnt tanks.

Our padre used to bury people. Go and bring them out of tanks. If he came to you and said, 'Would you like to come with me?' You couldn't say no, could you? It would be difficult! But on the other hand, you didn't want to! Some of them you had to very near cut them out of the tank. Because they were burnt and stuck on to the floor of the turrets. He had a little tin of creosote – with a little brush he put a bit on your moustache – so when you were moving the bodies that were burnt or decayed, you didn't smell it – you smelt creosote. As soon as we saw him with his can, we used to clear off out of his way, because we knew he was looking for volunteers.[32]

Trooper Jack Rex, HQ Squadron, 2nd F&FY

Doug Hayes felt it his duty as a lorry driver to step forward to help – he owed it to the tank crews.

Whenever the padre appeared and he was looking for somebody to come and dig a grave, I would go! With others, I used to take the attitude, 'They were our people, and they were mainly from the tanks, so the least I can do is not expect the tank crews to dig the graves!' They were quite shallow graves, because they'd come and salvage [the bodies for reburial] after we'd gone. The first time I saw a burial there were two very young officers. They arrived on an ambulance; they were tightly wrapped in an army blanket. The padre had obviously gone through their pockets and got anything for the next of kin. The padre would make sure they had a wooden cross with their name on.[33]

Trooper Doug Hayes, MT Section, 'A' Squadron, 2nd F&FY

John Buchanan remembered one funeral that was rudely interrupted.

We were out in the open burying some of our friends, about a dozen of us to say farewell. And the padre was there, he was droning on about this and that! And some of these damn German planes came over, flying around and dropping bombs. The infantry were firing; they had their own little ack-acks! There was shrapnel flying all over the place! I felt a wee bit scared that I was a coward, because I was no interested in burying the chaps, I wanted to get back into a slit trench.[34]

Trooper John Buchanan, 4 Troop, 'A' Squadron, 2nd F&FY

Overall, it was an extremely hard life for the tank crews. They were under an unremitting stress that never seemed to dissipate. So many of their comrades had been killed or wounded that it was difficult to maintain a positive mental outlook.

> I had a sort of pessimistic feeling – I always thought the worst was going to happen. Funnily enough, you sort of mentally prepare yourself for it. And there's another side to it – you always feel that, 'It can't happen to me, it won't happen to me!' There's also the worry that you won't be able to cope if something really did happen that required you to be steady in your thinking – would you go to pieces. Most of us had a worry like that: how are you going to cope? Am I going to crack up when the shots come flying at you? Your pride – you wouldn't like to let your mates down. That was the feeling all the crew had – none of them would want to let you down in a tight spot.[35]
>
> Trooper Ron Forbes, 4 Troop, 'B' Squadron, 2nd F&FY

Some men cracked under the strain. 'Pinkie' Hutchison's driver was one who couldn't cope.

> Perhaps I was unaware that he was losing his nerve, but it didn't boil up until the breakout. He in effect said to me, 'I can't go on! I just can't go on!' I saw that he was in a hopeless state. I'm afraid I took the view that the simplest thing was to relegate him to driving a lorry in 'A' Echelon. He never drove a tank again.[36]
>
> Captain Douglas Hutchison, HQ Troop, 'A' Squadron, 2nd F&FY

There was another way out for the really desperate: the self-inflicted wound. There were rumours that there were cases of this, but little hard evidence. But the very fact that there were rumours illustrates how there was a temptation, to end the dreadful suspense once and for all.

> The Sten gun was a very dangerous weapon. It was a very cheap mass-produced sort of thing, and it wasn't unknown

for someone to come in, let's say the tanks had stopped for the night, and say, 'Roll on my demob!' and take his Sten gun off and just drop it – and the thing would go off! They had a very loose bolt action.[37]

Second Lieutenant Charlie Workman, 1 Troop, 'C' Squadron, 2nd F&FY

But most men stuck it out.

13

ADVANCE THROUGH FRANCE AND BELGIUM

There we were just rattling along through places with names like Amiens, Somme, Ypres and so on, which had become horrifying legends only twenty-five years earlier; where hundreds of thousands of men, millions even, on both sides, slogging it out in muddy trench warfare had perished. All that ghastly business of going over the top, the barbed wire, the machine-gun fire, and yet here we were just driving through those places![1]

Major General Philip Roberts, Headquarters, 11th Armoured Division

ON 12 AUGUST, AFTER A REST PERIOD out of the line, the 11th Armoured Division was sent to relieve the 15th (Scottish) Division in the Lassy region. Meanwhile, great things had been under way, as the American Third Army had switched its line of attack to push north from Le Mans to Alençon, which was taken on 12 August, before pushing on to Argentan; while from 14 August, with Operation Tractable, the First Canadian Army and 1st Polish Armoured Division would try to break through determined German resistance to Falaise. Montgomery's intent was clear: to trap the German Seventh Army in Normandy by cutting their line of retreat to the east. As usual, the men of the 2nd F&FY were unaware of the larger picture. At this stage, the method of advance could often be roughly summed up as 'Two up, one in support!' Thus, the armoured brigade would have two regiments leading, with one in support; each of the regiments would have two squadrons pushing forward and one squadron in support. Mostly, given the nature of the country, they had to use roads, travelling forwards on parallel roads, separated by a couple of miles but heading in the same general direction.

After a couple of days in reserve at La Bruyére, the 2nd F&FY moved into action on 14 August, advancing towards La Rocque and ultimately heading for Vassy. Wireless operator Jack Edwards was in the tank commanded by the newly promoted Corporal Pat Ketteridge.

> We set off along the road, Mr Darke leading, we were second tank. As we were going along, I could see in the fields to the side of us our dead men from the 15th Scottish, still lying about from the recent operations. Another half mile or so and there was a couple of knocked-out Churchill tanks and some more of our dead lying about. It used to give me a funny feeling seeing our dead. I used to cast my mind back to the moment when they were shot down and think, 'What would they be thinking at the time?'[2]
>
> Trooper Jack Edwards, 4 Troop, 'B' Squadron, 2nd F&FY

His philosophical musings were to be rudely interrupted.

> We'd done about a mile up the road when Mr Darke hit a mine. He left his tank and came and took over ours. We carried on advancing, but we'd only done a few hundred yards when there was a terrific bang and the inside of the tank went dark with suspended dust – it came out of every crevice and you couldn't see across the tank. Mr Darke was reporting he'd hit a mine again. He left us to take over yet another tank. The column then left the road. They decided to try cross-country. The squadron plus a company of the 8th RB [Rifle Brigade] carriers and halftracks following them. We got out to have a look and the track was broken and a complete suspension unit had been

blown off the side of the tank. It had been blown about five or six yards away and had wrecked a five-bar gate. The eight bolts that secured it had sheered off and shot back inside the tank – they'd hurt the ankle of the driver – rattled against this ankle. Nothing we could do, so we got the stove out and boiled some water for a brew. Two Royal Engineer chaps came up the road, looking for mines. When they got to our tank they said, 'Oooh, must have been two mines, one on top of the other to do that damage! Just shift your stove a minute!' We shifted the stove and they dug up a mine up from where the stove was! There were lots of them around![3]

Trooper Jack Edwards, 4 Troop, 'B' Squadron, 2nd F&FY

An AVRE vehicle eventually arrived and towed them back. The crew then waited two days whilst the fitters repaired their tank, and they would only rejoin 'B' Squadron on the evening of 16 August.

As the 2nd F&FY approached the village of La Rocque, there was a great deal of trouble with German anti-tank guns, which kept moving their position in such a fashion that it was difficult to pin them down to enable an artillery counter-battery barrage. A further problem for the regiment was the collapse of Lieutenant Colonel Alec Scott from the after-effects of his earlier wounds.[4] Eventually, it was decided to send 'A' Squadron to sweep round the left flank of the La Rocque crossroads. This was successful, surprising the German gunners and resulting in the capture of some forty prisoners. But 'Pinkie' Hutchison had his mind on other things.

The leading squadron got held up, so we were sent round the left flank with infantry, who were pretty slow; they were beginning to get a little nervous, I think. Before we got to this crossroads, Sergeant Gale's tank was knocked out by either an SP or tank which then withdrew. We recovered his tank and towed it into the laager. It was burnt out – all the crew in the turret had been killed. I was upset about Gale[5] because he was such a quiet, unobtrusive fellow, but thoroughly effective, somebody I liked and respected. I had to take his charred remains out of the turret and bury them.[6]

Major Douglas Hutchison, 'A' Squadron, 2nd F&FY

By now they had gained a lot of experience as tank crews, which gave them a slightly better than average chance of surviving the mayhem around them. That and a large measure of luck.

With experience one became a bit more cautious. One became more skilful, I think, in not looking for trouble unnecessarily. If you're going up to a place – if you could make use of a building, or bushes, or trees, you'd sidle up alongside that, so that you'd be a less obvious target to anybody who was going to shoot at you. The more experienced tank commanders perhaps survived longest – Steel Brownlie and his troop of tanks were worked harder than any other troop and yet they survived. It may have been luck but perhaps because they became a little more skilful with battle experience.[7]

Major Douglas Hutchison, 'A' Squadron, 2nd F&FY

Next morning, there was a big surprise. When the infantry patrols went out to check what was in front of them, they found the Germans had gone. The regiment moved on, supporting the 3rd Monmouths as they took the high ground beyond La Rocque. As the Germans retreated, they left plenty of signs of their passing. The country was littered with debris.

There were dead horses, hundreds and hundreds of soft vehicles, trucks. Mostly horse-drawn vehicles. The odd tank. All their armoured stuff got away – the stuff that we were wanting – they got away! Smoke. Everything was on fire. Dead bodies, dead horses, cattle dead or dying all over the place. The legs were sticking up and blowing up like balloons. The smell. If you inadvertently hit one with a tank track, it released the gases

and the smell! They talk about skunks, but oh Jesus! You had
to have bags of water to try and wash it off. Or wait for a rainy
day! You had to be very careful you avoided going over dead
horses – or people for that matter. The roads had to be kept
clear, so they just got one of these bulldozers up and shoved
them off the road – dead, dying or wounded.[8]

Trooper John Buchanan, 4 Troop, 'A' Squadron, 2nd F&FY

The advance continued with no opposition to Vassy, held up
only by the blocked roads and the necessity to clear mines from
almost every crossroads. The Germans had also destroyed most
of the bridges, which triggered more delays while a passable ford
was located, or the engineers put in temporary bridging. Then
it was on to St Germain du Crioult. On 17 August they reached
the Rouie river just to the east of La Carneille.

After a recce it was decided that they could get across the
river using a scissors bridge, a moveable bridging unit attached
to a tracked vehicle chassis, which could be quickly moved
into position as and when required. The engineers came under
some fire from the opposing bank before the bridge was in
position, reinforcing the remains of the existing bridge. At
around 18.00, two troops of 'A' Squadron were sent forward
with a company of the 3rd Monmouths. With them was Wireless Operator Jack Edwards and Driver Cliff Pember, who were
in a tank commanded by Lieutenant Alexander Munro, who
was a recent reinforcement from the Lothians and Border
Horse. Once across the river they moved forward to support
the infantry.

The infantry were being mortared and we were told to advance
– and we did. We'd done about 400 yards, Lieutenant Munro
was in command, and he headed towards a gap in a hedge.
There was a big explosion in front of us. So he backed us off a
bit and then he machine gunned the hedge on both sides of
the gap. He went farther along the hedge to the left. Then he

started moving towards the hedge again, but a voice, I don't know whether it was a troop leader or some other officer, warned him that he was getting too near the hedge, he ought to come away from that hedge. He started reversing – you can only reverse slowly – we were sort of at an angle, so we weren't getting very far away.[9]

Trooper Jack Edwards, 4 Troop, 'B' Squadron, 2nd F&FY

By this time, some of the more experienced members of the crew were getting worried. They were coming under mortar fire and there was a serious risk of panzerfaust rockets emanating from the nearby hedge.

This lieutenant was a bit of a death or glory boy. We were going into an orchard, seemed like it – a lot of trees. I can remember hearing over the intercom, one of the fellers inside the turret, 'Get your head down!' But he didn't take any notice of him.[10]

Trooper Cliff Pember, 'B' Squadron, 2nd F&FY

Then, suddenly, they were hit.

I was looking through the periscope, seeing what I could see. There was a big explosion behind me, somewhere at the back of the tank, so I turned round – and I saw that the turret seemed to be full of flames. I did my very 'quick draw' on the fire extinguisher and started spraying where the flames were coming from. They eased off somewhat – amazing – I think they were coming through the engine bulkhead. I guessed something had hit us at the rear end of the tank – I guessed it was a bazooka. All the crew had disappeared except for Lieutenant Munro,[11] who was slumped over the back of the gunner's seat. I leaned over to have a look at him, and I thought, 'Well, he must be dead!' Because his blood was spattered all over the gun shield. He had a big hole thorough his neck, but it wasn't bleeding. I thought, 'If it's not bleeding now – he must be dead!'[12]

Trooper Jack Edwards, 4 Troop, 'B' Squadron, 2nd F&FY

Cliff Pember had only one thought on his mind – and who can blame him – to get out of the tank as soon as physically possible.

When the tank caught on fire, I really don't know what happened. I thought we'd got hit by a bazooka and the turret crew had been killed – the amount of flames that was coming out of there. The only thing I was concerned about was getting out! I couldn't get out of the escape hatch at all – there was not enough ground clearance. I couldn't get out of my hatch because the gun was over it. All I could see was smoke in the turret. I said to Viv Holden, 'Get out, Viv!' He wouldn't get out! So, I went over the top of him and out! Down by the side of the tank.[13]

Trooper Cliff Pember, 'B' Squadron, 2nd F&FY

Then Holden jumped out of the tank, but as he did so he was badly hit.

Viv got out and a sniper got him, right up the back. Must have got him as he turned round to jump down. I got Viv round by the side of me – and every time he groaned you could hear a burst of machine-gun fire coming like that, 'Brrrrrrrtttt!' There's a tow bar on the side of the tank, so I got on the bogie – hanging on there I was. Every time old Viv was groaning the machine-gun bullets were coming – I was all right – keeping my feet off the ground.[14]

Trooper Cliff Pember, 'B' Squadron, 2nd F&FY

Edwards was still in the Sherman; his only thought was to get away from the hedge and any German infantry that might be lurking there.

The turret happened to be in the right direction so I could wriggle through into the driver's seat. I started reversing, I thought, 'I'll try and get a bit farther away from the hedge before I get out'. 'Taffy' Pember who was outside, shouts, 'Stop! Stop!' I stopped and he said, 'Viv's hurt! And you're taking the tank away from him. We've been shot at as we bailed out. Get out, anyway, because the tank's on fire!' Which I knew! I said, 'One, two, three!' And I shot out like a streak of lightning on to the ground outside.[15]

Trooper Jack Edwards, 4 Troop, 'B' Squadron, 2nd F&FY

His first reaction was a totally irrational annoyance – at the actions of the now-deceased Lieutenant Munro in putting them into danger, at Viv Holden for being wounded, and at himself!

I looked around and I felt quite annoyed, because our tank was there on its own and the rest of the troop were about 100 yards or more behind us – and we were there poking about in this hedge all on our own. There was 'Taffy' and myself behind the tank. I was also annoyed at Viv Holden lying on the ground – pretending to be badly hurt – I couldn't see any blood coming out of him! And I was annoyed at myself, because I thought, 'If I had just thought on, I could have brought some smoke grenades or something out!'[16]

Trooper Jack Edwards, 4 Troop, 'B' Squadron, 2nd F&FY

At this point there was no sign of the gunner – they later found that he had jumped out and simply 'run like hell' to get as far away as he could as quickly as possible. The two remaining survivors tried to attend to Viv Holden's wounds.

Taffy says, 'Let's have a look at Viv!' I got Viv's field dressing out of his pocket and between us we started taking his jacket off. We got it half off and still couldn't see any sign of blood. Just then there was a long burst of machine fire came under the tank. Viv shouts, 'Margaret![17] Darling, I love you! Goodbye!' I said, 'Taffy, they've got me in the legs!' He said, 'They've got me in the legs as well!' Lots of wounds over both legs, they weren't bullet holes they were bits of ricochet, bits of rock shot up from the ground and all sorts. The legs were riddled – wounds all over them. I sat down with my back to one of the bogies. I

still had this field dressing in my hand – there is actually two
dressings in one – so I used one on the worst wound on one leg
and one on the worst wound on the other leg![18]

Trooper Jack Edwards, 4 Troop, 'B' Squadron, 2nd F&FY

It seemed hopeless, but then their hopes of rescue were briefly
raised.

While I'm doing this, the troop Firefly arrives and stop nearby.
The sergeant shouts, 'Get on the back of my tank!' I thought,
'We haven't got a lot of chance of that!' He'd no sooner said it
when I saw something come over from behind the hedge, shot
over, and it just missed the front of this Firefly and it exploded
somewhere in the space between the Firefly and us – terrific
bang! The Firefly went smartly into reverse and got out of it!
This explosion shot up a big cloud of smoke and dust. Viv
Holden[19] was lying on the ground, he made the most piercing
scream – and he came completely off the ground – umpteen
feet in the air – and then dropped back again. I presumed he
was dead or too far gone to worry about. I saw this cloud of
smoke and dust and thought, 'That'll give us cover! Hurray,
let's get out of here!' I said, 'Come on, Taff!' We both staggered
to some rocks about 25 yards away. Not very big ones, but we
dropped behind them. Then started to crawl to the other side
of the field. It wasn't a very big field.[20]

Trooper Jack Edwards, 4 Troop, 'B' Squadron, 2nd F&FY

Jack Edwards and Cliff Pember were both by then wounded
badly, but they tried their best to get away.

We both crawled across the field and got to a hedge at the other
side. There was an infantry patrol hiding behind the hedge.
One of them showed his face in a gap and said, 'This way,
mate!' We crawled through the gap he'd indicated. The other
side of the hedge I tried to stand up to walk and I couldn't –
just fell on the ground. We both settled down on a grassy bank

the other side of the hedge. The infantry disappeared, the tanks moved off, it was just very quiet – and it went dark. An infantry medical corporal arrived, he looked at us, cut our trouser legs off and did a good bandaging job on us. I'd put dressings on, but they'd dragged off as I'd been crawling. Whether it was the wounds, or the shock, or loss of blood, or what, I don't know. I just felt tired. I could have gone to sleep. I was at peace with the world.[21]

Trooper Jack Edwards, 4 Troop, 'B' Squadron, 2nd F&FY

The corporal disappeared, but shortly afterwards reappeared with a stretcher. They took Cliff Pember first, but then came back again for Jack Edwards. By then it was pitch black. He was carried back to the scissor bridge – he estimated it was about 600 yards to the rear. Then he was taken in a scout car to the dressing station. Here Edwards had a brief reunion with his gunner who had got away but was being treated for burns to his hands. Both would be evacuated back to the UK for more prolonged hospital treatment. Behind Edwards and Pember, the German resistance had soon ended. This was the pattern of the fighting in this period – a spasm of machine-gun fire, a splatter of mortar fire, shots from the deadly panzerfaust, or perhaps even a panzer, or self-propelled gun, before the rearguards fell back. Hold-ups were frequent, but progress continued.

Overall, it was evident that the Germans were staggering. Falaise fell on 16 August, and over the next few days the Falaise Gap was 'closed', although several of the German divisions had either slipped through or forced their way out, before it was finally 'sealed' on 21 August. Nevertheless, 50,000 men of the German Seventh Army were made POWs. Although a further 50,000 escaped, they had been forced to abandon much of their heavy equipment in chaotic conditions. They left behind some 10,000 dead, roads blocked with wrecked vehicles and hordes of the dead horses upon which so much of their transport logistical system depended. The Battle of Normandy was finally over, and it had ended in a crushing defeat for the Germans. Now it was time for an almost unopposed advance to the Seine.

Over the next few days, the 2nd F&FY crossed the Orne river and moved into position southeast of Habioville. After crossing the main Argentan–Falaise road, the 2nd F&FY occupied the high ground to the north-west of Argentan without meeting any opposition. They were then held up to some extent by the sheer thickness of the Forêt de Gouffern, before reaching the Bailleul area. On 21 August, the 2nd F&FY moved back to Argentan and then pushed forwards via Le Bourg St Léonard to Exmes on the road to Coulmer. Here came the next big challenge as they tried to get across the Touques river. 'Pinkie' Hutchison described what happened.

'B' Squadron were leading, and they got stuck on account of a bridge being blown in front of them. I was sent with my squadron round to the right to see if we could find an alternative place to cross. We found a minor bridge; it took the tanks and there was a little bit of a lane beyond the bridge and then this main road. The leading tank, one of Peter Northern's tanks, was hit by an anti-tank gun firing down the road. He dismounted and went forward to see if there was anything he could do – the exit onto the road was blocked by this tank. The gun fired again, and he was wounded in the hand. Colonel Scott was beginning to get a bit impatient about us getting on and clearing this road! We couldn't get out so I dismounted and managed to get a tank – it was Voller's – into a field where he could fire up the road, but he couldn't see properly. I was in front of it – and got into a ditch where I could see the gun up the road. I told him where to put a shot down, HE, which he did, and it burst in the middle of the road opposite the gun. I used a pair of German binoculars; they were very good – Zeiss – with graticules on them. I put my hand up and said, 'Right two [degrees]!' The next shot exploded above my head! It hit a cast iron signpost[22] saying two kilometres to wherever it was.

I thought, 'Oh, Christ! This is it!' But the velocity of the shell took all the blast forward. Voller thought that he'd killed me; he jumped down from his tank and said, 'Are you all right?' I said, 'Yes, I think so, but I think you may have hit me in the bottom. He said, 'Take down your trousers – and let's have a look!' It was just a fragment of shell – it just broke my skin! I still have the overalls with a sort of jagged cut from the splinter that had ripped the bottom![23]

Major Douglas Hutchison, 'A' Squadron, 2nd F&FY

Meanwhile, 'B' Squadron had faced some strong resistance from German anti-tank guns and infantry. By the time the German rearguards had been cleared, it was too late to resume the advance.

On 22 August, they continued to push to the east, coping with the threats of heavily mined roads often blocked with lines of felled trees. There were constant frustrating delays, waiting for sappers to help clear the way forward, but little or no opposition. The 2nd F&FY, along with the rest of the 11th Armoured Division, were then given a few days' hard-earned rest in a laager some 4 miles west of L'Aigle. More new officers and reinforcement drafts arrived to replenish their ranks. The men were growing accustomed to new faces.

On 28 August, they sprang back into life, with the 11th Armoured Division now assigned as part of the XXX Corps, recently reinvigorated under the energetic command style of Lieutenant General Brian Horrocks. They advanced at the fastest possible rate to the Seine, making a late crossing at the town of Vernon. This was part of Montgomery's mission for the Twenty-First Army Group – to push northwards and destroy the remaining German forces in north-east France and Belgium. He intended to secure the vital Channel ports in the Pas de Calais area and the Belgian airfields essential to maintain aerial domination. Then the port of Antwerp would be the next great objective, offering as it did a potential shortcut to their ever-lengthening lines of communication and supply back to Normandy. Once this had been achieved, Montgomery planned a thrust eastward into the Ruhr heartland of Germany. However, a change in his status was imminent, as in a couple of days the Supreme Allied Commander, Dwight Eisenhower, took direct overall control of operations, to reflect the increasing importance and size of the American element in the Allied armies. Montgomery, although still commanding the Twenty-First Army Group, would no longer be the man who set the parameters of future operations, but would be working as an equal alongside General Omar Bradley commanding the Twelfth Army Group, and under the overall command of Eisenhower. The somewhat prickly and arrogant Montgomery found this difficult to accept, but as some compensation he was promoted to field marshal on 29 August. Although always a difficult subordinate, he would continue to play an important role in the debates over Allied strategy for the rest for the war.

Meanwhile, there was little opposition as the 2nd F&FY advanced through the French countryside. Lance Corporal Ken Watson came from Deptford and had worked in the dividends department of a bank before being called up. He had been serving with a Tank Delivery Squadron before being assigned to the 2nd F&FY as spare personnel while they were in Cully back in June. Now he was serving as the driver of a Humber scout car for the regimental intelligence officer, Lieutenant Hudson. Watson fondly remembered talking to what he thought was a Frenchman in Vernon.

> There were flowers, bottles of wine, food if you wanted it! I spoke reasonable French and I used to speak to the locals when I got the opportunity. I was speaking French to one local and he said, 'There's no need for you to speak like that to me!' He was a Scot who'd married a French woman in the First World War and stayed there ever since! When I asked him if the Gestapo had ever cottoned on, 'No, I've never been interviewed,

stopped or anything!' 'Do you speak French? 'Yes, but I don't speak it very well, I still speak it like a Scot!' He'd gone right through the whole of the war without being stopped by the Germans at all.[24]

Lance Corporal Ken Watson, HQ Squadron, 2nd F&FY

The following day, the regiment was in the lead role for the division as it pushed on at a good rate, passing through Guitry with only minimal opposition. But resistance stiffened as they approached Etrépagne and 'C' Squadron were ordered forward. Lance Corporal Leslie Gibson was all for adopting a cautious approach.

It was pouring down with rain. We were using the leapfrog formation. I was the leading tank at the time. I was pushing on and I saw in front of me a little copse, which I was a bit suspicious of. So I stopped to have a look through the glasses. Of course, I couldn't see a damn thing. They all steamed up. The colonel came on and said, 'Move on, this place has been recce'd, move on!' He's hardly said that, when an 88mm in the copse hit me in the turret ring just in front of me above the driver. It wasn't very pleasant, I can tell you that. The gun turret was completely jammed, it couldn't move. The shell didn't penetrate but it must have fused the metal on the tank, because it wouldn't move one way or the other – it was absolutely stuck. Then the damn thing stalled, it wouldn't go. I just wanted out – we all bailed out. I don't know if it fired again – we were too busy getting out. I knew where they all were except the driver. I heard one of my crew – Cliff – being hit by snipers. I knew there was a sunken road and I thought, 'Now if we can get back there, we can get maybe back to the other tanks and sort this lot out!' I was going towards this road to try and get some help for us. I don't know why, but something said to me to turn round – and I did! And I went backwards – and I got shot through the foot, where my head would have been. I was so lucky; it went through the top and didn't break a bone. [The Germans] came out – there was quite a crowd of them. They knew we were in this turnip field. They treated us very well – they tended to our wounds. They took us into this railway station. There was the most hell of a bloody clatter – and half the wall came down. 'What the hell is this?' The Germans pushed off outside thinking there was something coming, but a German Red Cross corporal came in and he pulled Cliff and I out into the garden behind a wall. They said that they would be pulling out and put us into a barn. They said, 'You know how your tanks sometimes just go through things – if you hear them coming yell!' They went away – there was a battle – we could see the tracer back and forwards. We got picked up by some civilians, who took us into this village and put us into the biggest bed I've ever seen! The one thing both of us would have loved was a cup of tea – which we eventually got – but not quite the tea we were used to – it was laced with cognac! Some time after a big recce sergeant from some other unit came in and said, 'Oh, you're doing well there!' He arranged for us to be picked up![25]

Lance Corporal Leslie Gibson, 2 Troop, 'C' Squadron, 2nd F&FY

Later he met his driver in hospital back in Edinburgh.

Who do I meet but my driver, Frank McGlashan. I said, 'Frank, I'm so glad to see you, I didn't know what happened!' 'Oh', he said, 'I got away, I got back to Major Leith, the second in command, and I reported there were enemies in this railway station. They called up the 25-pounders, who knocked hell out of the place!' I said, 'Thanks, very much, we were in there!' He didn't know that, of course.[26]

Trooper Leslie Gibson, 2 Troop, 'C' Squadron, 2nd F&FY

Frank McGlashan was a well-known character in the regiment. In all he was 'brewed up' in different tanks on some eight or more occasions, but he was still alive![27]

There was also fighting a couple of miles to the north at

Doudeauville en Vexin. Here 'B' Squadron were leading when they ran into a battery of anti-tank guns. This was where Sergeant Reginald Osgerby was wounded. He had been with the 24th Lancers, before being transferred to the regiment after the Goodwood debacle.

> It befalls everybody to be a leading tank now and again. I was the leading tank at that stage. We passed Etrépagne, went through the little hamlet of Doudeauville, was waiting for the rest of the unit to come up behind. I was in a good hull-down position, we were firing our Browning at some Germans across the field, about 200–300 yards away. An anti-tank gun must have swivelled round and got me from the left. The shell came through the turret and killed outright my gunner and operator – and wounded me. I had my head out – I just looked down inside – it was a mess. The gunner and operator were certainly killed; there was no way of helping them. I finished up with a broken wrist and a gash in my side just under my ribcage. A bit of shrapnel in my eye. The only thing for me to do was to get out before the next shell came. I managed to get out of the tank, together with my driver and co-driver, but the other two – there was practically nothing left of them in the tank. I finished up in the ditch trying to find a first field dressing to slap on myself. They were buried at Doudeauville. That was the end of my war![28]
>
> Sergeant Reginald Osgerby, 2 Troop, 'B' Squadron, 2nd F&FY

Osgerby was flown back for treatment at the Bayeux field hospital, then evacuated back to England.

The date 30 August would live in many of the men's memories, as it proved to be truly a hard day's night. First, they made the journey to Hétomesnil, meeting little opposition, although en route they got the chance to shoot up a convoy of German vehicles and secured several prisoners. This had been an advance of some 40 miles and some of the tanks had already run short of petrol. In the normal course of events, they would have laagered at Hétomesnil, but instead they received orders to push on overnight all the way to Amiens in the Somme area. This was on the orders of Lieutenant General Horrocks, who perceived that the lack of resistance meant that if the 11th Armoured Division pressed on regardless that night, then they might totally surprise the Germans and 'bounce' them out of Amiens before the bridges over the Somme were demolished. 'Pip' Roberts had his own amusing perspective as to the genesis of this plan.

> It was the afternoon of 30th August, and I got a signal that General Horrocks was on his way to see me. He arrived at 16.15 hours at a little village called St Germer; at that time our leading troops were about 30 miles from Amiens and the burden of General Horrocks's visit was that we should carry out a night march and take Amiens at dawn. That sounds simple and straightforward, but there were problems. First of all, if we have to take a large town like Amiens, we must have infantry easily available; so the grouping of the brigades must be altered. And then there was the question of petrol; there must be enough to ensure that we could get there and fight a battle. Afterwards a wag said, 'It was quite simple! Ike said to Monty, "Amiens tonight!" Monty said to "Bimbo" (Dempsey), "Amiens tonight!" "Bimbo" said to Horrocks, "Amiens tonight!" Horrocks said to "Pip" Roberts, "Amiens tonight!" And then the planning started![29]

Major General 'Pip' Roberts, Headquarters, 11th Armoured Division

The officers of the 2nd F&FY were certainly caught on the hop after a hard day in the field. News of an all-night advance was the last thing they wanted to hear.

> All I wanted was sleep but had to await orders for next day. When they came, we were flabbergasted, for we were to move at once and drive through the night to Amiens. I don't know if Corps Commander Horrocks actually said: 'There's a moon

tonight,' but he did write later that this was a curious way to
employ an armoured division. If he had been in Hétomesnil,
he would have heard similar opinions, expressed more bluntly.
Thirty miles in the dark, can't see to fire, can't hear, who's
reading the map; we had problems. He also wrote later, 'It has a
shattering effect on the morale of the enemy to wake up in the
morning and find that some hundreds of tanks have penetrated
deep into their positions under cover of darkness.' True.[30]

Lieutenant William Steel Brownlie, 4 Troop, 'A' Squadron, 2nd F&FY

The advance was a sound tactical vision perhaps, but one hell
of an undertaking in practice – they would be travelling in the
pitch dark on minor twisting roads, with multiple junctions, on
an unreconnoitred route. The one saving grace was that there
was minimal German opposition.

We were to replenish, bomb up and continue advancing all
through the night. Extremely unusual – the first time this had
ever happened. The opposition at this stage was comparatively
light. We all thought it was a jolly good thing – we could see
the end of the war almost in sight! We started off at about six
in the evening. We were just told to keep nose to tail, keep in
touch with the vehicle in front and we wouldn't lose the way in
the dark. Quite late in the evening, the column was stopped,
and after a while I became suspicious as to why we were stopped
for such a long time. I walked ahead and found that all the
crew in the tank in front of me from another troop were sound
asleep! And there was not a vehicle in sight in front of them. I
knocked them up, went back to my tank, overtook that tank,
and just swanned on in the dark, hoping I would catch up.
Needless to say, we did![31]

Lance Corporal Roy Vallance, 4 Troop, 'A' Squadron, 2nd F&FY

At the front of the column was Corporal Byrne, who seemed
to be able to see and map read in the dark, as his performance
was much complimented in the regimental history, 'He made

scarcely a single mistake'.[32] John Buchanan had a slightly more jaundiced – and amusing – view of progress.

> This is what we were geared up for – the breakthrough. Somebody punched a hole, and we went through it. Our chance came and we weren't going to miss it – even day and night! You had to follow the tank in front – there was only a wee light to follow. You couldn't put your headlights on. More or less nose to tail. One laugh was the lead tank, the boy must have been bamboozled, instead of turning right, he went straight into this field! Of course, the whole British Army followed him! We were actually kind of sleepy then and everybody followed him. He went round in a circle in this field and came out! It took a wee while for to sort ourselves out! [33]
>
> Trooper John Buchanan, 4 Troop, 'A' Squadron, 2nd F&FY

In many ways, driving in a column behind the leader, with no effective lights, was even more difficult than being at the front. It is a well-known military phenomenon that even if the front vehicles are going at a reasonable speed, those at the back of the column will have difficulty in keeping up. But worst of all, these men were exhausted. Indeed some resorted to taking their Benzedrine tablets to try and stay awake.

> I was damn tired and so I got out of my tank and got into the scout car, a little lightly armoured thing, and I said, 'Look, I'm going to see if I can have some sleep, but for God's sake don't lose the tank in front – and if anything goes wrong, wake me up!' I collapsed in a heap in the bottom of this thing. We motored on. We went through Conty – quite a large town. Whoever was leading the columns had got lost – we were driving backwards and forwards through the place. The odd thing was, it was still occupied by the Germans, but they kept their heads down while we were messing around. Next day

there had to be quite a considerable attack put in before they cleared out.[34]

Major Douglas Hutchison, 'A' Squadron, 2nd F&FY

There were indeed substantial numbers of Germans in Conty, but they were not unnaturally disheartened by the sound of so many tanks charging through the narrow streets. They kept well out of the way, until next morning they were 'tidied up' by the infantry following up behind.

Over this madcap advance, it was inevitable that more and more tanks would run out of petrol, to be left behind by the wayside. However, some of the crews found it an absolute benefit to be momentarily 'out of the war' while they waited for the fuel lorries to catch up with them. When the villagers awoke they gave them a great reception.

> Bertie Moir had red hair. We got into this village and suddenly we ran out of petrol. We were lucky to stop in a village. Some fellows ran out in the wide open! The villagers came out full of the joys of spring – and there was one red-haired girl attached herself to Bertie Moir. I think he fell in love with her! The most enjoyable thing of the whole war was seeing these delighted people coming out and kissing you and whatnot! Buried wine emerged from gardens – some of it was too 'mature' for us. We were warned not to get ourselves too inebriated, because we wouldn't be fit for duty. The column eventually caught up.[35]

Trooper Ron Forbes, 4 Troop, 'B' Squadron, 2nd F&FY

Several apocryphal-sounding stories were told that German lorries – or even perhaps an unwary Panther – had 'joined' the convoy at some time during the night. The Panther was not mentioned by any outside of the regimental history, but several of the interviewees vaguely referred to brief sightings of 'enemy' lorries in the column.

A German convoy came off a side road and joined us. When they realised they were in the wrong convoy they disappeared. They were fleeing and they'd come on to the wrong road.[36]

Trooper John Buchanan, 4 Troop, 'A' Squadron, 2nd F&FY

As the tanks neared Amiens, come the dawn, it was evident that the Germans had indeed been taken totally by surprise, and several vehicles were shot up. Jim Thompson-Bell, a Londoner who had worked in dry cleaning shops before his call-up, was by this time a sergeant who had seen active service in Normandy with the 1st Lothians and Border Horse, before being transferred to the 2nd F&FY in August 1944. Initially posted as a driver in the Sherman commanded by Lieutenant Eric Lamont, he now had a bit of a surprise when they captured a German halftrack.

We went like the clappers, very rarely stopped, just stopped occasionally in a village. We arrived at one village in the morning and we stopped. Some of the population came out and one chap came up and said, 'Bosche, in here!' I got one of the crew members down and we went in and it was a German halftrack. The crew was asleep in their little bunks at the back! We just tapped them on the shoulder and woke them up! Fetched them out. We didn't want them as prisoners, because they are a bloody nuisance! We fetched them out and passed them back to the infantry. We couldn't be bothered with prisoners! But it was a pay-waggon! We opened the back and you've never seen such a sight! Bank notes galore: Belgian francs, French francs! We liberated a bit, a packet each for each member of the crew! Then we moved on![37]

Sergeant Jim Thompson-Bell, 2 Troop, 'C' Squadron, 2nd F&FY

Far more important was the capture in Amiens of General Heinrich Eberbach, who had just been promoted to command what remained of the German Seventh Army. Lieutenant Hudson, as the intelligence officer, was ordered to take Eberbach back to be interrogated. His driver, Ken Watson, remembered it well.

When they captured the German General Eberbach, we had
to take him back to brigade headquarters. He was a very surly
sort of gentleman. We had him right on the back of the scout
car, although I think he had his legs inside. I saw three Germans
running across the road into the woods. I said to this German
general, I don't know why Hudson never said it! 'Tell those
men, to come out here and get on the back of this scout car.' So,
he did – he spoke English in a broken fashion. These men came
out and jumped on to the back – and their eyes popped out of
their head when they saw the German general! We went across
this railway line and I saw a German walking along with his
helmet in his hands. We stopped him. I got out of the scout car
and had a look. In his helmet he had half a dozen eggs – which
I said were mine and told him to jump on the back of the scout
car. We delivered the German general to brigade headquarters –
he didn't say goodbye![38]

Lance Corporal Ken Watson, HQ Squadron, 2nd F&FY

Eberbach was then sent on to the Headquarters of the 11th
Armoured Division, where he met a delightfully acerbic
response from Horrocks.

It was thought possible that General Horrocks might be
intrigued with the spoils of his triumph, and this party was
accordingly shepherded together to await his arrival. But the
corps commander was evidently disposed to concern himself
only with the next stage of the pursuit; what the hell, he wished
to know, were all those Germans doing there, and would we
please get them out of the way as soon as possible? So General
Eberbach and his staff were evacuated through the usual
channels.[39]

Lieutenant Edgar Palamountain, HQ, 11th Armoured Division

Meanwhile the main body of the tanks were arriving. Gordon
Fidler remembered driving into Amiens, although he immediately broke down, which for him proved a blessing in disguise,

as he became a symbol of liberation to the French civilians, who soon surrounded his Sherman.

> We then were on the outskirts of Amiens; I think we had something to eat. Moved into Amiens, and in the Boulevard, we stopped dead! We had a piston come out through the side of the block! We went round to the rear of the tank, opened up the engine, absolutely flooded with oil, nothing we could do. The squadron goes through, leaves us on the side of the Boulevard. The recovery vehicle comes along, pushes us off the road into a line of trees, and we stay there for five or six days. We had the bivouac on the side of the tank. I've got photographs of civilians clambering up on the tank. Two schoolgirls, about eighteen, used to come down on their bikes and used to bring us tomatoes and all sorts of goodies! One of them was named Michelle, and her father invited us back for a meal at their house. He was a superintendent of police. We went up to this house and had a beautiful meal.[40]

Trooper Gordon Fidler, 4 Troop, 'A' Squadron, 2nd F&FY

Eventually they were picked up by a lorry and returned to their squadron.

By 11.00 on 31 August, the two main bridges over the Somme river had been captured and Amiens was secure. The Germans were in chaos throughout the whole area. After a brief rest, on 1 September the mad advance continued, pushing across the Somme and on to Aubigny. In the absence of serious German opposition, the 11th Armoured Division were directed to advance on the great Belgian port of Antwerp. Many German prisoners were taken and here again the Recce Troop made themselves useful.

> Having taken Amiens we got about 2,000-odd prisoners – probably more than that! My job then was to take these prisoners back to Amiens and hand them over. Very dejected they were. Still hostile. The biggest trouble we had was to

make sure that the French people didn't get at them as we were making our way back. That was the worst part about it – to get them back safe and sound.[41]

Lance Corporal Bill Knights, Recce Troop, HQ Squadron, 2nd F&FY

Jack Rex remembered one incident that provided him and his crew with a great deal of amusement at the expense of a somewhat pompous German officer.

Going through a village, an old Frenchwoman stopped us. She says, 'There's a German officer wants to give himself up!' Me and a pal of mine, we went upstairs and he was sat in bed. His hat was on the chair and his tunic on the chair back – with all these fancy decorations! He said in perfect English, 'And what rank are you two?' 'Why?' 'Well, I want to give myself up to somebody of my own rank!' This lad came from Dundee, he was a real hardnut! He reached by me, grabbed him by the scruff of the neck, threw him downstairs, and threw all his clothes through the window out into the street! All the French people were stood in a ring round him, while he was putting his trousers on! Jock said to me, 'The bugger, who does he think he is?'[42]

Trooper Jack Rex, HQ Squadron, 2nd F&FY

The plethora of abandoned German vehicles scattered about the countryside provided an opportunity for souveniring that proved too strong for Roy Vallance, although he later regretted it.

The following day were in a field, spread round the hedgerows, and there were a number of German vehicles in the vicinity that had been abandoned. I strolled across with some friends to one, and we found a German officer's greatcoat, hat and boots. Rather foolhardily, I put them on and said, 'Take me back as a prisoner!' For a joke to the squadron leader – I was almost shot as they took me into the squadron area. One of our crews said, 'Shoot the bastard!' I very quickly took them off![43]

Lance Corporal Roy Vallance, 4 Troop, 'A' Squadron, 2nd F&FY

The advance for the next couple of days blurred into a roll-call of French villages and towns. The occasional skirmish was all that marred their steady progress. The French were generally over-joyed to see them, but there was one aspect of the liberation that the soldiers did not enjoy – the treatment by members of the French Resistance of female 'collaborators', accused of 'crimes' with the Germans.

> We took up defensive positions in Oignies, and people gave us steak and chips. A family let me have a shave and a bath in their house. I was in the turret writing a letter home, when my front gunner brought a girl into his seat in the hull. I sat quiet until three or four French youths hauled her out. A pistol was drawn, but I persuaded Trooper 'X' to put it away. She was hauled away to have her head shaved, and to be ducked in a pond, for having been too friendly with Germans.[44]
>
> Lieutenant William Steel Brownlie, 4 Troop, 'A' Squadron, 2nd F&FY

This was a common experience and these humiliating punish-ments of 'collaborators' were generally frowned upon by the British witnesses. It always seemed to be women who were picked on.

> It's a shame really. They grabbed the women and put them out in the middle of the street. Sat them in a chair, tied their hands behind their back and then shaved off all their hair. Because they been 'doing' with the Germans – collaborating. But I felt kind of sad at that. Because no matter who you are, the first six weeks you might hate them, but you've got to live with them. Nature takes its course – these Germans – some of them nice blonde Aryans. If you're hungry you'll do anything – they couldn't help themselves.[45]
>
> Trooper John Buchanan, 4 Troop, 'A' Squadron, 2nd F&FY

On 3 September 1944, the regiment was following up behind the 3rd Royal Tank Regiment, joining them to overcome some stiff resistance at Seclin, moving round to the right of the town while the 3rd RTR attacked from the left. Shortly afterwards, they crossed the border into Belgium to scenes of great rejoicings. However, they were soon made aware that the Belgian people were starving.

> These four horses had got caught up in the crossfire and got themselves shot – they were lying in the road. As soon as the last shot died away, all the civvies rushed out and in less than ten minutes all there was left was a pile of hooves! Never seen anything so quick! There was just a pile of steaming hooves![46]
>
> Trooper Geoff Eason, Recce Troop, HQ Squadron, 2nd F&FY

Many of the men remembered this rapid advance as a 'golden period' of their wartime experiences. A sense of their collective achievement, the welcome from the civilians and the absence of serious fighting, contributed to this.

> The days were full. One started at first light and didn't go into laager until last light. And then you had to 'bomb up' and fill up with petrol. You got very little sleep. We were exhilarated, we thought everything was going well. We were winning the war. It was going to be over. Casualties at this stage were very light. We didn't mind at all. I was 21, 22 years old – it was a great adventure.[47]
>
> Lance Corporal Roy Vallance, 4 Troop, 'A' Squadron, 2nd F&FY

Steel Brownlie provides a splendid story illustrating – at least partially – why Vallance was 'enjoying' the experience.

> We reached Aalst, 20 miles north-west of Brussels. All the cafes were open, the streets were crowded, but our rendezvous was by the roadside a mile further on. Fortunately, Corporal Vallance had 'run out of petrol' in the town square, and I thought it my duty to go back in a scout car and see how he was getting on. He was getting on very well, and I joined him and his crew in their cafe for half an hour. Time for breakfast,

so we drove back up to the squadron. Buchanan had mine ready, but I lay down on the ground and went to sleep. An hour later it was, 'Move.' [48]

Lieutenant William Steel Brownlie, 4 Troop, 'A' Squadron, 2nd F&FY

Still, they pushed on, on, until they reached Antwerp on 4 September. This was the real target: it was essential to capture the port and keep its logistical infrastructure intact, as the British supply lines were severely overstretched, reaching as they did all the way back to far-off Normandy. Indeed, since they had crossed the Seine, they had advanced some 340 miles. Most of the German conquests attained in the much vaunted 'Blitzkrieg' of May 1940 had been reclaimed. It was a magnificent achievement by the 11th Armoured Division as a whole. On entering the city, the 2nd F&FY were deployed alongside 159th Brigade to clear up the remaining pockets of German resistance in the city. This was quite a tricky business.

On the outskirts of Antwerp, we were met by huge crowds of people. Cheering us on! Pressing drinks on us! We were in one street being mobbed and then we were told to advance, which we did with difficulty, because of all of the civilians all over the tanks. We went round the corner and there was hardly a soul in sight – and we were fired upon immediately. The contrast was enormous. We were being sniped from a large factory building. I put an HE shell through every window in the side of the factory that was looking at us.[49]

Lance Corporal Roy Vallance, 4 Troop, 'A' Squadron, 2nd F&FY

The British found the Antwerp docks almost undamaged, which, given their obvious value to the British, seemed to indicate how the sheer speed of the advance had wrongfooted the Germans. There was some resistance in the central park, where the Germans had built a system of linked concrete pillboxes and deep dugouts. The presence of the 'C' Squadron tanks seems to have intimidated the garrison, which surrendered after a short exchange of fire. Overall, there was considerable confusion as to what was happening, with a fair amount of sniping and shots from the occasional anti-tank gun. It was here that Terry Boyne, veteran of so many Normandy battles, finally seemed to have run out of luck when his tank was sent out on a recce mission.

A bridge had been blown and they wanted to know how much was destroyed. Down at the river there was a lot of sniping going on. An Inns of Court armoured car came up and the lieutenant in it had lost about the last quarter of an inch of his nose! Bleeding like a stuck pig! Telling us there was snipers everywhere. We fired shots off, but on getting back to the laager, as we got near, our tank went up, a shudder then this big 'WHHUUUFF!' Not a clue what had hit us. You get this roaring in your ears – the fire. I didn't stop to hang about. We all bailed out and rolled on the grass – we were all burnt. We were picked up and taken to a medical station. They bound the hands up – they could do very little for your face at that point. It wasn't bad, it was black and scorched, I'd lost my eyebrows and a bit of my hair. Somehow, we got separated. I was put on an ambulance and being sent to a forward hospital. When the ambulance stopped and the backdoors opened, I was helped out of the ambulance by a German. All I could hear was German being spoken – it was a German hospital – the ambulance had lost its way. Then I was on a mattress in a corridor. I just lay watching these big boots going backwards and forwards. There was no English there at all – the Germans were still running it. I was in their hands, as it were. They were pulling out their walking wounded fairly rapidly. It must have been a couple of days I was lying there. A doctor came and looked at my hands and they bound them up with paper bandages. Everything was ersatz. They fed you – a watery sort of soup that tasted of nothing and the bread was like dark bread, looked like chipboard – tasted like it, now I come to think of it! But at least they gave you something. Then late one evening, I was woken by a light being shone in my eyes, and a very soft voice said, 'All right, old son! Stay where you are, I won't be a minute!' In English! He looked at my face and hands. There was an orderly with him. He was a medical officer. He said to the orderly, 'Put the 'E' label on this one!' The bloke stuck a tag on me – and 'E' stood for evacuation. He said, 'You'll be going out in the morning!'[50]

Trooper Terry Boyne, 4 Troop, 'A' Squadron, 2nd F&FY

His luck had held after all! The hospital had been liberated and Boyne was evacuated by air to the UK where he was treated for his burns. There were several such incidents during the 2nd F&FY's brief time in Antwerp.

We went straight along a road to the outskirts. We ended up on a bridge near the docks. It was one of those bridges that goes up and over. We went so far up there, and we were hull down. We thought we weren't showing. We were stood there just on observation jobs. I couldn't see, we were all hull down. We were sat there quite a long while. Looking round. Then I heard Sergeant Heard say, 'Hey, there's something hitting them buildings behind us!' There was a couple of shots and then all of a sudden, I was told to get out! It shows just how good the sights of the German guns were; the gun had seen us hull down, it could only see a very little bit, and he'd brought his gun down and fired – it skimmed right across the top of the turret! Willie had had his head half out. So he just said, 'Bail out!' We jumped out and left it there! They recovered that tank that night! It had only skimmed along the top, taking a groove.[51]

Lance Corporal Harold Wilson, 4 Troop, 'C' Squadron, 2nd F&FY

The regiment was in a laager to the south of Antwerp, where much valuable maintenance and repair work was carried out over the next couple of days. There were still duties to perform, thus tank patrols were sent out into the city suburbs, guards were set up on possible canal crossings and there was also a brief abortive attempt to cross into the Meuse–Escaut Canal to the north of the city, which was abandoned when the bridgehead was found to be too insecure. It seemed that the German resistance had at last begun to stiffen.

Then came opportunity, as the Guards Armoured Division established a viable bridgehead over the Albert Canal at Beeringen. On 8 September, the 29th Armoured Brigade as a whole were moved up and the 2nd F&FY went into laager overnight, ready for action next day. Moving into action was no longer a novelty for the regiment. After just three months they were hardened veterans. As a result, 'O' Groups under Colonel Alec Scott had become much more informal, and often very brief, as Scott was confident that his officers knew what they were doing.

> Scott was a shy man, inclined to be a bit silent, but he had a dry sense of humour and was very nice! I liked him – very straightforward. 'O' Groups were as short as possible! More often than not a brief affair in a laager, maybe he had to take people in turn – give instructions to one squadron because the other squadron leader wasn't immediately available. We always had maps – not bad, some places better than others, but perfectly adequate.[52]
>
> Major Douglas Hutchison, 'A' Squadron, 2nd F&FY

They were used to a rota of switching the 'lead' regiment and squadron in the line of advance by 29th Armoured Brigade, just as within each squadron the troops took it in turns to lead, although within 'A' Squadron sometimes Steel Brownlie gave the impression he was still determined to lead whenever possible.

> Driving, stopping and waiting! You have to bear in mind it wasn't every day that you were the leading squadron or troop. You could just be following on those. You would stop and wait if for some reason they were held up. A lot of your time was spent just sitting and waiting – expecting at any minute to be told to go round the flank, or through the leading troop,

or carry on! All the time you were listening on the air to the regimental net, you could hear what was going on, so you had a good idea of what was likely to happen in the near future. A soldier's lot is waiting, expecting, hoping – dreading![53]

Lance Corporal Roy Vallance, 4 Troop, 'A' Squadron, 2nd F&FY

They were also thoroughly integrated with the infantry, in sharp contrast to the situation during Operation Epsom. Both infantry and tank crews knew the value of each other and were determined to keep as close as possible.

We very often carried the infantry. If we were not the leading squadron, we would certainly be carrying infantry. They would be all over the tank; we'd probably have a dozen or more clinging on to the top of the tank. Which they were quite happy to do – it saved them walking! They were very nice chaps. We had the same platoon time and time again, so we got to know them a bit. We didn't talk much about tanks – more about females![54]

Lance Corporal Roy Vallance, 4 Troop, 'A' Squadron, 2nd F&FY

On 9 September, the 2nd F&FY crossed the Albert Canal and relieved the Irish Guards from the position they were holding in front of the village of Helchteren. There was considerable fighting during the day as 'B' and 'C' Squadrons, supported by their old friends of the 8th Rifle Brigade, tried to make further progress. Towards the early evening they were joined by the 1st Herefords in some woods just to the west of the village. A company attack was put in by the Herefords with the intention of clearing the eastern end of the village. By then the German positions had been identified, with approximately two platoons located in houses on either side of the road, while another platoon was dug in on the north-west village outskirts around a prominent windmill. These positions were in turn covered by machine-gun and mortar fire from nearby woods and a sunken lane. It was during these operations that James

Donovan, the driver in the tank commanded by Sergeant Frank Carrison, became involved in a dramatic incident.

> We took over from the Guards Armoured. They had a couple of tanks knocked out. We were in this position sitting in the fields, looking across. I could see a black-painted windmill. We were asked to go out with a patrol of infantry, to give them protection. They would go along behind and alongside our tank – and reconnoitre what the situation was – towards the windmill. We got too far in front and they turned round and went back – so we were left on our own. We kept going across this field, running parallel with this small road. We saw one German come out from underneath the base of the windmill – I was watching him through the periscope, he just had his rifle slung on his shoulder, as if there was nobody about. I said to the crew commander, 'He's probably been spotting and he's going in the direction of the anti-tank gun that had done the damage to the other tanks!' He said to the gunner, 'We'll lob a couple of HE shells over in that direction!' Which they did do! Then we carried on.[55]
>
> Trooper James Donovan, 'B' Squadron, 2nd F&FY

In the event they probably went rather too far, unsupported as they were. As driver, Donovan was also beginning to have problems with the amount of mud in the fields.

> Eventually, I thought the ground was getting a little bit boggy and the crew commander didn't seem to realise. I said, 'Well can you get me up on to that road and we'll try and make our way back! I want a bit of firm ground!' There were drainage ditches down each side of this road. He said, 'Oh, I can see a ramp where we can get out of the field!' I suppose what the farmers used! He got me onto the ramp and then turned right onto the road. The tank virtually filled most of the road. I thought, 'Right! Put your foot down and we'll get rolling!' I started belting back to our own lines. I thought, 'Smashing!' All

of a sudden, as we came round a slight bend, there were these German infantry in Indian file moving up. As we started going through them, the co-driver (it was one of the days he hadn't been drinking wine) he opened up with his gun – and the turret gunner opened up. We were getting well past them.[56]

Trooper James Donovan, 'B' Squadron, 2nd F&FY

Both sides were taken by surprise and the Sherman created havoc with its machine guns. But had they got the one man in the German section who could really harm them? No, they hadn't.

The Germans dived into the ditch, but the one we needed most – with the panzerfaust – after we got by, he fired out of the ditch and whacked it straight up the back. Next thing you know, the tank suddenly lurched, so I banged it down one gear; it lurched again, I banged it down another gear. It lurched again and all of sudden all the power was gone! As I looked round in the turret, it was just all burning! Trying to pull my headset off. The crew commander shouted, 'BAIL OUT!' I went to push the hatch up, I found they'd left the gun over it and I couldn't get the hatch up. I was screaming at the co-driver to get out! Because it was burning! He's getting out – and there's me behind him trying to give him a push up to get him out of his hatch! 'Get out! Get out!' I had to climb over the gear box, scramble over there and get out of his hatch! The others got out of the turret.[57]

Trooper James Donovan, 'B' Squadron, 2nd F&FY

As the desperate men clambered out of the flaming death-trap, they immediately found that they were now excruciatingly vulnerable to the small arms of the nearby German infantry.

The one that was badly wounded was the crew commander – Frank Carrison – he got a burst right down his thigh. That was opened up like a butcher's shop – it just spewed open – his thigh was all one big gash. We grabbed him and pulled him round – we lay to the front of the tank – it was burning fiercely by now. We crept away from it a little bit. The next thing we knew a couple of Germans had come up alongside of us and they were just sitting there guarding us in the ditch – they never said a word.[58]

Trooper James Donovan, 'B' Squadron, 2nd F&FY

Donovan and the rest of the crew were prisoners. His first instinct was to look after his crew commander, whose leg was a ghastly sight. With blood everywhere, his field dressing was almost useless. But it wasn't just physical – there was the emotional trauma, which was almost too much for Donovan, who was after all only a youngster.

I was looking after Carrison. I took his field dressing and just tied his leg together as best I could. Then I took my own field dressing out of my pocket and I tied his leg again, pulled it together – that was all I could do! He'd lost his wife in the air raids on Hull – and he had two young children. He was giving me his last will and testament. I was thinking to myself, 'I'm a youngster and he's telling me to go and look after his children because he was going to die!' We talked him out of that – told him he was going to be all right! We lay there – even got cigarettes out of our pockets and had a light up! I lit one for him! We thought, 'What are they going to do with us?' They must take us back – we're prisoners!'[59]

Trooper James Donovan, 'B' Squadron, 2nd F&FY

The trouble was that the Germans themselves were undoubtedly under severe stress, knowing they were outnumbered and expecting an armoured and infantry assault at any moment. It was a tense situation, with an underlying fear for the Sherman crew that they might all be shot out of hand.

A couple of hours had gone by – we're still lying there. They're looking across from this ditch across the fields – firing a rifle now and again. Apparently, we were being watched by our own people through binoculars. They could see what was going on – and they tried to send a halftrack ambulance out. The Germans fired on it and sent it back. We could see across to this small anti-tank gun – one of those little ones the soldiers themselves used to pull along. One of our HEs must have dropped right on it, because the crew were just lying there. We must have had a direct hit on them. Carrison was getting a bit delirious and all of sudden he decides that, 'If I'm going to go, I'm going to take one of them bastards with me!' I looked round and he's waving this revolver about! Luckily, the two Germans who were guarding us were looking out across the fields where the action was going on! I hit him and snatched the revolver away from him! There was a steel pipe there and I slid it into the pipe![60]

Trooper James Donovan, 'B' Squadron, 2nd F&FY

They couldn't fight it out with heavily armed German soldiers, but their options appeared to be diminishing by the minute. Perhaps these Germans would not respect their rights as prisoners when it came to making a dangerous withdrawal under fire. Perhaps they would just shoot them! What should they do? This was a life-or-death decision.

We kept talking to Carrison, trying to keep him awake. Eventually, Geoff Marshall and I said, 'They're not going to take us back behind the lines – when they pull back, they'll shoot us!' There was a lot of SS among them. We decided that by six o'clock, if they don't do anything we'll make a break for it! And hope! Carrison picked up this conversation – and he pleaded with us not to leave him. We said, 'Well you're too big for us to carry!' He weighed about 12 to 14 stone! 'You can't walk! You're crippled, you've only got one leg!' We decided the only way that we could help him was to roll him over on his back, Geoff would take one hand, I would take the other one, and we would run up the road dragging him!' We said, 'You want to chance it – we'll do it!'[61]

Trooper James Donovan, 'B' Squadron, 2nd F&FY

The moment came and off they went. It was madness, but they had heard too many stories of SS behaviour with inconvenient prisoners to risk staying. They did not get far. It must have been agony for poor Frank Carrison as he was dragged along on his back, his severely wounded leg banging along the ground.

We ran – and he was screaming – you imagine the pain he must have been in with his leg bobbing up and down on the road. There was all hell let loose – there was bullets flying everywhere! The first indication that something had happened to Geoff was he shouted and dropped Carrison. I couldn't drag him on my own and I turned round to Geoff. I thought his nerve had gone and he'd given up. As I turned round, I got whacked right in the face. There was blood everywhere. I had enough sense then to dive off the road back into this ditch that's still running along the road. Geoff Marshall hadn't panicked – bullets had gone straight under his armpit and come out of the top of his shoulder. So he was in a bit of a mess as well. He was still out in the road with Carrison.[62]

Trooper James Donovan, 'B' Squadron, 2nd F&FY

On diving into the roadside ditch, Donovan got another surprise.

When I dived in there, I landed on top of one of these blokes out of the Lothian Borders. After a few minutes he's screaming, 'I've been hit! I've been hit!' I said, 'What's the matter then?' He said, 'I've got blood all down my back! I can feel it!' I said, 'Well that's not your blood, mate – that's mine – that's coming off of me!' I said, 'Give me your field dressing!' I'd already used my own on Carrison. We lay there another couple of hours at least. There was odd firing going on. Then when it got dark, we – Geoff and I – said, 'Well, we'll have a go to creep away in the dark.' But all the time we were getting weaker with loss of blood. We heard shells coming over – but no explosions! We realised as they got nearer that they were smoke shells. Out of the smoke came our infantry – first time I'd ever seen fixed bayonets![63]

Trooper James Donovan, 'B' Squadron, 2nd F&FY

Even this posed dangers in a darkening battlefield, covered in smoke; they were reliant on the soldiers spotting they weren't Germans.

The infantry approaching them were probably led by the redoubtable Private D. Evans, who had taken over command of his 1st Herefords platoon after his officer and section NCO had both been wounded in an attack on the houses at the end of the village, Evans had calmly assessed the situation, then launched an attack towards the windmill, braving heavy mortar and machine-gun fire. His later citation for a well-deserved Distinguished Conduct Medal (DCM) notes that Evans personally captured the panzerfaust that had put tanks out of action. Evans then moved forward to organise the evacuation of the wounded – all the while still under fire. Here was an ordinary soldier 'making the difference'. But Donovan was also very grateful to his squadron commander, Sir John Gilmour – another man capable of going the extra mile.

The Germans must have started pulling back. And through the smoke also came Sir John Gilmour – and he'd got a stretcher on his shoulder. They'd been watching everything that had happened. He said, 'What's the situation?' We said, 'Well, we can walk, but Carrison can't!' We put Carrison on the stretcher and Sir John Gilmour took one end – I took the other end – went to pick it up and dropped him – I was too bloody weak! So we did the obvious thing – I took one side of the stretcher and Geoff with his good arm took the other and we carried him back like that. I'd got hit in the face and I lost part of my nose as well. I lost a lot of blood, but I didn't realise how much until I went to help carry Carrison on the stretcher! The wounds weren't too bad really, the great thing was, like all of us, I worried about my eyes, whether you were going to be blinded. If you get part of your nose taken away without touching your eyes – to me it was a gift![64]

Trooper James Donovan, 'B' Squadron, 2nd F&FY

Donovan never forgot what Gilmour had done for him. He may have been landed gentry, he may have been an officer, but he was a decent man who really cared for his men.

It is interesting to follow the medical treatment given to James Donovan, who was first evacuated to a field dressing station, where his wounds were given a preliminary dressing. He found that everything below the bridge of the nose had been smashed away by the bullet. From there he was taken back to the field hospital, where he and his wounded comrades were split up, as both Frank Carrison and Geoff Marshall needed urgent operations. Donovan was taken to Brussels and flown back to Swindon before being treated at the Hereford General Hospital. His traumatic ordeal and the deeply personal nature of his facial injuries were obviously having an impact, as he was suffering from severe insomnia – despite an overwhelming sense of fatigue.

You got there, my hair hadn't been cut for weeks, it was now Wednesday morning. I was pretty grubby. The only thing that had happened, everywhere we went, is they changed the dressing and passed you on for evacuation. They said, 'Well, get into bed!' I said, 'No, let me have a bath!' 'No, all you want is sleep, it doesn't matter about how dirty you are!' I thought to myself, 'Lovely, well I'll sleep for three or four days in this bed!' Got in there and I couldn't sleep, I said to them, 'Well if you let me lie on the floor, I'll be able to sleep!' It was a rather weird sensation. I just could not go to sleep![65]

Trooper James Donovan, 'B' Squadron, 2nd F&FY

His wounds were tidied up, but, at this stage, there was no reconstructive element to his treatment.

> I had a couple of operations at Hereford, just to clear all the bits of flesh that had gone up into my nose. They froze my face with injections and just operated while I laid on the table. It was quite nice holding the nurse's hand on the operating table![66]
>
> Trooper James Donovan, 'B' Squadron, 2nd F&FY

He was lucky enough to be sent to Queen Victoria Hospital at East Grinstead, which had earned a pioneering reputation in plastic reconstructive surgery based on their work there during the Great War. Since then, there had been further significant advances in medical knowledge and of course – tragically – plenty of opportunity for practise in rebuilding the faces of burnt RAF air crew.

> I was taken to East Grinstead Hospital, which was a great plastic surgery hospital. I had about five different operations there – they do it in stages and eventually built my nose up. They cut the muscle from my right forehead, then that was rolled down and stitched into my face. Then after four or six weeks they separate the bit at the top that's joined to your forehead and stitch that on above the nose. Then that's left for another six weeks. Then they start to shape it and build your nose up! It's a long process! I can't say it caused a lot of pain, not really.[67]
>
> Trooper James Donovan, 'B' Squadron, 2nd F&FY

Donovan was eventually given a medical discharge from the army in February 1945. It was made evident to him that he had no choice. Thank you but no thanks, was the apparent attitude.

> I had to go to Farnborough in Hampshire for a medical. They said, 'What do you want?' I said, 'I want to stay in the army; I want to do twenty-one years! I'll stay in – and I don't mind going back!' They said, 'Oh, no, no, no! You've done your bit

and that's it!' Which I didn't agree with. I was still A1 bodily. Perhaps they didn't want disfigured people in – I don't know! When I first came out, I got a 100 per cent pension, but that was reduced once I was fit enough to 30 per cent, which it has stayed at all these years.[68]

Trooper James Donovan, 'B' Squadron, 2nd F&FY

He always remembered the irony that on an early exercise in England he had been chosen by umpires to be counted as 'wounded' with facial wounds. For him, the exercise had come true.

*

BACK AT HECHTEL the war went on. On 10 September, the 2nd F&FY took part in an attack on the village in conjunction with the Welsh Guards. 'A' Squadron was in the lead, supporting by a company of the 1st Herefords, while 'C' Squadron moved to flank the village from the right, attempting to cut the road between Hechtel and the town of Peer. As 4 Troop advanced across the fields, they became aware that they were not alone. The field was riddled with a mixture of trenches and individual foxholes occupied by the 10th Parachute Regiment. Steel Brownlie remembered the moment of realisation well.

There were a dozen Germans running, 800 yards, so I halted and was leaning out of the turret giving orders to the gunner, Buchanan, when suddenly the tank was spattered with bullets. I ducked down sharpish. Only a few enemy had run, and it soon became obvious that we were in the middle of a large area of dug-in Germans, who were firing at us from all sides with small arms and panzerfausts. What to do? Certainly not sit still: either retire, or keep moving and firing. I decided on the latter course.[69]

Lieutenant William Steel Brownlie, 4 Troop, 'A' Squadron, 2nd F&FY

Arriving to join 4 Troop was Captain David Voller, who had the reputation of always looking to be at the forefront of the action. Having swiftly assessed the situation, Steel Brownlie flew into action.

> I gave the order that we would keep moving among the enemy positions, never halt, run over trenches, fire at all possible targets. They kept appearing and disappearing as we drove round and round, flat out. We shot them, crushed them, blew them out of their holes, but as soon as we passed others popped up and let fly at us.[70]
>
> Lieutenant William Steel Brownlie, 4 Troop, 'A' Squadron, 2nd F&FY

It was an exciting – and dangerous – operation with the very real risk of being 'brewed up' by panzerfausts.

> The infantry were pulled back and we went haring round this field with our guns depressed, blasting into everything that moved. Every little hole we saw, we tried to put machine-gun bullets in. That's where the co-driver came in handy, because he could do the same. He was more or less at a level. Eventually the paratroopers gave up. There was a lot of tanks in this field. Voller was in one of the tanks, and he was standing up. All the Germans were crowded round our tanks, with their hands above their heads. There was some of our infantry in among them – herding them, you might say. All of sudden, Brownlie says, 'He's been wounded. Buck, shoot him!' There was one man alone. All the rest of the parachutists moved away and left him standing isolated. He had pulled out a Luger and shot Voller in the back of the neck. I traversed my gun on to him, but really, I couldn't shoot a man in cold blood – he just stood there. I had the opportunity to do it – use the machine gun and blow him to bits. If he'd pointed a gun at me, I'd have shot him! Just at that time – to save my bacon more or less – two British infantrymen stepped in and prodded their bayonets into him. He dropped his gun, put his hands up and they marched

him away. They took him prisoner. One of these Nazi fanatics. Bearing in mind Voller was his great friend, Brownlie wasn't very happy I didn't fire, but I just couldn't.[71]

Trooper John Buchanan, 4 Troop, 'A' Squadron, 2nd F&FY

Captain David Voller was evacuated to have his wound treated, but he recovered enough to rejoin the regiment about seven weeks later. In all they took some 350 prisoners. The intensity of actions like that at Hechtel was slowing the rate of the British advance, as after their chaotic retreat from France, the Germans at last got some kind of a grip on the situation. Recognising the changing situation and increased difficulties, Montgomery was intent on building up his strength before launching a proper attempt to cross the formidable Meuse–Escaut Canal.

On 11 September, the town of Peer fell to the 2nd F&FY as the Germans pulled back – just as the tanks were about to launch an attack. Hechtel would fall the next day. But even on an 'easy' day there could be fatalities. Tommy Willmott remembered another example of the padre's willingness to do all he could for the dead and dying.

The padre, Captain Oswald Welch, he just didn't have any fear at all. One of the tanks had been hit up at a crossroads, just over the Albert Canal. It was one of our Honeys. A young lad called Milne[72] had been killed. He was half in and half out the tank by the time we got there. Oswald just wanted to be there with him. He was always getting into trouble for being too far forward, always wanted to be up with the tanks. He was really a superb person.[73]

Squadron Quartermaster Sergeant Tommy Willmott, HQ Squadron, 2nd F&FY

The regiment would spend a week at Peer, engaged in the usual maintenance activities and resting as best they could. Ready for the next stage in the advance.

14

ADVENTURES IN HOLLAND

We were bivouacked for the night in an apple orchard. I was on guard; we all took our turn at being on guard duty. They lobbed over some 88mm high explosives and I got hit in the leg. It took a lump out of the side of my leg. I could walk all right, and I got in the bivouac and the crew put a field dressing on it – and in the morning I wound up in Brussels hospital.[1]

Trooper Don Fairweather, 'B' Squadron, 2nd F&FY

THE HOUSEHOLD CAVALRY proved their worth during the 2nd F&FY sojourn at Peer. Not only did they uncover a gap in the German lines, but they also discovered an undemolished – and even more to the point – unguarded bridge across the Meuse–Escaut Canal. The Irish Guards were rushed forward to create and hold a bridgehead. This allowed a general move to the north by the 11th Armoured Division, now back in VIII Corps, to cross the canal, which appeared to offer the chance to free up the stalled campaign before winter and the glutinous nature of the South Holland mud slowed it to a complete halt. The division would now be charged with guarding the right flank of the Guards Armoured Division and the rest of XXX Corps as they surged forwards, in conjunction with a mass airdrop of the American 101st Airborne Division in the Eindhoven–Veghal area; the American 82nd Airborne Division dropping in the Grave–Nijmegen area; and the British 1st Airborne Division landing at Arnhem. Ultimately, the intention was to create new bridgeheads across both the Maas (Meuse) and the Rhine where they drew close to each other at Nijmegen and Arnhem respectively. This bold scheme, Operation Market Garden, was the brainchild of Montgomery, who proposed thereby out-flanking the German defences of the Siegfried Line to secure the all-important Rhine bridgehead before the Germans could amass sufficient forces to prevent it. Bold it may have been, but it was also an over-optimistic gamble reliant on a compliant German opposition. Nevertheless, Eisenhower acquiesced, and the operation began on 17 September. The result was disaster, as the XXX Corps were unable to keep up with the ambitious requirement to advance some 65 miles in three to four days in order to relieve the forward airborne troops. The Germans had managed to reorganise their forces and proved that they were not to be underestimated.

For the 11th Armoured Division, the operations had a far more conventional aspect. On 19 September, the 2nd F&FY crossed the Meuse–Escaut Canal and advanced to Hoek. Next day, the advance continued across the Dutch border to Heeze. Occasional delays caused by German anti-tank guns, or demol-ished bridges, were overcome, until, by very late in the evening on 20 September, they reached the Zuid Willems Canal at Someren, where the bridge across to the village of Asten was blown up just as a strong fighting patrol of the 1st Herefords arrived on the scene. A recce to right and left failed to find an alternative crossing, so it became a job for the infantry and the Royal Engineers working in tandem. At 19.30 on 21 September, the Herefords forced a crossing of the canal, with two compa-nies using assault boats, while a third company followed up, rushing across the lock gates, which had not been destroyed. Despite considerable opposition, they managed to establish a small bridgehead around the other side of the destroyed bridge facing the village of Asten. Strong German counter-attacks fol-lowed almost immediately, with concerted efforts to infiltrate the Herefords' defensive positions. The situation became wildly chaotic, with Lieutenant Colonel G. R. Turner-Cain just about holding things together during bitter hand-to-hand fighting in the pitch dark.

> About 02.00 hrs the Germans made a determined attack on our bridgehead with artillery and mortar fire. I was ordered to take my section on foot across the lock gates to support 'C' Company and cover the road about 500 yards towards Asten. The night was pitch black and machine-gun fire from the right flank was very worrying. About 03.30 hrs a burst of fire brought down the overhead electric cables, arcing and sparking along the road. From the screams we heard, we were sure some of our lads were electrocuted. The Germans were coming closer calling 'Tommy surrender!' I threw six or seven grenades at them. All movement on the road stopped.[2]
>
> Sergeant Frank Moppet, 1st Herefordshire Regiment

At one point, Captain Lucas, the forward observation officer of the Ayrshire Yeomanry, found the Germans swarming through the house he was occupying and only escaped by switching off his wireless and hiding in a cupboard. Surreally, he was not discovered and later counter-attacks by the Herefords drove back the Germans and he escaped unscathed. Behind them, it was the sappers' turn to shine as they moved forward and began erecting one of their invaluable Class 40 Bailey bridges across the canal on the site of the demolished bridge. It was a fraught business, as they were under harassing mortar fire and further held up by the incessant German counter-attacks battering against the somewhat flimsy bridgehead defences. Nevertheless, they persevered, and by the morning of 22 September it was complete, the bridge ready for the armour to move across.

The task was given to 'A' Squadron. After a preliminary barrage by the gunners, they would charge 'cavalry style' across the new bridge, smash through the German defences, penetrate the village of Asten, which lay about a mile further back, and then deploy to cover all routes into the village to prevent any German reinforcements getting through. Lieutenant Don Bulley and 1 Troop would lead the way, followed by Lieutenant Steel Brownlie with 4 Troop. Then Major Hutchison with the 'A' Squadron headquarters, accompanied by an armoured car from the Recce Troop would support 1 Troop, and finally 3 Troop under Lieutenant Samson. This was a desperate undertaking, and all tanks were ordered to go flat out, deploying all armaments to maximum effect to try and 'shock and awe' the German defenders. Contrary to usual practice, the officers would lead each troop from the front.

> On this occasion Don Bulley proposed that troop leaders should go first, which meant that he would be leading the whole show, and this was agreed. He was a fair-haired, cheerful young man of about my age, who had a habit of singing to himself popular tunes, like: 'I'm just biding my time, that's the kind of guy I am!'[3]
>
> Lieutenant William Steel Brownlie, 4 Troop, 'A' Squadron, 2nd F&FY

Major Hutchison sets the scene for us.

> There were small warehouses which slightly concealed the bridge, which was probably a help in getting it rebuilt. There was very flat wettish ground between there and the village of Asten, which was a few hundred yards away. The road, quite soon after you'd debouched from the buildings, there was a dogleg to the right, and then it went more or less straight in towards the village. The idea was that the first troop would drive flat out, firing their guns as they went, bunging hand grenades out of the top of the turrets, and hope to God they'd get through all right. They were to go straight through the village, out the other side and then stop and try to prevent anyone coming back into it. That was what Don Bulley was supposed to do. Then Steel Brownlie was going to go into the village and up to the left, then

I followed, and I was going to go out beyond to join Bulley. The other troop was to go right out of the village.[4]

Major Douglas Hutchison, 'A' Squadron, 2nd F&FY

'B' Squadron would follow them up accompanied by a company of the 4th KSLI. However, it was evident that if anything went wrong, then there was a strong chance the whole of 'A' Squadron could be marooned.

It was a bold if not desperate plan, for if anything halted us beyond the bridge, the entire squadron would be sitting immobile in line ahead among the enemy defences. We would have been finished off at leisure. If there were mines or anti-tank guns, if any of the leading tanks were knocked out and blocked the road, if anything unexpected turned up, we had had it. This is why we were shocked.[5]

Lieutenant William Steel Brownlie, 4 Troop, 'A' Squadron, 2nd F&FY

The bulk of the regiment were laagered behind Someran, so the intelligence officer and his driver were sent forward to report on the progress made on the Bailey bridge over the canal.

Harry Axton and I went up to the bridge in the scout car at about 4 o'clock in the morning, so that when the bridge was completed, we could radio back and say, 'It's completed, charge over!' I can remember this major, or lieutenant colonel, in the Royal Engineers, standing on this bridge smoking a pipe as calm as you like, giving these engineers instructions – bearing in mind there's a lot of fire coming from the Germans on the other side. That impressed me more than any other action I saw during the whole war – the calmness of this bloke under fire. Then telling us that the bridge was ready to go over. Harry Axton then radioed back, and the first troop went over. We could see all the shots coming over, the tracer, hear all the explosions, saw the tanks go over.[6]

Lance Corporal Ken Watson, HQ Squadron, 2nd F&FY

Lieutenant Don Bulley's Sherman was the first across and it was evident immediately that the Germans were a lot closer than they had thought.

> Don Bulley shouted over the air, 'We're off!' We motored over the bridge and through the little cluster of houses. Don had got about 50 yards beyond the last one, when his tank disappeared in a cloud of smoke and flame. His second tank swerved to the right, in an attempt to by-pass over a field, but it stuck fast in the ditch. His third tank tried to do the same to the left, but also stuck. Me next. All I could see dead ahead was smoke and dust, but this was no place to hang about, so we just drove on. There was a tremendous crash, but the tank kept moving and emerged with a rush, still on the road.[7]
>
> Lieutenant William Steel Brownlie, 4 Troop, 'A' Squadron, 2nd F&FY

John Buchanan picks up the story.

> Bulley was wounded by a bullet through the neck, because he had his head stuck out of the turret. I can still hear them yet, 'Sunray is lying on the floor – he's bleeding badly, can we get "Niner" [code for medical help]?' You couldn't – he just had to try and stop the blood. Hutchison says, 'Now just hold on and we'll be there shortly, just hold on, hold on!' He couldn't stop the war to sort that one man out. His tank was in the ditch. The crew bailed out when Bulley died. It was a silly thing to do; if they'd have stayed in the tank, they'd have been all right. They were all shot down, it was full of Germans all around.[8]
>
> Trooper John Buchanan, 4 Troop, 'A' Squadron, 2nd F&FY

Reports indicate that Don Bulley[9] was fatally wounded while firing his revolver at the Germans clustered round his Sherman, which some thought had been mined. With Bulley out of action, the second tank also ran into terrible trouble. At the speed they were travelling, everything was happening in a blur. Split second decisions could have fatal consequences. Hit by a panzerfaust,

Sergeant David McMahon and his crew decided to bail out – and were shot down by the German infantry. McMahon[10] and three of his crew were killed.

> The second tank, he tried to go past him. He went in the ditch on the right-hand side. He was under fire, too. The third tank couldn't get through. I think he panicked – and he went in the ditch. Three tanks – and ours was the fourth one. They were going at speed; we were doing about 30 miles per hour. I got hit. I thought it was a bazooka hit. There was a bang, a flash, a bang and dust. It's funny where dust comes from when you get hit. That's where I thought that was the end of me. Later on, I found we had hit Bulley's tank, his tail was hanging over the road, we'd hit it, probably knocked it back into the ditch – and we carried on. A Scotch mist had come down and you couldna see, you could only see the height of the tank – 6 feet. I was dead scared, because I was [now the] first tank.[11]
>
> Trooper John Buchanan, 4 Troop, 'A' Squadron, 2nd F&FY

Behind Scott-Brownlie's 4 Troop was the squadron headquarters led by Major 'Pinkie' Hutchison. He reviewed the situation as he found it and as an experienced officer adapted his plans to the situation.

> When Bulley got just beyond this dogleg, he got hit. He pulled his tank off the road, so that it didn't block the road. The next tank got knocked out too – Sergeant McMahon – he didn't block the road either. There were just two tanks in Bulley's troop. Steel Brownlie then found himself in the lead. He went on flat out. He got hit by a bazooka – not penetrated – the tracks were damaged, but it didn't prevent him from getting on. He got through into the village. Then I was immediately behind him. We had to then do Bulley's job and go straight through the village, which we did: I hurled hand grenades – Tom Dines was feeding me hand grenades and I was bunging them out the top. We were firing machine guns – spraying them around, help

to keep people's heads down. The Germans were for the most part between the canal and the village, more than in the village itself, because we got through and out the other side without difficulty, once we got past where the German infantry were dug in. Bulley was right in among them, he defended himself as nobly as he could in his tank, trying to use his pistol against them and he was killed. Those killed and wounded were the crews of those two tanks.[12]

Major Douglas Hutchison, 'A' Squadron, 2nd F&FY

Geoff Eason, with his driver Harry Gregory, was in a scout car near Hutchison.

Rattled over the bridge. There was another bridge the other side too, over a little river. The road ran on through a floodplain on an embankment. Before we'd gone 100 yards, the two tanks in front of me were on fire. There'd been somebody squatting down in the ditch with a panzerfaust – and set these two tanks on fire. We had a mortar shell land on the front. Harry couldn't hold the car and it went in the ditch. Ended up at an angle. The ditch was full of Germans. There was hell's delight going on outside. Firing and shots all over the place. It was a hell of a row! Harry, I shouldn't say this, but he panicked. He couldn't bear being shut up in there with all this action going on; he got a pistol and he thought, 'It's not far back!' I'm afraid he was dead before he hit the ground.[13] I stayed put! A Jerry climbed on the front of the car and had a look through Harry's hatchway; he thought I was dead! Briefly, momentarily, I considered suicide, because I thought I was a goner! There were so many Germans milling around the vehicle. There was so much noise going off. I'm glad I didn't, but these things go through your mind. I tossed out a couple of hand grenades, little pineapple things. I always had four-second fuses on them, terrified of someone picking it up and throwing it back. Ten seconds is a long time, you know. In the back of my seat there was a little porthole that could be opened. Looking through there I could see I was behind some German machine-gun pits along the riverbank. I reported these; somebody might run into them. I didn't do a lot more! I sat there for a couple of hours while all this mess was going on. I couldn't do much! I sat it out until things sounded to have calmed down a bit. I had a cautious look, walked back along the ditch, waded over the little river, and reported my presence.[14]

Trooper Geoff Eason, Recce Troop, HQ Squadron, 2nd F&FY

Eason was awarded the Military Medal for his actions. Meanwhile, Steel Brownlie's Sherman was now in 'point' position, exactly where he liked to be, careening through the streets of Asten.

There were enemy infantry all over the place, so I kept the guns firing and threw grenades out of the turret at random. I never went into action closed down, because the periscopes were inadequate and the only way to know where you were and what was going on was to put your head up over the cupola ring. It was the only way to judge what to do next, rather than blunder about. There was some protection from the two raised cupola lids, but on occasions like this, the trick was to duck up and down, taking a look then shouting something down the intercom, taking another look, and so on. We were issued with steel helmets, but I for one never wore one, as it cramped movement.[15]

Lieutenant William Steel Brownlie, 4 Troop, 'A' Squadron, 2nd F&FY

His gunner, John Buchanan, was worried – to say the least!

We went through this village waiting for an anti-tank gun. I had my gun; the first thing I was going to do was blow the church steeple off, because that's where you get snipers – but I couldn't see, it was that foggy. It was cobbled roads and the driver turned left and went straight up this street – where we should have gone. When we got to our position the tank ran into the ditch

– and that was it – the tank track came off – we were stuck!
'God!' I said, 'Here we are!'[16]

Trooper John Buchanan, 4 Troop, 'A' Squadron, 2nd F&FY

There they were – unable to move. But by chance they were in
the right place to continue playing an active role in the battle,
almost as planned.

In front of us, the road led into this wood, so that gun of
mine stayed on that wood, to make sure any enemy coming
were going to get it. Our idea was to stop any reinforcements
reaching the Germans – so we were in the right position – it
was an orchard. When you're in a tank you don't know what's
behind you; it wasn't until later in the evening I found a Bren
carrier and two other tanks had followed us. We were safe
enough. I thought we were all on our own! I turned the gun
round – searching the area – and I saw these Germans – two
hundred of them – marching across the fields from the canal.
They were going to the bridgehead to relieve or help. I say to
Brownlie, 'Look there!' He says, 'Right, we'll give them an
airburst!' Bounce it in front of them. The shell – it was a perfect
airburst – you've never seen anything like it. One shell, it
bounced above their heads – and every one of them collapsed.
Two hundred: all wounded or dead. Those who could stand
on their feet dived into the hedges. One shell and that was it. I
saved the British government a lot of money there![17]

Trooper John Buchanan, 4 Troop, 'A' Squadron, 2nd F&FY

Not everything was conducted with such a commendable and
rigorous military efficiency, as his next story demonstrates.

Beside this wood was a hut. There was a lot of fluttering going
on in the hut. I say to Brownlie, 'There's somebody in that hut!'
'Well,' he says, 'Brass it up!' I got my machine gun on to it – I
discovered it was a fucking henhouse![18]

Trooper John Buchanan, 4 Troop, 'A' Squadron, 2nd F&FY

There was a further amusing postscript to their breakdown.

> The damage was that the sprocket wheel that held the track
> had sheared off. We had to get the big boys up, the ARV, to
> give us a new sprocket after the battle was over. This sprocket
> was left lying in the orchard. Fifty years later, I went there for
> the celebrations. This woman had our sprocket wheel, painted
> white – and she'd put flowers in it.[19]

Trooper John Buchanan, 4 Troop, 'A' Squadron, 2nd F&FY

Behind 'A' Squadron, 'B' Squadron and the KSLI infantry had
arrived in Asten and soon they had a firm grip on the situation. But it had been a wild morning, long remembered by the
survivors. Afterwards, Steel Brownlie pondered on what had
happened.

> The chief factor, resulting in the crossing of a formidable water
> obstacle and in opening the way to north-east Holland, was
> the boldness of the plan, which had shocked us when we heard
> about it. Who devised it I do not know, but it certainly worked.
> On a much smaller scale obviously it could be compared with
> the main Arnhem thrust, which did not work. In such matters
> there is only a thin line between success and failure. But for
> a few chance circumstances, Arnhem would have worked,
> and only hindsight says otherwise. And if my driver, Jock
> McKinnon, had steered about a foot further left we would have
> hit Don's tank hard, and maybe slewed round and blocked the
> road. What then? The whole squadron trapped? Could be.[20]

Lieutenant William Steel Brownlie, 4 Troop, 'A' Squadron, 2nd F&FY

Truly, the narrowest of margins.

Next day, the 23rd Hussars took up the advance, pressing on
down the road to capture Deurne. The 2nd F&FY remained in
Asten, where they passed under the command of 159th Brigade
for the next phase of operations. In the afternoon of 24 September, they took up the advance from Deurne towards Bakel.

Don Fairweather, a recent arrival in the unit, who hailed from Chalfont St Peter, had had an interesting career as a junior engineer with a building firm on airfield construction work before he was eventually called up in December 1942. Now he was the co-driver in a tank commanded by Lieutenant Roger Gregory. Fairweather had a personal perspective on the reality of a 'divisional advance'.

> You talk about divisions advancing, but then it comes down eventually to regiments advancing, then to squadrons advancing, then to troops advancing, and then you find *you* are the lead tank! You know very well that when you're going down the road, if anybody's waiting, you're going to be the first to cop it! We all had various map references to go to, so you're sweating a bit that you'd get to your map reference before somebody knocked you out. Then the others would come through you! It used to come round quite frequently this lead tank lark! I used to find it quite traumatic.[21]
>
> Trooper Don Fairweather, 'B' Squadron, 2nd F&FY

As they pushed towards Bekel, they were ambushed by Panthers and two of 'C' Squadrons' tanks were knocked out.

> My life was probably saved by a few words! 'Dickie' Leith, who was the squadron commander, ordered 2 Troop to lead towards Deurne. At the last moment he amended that order for 1 Troop to lead! It was a lovely straight road and not a thing moved. One is always suspicious under these circumstances! Anyway 1 Troop went ahead. Well, they were caught out and they lost two or three tanks, including a friend of mine, Cliff Colley.[22] Lamont did the right thing, he immediately directed our troop off the road to the left and we raced across an open field to a big wood. These two tanks – which we think were Panthers – fired on us but they missed us! So we got into the safety of the wood. You can't creep around in a tank, but we crept around in this wood until we got to a position where we could see them

behind a thick hedge. Lamont brought up his 17-pounder, and standing on the engine covers at the back of the turret he directed the 17-pounder and took a couple of shots at these Panthers – and we retreated rather rapidly. We don't know whether he hit, you're not going to wait around! Lamont wasn't that stupid! I think probably one of them was hit. Next morning they'd gone, and we were able to get into Deurne![23]

Trooper Robert Nurse, 2 Troop, 'C' Squadron, 2nd F&FY

Troop commander Lieutenant Eric Lamont had been a management trainee with Woolworths before the war. Now he was considered an excellent officer, good looking, debonair, although a bit ruthless.

On 25 September, they resumed their advance on Bakel. This time 4 Troop of 'C' Squadron was leading, but they took sensible precautions, avoiding the road. However, they still ran into trouble.

We led, but we didn't go down the road, we got over. Somewhere there was a bit of a bridge over this dyke, and we got into this field. We set off and got to this clump of trees. McGrigor twigged a Panther near a house at the outskirts of this village. He reported it, so they fetched the 5.5-inch down on it. We moved forward under the 5.5s, then we were due to come in off a little side road into the village. We poked our nose round the corner on this main road, that we'd rejoined – and got fired on! The thing was in reverse before he had time to tell me! I reversed back, he didn't look to see where we were going, and I couldn't see, so we backed straight into a ditch! We'd got to get out, somebody had to stop and take the firing pin out of the gun. I said, 'That's no worry, Sir, I'll do that!' I was the lance corporal of the crew.[24]

Lance Corporal Harold Wilson, 4 Troop, 'C' Squadron, 2nd F&FY

Later, when the situation became calmer, their tank was recovered. It was found that one of the Panthers had been destroyed by a 5.5-inch shell, while the other had been ditched and abandoned when trying to escape the vengeance of the rest of 'C' Squadron.

Although few of the 2nd F&FY were aware of it, it was already obvious by 21 September that the Arnhem operation had failed. It is usually excused as 'a bridge too far' and bad luck, but it was really the result of over-optimistic planning and a determined German resistance.

A welcome brief rest over the last few days of September followed, spent at the village of St Antonis, close behind the town of Brabant. Then they were withdrawn for a proper rest at Handel, about 10 miles further back to the west, while the American 7th Armoured Division took over the front line along the Maas. During this period one of the 'old hands', Sir John Gilmour, was removed from his command of 'B' Squadron and promoted to second in command of the regiment.

> One's main role was in communication with brigade headquarters. Because the commanding officer was on the regimental net commanding the regiment and as second in command you were in direct contact with brigade headquarters, therefore you were the intermediary as you might say for passing information back and giving any orders or changes of plans to your CO. You were responsible for keeping a tally of casualties and replacements, of vehicles needed and that sort of thing.[25]
>
> Major John Gilmour, Headquarters Squadron, 2nd F&FY

Gilmour was replaced as 'B' Squadron Commander by Captain Peter Loram. A similar fate befell Steel Brownlie on his own well-deserved promotion to captain, as it meant he was moved away from his beloved 4 Troop to the Headquarter Troop of 'A' Squadron,

> Colonel Alec came round just before the gin ran out. I had mixed feelings. Aged 20, I had only recently got my second 'pip'. Maybe the third was for services rendered – after Asten the

Colonel had congratulated me for 'going on through the mass of burning vehicles and saving the day'. On the other hand, it was dead men's shoes. We had had so many casualties; and it meant losing my troop. I would be third in command of the squadron, with only one tank, and a bit of a dogsbody. So be it.[26]

Captain William Steel Brownlie, Headquarters, 'A' Squadron, 2nd F&FY

At the same time Roy Vallance was promoted to sergeant.

At this point it may be worth bringing up a slightly humorous incident fondly remembered by some of the men. This was reputed to have taken place in several locations, sometimes near Deurne, although the regimental history avers it was near Bree in Belgium. Of course, it could have been different incidents, but the essence of the story remains the same.

We thought we were the first unit to put a shell onto German territory. We were on a big farm, with a rather grand-looking farmhouse with all the front covered in little square windows. A very smart-looking place; a very prosperous-looking place. With us we'd got a Firefly, a Sherman tank with a 17-pounder gun, which was rather 'upmarket', better than the 75mm that most had got. Somebody said, 'You know, if we ran that up a bank, maximum elevation, I reckon it would reach about 11 miles!' So they did a bit on the back of an envelope – so to speak – and said, 'Yes, we could do that!' We did this, ran this tank up a bank, maximum elevation, told the civvies to cover their ears and take cover! We were going to fire this shell into Germany! When the shell had been fired, we slunk away with our tails between our legs! Because every window in this farmhouse had disappeared – every one of them blown out clean as a whistle! We crept away! Oh dear, oh dear! Probably still putting the windows back![27]

Trooper Geoff Eason, Recce Troop, HQ Squadron, 2nd F&FY

                              *

WITH THEIR REST OVER ALL TOO SOON, on 7 October
the 2nd F&FY moved back towards the front in support of
the 159th Brigade back in the St Antonis sector. The defeat at
Arnhem had left a stalemate situation, with the British facing a
narrow German bridgehead west of the Maas river that ran from
the north of Belgium across the south-east of the Netherlands.
At first the 2nd F&FY were just helping hold the line, sending
out daily troop patrols forward to Boxmeer and the neighbouring village of Sambeek. Then they were moved to the Overloon
area to support ongoing operations by the 3rd Division, who
for the last few days had been fighting to capture the town of
Venray and eradicate a German pocket. On 15 October, the 2nd
F&FY and the 4th KSLI made an attack through a wooded area
towards the railway line at Smakt, with the intention of distract-
ing attention and drawing German reserves from the main focus
of the attack at Venray. Here John Thorpe came to the end of his
time with the regiment.

> Every day came nearer to the fact that I should die or be
> seriously wounded. I accepted it, there was no getting away
> from it, there was nothing I could do about it; in fact it would
> be a relief to end it all. This day is different, I feel this is my last
> day, I'm really morose, they all tell me, 'Go on with you, it's
> no different than any other time!' But somehow, I know, as a
> matter of fact, I don't tell them but I think I am going to be
> killed! In the late afternoon, we begin to be mortared, I turn
> round in my seat to shout to Cliff that it's getting too close
> and he should close his hatch for a bit, or we shall have one in
> the turret and every one of us will have had it, when one lands
> on Robby's periscope and blows it in, Robby and I are both
> wounded and Robby attempts to scramble over me to climb
> out through my hatch, but I try to reassure him and hold him
> in. Robby's ears are bleeding, besides facial cuts. I was wearing

my headset so that I avoided the concussion to my ears, but my face is opened from my eye to my mouth and I cannot see with that eye; it was as if I had been hit in the face with a red-hot cricket ball. The turret boys get us up in the turret, one at a time, and apply field dressings to both of us. Cliff requests for us to withdraw over the radio, but permission is not granted, we must stay till stand-down. No one else can drive, and when clearance comes Robby has passed out, so I take over and as there is no periscope I open up and drive us back to our start. We are both helped out and taken to the first aid post, examined and both detained to go back for further attention. We are put into a jeep and taken sitting up to Deurne, and from there further still to Helmond where a school room has been converted to a hospital. Gosh, there are female nurses here: fresh, crisp English girls, marvellous to see them, something I've missed without knowing; I could have cried with the joy of it! I was wounded, but not too badly, I would sooner have been able to have stayed with my crew till the end, but it was not to be.[28]

Trooper John Thorpe, 4 Troop, 'C' Squadron, 2nd F&FY

It was indeed the end of his active service. Meanwhile, the regiment were then withdrawn back to laager at St Antonis.

On 17 October, there came a real challenge, as they were sent back to the Deurne sector, from which they were to advance across the marshy ground around Peel to launch an attack on the village of Veulen. The Herefords and the 15/19th Hussars had managed to cross the Deurne Canal to capture Ijsselstein, which was a good start for the 2nd F&FY to build on. The Germans clearly intended to make a stand in the Veulen area, with a plethora of mines and demolition charges laid in and around the village, coupled with infantry, a self-propelled gun, anti-tank guns and panzers in attendance. On 18 October, Major Richard Leith led 'C 'Squadron into the attack. At first, they made good progress, but the German resistance stiffened towards the eastern end of the small village. The Germans counter-attacked and then 'B' Squadron was sent into the fray. Don Fairweather always regretted his actions that day.

> Lieutenant Gregory was my tank commander. We'd got stuck in a ditch and Gregory was instructed to take over another tank, because he was troop leader. He said to us, 'Look, would you blokes like to come with me?' We said, 'No, you go on your own, mate! We'll stay with the tank!' Poor old Gregory got killed.[29] I felt a bit mean about it. We were still in the ditch and we had to get towed out of it.[30]
>
> Trooper Don Fairweather, 'B' Squadron, 2nd F&FY

Trooper Ron Forbes also had a close escape from a self-propelled gun.

> We had to run the gauntlet between two wooded areas. In doing that I was fired on and I had to turn a bit. In doing so I slowed down enough for four or five hits with HE. There was one on the turret ring, which made a dent in it but didn't penetrate, one on the periscope and two on the side. The fifth one hit the gun muzzle and glanced off – it's hard steel and it wouldn't penetrate that. There was a slight mark on the barrel. I was extremely lucky there. If the self-propelled gun had had armour-piercing shells, it would have been a different story. Where the first one hit at the side of the tank was practically where my head was. Having a fairly good close set of earphones you got a sort of shock, but you couldn't say you got noise. If your ears were exposed, it would be quite a 'BANG'. I think I had nine lives like a cat![31]
>
> Trooper Ron Forbes, 4 Troop, 'B' Squadron, 2nd F&FY

Both sides had their successes, with guns and tanks knocked out, but neither could break through. In all the 2nd F&FY lost seven tanks that day. After laagering overnight in the village, next day they moved back out to face the Germans, often at close range. The Germans shelled the area with increasing intensity, deploying both their artillery and the wailing nebelwerfers. The fighting would rage for days on end in this area with no real progress in a landscape that was gradually turned to rubble. It was rumoured that the Germans were fighting 'harder' as they fell back on the Maas, the last river defence line before the Rhine and their homeland. During the whole of this period in the Peel marshes, the static nature of the fighting, the flat terrain and miserable weather acted to wear away at the men's nerves.

> They put us in in the morning, brought us back at night –
> because we were no use at night. So we got plenty of rest. It was
> the mornings! It's like getting up in the morning and you don't
> feel like going to your work! You knew you had to go up and
> relieve the infantrymen who were holding the line. When you
> came back at night there was always one man short, one tank
> short. Every night there was always one tank short! At the back
> of your mind is, 'Who's it going to be today?'[32]
>
> Trooper John Buchanan, 4 Troop, 'A' Squadron, 2nd F&FY

On 23 October, the 2nd F&FY were partially relieved, pulling back to laager up with 'B' and 'C' Squadrons on rest back at Deurne, while the regimental headquarters and 'A' Squadron were acting as brigade reserve, a little further forward at Ijsselstein.

> We went into the village – there was nobody there, no civilians
> there. We found this house with a nice roof on it, the walls had
> been breached a bit. Bert and I thought, 'We'll have a bit of
> comfort!' We decided to have a bed down in this house with
> a roof over our heads. Andy Mathers was asleep in the turret;
> he could sleep in any position. Some hours later, when we'd
> stopped talking and settled down to sleep, these rats appeared –
> climbed all over us! It was a quick rush to get back in the tank.
> Instead of bailing out, we bailed in that time![33]
>
> Trooper Ron Forbes, 4 Troop, 'B' Squadron, 2nd F&FY

Whatever they did, the long winter nights were an uncomfortable ordeal.

> I slept in a dugout, but it became waterlogged in the night. I thought, 'To hell with this!' So I slept in the tank. It was ever so cold – I froze to the tank wall from condensation. Took me ages to get free – ages![34]
>
> Sergeant Jim Thompson-Bell, 'C' Squadron, 2nd F&FY

For the best part of a month, the 2nd F&FY would remain in the area, with a duty squadron stationed forward in or near Veulen in case of emergency, while troop patrols scoured the area. The commander of 'C' Squadron, Major Richard Leith, wrote a pithy description of that time.

> Few will forget our sojourn in the Peel country. Casting one's mind back, the pictures which appear are the never-ending rain and mud, the Bosche night patrols; the shells which landed in Ijsselstein with unfailing regularity, much too near RHQ and other billets for comfort; and the stonks on Dead Horse Corner. Then there were the standing patrols along the log road keeping watch on the area of St Henricus-Hoeve, and St Helena-Hoeve, and the squadron's shoots on Amerika (a small village in enemy-held territory). As to Veulen itself, as the weeks went by it became more and more battle-weary, ultimately becoming wholly repulsive. In Veulen, livestock were constantly setting off trip-wires in the night; the place was littered with rotting apples, dead horses and cattle. The enemy sent over mortars which one couldn't hear going off or coming down, and overall there was an awful stench. While at Veulen we had quite a number of casualties, including Lieutenant O. C. Davies killed.[35] However, our stay in the Peel had its compensations. When we were not in Veulen as duty squadron, we lived well. It was curious how many turkeys, chickens and suckling pigs became injured by shellfire and were still fit for human consumption![36]
>
> Major Richard Leith, Headquarters, 'C' Squadron, 2nd F&FY

Harold Wilson remembered a typical incident from one of these forward Sherman patrols.

> We were static there, holding the ground for quite a while. There was a troop went out every day, up to the front, right up to the infantry lines. To observe with the infantry over towards Venlo. The day my troop went we drove up and parked in an orchard. They 'stonked' us as we went up – and they gave us a good old 'stonking' when we came out! We got parked up and camouflaged in this orchard. My job that day was I went up and spent three or four hours with a lance corporal out of the Shropshire Light Infantry in this slit trench. With a pair of binoculars, just sat there with him and chatted. He was a very old hand. He'd made a slit trench – it was covered to save him against shrapnel anyway! He'd had some board put in, some grass sods at each end and then this place where just one of you could sit and look out! He sat there smoking his pipe and I had a couple of fags. We chatted, by this time we were a proper 'old family', our infantry and tanks! He could see me wince when these here blooming shells came over. He said to me, 'Now, you needn't worry about that – the one that gets you you'll know now't about it – you'll not hear it!' You didn't see a lot. You were looking for these [German] patrols that used to come over. Really, we were watching the river to see that there were no main body crossings.[37]

Lance Corporal Harold Wilson, 4 Troop, 'C' Squadron, 2nd F&FY

Harold Brown, Sir John Gilmour's long-suffering batman, recalled the dishevelled, filthy state Gilmour's uniform would get into after a long patrol.

> Gilmour would go out for maybe three days on patrol or just sitting in a tank for three days. You can imagine what his clothes were like when they came back! I got a telling off from Major Grant – he just happened to come along – as I was washing his shirt using a nail brush on Gilmour's collar with

three days' dirt on it, 'Your mother wouldn't do that!' 'No, she had a scrubbing board!' That was Major Grant for you![38]

Trooper Harold Brown, B Echelon, HQ Squadron, 2nd F&FY

One well-remembered old 'Dundee' face rejoined the regiment at this point: Alex Gilchrist had joined as a trooper back in 1939, had been rapidly promoted to sergeant, and was now an officer! After leaving the 2nd F&FY in 1942, he had attended the Royal Military College, Sandhurst, and been commissioned into the 12th Lancers in May 1943. During a period as adjutant at the Gunnery Training School, Lulworth Camp, in 1944, he requested an active service posting and was sent to Officers' Holding Unit in Brussels that autumn, pending assignment to a unit. Here he had a fortuitous encounter.

I went into an officers' club in Brussels and I saw an officer coming in. I looked at him, 'Christ, that's John Gilmour!' I went over and said, 'Excuse me, Major, do you remember me?' He looked, 'Christ, you're Gilchrist, aren't you? What the hell are you doing here?' I said, 'I'm at the Officers' Holding Unit looking for a regiment!' He said, 'Well don't look any blooming further, I'm over here to get reinforcements!' Within two days I was in the front line up in Holland. Everybody gave me a wonderful reception, right down to the lowest trooper! I never had any problems whatsoever being an officer, although I'd been a trooper, a corporal and a sergeant. Ronnie Forbes, who had been a great friend of mine, became one of my drivers. He accepted it; he always says to me, 'The only reason I wanted you was I knew you could make the best tea in the regiment!'[39]

Lieutenant Alex Gilchrist, 2 Troop, 'B' Squadron, 2nd F&FY

One man who soon made a good impression on Gilchrist was the redoubtable Padre Oswald Welsh.

One of the tanks was hit. It stopped; it didn't go on fire. We knew that the chaps were in the tank, but there was no movement whatsoever. I radioed back to say that this tank had been hit. There was light fire coming down, [the Germans] firing in case the chaps were coming out and trying to escape. Suddenly, a jeep came up behind me and who steps out of it but Oswald Welsh, our padre! He came and spoke to me and said, 'Do you think there are fellows alive in that tank?' I said, 'Well I haven't seen anybody get out!' He walked forward anything up to 200 yards, just with his steel helmet on. He walked right up to that tank. As soon as he got near, the firing that had been going on stopped completely. Now I'm not a religious man at all, but to me, as he approached that tank there was like a halo round his head – whether it was tears in my eyes I don't know! He climbed on to the tank, opened the hatch, and helped out the three men that were inside. He then went round the front and helped out the driver and co-driver. Not a shot fired at all. He walked back with these men past my tank. I won't forget it as long as I live. To me Oswald Welsh was an absolute hero.[40]

Lieutenant Alex Gilchrist, 2 Troop, 'B' Squadron, 2nd F&FY

During this period, another new officer arrived to join the regiment. Thomas Heald was born the son of a chemist and lived in Byfleet and Northwood before attending the Merchant Taylors' School, where he trained with the OTC and even served with the Home Guard based at his school. He attended Oxford University in 1942 before moving on to Sandhurst in 1943. After a brief period with the Sherwood Rangers Yeomanry, he was posted to 2 Troop, 'A' Squadron, a three-strong Sherman troop. As a young and unproven officer, it was inevitable that the older, more experienced, and hence exhausted officers would foist things upon him. Occasionally, the squadrons were required to send out foot patrols. There are no prizes for guessing who was given this task for 'A' Squadron!

The first day, the squadron was required to send out a patrol: one officer and six men on foot. Being the new officer, I was

delegated this duty. Our task was to go about half a mile in front
of our lines to a trench beside the road to Amerika, and report
back every hour by field telephone as to what was happening.
Very near a village called Veulen. We spent the night there,
two hours on, two hours off, as it were. A certain amount of
machine-gun fire, probably trigger-happy men on our own
side. Every hour the field telephone rang if we didn't ring them
beforehand! Eventually, at about 5 o'clock, a cold, rather foggy
morning, there was the sound of what appeared to be marching
feet down this road! It did occur to me that the Germans
weren't likely to be marching down the track! Also, I would
be rather surprised if the British were marching! Anyway, we
gave them the benefit of the doubt and thought there must be a
patrol out which we didn't know about! We were just about to
open fire when in came a herd of cows coming in to be milked –
on their own volition! That was my first bit of action![41]

Lieutenant Thomas Heald, 2 Troop, 'A' Squadron 2nd F&FY

These infantry patrols were well outside the comfort zone of
any of the tank men. Harold Wilson certainly found it a tense
and scary business when he was sent out on one in similar
circumstances.

One night they dragged eight or nine of us out us out to go on
an infantry patrol. Now this was an experience! Mind you, I'll
tell you what, we didn't treat it as a joke at all! We went out, but
it wasn't a bad night. It was semi-cloudy, but it was moonlight,
so there were times when it was fairly light. We must have
crept maybe's half an hour. We had Sten guns and revolvers. It
was just to give us something to do! Maybe's to warn us, keep
us aware of what happens. We went so far out there, and we
squatted, just sat round there to see if we could find out what
was going off. True enough, we saw a German patrol on our
side. As the moon came up you could see the silhouettes of
them! They were crouched. We were right down on the 'deck'

looking up a bit. They weren't that far away; you could hear them talking – low murmuring. We saw it go up past us towards our lines – and we saw it come back. I talked to infantrymen afterwards and they said, 'That goes on all the time, where we get through their lines – and they get through ours! A lot of times they either just come and plant mines, especially – if they can under tanks – or anti-personnel mines. Or they just come to find out what there is and where they are. In a lot of cases, you don't stick your neck out!'[42]

Lance Corporal Harold Wilson, 4 Troop, 'C' Squadron, 2nd F&FY

On 19 November, the whole regiment were concentrated at Deurne, in preparation for Operation Nutcracker, which was intended to eliminate the 'Venlo Pocket' occupied by the Germans. The 2nd F&FY were intended to support the 1st Herefords in their attack on the village of Amerika. However, a thorough reconnaissance showed that the ground was far too muddy for the tanks, while the roads had been smashed up by artillery and demolitions – and hence the infantry had to attack alone as the 2nd F&FY returned to Deurne.

At Deurne, the regiment were given a rest and spent the time on running a crew commanders' course for all the recently joined officers and NCOs, utilising the chance to study what had actually happened on the former battlefields that surrounded their billets. They then moved even further back to Helmond, where they had some excellent news. The 2nd F&FY were to be the first to be equipped with the brand-new Comet tanks – a British tank in contrast to the American Sherman they had been used to. While resting, the regiment underwent some familiarisation training on the Cromwell tank, in preparation for their imminent conversion to the similar but far more up-to-date Comet. The drivers enjoyed the chance of driving the Cromwells on the nearby Valkensward Heath, while the drivers and gunners were also introduced to the British BESA machine gun. Some of the NCOs were even sent back to the Bovington Royal Armoured

Corps Depot for a detailed course in the new tank. In the meantime, many of the Shermans were sent off to Brussels by tank transporters.

Captain Steel Brownlie seems to have kept himself busy as well, as John Buchanan hints that he wasn't only interested in chasing Germans.

> Brownlie was all right. As long as he got scooting about at night in his armoured car or scout car – chasing up the girls he was quite happy! He was a ladies' man. He made a lot of lady 'friends' in Holland while we were there.[43]
>
> Trooper John Buchanan, 4 Troop, 'A' Squadron, 2nd F&FY

After a pleasant couple of weeks, the regiment were delighted to hear they would be spending Christmas and New Year re-equipping with the Comet back in Belgium. They arrived at Ypres on 14 December, moving into generally comfortable billets in the town, which had been completely rebuilt after being reduced to rubble in the Great War. The last of the Shermans and Fireflies were surrendered with scant ceremony.

> You just handed your tank in, got into trucks, and went back to Ypres. In wartime you didn't have really much sentiment with equipment. You just handed the thing in and hoped that you would get something better – that's all![44]
>
> Trooper Ron Forbes, 4 Troop, 'B' Squadron, 2nd F&FY

Many of the men were intrigued by their first glimpses of the new Comets, but few of them had the chance to get seriously acquainted, as there were only a few available at that time.

One tragedy afflicted the regiment, when it was decided to allow selected leave parties to go back to Brussels. Alex Gilchrist was placed in charge of the party on 16 December.

> The adjutant decided that some of the chaps, including Geoff Hayward, had been having a very rough time of it; he decided that they should go back to Antwerp for a few days' rest. He

sent me back with a troop of about twenty men in 3-tonners. A few of the chaps, all other ranks, went to the Rex Cinema. I didn't go. I decided to go to the zoo.[45]

Lieutenant Alex Gilchrist, 2 Troop, 'B' Squadron, 2nd F&FY

Geoff Hayward was another who decided not to go to the cinema that afternoon. He, too, was lucky.

I had my first local leave down to Antwerp. They were arranging short 36-hour passes. We'd arrived by truck, were put up in this hotel and we were allowed to wander about, do what we like! The Germans had started firing V2s at Antwerp. We could hear occasional thuds as these things landed. The next day some of them had decided to go to the Rex Cinema, which was not far away. I'd chosen not to go to the cinema, I'd chosen to wander around the town and see the sites. I went down to the riverside and saw this old Het Steen fort down there. I'd come back to the hotel. It must have been late afternoon. We'd left our bedrooms, got our kit out. We were told to form up in the corridor on the upper floor. Just as we were formed up there was this almighty, 'THUD!' and we heard all the glass in the windows tinkling down inside, blown out with the blast.[46]

Trooper Geoff Hayward, MT Section, HQ Squadron, 2nd F&FY

The V2 rocket had fired from a base in the Netherlands and crashed down on the roof of the Cinema Rex at 15.23. Inside were approximately 1,200 people watching a matinee performance of the cowboy film *The Plainsman*. It killed 567 people and a further 296 were injured. In consequence of this utter disaster, a limit was introduced of only 50 people to be allowed to gather in the same place in future in Antwerp.

As Alex Gilchrist returned from his visit to the Antwerp Zoo, he heard the terrible news.

As I was coming back, I was told a V2 had landed on the Rex and there were literally hundreds of casualties. I was absolutely shaken. Four men didn't turn up – one of them was Bill Tyrie[47] – a great friend of mine from Dundee, who I had known before the war. Poor old Bill had been killed. We were all shaken rigid.[48]

Lieutenant Alex Gilchrist, 2 Troop, 'B' Squadron, 2nd F&FY

Geoff Hayward was certainly shocked. He suddenly gained an appreciation of what civilians 'back home' had to go through.

We were most anxious to leave Antwerp. We thought that of the two, being in the front line in Holland was preferable to being in Antwerp when those rockets were about! I am sure the people of London at that time felt the same. We were glad to get into that truck and away. It was only later that we heard news of what had happened in that cinema. [49]

Trooper Geoff Hayward, MT Section, HQ Squadron, 2nd F&FY

After such a crushing blow it is pleasant to be able to report that Hayward's luck improved markedly once he got back to Ypres, which seemed like a haven of peace and tranquillity compared to the evident perils of life in Antwerp.

For the first time in the campaign, we were actually sleeping in houses. The billet I had was a bedroom over a wine shop in one of the main streets of Ypres leading down into the market square where the Cloth Hall is. The couple who ran this wine shop were not particularly friendly. I found out later they were regarded as collaborators! All the time we were in that wine shop billet, we didn't get a drink of wine! I was in this billet with a chap called Willie Peyton, who was the squadron armourer. Quite a character, a very short Scottish chap! His main object in life was 'entertainment'! It was a very cold winter. Willie Peyton said, 'I've already found a friendly home to go to in the evenings after duties; why don't you look around for somewhere?' Our lorries were parked at the edge of a park in front of the station. There was a little parade of shops near this park – and it was in one of these shops that my future wife was serving. We used to go in there for our morning break, one of the lads said to me, 'Why don't you have a chat with that young lady and see if you can worm your way in there!' I was a bit bashful but, in the end, I came up with, 'Would you like to learn English?' She was a bit taken aback but said she would! Her father was very suspicious of this initial relationship, because he'd been a Great War veteran and served in the trenches in the Belgian Army, but he suffered it – and I was able to gain entry to the house in the evenings.[50]

Trooper Geoff Hayward, MT Section, HQ Squadron, 2nd F&FY

He would be engaged to his Mary on 18 February 1945. Their marriage would be long and happy.

15

ARDENNES INTERRUPTION

A chap in a tank that was knocked out, came up on the air,
saying he'd lost his leg and the rest of the crew had gone –
they'd been captured. Asking what he should do – and for help.
He was keeping quiet inside the tank. I think he actually died
there. They couldn't go and get him.[1]

Sergeant Roy Vallance, 4 Troop, 'A' Squadron, 2nd F&FY

CHRISTMAS WAS COMING and the men of the 2nd F&FY
were intent on enjoying the festive season ensconced in comfortable billets in Ypres. For the Scots among them, the siren
call of the New Year's Eve was beckoning. After all they had
endured, this was going to be a time to remember, even in the
middle of a world war. But the Germans had other plans, intent
on spoiling everyone's festivities. The Allied offensive had been
effectively stalled since October, and the Germans had used this
breathing space to reorganise and amass an intimidating force
with the specific objective of launching a concerted offensive to
disrupt the already fragile American and British supply routes.
Over 400,000 men, 4,000 guns and 500 tanks were assembled covertly, with bad weather concealing troop movements
from the Allied reconnaissance aircraft. On 16 December, the
German Army Group B (Fifth, Sixth and Seventh Armies)
were unleashed in a devastating surprise attack on the American First Army in the wooded Ardennes area. They intended to

smash their way – via Dinant and Brussels – all the way through to Antwerp. The Germans broke through and for a while the situation was critical as the Americans had few reserves in the Ardennes sector. However, isolated American units fought some brave rearguard actions, holding on to key points and carrying out demolitions to slow the German headway as far as possible. At first this 'Battle of the Bulge' seemed irrelevant to the 2nd F&FY, but on 20 December Colonel Alec Scott was called to a 29th Armoured Brigade briefing. They were all to move to the east as quickly as possible in order to stop the Germans crossing the Meuse river and threatening Antwerp. This caught many of the regiment by surprise.

> We had organised 'A' Squadron dance and the following morning there were a good many hangovers! I'd been to the dance and certainly I had a hangover! Then we got the warning order that the Germans had broken through in the Ardennes and we were to stand by to go back, pick up our old tanks in Brussels and get down to the Ardennes.[2]
>
> Major Douglas Hutchison, 'A' Squadron, 2nd F&FY

Hungover or not, an advance party was immediately dispatched to Brussels to locate billets and to find out which tanks they were to be equipped with – and exactly where they were to be picked up.

> Bombshell. We were to move to the Ardennes soonest. Forget the Comets, leave all heavy kit behind, pick up our old Shermans in Brussels, get to the Meuse and help stop von Rundstedt. Advance party to leave at 13.30, self for 'A' Squadron, Jimmy for 'B' Squadron who were short of officers, in scout cars. Cup of coffee in Aalst, Brussels in turmoil, population very scared. We laid out areas for billets, there being no time for details, and I was sent as regimental guide to a point in the suburbs where our column of trucks was expected. They

were late, it was cold and pouring with rain, V1s were passing overhead, very depressing.[3]

Captain William Steel Brownlie, Headquarters, 'A' Squadron, 2nd F&FY

They were followed that afternoon by the mass of Sherman crews, all heading for the Laeken Reinforcement Tank Park. Here there were row after row of Shermans in various states of repair. Many searched for their old tanks, which they had handed in just days before, as they had been 'customised' to their own specific taste. Ron Forbes was fortunate enough to find his old 'steed'.

When we went back to Brussels to pick up the Sherman, Bert Moir and I, we said, 'Right boys, we'll see if we can get "Annsmuir" back!' Lucky enough, when we got into the big tank park, we managed to get hold of Annsmuir, a 17-pounder! It was snowing a lot. We got white paint and painted the tanks white. And we had these winter tank suits, insulated material, which were very good.[4]

Trooper Ron Forbes, 4 Troop, 'B' Squadron, 2nd F&FY

These tank suits were much appreciated, given the appalling weather.

Before we had the 'zoot' suit, we just had our normal battledress blouse and trousers. When it got cold you put a pullover underneath the blouse. Some people had balaclavas that were sent from home. 'Zoot' suits were a type of heavy cotton, the lining was khaki, a sort of flannelette type thing – and they used to keep the cold out.[5]

Sergeant Jim Thompson-Bell, 'C' Squadron, 2nd F&FY

Not all the Shermans and Fireflies were 'ready for action' and the men spent a day selecting, checking and carrying out minor modifications or repairs to their selected tanks. By 10.00 on 21 December, eight tanks from 'C' Squadron and five from 'B' Squadron were ready for action and set off for Namur. Within a few more hours the rest of the regiment followed. This rapid mobilisation was a substantial achievement, but it was just a small part of a much larger response. On arrival, they found they were to be part of the hastily thrown together 'R' Force, with several assorted infantry units, sappers and an anti-aircraft unit. Their role was simple: 'They shall not pass the Meuse!'

> First light we went through the town and over the Meuse bridge, which was wired for demolition and defended by a scratch force collected from all kinds of units, looking nervous and checking everyone's papers. There were latrine rumours about German parachutists disguised in captured American uniforms, but our main worry was that some bloody fool would blow the bridges with us on the far side. We motored on a few miles to Erpent and deployed in defensive positions on high ground. All we knew was that the situation was 'fluid', so that an enemy thrust could come our way. This was welcome in a way, for we were camouflaged with a good field of fire, quite the opposite of the situation in Normandy. But nothing came![6]
>
> Captain William Steel Brownlie, Headquarters, 'A' Squadron, 2nd F&FY

'A' Squadron crossed the river and climbed the high ground around Erpent to the Andoy Ridge to try and block any approach from Liège, while 'C' Squadron covered the various Meuse bridges, and 'B' Squadron was held in reserve, ready to leap into action as required.

> The whole of the battle area up till about Christmas was in a dense fog, and the Germans had taken full advantage of that, because of course the one thing we had command of was the air! We couldn't use it. Our role was to go forward a few miles onto the Andoy Ridge with a very good view of the main approach road – no infantry with us – just tanks. Every morning we were out there by first light and then we came back into Namur at dark. We never saw any Germans there.[7]
>
> Major Douglas Hutchison, 'A' Squadron, 2nd F&FY

For a while, the situation was extremely tense. As reports came in, fevered calculations were made to try and plot the German movements as best they could on their maps. On Christmas Day, instead of celebrating in comfort in Ypres, the 2nd F&FY were replaced by the Welsh Guards at Namur and ordered south along the Meuse to the Dinant crossings, which seemed to be where the Germans were heading. Ice and snow made the journey a challenge.

> I was leading the squadron. I had a balaclava on – and it was absolutely freezing. I had my head out of the tank the whole time, driving all that way. When I got down to Dinant, I tried to report back to the colonel – and I found I couldn't speak! The air had frozen my nose to my lip underneath my balaclava![8]
>
> Lieutenant Alex Gilchrist, 2 Troop, 'B' Squadron, 2nd F&FY

On arrival, they discovered a strong force of American tanks already *in situ*, so they fell back a little to a bare ridge and glumly waited for their next orders. Most had to make do with nothing for their Christmas dinner but a cheese sandwich and a mug of tea. Ron Forbes was one of the fortunate few to benefit from some unexpected American largesse.

> We were out in the open and there was a little spotter plane. It came round in circles and it was obviously observing us. It landed in a field and this American came out looking like some gangster: he had a soft hat on, a fedora, a leather jacket and a cigar in his mouth. He came across and he shouted, 'Have you guys had any Christmas dinner?' We said, 'No!' He said, 'All right!' He went back to his plane and he took off. A while later four trucks came up with these insulated hot [containers] in the back. We went up with our mess tins and we got a little bit of turkey – it was very nice! This was American hospitality.[9]
>
> Trooper Ron Forbes, 4 Troop, 'B' Squadron, 2nd F&FY

The American resistance had dissipated all the German

momentum as the offensive ground to a halt. Periods of improved flying weather meant that the Allied air forces could attack the German columns and devastate supply depots, railways and roads. As a result, fuel shortages halted the progress of the 2nd Panzer Division which had got closest to reaching the Meuse. Hitler's last gasp gamble was falling apart at the seams.

Next day, the 2nd F&FY moved forward through Dinant to act as the brigade reserve in the Falmagne area. Between the heavy snow falls and icy roads it was another difficult journey.

> The ice – the tanks were swivelling all over the road, and off the road, tracks were coming off – it was a horrible journey. A matter of driving with extreme care! Instructing your driver, 'For God's sake ease up a bit!' If you lost control – you lost control! Once the tracks started sliding you couldn't do a thing about it. You had to just let it go! Before you knew where you were, you were on your side in a ditch.[10]
>
> Lieutenant Alex Gilchrist, 2 Troop, 'B' Squadron, 2nd F&FY

Here, on 27 December, they had some minor contacts with the Germans, with the Recce Troop excelling itself in taking eight prisoners from the 2nd Panzer Division, of which three proved to be officers – a valuable haul. The Germans were clearly in the vicinity, but a search next day to the north of the Lesse river failed to make contact. On 30 December, the Americans began a counter-attack on the German salient pressing in from the south. Meanwhile Montgomery was preparing a thrust from the north, timed to begin on 3 January 1945.

There was no New Year's Eve for the Scots in the regiment as they moved forward via Chanly to the village of Resteigne, which they reached on 2 January during a snowstorm that for a while reduced visibility from the tanks to almost nothing. Over a foot of snow descended, and once again they found themselves at risk of sliding all over the road.

We got to Resteigne, it was getting dark – after all it was January, so it got dark at about 4 o'clock. I was asked to recce a track up to the top of a feature called Chapel Hill, to see whether it was passable by a tank. The three tanks in my troop went up about half or three quarters of a mile up this track. It seemed perfectly passable. We came to a spot where we could turn round, and we were ordered to turn round and come back down to Resteigne for the night. It was very rare for tanks to spend a night 'out' unless they've got infantry support. And we had no infantry support at the time.[11]

Lieutenant Thomas Heald, 2 Troop, 'A' Squadron, 2nd F&FY

They parked overnight by the first house in Resteigne. Next morning the freezing cold had its impact on Heald's Sherman.

When we wanted to start it again, the tank wouldn't start. The starter motor had packed up. One would have thought a starter motor was a simple thing, but the way we had collected the tank, we hadn't got proper spares in the squadron – and they had no spare starter motor. The result was that my tank was out of action for the next day. Which as it turned out was a bit of good luck, because I would undoubtedly have been the leading troop the next day, and we had four tanks out of twelve in the squadron knocked out next day. They split up the other two tanks into the other troops. At the time I was furious that there was no other tank for me![12]

Lieutenant Thomas Heald, 2 Troop, 'A' Squadron, 2nd F&FY

On 3 January, 'A' Squadron moved forward to take the village of Bure. This was part of the Montgomery counter-attack to be conducted by XXX Corps, whereby the 6th Airborne Division, the 29th Armoured Brigade and the 34th Tank Brigade would launch their assault from a general concentration area to the east of Givet. On Chapel Hill, the 2nd F&FY would be acting in conjunction with the 7th and 13th Parachute Battalions of the 6th Airborne Division. Under the plan, 'A' Squadron was to take Chapel Hill, some 1,000 feet high, and then give fire support as the 13th Parachute Battalion put in an attack on Bure, 'C' Squadron would take over when Bure fell, while 'B' Squadron would support the 7th Parachute Battalion in attack on the village of Wavreille a couple of miles due north of Bure. As 'A' Squadron crossed the ridge just south of Chapel Hill, they came under fire and lost one tank immediately.

We were going up into some huge, forested hills, covered in snow. On one which we called Chapel Hill, because there was a little chapel some way up on the side, there was a German SP gun beside the chapel and the tank next to me fired at it, missed and it left a neat round hole in the chapel wall! If I remember rightly, Corporal Finlay, his tank got the SP. On the opposite slope to us, about a mile from us, we fired on some Shermans which were firing at us – they had captured them from the Americans, and they had black crosses painted roughly on. It seemed very strange! I brewed one up! I watched the trace of the shot all the way. Which was a change![13]

Sergeant Roy Vallance, 4 Troop, 'A' Squadron, 2nd F&FY

It was a good day for John Buchanan.

We were sent to chase them up Chapel Hill. We were sent along the top of the ridge. There was a big valley, it swept to the other side of the hill. You could look across; the Germans were at one side of this valley on the hill and we were at the other side. The snow was very thick. I saw these two German tanks – they were Mark IVs – we knocked them out. Just belted at them, kept hitting them at the side as they were running across away from us – until they stopped! Armour-piercing, it went straight in. The smoke came out of them. I got credited with the two.[14]

Trooper John Buchanan, 4 Troop, 'A' Squadron, 2nd F&FY

Various delays meant that the crest of Chapel Hill was not cleared until 12.00, at which point 'A' Squadron poured fire into

Bure as the paratroopers charged forward, meeting a very strong resistance.

Throughout this period, German self-propelled guns proved a real threat. George Davidson, usually known as 'Dod', remembered being ambushed by one in the approach to Wavreille.

> We moved off to the top of this hill to go down to the village down in the valley. The Airborne is supposed to be coming down one side, we were going down this side. I was driving with Lieutenant Hale. We just got down the bottom of the hill and the tank in front of us stopped, that had been hit. I was watching through the periscope, the crew jumping out, to see they were all safe, you see. Geoff Hale said, 'All right, "Dod", drive on!' I put my foot down on the pedal, nothing happened! I looked around at the dials, no needles flickering! All of a sudden, 'BAIL OUT! BAIL OUT!' We'd been hit! I never felt it. It went through the engine doors at the back. That one brewed up. Anyway we all got out and got back. The only casualty was the wireless operator from the tank in front of us – he hurt his ankle as he jumped down from the tank! There were some trees up on the top of the hill and there's been a German SP tank stationed. That had let us go past and shot us through the engine doors.[15]
>
> Trooper George Davidson, 'B' Squadron, 2nd F&FY

Ron Forbes was also involved in a 'duel' that had unexpected consequences as their 17-pounder let rip at a German self-propelled gun.

> We were up on a slope, tucked in under the eaves of a house. When this SP came out of the woods, we fired on it. In firing the flash and the explosion of the gun going off – all the slates fell off the sloping roof and we were covered in slates! We missed it and it disappeared – withdrew quickly. We had to get out gingerly and clear the slates off – we couldn't traverse the turret or anything![16]
>
> Trooper Ron Forbes, 4 Troop, 'B' Squadron, 2nd F&FY

Meanwhile, the fighting raged on in Bure. As 'C' Squadron moved into Bure, the weather again degenerated into a series of blizzards that reduced visibility to almost nothing – a 'white out'. One tank was lost to a mine, then another to an AP round from an unknown origin. When night fell, the parachutists had only about a third of the village and it was decided that one troop of tanks would have to stay with them to give them close support, while the rest of 'C' Squadron moved back a couple of miles to laager overnight in Tellin. The supply lorries had great trouble getting through.

> We had to slither, rather than drive, over these icy roads, following this column led by a sergeant from Falmignoul to the village of Bure, where we could hear gunfire in the darkness. As we got down into the village the shelling started, and I and the petrol truck driver both jumped out of our vehicles, because we sensed that there were things landing close. The nearest shelter we could find was crouched down behind a garden wall, between the house and the wall in the garden, until the shelling stopped. Then we got back in our vehicles and did whatever we had to do in the way of supply. As we were getting back into the lorries this other chappie said he'd got a pain in his back. When I looked, I could see his clothing had been ripped. He managed to drive back, but he got whisked away; he'd got shrapnel in his back – I was right next to him and I'd escaped.[17]
>
> Trooper Geoff Hayward, MT Section, HQ Squadron, 2nd F&FY

On the morning of 4 January, the Germans accurately targeted the remaining 'C' Squadron tanks left behind in Bure, knocking out all three. A further troop was dispatched forward, but one of these was also promptly 'brewed up'. A stalemate had developed, with both sides pouring in shells, but neither able to get any further forward. There were numerous close escapes, but somehow, despite the shells exploding all around the squadron, there were few casualties. After a day that seemed to last for ever, the squadron was withdrawn at night to laager back in Tellin. One of the luckiest men in the regiment was Robert Nurse, who had missed the earlier fighting as he had been dispatched to collect rations. On rejoining his tank, he found the man who had replaced him, Trooper Leslie Lines, had been killed.

> I found Lamont and was told where the tank was. Got into the tank – with one of those peculiar-shaped American torches – and it was covered in blood. I had been replaced by another guy called Trooper Les Lines.[18] He had an 88mm shell go through just above the periscope – and it had just taken his head off. Again, I was extremely lucky.[19]
>
> Trooper Robert Nurse, 2 Troop, 'C' Squadron, 2nd F&FY

Throughout this period, 'A' Squadron and the regimental headquarters had remained up on Chapel Hill, providing the fire support which was crucial to any successful defence of – or attack on – Bure. Up on a 1,000-foot snow-covered hilltop, they also suffered. It was absolutely freezing and as lorries couldn't get up the hill, their supplies had to be dragged by hand up to the top.

> With darkness we harboured near the chapel, which was in ruins. A body lay in the brushwood, apparently the commander of the SP. We sat and ate in the tank. There was no wind, no more snow, but it grew colder and colder. The ground was too hard for digging, so we decided to sleep in the tank. Jock McKinnon (driver) and MacKenzie (co-driver) in their seats down front; 'Buck' Buchanan (gunner) on the deck below the gun, Norman Ingram (operator) on top of the gun, self on the floor with feet in one sponson and head in the other. Sleep? Within minutes the icy cold of the metal seeped through your clothing, and the breath froze on your lips. I lit a candle in a tin lid, and a fat lot of good it did![20]
>
> Captain William Steel Brownlie, Headquarters, 'A' Squadron, 2nd F&FY

It says something for the British soldier that Roy Vallance was perhaps typical in finding the worst thing over the period was the difficulty in maintaining a steady supply of hot tea!

On 5 January, they were relieved by the 23rd Hussars and moved back in convoy to Wellin, behind Resteigne. On the way at least one convoy was shot up by some American fighters, as John Buchanan recalls.

> We were winding our way through the countryside. We were dive-bombed by American planes! The Americans said it was Germans, but we say it was American planes. One of our boys was killed. The tanks were all nose to tail and I was the lead tank. I said to my driver, my officer had gone somewhere, I says, 'Let's get out of here!' We were trapped with this wood on one side, hills on the other! I landed in a field. One tank in a field and the planes came for me! I was trying to hide underneath the engine, inside the tank. I said to Norman, 'Can you get her out?' He said, 'No!' He was underneath the gun! Mackenzie, the co-driver, he was outside with the Bren gun, trying to shoot them![21]
>
> Trooper John Buchanan, 4 Troop, 'A' Squadron, 2nd F&FY

They would remain in a reserve role in Wellin for a week, which, as the weather improved, allowed the men to relax a little.

The German offensive had by this time run out of steam. The improved weather left the Germans wide open to air attack, and although the Americans occasionally made their much-criticised mistakes in targeting, they were also capable of harassing the Germans to distraction. The 2nd F&FY were not required for the counter-attacks and it is said that in the days that followed, the Recce Troop even found time for a spot of boar hunting in the woods! Then, at last, came the news they had been hoping for: they were to be once more pulled out of action, dump the Shermans and then resume their delayed training on the new Comets at Ypres. For them, the Battle for the Bulge was over, although the Americans would continue fighting hard until the end of January, by which time they had eradicated the 'Bulge' and the Germans were back where they had started. It was one more nail in the German coffin.

*

IT SEEMS STRANGE THAT BRITISH SOLDIERS would ever rejoice at the idea of a return to Ypres after their suffering and torments there throughout the Great War just twenty years before. Yet in January 1945 it offered a safe harbour, far from the ever-present strain of life in the front line of battle. Once the Shermans had been returned to the Brussels tank park, the crews moved back into billets in Ypres, where they faced a mild disappointment.

> We got back to Ypres and we discovered that our Christmas fare, which had been locked up, had been stolen by the locals. Nobody was offended, because they were starving people. Good for them! The CO called up the Royal Army Service Corps and they sent up another load of Christmas stuff. So, we had our Christmas dinner on 25 January! Traditionally the officers serve the men.[22]
>
> Trooper Ron Forbes, 4 Troop, 'B' Squadron, 2nd F&FY

The belated Christmas festivities seem to have been enjoyed by all concerned.

> Next day it was visits from one mess to another, then the officers and sergeants converged on the men's cookhouse to serve them their festive meal, a well-established army tradition. We were surprised to be met by the whole regiment of other ranks, armed with snowballs. There was quite a battle. In the dining hall, which was so small that normally there had to be two sittings, all were crammed in, and we had to walk on the tables to get the piled plates to those furthest away. It was not

elegant, but it was a successful regimental occasion. I could write a slim volume about our spell in Ypres, the reputable and disreputable liaisons, the parties, the brief leave I enjoyed in Paris, and other non-military matters. Better not![23]

Captain William Steel Brownlie, Headquarters, 'A' Squadron, 2nd F&FY

Most of the men were made welcome as they moved into their billets in Ypres; some more welcome than others!

I was billeted on an elderly couple with a daughter of 25, who took to me! One of the things in my life I had to keep quiet about! When I was taken ill, I had flu, for two or three days in bed, she used to bring me up food. No heating in the house – absolutely freezing cold – and she'd pop into bed with me and keep me warm! She knew I was married! She was a nice woman, church every week – but she hadn't got a man – that was it and I filled in the breach for her![24]

Sergeant George Cozens, HQ Squadron, 2nd F&FY

They were young men, in the prime of life, all too aware that they might be dead in a matter of weeks. The hunt for beer, women and sex was of paramount importance to them.

Bob Haynes and I, we found a little estaminet to enjoy our evenings. There were two girls there – Rachel and Mariette. They wanted to learn ballroom dancing – and that was Bob's thing – he was a trombone player in a dance band – and he was an excellent dancer. So, we used to go round there every night. It had a nice big place where there'd been a lounge, but the Germans took away a lot of their furniture. It was empty – plenty of space to dance in. They managed to get drinks from somewhere, Belgian beer – a slightly bitter lager tasting stuff. Not to my taste, but if you drank enough of it you would get some effect![25]

Trooper Ron Forbes, 4 Troop, 'B' Squadron, 2nd F&FY

While they were at Ypres, Charlie Workman rejoined them, having recovered from his wounds suffered in late July. He soon fitted back into his troop. He was given helpful advice on the thorny question of romance by – of all people – his driver.

> You live with them all the time; you knew them all. My driver, Hutchinson, always used to say to me, 'Have you got a woman yet?' I would say, 'Not yet, Hutchinson!' 'Well, if you come down to the pub with me, I'll get you a woman!' I'd say, 'Hutchinson, I've seen your woman, I want a woman that looks like a woman!' 'Oh, you can't be too fussy!'[26]
>
> Second Lieutenant Charlie Workman, 1 Troop, 'C' Squadron, 2nd F&FY

Hutchinson was clearly a bit of a character and Workman, at the grand old age of 24, had to stand in *loco parentis* to his amorous driver when he became overly involved with a Belgian woman.

> A lot of them spoke excellent English – we got on terribly well with them. In fact, one or two of our people married them. Hutchinson came up to me and said he wanted to marry a Belgian girl. I said, 'But Hutchinson, you don't speak English let alone bloody Walloon! You're not marrying any Belgian girl!' He said, 'Ohhhh!' He was a great romantic![27]
>
> Second Lieutenant Charlie Workman, 1 Troop, 'C' Squadron, 2nd F&FY

Overall, the men became very friendly with the locals, trying to help them wherever they could. They were well aware of the privations the Belgian civilians had suffered under the lengthy German occupation.

Workman was also well aware of the grim history of the British Army in Ypres, which had resulted in there being tens of thousands of soldiers with no known grave. These were commemorated on the magnificent imposing structure of the Menin Gate, which guarded the road along which so many men had tramped to their deaths on the low Passchendaele ridges.

We mounted a quarter guard on the Menin Gate. We were shown round some of the trenches that they keep – and I must say it made my blood run cold. We had been right through Normandy, but the idea of these chaps in the First World War, spent month, after month, after month, being shelled. Just sat facing each other. The conditions that they had. It made my blood run cold.[28]

Second Lieutenant Charlie Workman, 1 Troop, 'C' Squadron, 2nd F&FY

Doug Hayes found the weight of the past weighed down on him when he was on sentry duty.

Ypres was an eerie place at night if you did a guard there. The background noise could be very quiet in a Belgian town in the middle of the night. It was almost like ghosts from the past – the amount of men that were lost there. I had a very imaginative mind. Everything echoed. There were patrolling guards all over Ypres. A click of a foot. If somebody the other side of town put one 'up the spout' you would here the click of the bolt echoing through the night! It was eerie.[29]

Trooper Doug Hayes, MT Section, 'A' Squadron, 2nd F&FY

*

THE NEW COMET TANKS ARRIVED and created a good initial impression on officers, NCOs and men. They were a vast step up on the Sherman. It gave them a confidence that they had lost in the Sherman.

It was a 'proper' tank. I loved the Comet tank – from the day I first saw one I fell in love with it. I thought it had everything that I was expecting in a tank. From the moment I got into it, I felt more confident. I had something around me I could trust.[30]

Lieutenant Alex Gilchrist, 2 Troop, 'B' Squadron, 2nd F&FY

Charlie Workman was another admirer of the Comet.

Very favourable: the Comet was a lower lying, more compact
tank than the Sherman; it had a Rolls Royce engine, faster, with
a bigger gun – the 77mm. It was armoured reasonably well. It
hadn't quite the space inside it that the Sherman had, but the
ammunition was much better protected. It had a heavy lid over
the bin where the shells were kept.[31]

Second Lieutenant Charlie Workman, 1 Troop, 'C' Squadron, 2nd F&FY

Driver Ron Forbes certainly appreciated the extra engine power,
amid the whole 'package' of improvements on the Sherman.

The Comet was a revelation to us. The speed was something we
enjoyed – the acceleration was terrific – you could take off very
quickly. It was governed to 42 miles per hour, but you could get
up to 45, on a slope up to 50! The non-maintenance engine. It
was a Rolls Royce engine – same engine as the Spitfire. It was
sealed, there was nothing to do on it. Never had a bit of trouble.
A better gearbox – changing gear was easier. It was a better
vehicle mechanically all round. The armour was thicker, the
turret was 'cast'; it was solid. The 77mm gun fired a 17-pounder
shell, same as the Firefly – but we all had it! You felt this is what
you wanted from the start. If you'd had this from the start it
would have been a little bit pleasanter war![32]

Trooper Ron Forbes, 4 Troop, 'B' Squadron, 2nd F&FY

Overall, the Comet was a far more modern tank, with a high
technology precision-engineered engine. Basic routine maintenance was easy enough, but if anything serious went wrong they
would have to go back to more highly qualified engine fitters in
the brigade fitter workshops.

There was no comparison. They were a much more powerful
engine, the Merlin. It was a de-rated fighter aircraft engine,
really, the Merlin. They were an excellent engine, but we could
hardly touch them; they were nearly all sealed by Rolls Royce.
They were beyond our technical expertise and our fitters would

very seldomly touch them. They could have a go at the Sherman tanks, because they were built in a very rugged sort of way. But certainly not the Merlins. They were a very sleek piece of engineering. They very seldom gave trouble, but nevertheless if they did it wasn't a job for us, it was a job for brigade.[33]

Trooper Doug Hayes, Fitters Section, 'A' Squadron, 2nd F&FY

As a gunner, John Buchanan was pleased with the general performance of the 77mm gun. However, they were all aware that the 77mm AP shells still did not have the means of penetrating the armour of either the Panther or the Tiger. But at least their hitting power had been increased.

It was a good gun – it could take on a Mark IV and destroy it. It could stop a Panther, maybe not penetrate, but it could stop it. We put a German Panther we'd captured out on the range and we fired at it. The shells wouldn't go through. We felt a wee bit despondent because of that. But we went to the tank afterwards to have a look at it – and although the shells hadn't gone through, they had left a bulge where the AP shell had hit it. The officer said, 'Well, it's not going to go through, but if you're sitting in a tank and you get belted by one of these APs you're not going to be very happy! You'll probably bail out! Still couldn't get the Tiger![34]

Trooper John Buchanan, 4 Troop, 'A' Squadron, 2nd F&FY

With any tank there was always this balancing act. Improved performance in one area meant a commensurate sacrifice somewhere else, or a likely loss in manoeuvrability and speed through increased weight.

The crews worked hard to get the Comets just as they liked them. They also named their tanks and personalised them to their own requirements.

We prepared the tanks. You may think that when a tank is delivered it's prepared for you already, but you won't have things in your own proper positions. I would make sure I knew where everything was – make sure that I had plenty of room for my bed roll, etc. To just get the tank as though it was something you lived in, because we were going to live in them for weeks and possibly months. We all had to give names to our tanks: Ken Howard I put in charge of giving the names. He thought of one – 'Desert Rose'. They were all beginning with the letter 'D'. I believe mine was 'Dante'. You had to paint the names on the tanks.[35]

Lieutenant Alex Gilchrist, 2 Troop, 'B' Squadron, 2nd F&FY

While they were getting the tanks ready and training up the crews on the Comet, there was an amusing incident that could have had terrible consequences.

Alongside the canal there is a big wharf. When we came in from anywhere, you elevate your guns to the highest, so the gun's pointing up in the air before you unload the shell. For some strange reason I must have pressed the button – and the thing went off. It must have been an AP shell because it went through the roof – and disappeared. There was a stunned silence – and Brownlie came up and says, 'What happened?' 'I must have pressed the button – the shell's away!' The gun was fully elevated so it would go between 5 and 6 miles before it landed. Lieutenant Samson and Brownlie got a scout car and went haring off to look for it, see if they could find it! They couldn't find it! He came back and said, 'Anyway, it will be in a farm – some field, nobody's said anything about it!'[36]

Trooper John Buchanan, 4 Troop, 'A' Squadron, 2nd F&FY

The training intensified as each crew member mastered their role in the new tanks. Jack Edwards, hitherto a wireless operator, decided to convert to being a gunner and was posted as such to the Comet commanded by Corporal Paddy Purcell.

I was told there was a vacancy for a gunner – so I became a gunner. I always had the impression that people could have fired more. They could have put down more fire in various situations. That if they'd done a bit more shooting it might have done a bit more good instead of being conservative with the ammunition. It's not as if we were short of ammunition – we had stacks of ammunition all the time. I thought, 'Well, I'll be a gunner! Then I can shoot when I want to!'[37]

Trooper Jack Edwards, 'B' Squadron, 2nd F&FY

Whatever their 'trade' they had to be ready, as even a moment's hesitation could be fatal in action. The weeks passed pleasantly enough, the men working hard but enjoying the sybaritic pleasure of Ypres as best they could. By early March they were generally considered to be once more ready for war – and the invasion of Germany that was beckoning.

On 10 March, they had a visit from Montgomery, who carried out the award ceremony for various medals, but also briefed the men of the 29th Armoured Brigade as to what lay ahead.

We all went to a large theatre and General Montgomery came along to address the whole brigade. Most people at that time smoked – General Montgomery was a non-smoker. Everybody in the whole of this theatre was not smoking – and they were all chaffing at the bit dying to get a fag going. Montgomery was a bit of a humourist and he sort of sensed the feeling about these cigarettes – and he purposefully delayed the 'permission' for everybody to light up. Then after about five minutes, as by way of an afterthought, he said, 'Gentlemen, you may smoke!' A large cheer went up! We were seated in the upper circle and from my vantage point a huge cloud of smoke arose up to the roof. Being a non-smoker, I wasn't very pleased! I was very impressed by Montgomery; he was missing a vocation – I think he would have done extremely well on the stage. He knew how to conduct things, he was humorous, he put backbone into people, and he created 'esprit des corps'! Which is most important! I thought he was a brilliant chap![38]

Lance Corporal Ken Watson, HQ Squadron, 2nd F&FY

Steel Brownlie was one of those presented with their medals, in his case the MC.

Centre-stage was a chalk circle into which each recipient marched, exchanged a few words, had his ribbon pinned on, and marched off again. Comparing notes later, we found that he had six stock questions, of which he asked each man three. Mine were: 'What were you in civvy street?' Music hall reply, 'Happy!' but I restrained myself! 'When did I come over?' 'D + 10 – same as the King!' 'What did I intend to do after the war?' 'No idea!'[39]

Captain William Steel Brownlie, Headquarters, 'A' Squadron, 2nd F&FY

It was evident to most that Montgomery was an egotist, but that his forceful character and absolute confidence was probably just what they needed.

We had a great respect for Monty; he was a great morale booster. He always had the Royal Tank Regiment badge on! He came to see us in a theatre. The brigade officers crammed into this theatre. Monty stood on the stage with a big map behind him and it was 'I', 'I', 'I' – 'I shall cross the Rhine! I shall give them a bloody nose!' You sat and you said, 'Hang on a minute! He's not in the tank – it's me!'[40]

Second Lieutenant Charlie Workman, 1 Troop, 'C' Squadron, 2nd F&FY

'Twas ever thus.

16

INTO GERMANY

> Our state of mind at that time: we were used to death. We
> considered we were the tops. We were a good regiment. We
> were in a good division. And we knew we were about to go into
> Germany, so there weas no stopping us![1]

Second Lieutenant Charlie Workman, 1 Troop, 'C' Squadron, 2nd F&FY

THE DAY FOR DEPARTURE DAWNED on 12 March as they
waved a metaphorical tear-stained handkerchief to the good
burghers of Ypres. Their first destination was the small town of
Montaigu. Once they had settled in, they began work on the
various alterations that they had identified were needed on the
Comet. One minor problem that arose was referenced somewhat wryly in Steel Brownlie's memoirs – the difficulty in getting
the fitters up in the morning when they had been unwisely billeted in premises that were effectively acting as a local brothel.
However, eventually, they set to work.

> There were official modifications to the Comets, like taking all
> the tracks off and fitting a new part to each sprocket and idler,
> plus many more. There were unofficial modifications, like fixing
> bins and boxes to the outside, to leave more room inside. The
> Comet was cramped compared to the Sherman. We, the users,
> increased the capacity of sixty rounds per tank to eighty-five
> and that of machine-gun ammo by over 50 per cent. All this

with no loss of living space. Why hadn't the designers consulted us?[2]

Captain William Steel Brownlie, Headquarters, 'A' Squadron, 2nd F&FY

Then, for the rest of that reasonably dry and sunny month, they were put through their paces in a series of troop, squadron and finally regimental tactical exercises held in conjunction with companies from their old friends the 8th Rifle Brigade and the 1st Herefords. Since the fiasco of failed cooperation at Epsom, the tanks and infantry had mastered a variety of methods to work together to best effect. In general terms, the leading squadron would push on alone, with the other two squadrons following up, each carrying a company of infantry clinging to the back of the tanks – about twelve men on each tank.

Taxi service! To save the infantry having to embark on trucks to catch up, you had your infantry on your tank! It was handy to have them there, because when you met an obstacle, or were fired on, the best people to clear it was the infantry on the ground. The Herefords were with us most of the time. Sometimes there would be a rifleman on the front, sitting talking to the driver. As long as there was no stuff flying about – it was quite friendly![3]

Trooper Ron Forbes, 4 Troop, 'B' Squadron, 2nd F&FY

Major 'Pinkie' Hutchison explained what was happening – and why it would be so essential to have infantry close at hand in Germany. It was increasingly apparent that the main threat would no longer be the panzer, 88mm gun or self-propelled gun, as it had been in Normandy. Now the real threat was the humble panzerfaust.

The bazooka, which the Germans were perfecting, was a very effective weapon against tanks. It could knock out a tank very easily and was fired at very close range so that it was difficult to miss, fired from a ditch into the side of a tank, which is what they generally did. If there was infantry around, they could be the greatest help as protection. We were working ever more closely with infantry. When we were out of contact, the first squadron of tanks would be operating separately in front. The next squadron would have the infantry on the top of the tanks so that they were ready to deploy to one side or the other to help clear the obstructions. The remaining infantry would be on lorries, ready to mount the tanks if need be. We worked particularly closely with the Herefords throughout that period. Colonel Scott got on very well with their commanding officer and they moved together. It worked very well working with the same battalion, knowing the same officers, one got to know them; that was a help. It was the most sensible way to operate and to push on. It enabled us to go so much faster than we would otherwise have been able to do.[4]

Major Douglas Hutchison, 'A' Squadron, 2nd F&FY

They had also greatly improved their cooperation with the true maestro of the Second World War battlefields of 1944–5 – the Royal Artillery.

As likely as not at squadron headquarters we would have an OP from the field gunner regiment, who was supporting our group. He'd have one set on our net so that we could talk to him and another set [going] back to his guns. So one could get fire not only from one's own support regiment, but also if need be from the regiments supporting the other brigade group if there was a sufficient priority target – and you might even be able to get the support of medium artillery that was within range. If we didn't have an OP near us, we did develop a technique for directing fire ourselves: a fairly rough and ready system, but as long as you could pinpoint the place and give a six-figure map reference of the target, then they would put a round down and you would correct that by saying, 'One 100 yards north-east!' or whatever the direction you judged it to be, and try to bracket the target in that way. It worked up to a point![5]

Major Douglas Hutchison, 'A' Squadron, 2nd F&FY

On 28 March, with their training complete, the 2nd F&FY were ordered forward into the front line. They were moving into a new situation – as was recognised by 'Pip' Roberts.

From a divisional commander's point of view it is interesting to compare the situation, at this time, to the situation in Normandy. In Normandy there was always real anxiety; if one made wrong decisions, if the front were penetrated by the Germans, if our line of communication was cut, the result could be catastrophic. Now, mistakes or failures could only delay the end. Of course, we wanted to finish the war as quickly as possible, but at what cost? Unless morale was high, we would not achieve our objectives; heavy casualties in a fruitless battle will not help morale. We must try to win our battles without heavy casualties – not very easy. So, the divisional commander had all the time to be thinking of how to achieve the objective with the least cost. And if there were likely to be heavy casualties, or if there had been heavy casualties, it was important that he should be seen among the forward troops so that they knew that he knew the sort of hell they were going through. Occasionally we did have heavy casualties, but I am quite certain morale stayed high.[6]

Major General 'Pip' Roberts, Headquarters, 11th Armoured Division

In the interval, the Twenty-First Army Group had launched Operation Veritable to clear the area of ground between the Maas and the Rhine, pushing south-east from the Nijmegen sector. It was a good campaign to miss, fought as it was across low-lying land, a contrasting maze of dykes, streams, low ridges and thick woods, with the margins deliberately flooded by the Germans. Here the Germans had prepared three successive lines of multiple trenches, minefields and barbed wire, with the most fearsome challenge in the Reichswald Forest sector, stretching between Goch and Cleve. Commencing on 8 February, the XXX Corps and Canadian II Corps had battered their way forwards, aided by a stupendous series of concentrated artillery bombardments. It was an awful slogging match, hampered by bad weather which at times restricted air support, but still they had inched their way forwards, taking first Cleve and then Goch, beating off the usual German counter-attacks. On 23 February, the American Ninth Army joined in the fray, launching Operation Grenade with a crossing of the Roer river and thrusting to the north-west to take Venlo and Munchen Gladbach – just across the Rhine from the great German city of Düsseldorf. The two offensives would link up as the Germans were forced to flee across the Rhine on 10 March. Next would come the crossing of the Rhine. This was no minor undertaking: it was some 500 yards wide, it was in flood, and the Germans lay in wait on the other side. All told, it was a logistical nightmare.

Behind them, the Maas still had to be properly bridged, rail and road communications restored and extended, hundreds of special amphibious DD floating tanks and Buffalo infantry carriers deployed. Huge artillery concentrations coupled with massed bombing reduced key German defensive locations to rubble. Whole towns – such as the communications hub of Wesel – were almost erased from the map. On 23 March, the Twenty-First Army Group began Operation Plunder with a series of Rhine crossings, in conjunction with Operation Varsity, a massive strike by the First Allied Airborne Army. German opposition was variable, but the fateful step had been taken and the final campaign had begun.

The 2nd F&FY and 29th Armoured Brigade came somewhat late to this 'party'. At this point the 11th Armoured Division were still part of the VIII Corps, now commanded by Lieutenant General Evelyn Barker (11th Armoured Division, 6th Airborne Division and 1st Commando Brigade, shortly to be joined by the 15th (Scottish) Division and the 6th Guards Armoured

Brigade). With the Dutch roads clogged with heavy traffic, the tanks were often forced to go through the surrounding fields if they were to hope to make any progress at all. But that brought its own problems, with the threat of getting bogged in. On 28 March, the 2nd F&FY moved forward through the Netherlands, crossing the Maas near Venlo, and entering Germany for the first time. They found most of the German civilians they encountered were cowed, staying out of the way of the invaders, trying to avoid trouble. Some thought they were sullen, but in truth what else would one expect? Their homes had been amidst a battleground for weeks, they feared for their own lives, their armies were being defeated, their homeland invaded, and they seemed to have lost all control over their lives.

The scale of operations envisaged by Eisenhower was enormous and somewhat controversial, as he had abandoned hopes of getting to Berlin before the Soviet Army. Eisenhower's focus was on the destruction of German military strength, not on the political consideration of capturing the German capital. He regarded the 'bird in the hand' of the Baltic ports as more important than a speculatory 'race' with the Soviets, with all the diplomatic and possible military clashes that might be triggered. To Montgomery's chagrin, the Twenty-First Army Group was assigned the less stellar role in advancing to the Leine river, to capture Bremen, before pushing on to the Elbe. Montgomery would be protecting the left flank of General Omar Bradley's Twelfth Army Group, which was charged with encircling the Ruhr, while the Sixth Army Group would advance to protect Bradley's southern flank. Once the Ruhr was controlled, the Twenty-First and Twelfth Army Groups would advance on Leipzig, while the Sixth Army Group moved on Nuremberg to control southern Germany. Meanwhile Eisenhower was liaising with the Soviet armies approaching from the east. Germany was finished – it was only a matter of time.

During the next phase of the operations, 'Pip' Roberts had a difficult task on his hands. He had to reign in the rash enthusiasm of Brigadier Harvey Roscoe, of 29th Armoured Brigade, full of the old 'Prince Rupert' dash and bravado, while simultaneously pushing on the far more cautious Brigadier Jack Churcher of 159th Brigade. One slightly apocryphal story was told by one of his staff officers, Lieutenant Colonel Robin Hastings, which will perhaps illustrate the problem Roberts faced.

Roscoe commanded the Armoured Brigade in 11th Armoured Division when I was GSO1. He was definitely a cavalry officer turned tank commander and had an irresistible desire to press on. He was always at a prominent position himself and, though he did not adopt the front-line tactics of some of his misguided contemporaries, he was always stationed where he could see what was going on. As one squadron leader said, 'You liked to know that if you wanted him, you only had to look over your shoulder to see the brigadier!' The Infantry Brigade was commanded by an excellent infantry officer whose methods were the opposite of Roscoe's. He liked to make the most thorough preparations and move as little as possible. Their aims and talents were exactly opposed. General 'Pip' Roberts, a brilliant soldier, a good tactician and experienced in tank warfare, was not keen on getting himself involved in the minor squabbles between these two. It was for the GSO1 to sort out the differences between the brigade commanders. General Pip often used to sit in the corner of the armoured command vehicle and laugh at my efforts to appease both.

When we were approaching the Elbe, I think it was, the Armoured Brigade reached the river and held one end of the bridge. They urgently needed infantry support, the task which Brigadier Churcher's brigade was expected to perform. But his brigade was very slow in coming up to scratch. Roscoe protested to me and then said on the wireless, 'Tell Churcher we need him. And to encourage him to go faster tell him we've captured a wine store near the bridge and if he gets here by tonight, I'll give him a case of 'ock – a whole case of 'ock – the lucky chap!' The ploy worked.[7]

Lieutenant Colonel Robin Hastings, Headquarters, 11th Armoured Division

*

THE 2ND F&FY CROSSED THE MIGHTY RHINE RIVER at first light on 29 March, by means of a pontoon bridge created by the apparently indefatigable Royal Engineers. The crossing proved a frightening undertaking, as the pontoon boats plunged up and down beneath the Comets – and they knew that if they came off, they would sink like a stone, with little or no chance of escape from a watery grave.

> The Rhine is a very wide river! These pontoons, as you actually got on to it the pontoon would disappear under the water, so the water was lapping the bottom of the tracks! The drivers were just looking ahead, they had to keep a certain spacing to offset the weight, I guess! Going across each pontoon and watching the thing disappear under the water wasn't a very pleasant sight! Then they'd pop back up! I was quite pleased to get to the other side, that's for sure![8]
>
> Trooper Terry Boyne, 4 Troop, 'A' Squadron, 2nd F&FY

Driver Ron Forbes realised that it was easy enough to drive in a straight line. The main requirement was to do nothing!

> The bridge was a magnificent Royal Engineers design – a pontoon bridge right across three quarters of a mile or something! You were a long time on the bridge. As you went over, as the tracks hit each pontoon it went down almost to submerge until you got over. Very flexible the whole thing. A tank was quite wide, but, being equal on both sides, if you sat [still] it would have gone across without you steering – dead straight – so there was no bother![9]
>
> Trooper Ron Forbes, 4 Troop, 'B' Squadron, 2nd F&FY

Charlie Workman, as a tank commander, was higher up in the Comet and he found the crossing a nerve-wracking business.

> I think I was the first over. It was this pontoon bridge, and these were Comets, heavier tanks! I said to Hutchinson, 'For God's sake, I'm not a good swimmer – take it easy!' As we got on the pontoon bridge – rows of little boats all strung together – and as we started going over, it dipped! Hutchinson would make comments, 'It's a bloody fast river that!' 'Never mind the bloody river, Hutchinson, just get us to the other side, will you?'[10]
>
> Second Lieutenant Charlie Workman, 1 Troop, 'C' Squadron, 2nd F&FY

However, Workman soon recovered his spirits once he got to the other side. He was now in the Rhineland, the heart of Germany. His reaction was typical.

> When we got to the other side, 'Boy, this is Germany! This is us really in Germany now!' That was a great feeling. 'We've taken all this hammering from the Germans, and here we are now – here's us giving them what they've been giving everybody else for a long time! Now we've got these bastards! Here we are!'[11]
>
> Second Lieutenant Charlie Workman, 1 Troop, 'C' Squadron, 2nd F&FY

The town of Wesel, on the other side of the river, was not a welcoming sight as it had been bombed and shelled to rubble, but they soon passed through the grim devastation into the German countryside, heading in the first instance for their rendezvous at the village of Bunen. The ground was soft and they became aware that the Comet had a tendency to bog down in muddy conditions.

> There were quite a few incidents of bogging down in Germany. I think the tracks weren't wide enough – really. If you looked at the Tiger the tracks were about twice the width. If the tracks wouldn't take you out, then you just had to wait until the Light Aid Detachment came up and you got towed. On some

occasions, another tank on drier ground could tow you out with a couple of tow ropes.[12]

Trooper Ron Forbes, 4 Troop, 'B' Squadron, 2nd F&FY

On 30 March, 'B' Squadron led the way, passing through Velen and heading towards the village of Gescher, with initially no opposition. After a minor scrap with some German infantry armed with the deadly panzerfaust at Gescher, 'C' Squadron took over the lead. A little further on they approached the village of Legden. In the lead were the Comets, commanded by Lieutenants Eric Lamont and Charles Workman.

As we went through, they would put out white things in the window – 'the washing', as we used to say, to show that there were no troops in the area. It had been fairly straightforward. Eric Lamont and I came up to this village, Legden, and there was no 'washing' up, no sign of surrender. We went into the village square and then suddenly the place erupted with SS with small arms coming out of the houses. They were right round us; the tank machine gun hadn't got the freedom of movement that we needed to dispose of this opposition. We decided, 'Let's get out of here and sort these guys out!' We both got out with our crews with machine guns – Brens and Sten guns – and just did a John Wayne – just shot away – banging on. I came round a corner and ran into this guy. He shot at me – luckily, he missed! I had a Bren gun and I didn't miss. It was the first time I had ever killed a chap face-to-face.[13]

Second Lieutenant Charlie Workman, 1 Troop, 'C' Squadron, 2nd F&FY

The crew scattered hand grenades all around to force the Germans away from the tanks. It might have ended badly, but, just in time, the rest of the squadron came barrelling into the square and to their rescue. But they did suffer casualties and the news of one caused much grief and heart-searching for Ken Watson.

When I got back from leave, my best friend Corporal Alf Wedderburn,[14] who came from Blyth in Northumberland, had been killed at a place called Legden. I think he was killed by machine-gun fire while outside his tank. I had to write to his mother and father a letter of condolence – with some difficulty. He was a very, very nice chap. I'd known the chap for two years. I stated that I'd really enjoyed his company and friendship during the whole time that I'd known him – and that I was very, very sorry that such a tragedy had occurred so late in the war. He'd gone right through from the beginning. I told them that he didn't suffer, that he was killed instantaneously. He had been an adopted child, nevertheless he was loved. When I visited his house with him when we were on leave one time, I could tell that his adopted mother and father really thought the world of him. They were obviously of a religious persuasion. Owing to my experiences, I had become a confirmed agnostic. I saw no evidence of 'the Lord'. It's something I've never altered for the whole of the rest of my life. In fact, I had it entered into my army paybook. An agnostic being one who doesn't know, compared with an atheist who states there is definitely no God – I'm not big-headed enough to say there is no God, but I am a non-believer in Christianity as such and the 'life hereafter'.[15]

Lance Corporal Ken Watson, HQ Squadron, 2nd F&FY

The drip, drip of casualties continued. Every man lost was some-one's best mate, but they had to carry on regardless.

On 31 March, the advance continued unimpeded to the village of Laer, where they laagered for the night. Warnings of a German counter-attack next morning proved groundless, and they moved forward via Emsdetten to cross the Ems river at Mesum. Not so far away was the Dortmund–Ems Canal. This would prove a more challenging prospect. Although the bridge had been destroyed, a squadron of the 3rd Royal Tank Regiment had been ferried across and, with the help of the Shropshire Light Infantry, hammered out a bridgehead. Within a few hours the Royal Engineers had managed to improvise a workable temporary bridge and the 2nd F&FY were ordered across. Much against his will, Steel Brownlie had been left out of battle (LOB), but he now found himself rather closer to the 'wrong' sort of action.

> My LOB tanks pulled off into a field about 300 yards away on the near side. The din was terrific, with our 25-pounder shells whistling over our heads, and our forward tanks getting to work on the wooded ridge. A number of Focke-Wulf 190s appeared overhead, intent on destroying the bridge. Our anti-aircraft guns opened up on them, as well as every kind of suitable gun in the area, including a Bren fired from the shoulder by a very small sapper. It was too heavy for him and kept wandering down till the bullets were spraying us! With this and all the other shit flying about, I shut down all the hatches and just sat. Four enemy planes were shot down, and the only bomb that landed near the bridge was a dud![16]
>
> Captain William Steel Brownlie, Headquarters, 'A' Squadron, 2nd F&FY

When they got across the bridge in the late afternoon, the LOB tanks laagered up close to the bridge when there was another air attack.

> As dusk came, the Germans planes came over – an assortment of planes. There were dive-bombers, fighter-bombers there – as if they were scraping the barrel to try and destroy this bridge. There was ack-ack guns, one double-barrelled gun was straddled by bombs, but it came out 'smiling' – it was still firing away. They weren't aiming at me – they were aiming at the bridge, so I got out on the turret and I got my Bren gun. I stood on the turret and I was hosing them. This one came – and I hit it – the tracer bullets hit it, but you could see them bouncing off – it must have been armoured. A dive-bomber is armoured at the front. I said, 'Stuff this!' Then I saw coming from its 'belly' this big black bomb! I looked at it and it was coming straight

for me. I dived into the back bin, which was open – I'd taken
the Bren gun out. This red-hot Bren landed on top of me!
My hands were all burned. There was one massive explosion.
I opened my eyes, looked up and here's this black mountain
of dirt descending on me! The tank was covered with about
2 inches of dirt. That's what saved us, the fact we were in a
ploughed field – it was soft – and the bomb had buried itself
in before exploding! If it had been hard ground, it would have
blown up – me, the tank and everything.[17]

Trooper John Buchanan, 4 Troop, 'A' Squadron, 2nd F&FY

The bridge survived unscathed – and so did the 2nd F&FY.
Several aircraft were reputed to have been shot down; indeed
one Messerschmitt 109 plunged to earth some 200 yards from
their headquarters. It was symptomatic that the Luftwaffe was
no longer the mighty engine of war that had driven the Blitzkrieg to such successes earlier in the war.

In front of them lay the steep escarpment of the Teutoburger
Wald, an imposing, thickly wooded natural feature that rose to
over 1,000 feet above them. About 30 miles long and 2–3 miles
wide, it was a tough proposition, as the 'pupils' from the local
NCOs' training school were holding this superb defensive position with a grim, if not fanatical, determination. It had been
reported that the 3rd RTR had taken the pass leading up and
over the escarpment, but, in reality, they had been stopped dead
in their tracks. Now the 2nd F&FY moved forwards to take their
place. There were only two passable roads across the Teutoburger
Wald, one running from Munster to Ibbenbüren and a smaller
road through the village of Brochterback up to Holthausen. For
two days the fighting raged, but tanks were of limited use in this
terrain, although they tried their best – blasting away at the edges
of the woods. For the 1st Hereford and 3rd Monmouths it was a
terrible battle, sucked into the maw of the woods while struggling
against a skilful and determined opposition. Even massed artillery
barrages did not seem to break the cadets' grip on the ridge line.

The infantry and an armoured regiment were held up and we were ordered to go through them – and carry on. 'A' Squadron were the leading squadron – and 4 Troop were the leading troop! I think I was the leading tank. It was a high ridge, and the road went over it – it was densely wooded. We had to approach where the road went up into the hill and wood – and we were fired upon. I swung off left immediately, in a big circle, and put out some smoke. Even as we swung off, we'd swing the turret round and fire up where the gun was firing from. You wouldn't stop; you had to keep moving. Then across the road again into a farmyard, where we were under cover. The other tanks in the troop all swung off right, where the ground was boggy – and they got bogged in – which rather pleased me! We all fired up there and it stopped firing back. I was ordered to go on foot and see if I could see what was up there. My driver came with me and we crept up by the hedgerows and so on. Couldn't see a thing. After a bit I said, 'I think we've gone far enough!' and we went back. It wasn't our role – we felt very naked going up on foot. The infantry suffered dreadful casualties there and I think the Monmouths were disbanded after that, with something like 300 casualties.[18]

Sergeant Roy Vallance, 4 Troop, 'A' Squadron, 2nd F&FY

The 2nd F&FY were perhaps fortunate that they played a relatively brief role in the fighting to force a passage up and over the Teutobürger Wald. On 3 April, the task was handed over to 131st Brigade of the 7th Armoured Division, which took a further three days to seize their objectives. The remnants of the 3rd Monmouths were pulled out of line and were replaced by the 1st Cheshire Regiment in the 159th Brigade. It had been decided that the LOB tanks retained near the regimental headquarters should now be returned to their squadrons. Steel Brownlie was called in to an interview with Lieutenant Colonel Alec Scott to get the welcome news.

I found Colonel Alec squatting in a barn, looking very tired and eating cold 'meat & veg' from a mess-tin, headphones round his neck. I had the greatest respect for this man. He had a grip on everything, he never spared himself, and when I had an extra 19 wireless set in my tank I tuned it in to the brigade frequency – and listened to him arguing things out with Brigadier Roscoe Harvey about what to do next. He was always logical, and anxious that there should be no unnecessary casualties in his regiment.[19]

Captain William Steel Brownlie, Headquarters, 'A' Squadron, 2nd F&FY

Meanwhile, on 4 April, the 3rd RTR excelled themselves with a splendid night march to seize a bridge over the Ems–Weser Canal at Eversheide, just north of Osnabrück. The 2nd F&FY followed up, but Charlie Workman found to his cost that not all German resistance had been stamped on.

We were moving up on Osnabrück; I was lead tank on the centre line. Normally the troop leader would be in the middle. You made use of the roads as much as you could until you bumped into opposition. Then you got off. We were moving quite fast. We didn't know this, but they'd put a whole bunch of SS into Osnabrück. We got into Osnabrück; we were in narrow streets. The Comet had a ring of periscopes right round the turret. So when I saw these guys were firing at us from the houses, I closed down, put the lid down. A panzerfaust hit the rim of the turret, shattered the periscopes, it went into both eyes – so I couldn't see! And I was quite deaf! We were still under fire – they put the infantry in to clear this crowd out. They pulled me out.[20]

Second Lieutenant Charlie Workman, 1 Troop, 'C' Squadron, 2nd F&FY

The periscopes were designed to shatter into dust rather than little bits, but for a while it was uncertain how much damage had been done to his eyes. Workman was therefore evacuated back first to hospital and then all the way back to Catterick – his fighting war was over.

On 5 April, progress accelerated dramatically as the regiment passed through the 3rd RTR at Lovelsloh, moving forward alongside the 23rd Hussars in an informal 'race' to reach the Weser river.

> Between villages, it was the custom for the leading troop to 'brass up' every wood and bit of cover where there might be tank-hunters, who might be scared off or at least put off their aim with their panzerfausts. These were feared more than anti-tank guns, which might be spotted after they fired their first shot and then dealt with. A man with a panzerfaust shot just once, and it was another one nearby you had to worry about. We loaded our BESA machine-gun belts with a proportion of incendiary bullets, so that forest fires and burning buildings marked our progress. It was often an impressive sight to look back at the pall of black smoke along the 'Charlie Love', the centre-line. Everywhere there were non-combatants straggling along the roads, or resting in the ditch. With no pressing military tasks, I used my Greenock Academy French and German to talk to as many as possible. Information could sometimes be got from prisoners or civilians who were willing to give it. There were thousands of DPs, displaced persons, and released POWs, prisoners of war. They would often ask what was the safest way to go, accept a few cigarettes or biscuits, and plod on. Germany in 1945 was not a pretty sight.[21]
>
> Captain William Steel Brownlie, Headquarters, 'A' Squadron, 2nd F&FY

Village after village was passed without any problem until they arrived at Glissen, just a mile or so from the Weser. Here there occurred one of those brisk engagements that were 'something and nothing' but which could end lives in an almost haphazard fashion.

> Approaching Glissen, still at full speed, Frank Fuller's troop was in the lead. His corporal was first tank, and the operator reported on the air 'no washing' in the village ahead. Therefore,

they slowed down. The corporal reported enemy in the ditches on both side of the road. Frank reported that he had been hit, and then was silent. His corporal reported that he seemed to have gone right through the enemy pocket and was told to stay where he was. The squadron deployed off the road, myself going left over the fields looking for a position to fire onto the road, or into the village. The following troops unloaded the infantry who were travelling on the back of the tanks, to start a clearing action. Meantime Frank's tank sat alone and silent, round the bend in the road. Suddenly his operator, Trooper Oxley, came on the air and said very quietly that the rest of the crew were dead, that the enemy were all around, and he proposed to lie doggo till he could escape. He was told to do that. I found a good fire position, and saw our infantry deployed and advancing. I fired in front of them to help them forward, but they went to ground – maybe they mistook my stuff for enemy fire. More of our tanks came up, a few prisoners were taken, and casualties inflicted on others trying to escape. I shot at some crossing open ground to my left, and Glissen was taken without much trouble: more prisoners. They were from 12th SS Panzer, very young, blubbering and weeping as they ran back along the dusty road, urged by the boots of our infantry. I helped by brandishing a pistol from the turret, and shouting 'Schneller! Schneller!' We found bicycles and panzerfausts in the ditches. Obviously, the enemy were now scraping the bottom of the barrel, but they could still kill people.[22]

Captain William Steel Brownlie, Headquarters, 'A' Squadron, 2nd F&FY

They later found out what had happened. A panzerfaust had hit the front of Frank Fuller's Comet tank which shuddered to a halt on the road, with German infantry in the ditches on either side. The driver had been hit and when Fuller jumped out to try and do something, he was riddled by machine-gun fire and hit by another panzerfaust for good measure. The gunner also jumped out and was killed. Lance Corporal Oxley stayed put and survived. When Steel Brownlie got to the scene the tank had already been unceremoniously shoved off the road and Fuller's almost unrecognisable body was lying mangled in the ditch. That evening Lieutenant Frank Fuller,[23] and Lance Corporals Arthur Axtell,[24] Herbert Grossmith[25] and Frederick Marris[26] were buried in the midst of a German air raid. Padre Oswald Welch did not seem to turn a hair, but the rest of the observers, even Steel Brownlie, had to resist a strong urge to dive for cover.

Next day, the bulk of the regiment remained in the area, but 'B' Squadron was sent north to Stolzenau to try and locate a river crossing. Here they found both the bridge and ferry had been demolished, but a bridgehead had been established and the Royal Engineers were hard at work creating a new bridge over the Weser. In the event the bridgehead was withdrawn, and on 7 April the whole regiment was moved south to cross the river at Petershagen in the area captured by the 6th Airborne Division. They then sped on until they ran into trouble at the village of Loccum which was held strongly. 'A' and 'C' Squadrons were sent into the attack, with 'B' Squadron holding a forward line in support. 'C' Squadron ran into considerable trouble, with estimates of up to eight 88mm guns facing them. Jim Thompson-Bell certainly encountered one.

> We pulled up at Loccum and there was a field and a row of houses directly in front of us, then the road swung to the right, and there was a row of houses, a gap and another row of houses. We didn't know what was behind these houses. I got down off my tank, which was unusual, to go and have a look. Fortunately, there was a sheltered road from the houses that I got up to – and I found a barn at the end. In the barn there was a load of German equipment. So, I looked through the back – and there was an 88mm gun and a full crew, pointing down the gap between the houses. I then moved my tank across the front, to the gap, traversed the gun and opened fire – we brassed it up with HE and we also put an AP up there – we destroyed the

gun. Then I got stuck – the ground was too bloody soft! The tank went down, and I couldn't move! We hopped out of the tank rather rapid! We were pretty certain we'd 'done him up', but we weren't quite sure![27]

Sergeant Jim Thompson-Bell, 'C' Squadron, 2nd F&FY

This was not untypical, for several of the Comets got bogged down that day in the thick, glutinous mud. Bell-Thompson reckoned that it was for this incident that he was later awarded the Military Medal. Meanwhile, to their right, 'A' Squadron was also pushing into the village.

Off we went over the fields towards the houses, and almost at once I bogged. I called for the ARV, or rather bawled for it, as I was a sitting duck. It pulled me out, and I caught up with the others 100 yards short of the road leading into the town. There one tank bogged, then another, till over half the squadron were stuck. Desmond Chute was put in charge of the de-bogging, while the rest of us, only five or six tanks now, got onto the road and went left towards the centre of the place.[28]

Captain William Steel Brownlie, Headquarters, 'A' Squadron, 2nd F&FY

Luckily, they were still unopposed, although over the wireless they could hear that 'C' Squadron was having a tough time.

Jimmy Samson with two tanks went up the gardens on the right of the road. 'Pinkie' Hutchison with only three tanks was advancing towards the town centre, not really a proper job for a squadron leader. He called me up urgently to join him. The infantry were complaining about lack of tank support, and Colonel Alec was worried for the same reason, so I went flat out along the narrow streets. At one point a civilian family were desperately removing furniture from their burning house, and I hit a huge chest of drawers at 30 mph with 45 tons of Comet. Clothing and underwear were caught up and whirled round in the tracks. I found 'Pinkie' near the centre; the infantry having gone further on. He sent me to join them, with his only two remaining mobile tanks, but within a couple of hundred yards they were stuck, as was Jimmy Samson's party. The hazard was the sewage pits attached to each house, invisible but lightly covered and ready to trap a tank in stinking muck. No credit to me, I was now the only advancing tank in the squadron. With a platoon of the infantry, I reached the railway line and blazed away at likely targets in front. Four hundred yards to the left the line ran into a cutting, and suddenly a stream of Germans came pouring down one side and up the other, obviously fleeing from 'C' Squadron's assault. I fired rapid with HE and machine gun, they were soon in confusion, and our infantry went out to bring in the survivors. They were the crews and covering infantry of seven 88mm guns, which amazingly 'C' Squadron had overwhelmed without loss, I learned later. Was it cruel to batter retreating troops? There was always the thought that they might be reorganised and waiting for us next day or the day after, as well as thoughts about Frank Fuller and many like him. Not far away was another family rescuing furniture from their burning house, but in the circumstances one's reaction was simply, so what?[29]

Captain William Steel Brownlie, Headquarters, 'A' Squadron, 2nd F&FY

However, during the fighting, there had been a wretched incident when Major Peter Loram,[30] the officer commanding 'B' Squadron, was killed.

I was in a forward position and I was speaking to Peter on the radio. I said, 'I think there's possibly some Tigers or some tanks somewhere forward of me!' He was behind me. He said, 'Well, I'll come up and have a look!' I said to him, 'Well I think it's a bit risky!' 'Oh, I think I'm all right, I'll come up.' He came up in a Dingo scout car. Right in front of my eyes, 300–500 yards in front of me, near a crossroads, there was a hell of an explosion and the Dingo went into pieces. Something fired at it. What

German gun it was I don't know. It knocked the Dingo to
pieces. I think he took the wrong road. I expected him to come
up behind me, and he came up at a road junction in front of
me.[31]

Lieutenant Alex Gilchrist, 2 Troop, 'B' Squadron, 2nd F&FY

On the morning of 8 April, the 2nd F&FY first followed behind
the advancing 15/19th Hussars, before taking over the lead in the
late afternoon. Now Thomas Heald and his 2 Troop took the
chance to make their mark. With him was a young Glaswegian,
Lieutenant Norman Miller, only 19 years old, he was looked at
askance by the likes of Steel Brownlie as a teetotal non-smoker,
but clearly he was made of the 'right stuff'.

There were three tanks in the troop, my own, Norman Miller's
and Derek Collis as the sergeant. We had made up our minds
– I think a young officer who is keen makes the difference
– that we would go as fast as possible. Apparently we did 10
miles in an hour! Continuously firing the whole way, going
flat out. If there were hedges, down either side, one fired –
that's where somebody with a bazooka might hide. There
was probably nobody there at all! One fired a tremendous
amount. On that basis, with any luck the first tanks can get
through any bazookas. Once the tanks are through, they can
deal with any bazookas – it makes the bazooka man's position
almost impossible having tanks beyond him. I think that was
probably the longest advance by anyone in the Fife and Forfar
Yeomanry in the whole of the campaign. Certainly, if one went
fast enough – providing there were no mines on the road – you
could get through most things.[32]

Lieutenant Thomas Heald, 2 Troop, 'A' Squadron, 2nd F&FY

Once this would have been Steel Brownlie charging ahead, but
this marked a new generation of young officers. At Ober Bauerschaft they encountered a roadblock, and once the follow-up
squadrons had arrived there was a brisk fight.

Colonel Alec laid on an attack. We had no infantry on the back of the tanks, so had to wait for them to come up in their trucks. Meantime we plastered the village and started many fires. The infantry deployed, and we moved forward to cover them in. Things became very confused. The wood to the left of the entrance to the place was strongly held; we thought including some kind of pillbox, for no amount of fire from us could shut them up. We bypassed and worked our way through the burning houses behind the infantry. It was eerie to creep along in the gathering dusk and the smoke, watching them dodge from one place to another, an occasional casualty crawling back covered with blood. We did reach the far end of the place, and my last position was in the fields, watching out into the darkness. Maybe we could have held the village, but there was still machine-gun fire from the pillbox or whatever it was, so that our echelon could not come up to replenish. Therefore, the CO withdrew us and the Herefords company for what was left of the night. We took the infantry on to the back of the tanks. On mine was a so-called platoon, normally thirty or so men, under command of a corporal. We crawled back through the red-hot ashes and rubble to Laderholz.[33]

Captain William Steel Brownlie, Headquarters, 'A' Squadron, 2nd F&FY

There they laagered up. Next morning the Herefords attacked again, covered by a mass of smoke shells. By this time there was very little left of Ober Bauerschaft and the German resistance soon crumbled. Then the 2nd F&FY were back on the endless road, travelling south to cross the Leine river at Neustadt, within the 6th Airborne Division sector, before moving north to concentrate at the town of Esperke. 'B' and 'C' Squadrons were then ordered to clear the eastern bank of the Leine as far as the junction of the Aller river. They soon ran into trouble as they approached a wood in front of the village of Schwarmstedt. Jack Edwards remembered the sudden bouts of vicious fighting as they moved forward.

An infantry lieutenant and a sergeant came walking around, searching the area. They said, 'Have you seen any of our blokes? We said, 'No'. They said, 'We had a three-man listening post near the edge of this wood, and it disappeared in the night – they must have been taken prisoner!' We advanced up a road, and the second lieutenant [tank commander] told me to put some HE into a wood we could see in front – which I did. But then we turned left off the road and advanced cross-country. As we were advancing across this field, slanting towards the right-hand edge, we were the right-hand tank of the right-hand troop. There were no orders from the lieutenant and I didn't like this hedge, so I started to spray the base of it with the Besa. Spike, the driver, who was having a spell in the co-driver's seat, he joined in with his Besa, so between us we gave the hedge a good dose of lead all the way along. Then we went through the hedge, stopped on the other side. There'd been a bazooka party – half a dozen enemy hiding behind the hedge, with their bazookas – and they'd all been wiped out with our machine-gun fire – which was fortunate for us and not so fortunate for them. Spike opened his hatch and had a look round. He saw these dead Jerries. He came on to the commander, 'Hey, commander, some of these Jerries aren't properly dead, and they've got bazookas and how about hand grenading them!' No answer from him, so Spike said, 'Tell him, Jack!' So, I tapped his leg and repeated the message. Still no response from this lieutenant. Next thing I heard was, 'Bomp! Bomp! Bomp! Bomp!' Spike was out with his Luger, finishing off the ones that weren't quite dead. Not quite Geneva Convention, but he was frightened of them coming to life with a bazooka.[34]

Trooper Jack Edwards, 'B' Squadron, 2nd F&FY

At this point, their squadron leader, Captain Peter Ryde, arrived in his Comet accompanied by an infantry officer in a Bren gun carrier. But this area was emphatically not 'clear'.

The infantry officer got out of the carrier and was crouching on the back of the tank conferring with Captain Ryde, when he got shot in the shoulder. They helped him back in his carrier. Captain Ryde had his head out watching them go, when he got shot in the face! So he turned round and he disappeared, so we were there on our own again! The lieutenant said, 'Start the Besa up again!' So we were blazing away with the Besa at everything – every hedge of every field we could see. After a bit, we'd fired nineteen belts. The gun must have been red hot! On front of the gun mantle was a waterproof canvas cover, and it had caught fire. I was choking and suffocating in this dense white smoke inside the turret. I thought, 'Hey, what's going on?' The operator got up, he had to keep dodging up and down, because Captain Ryde had got sniped, and he thought he might be as well. So, he was dodging up and down, squirting the fire extinguisher at this thing. He used both fire extinguishers which we'd got in the tank. It was still smouldering. Myself and the other two in the turret, we all peed in an empty shell case – and the operator tipped that on it! And that sort of finished off the smouldering.[35]

Trooper Jack Edwards, 'B' Squadron, 2nd F&FY

As suddenly as it had begun, the resistance collapsed as the Germans either surrendered or pulled out. They were then all ordered back to a regimental laager at Esperke. Here there was a tragic event which removed one of the key characters from the regiment.

The infantry dismounted and filed away to their area. John Gilmour was on foot guiding everybody in. Mike Adams dismounted to shepherd his lot. I was looking back at this commonplace scene when there was a huge explosion, and the little figures were drowned in dust and smoke. I shouted to speed up and load the guns, as it seemed to be a counter-attack.[36]

Captain William Steel Brownlie, Headquarters, 'A' Squadron, 2nd F&FY

In fact, there had been a terrible accident. Sir John Gilmour picks up the story.

> At the end of day, it was my job as second in command to get the regiment parked for the night. I had parked my own tank and had gone over to where 'A' Squadron were coming in, to tell them where to go. We were still worried about air attack and so we tended to harbour under trees if we could. I was directing 'A' Squadron as to where they were to park, when unfortunately somebody fired a gun in one of the tanks – the gun hadn't been unloaded. The HE shell hit a tree soon after it left the gun and it burst. I got a bit in the groin and one of the drivers of the tanks – alongside where I was – was actually killed in the tank. I was hit in the groin and the thing was bleeding fairly profusely. I didn't really know what had happened. I was taken down to a field hospital.[37]
>
> Major John Gilmour, 'B' Squadron, 2nd F&FY

Tommy Smith[38] was the driver killed by the cruel blast of that random 77mm shell.

> Trooper Smith was my driver at the time. There had been a lot of action during the day, but we were in reserve. Eventually, we went into laager with the regimental headquarters. It wasn't a proper laager; it was in a sort of farmyard and it was very close to Belsen. We came into laager and there had been reports of a Tiger tank about. We were just getting out of our tank – Smith was half in and half out of the driving hatch. Sidoway, the co-driver, he was getting out. I was half out of the turret. I think Mackenzie, my wireless operator, was half out. We were just getting ready to dismount. The colonel's tank, or the second in command's tank, had not cleared his guns. The gunner obviously pressed the trigger – and it fired a high explosive shell – he was only 15 yards from us – which hit the tree immediately beside my tank. I just had the tree on top of me, but Sidoway and Tommy Smith both were hit by shrapnel. The regimental

second in command [Major John Gilmour] was hit by shrapnel
and wounded. Nobody realised what had happened; they
thought, 'Well here's the Tiger tank arrived!' It was just one of
those accidents, which was very unfortunate.[39]

Lieutenant Thomas Heald, 2 Troop, 'A' Squadron, 2nd F&FY

Gordon Fidler was in the tank behind them when it happened
and saw the whole thing.

I'm shouting across to him. The engines are still running.
Headquarters were cleaning their guns – and one had got an
HE up the spout. It hits the tree above Tommy Smith and kills
him outright, he went backwards over the tracks. I tried to
get back down inside, with a hell of a struggle! There was an
infantryman injured, Tommy Smith is killed, and his co-driver
is injured. If it had been an AP shell, there would have been no
problem, it would have gone through the tree, but it was just
like an airburst and spattered the tank in front of it. These are
things that do happen – and always will happen. You can't cater
for these types of things.[40]

Trooper Gordon Fidler, 4 Troop, 'A' Squadron, 2nd F&FY

Sir John Gilmour was evacuated and had an exploratory
operation in a hospital in Belgium. He was unlucky in the circumstances of the accident, but very lucky in that not too much
damage was caused 'down there'.

I was in hospital for several days before I was operated on. It
was such a small bit of shell that they left it in as they said they
would do more harm than good digging it out. I can confirm
that because years later I had an operation for varicose veins,
the surgeon had me X-rayed before he did the operation – and
the X-ray showed up the bit of shell in the groin and top of my
leg.[41]

Major John Gilmour

Gilmour then was flown back to recuperate in the UK. His departure caused a considerable reshuffle in the senior ranks of the regiment. Firstly, Major Hutchison took his place as second in command. 'Pinkie' was not best pleased.

> As the senior squadron leader, Colonel Scott asked me to become his second in command, so I had to abandon the squadron – I would much rather have stayed with 'A' Squadron. It was for me a bit of an anti-climax to be relegated into being a second in command and doing nothing really very much except following behind the leading squadron – as a general rule. When we were operational, Colonel Scott was very much in command and directing operations.[42]
>
> Major Douglas Hutchison, RHQ Squadron, 2nd F&FY

In Hutchison's place, Captain Desmond Chute was appointed to command 'A' Squadron, while Captain Steel Brownlie became his squadron second in command. Chute proved to be an unfortunate choice for command. Although generally accepted as a 'nice chap', he was not considered 'bright' enough and his junior officer resented his inability to issue clear orders, and as a result very soon lost all confidence in him. Captain David Voller was promoted to command 'B' Squadron after Peter Ryde was evacuated due to his head wounds. A somewhat wild, happy-go-lucky officer, who enjoyed a drink, Voller had a reputation for clowning around, although he proved serious enough when running his squadron. Captain Mike Adams had also been wounded by the blast, but was able to remain with the regiment, though he was consigned to light duties for a period.

The campaign seemed to be degenerating into one river crossing after another. Nothing ever seemed to change. They advanced along the roads, encountered opposition with the sudden blast of a panzerfaust or 88mm gun, called up the infantry and deployed to the flanks to encircle the opposition and having killed or captured most of them, they would then pursue the remnants into the middle distance. Germany seemed an endless slog. Victory would be theirs, but when?

*

IN GERMANY, STORIES BLURRED TOGETHER. As in Normandy, it was a period of intense fighting, where the men often had no real idea of where they were day to day. But their general accounts of this time still have value in giving us a sense of how it was. Of particular interest was the way in which this material shows how every new officer joining the 2nd F&FY was inculcated in the same basic tenets of the 'trade'. They experienced the same challenges and usually came to the same conclusions that their predecessors, an earlier 'generation' of officers – men like Charlie Workman, or before him 'Pinkie' Hutchison – had reached. But for the men and their experienced, wary NCOs, every new young officer was assessed by one basic question: would he get them killed? John Buchanan explains their thinking.

> At this time in the war, we were getting reinforcements sent up. Some of them had only been in the army about six to eight weeks. They were all dead keen to get into action, get at the Germans, make a name for themselves before the war finished. We got a couple of young officers who were wanting to get their MCs before the war finished. We, being old soldiers by that time, our main effort was to end the war as we were – fit and well. [43]
>
> Trooper John Buchanan, 4 Troop, 'A' Squadron, 2nd F&FY

By the time they got deep into Germany, Lieutenant Thomas Heald had become an accepted member of his crew. Over a period of weeks, he had proved himself to be a steady enough officer, willing to 'do his bit', but not a 'glory hunter' by nature. He was well aware that junior officers had to earn the respect of their men.

I suppose my background was different from theirs. I had confidence in them; I think they had confidence in me. For a month I slept with them in a bivvie beside the tank. I'd eaten with them. We had the same troubles. I hope I was as good a commander as I could be – and they were as good a crew as they could be. I called them by their surname always. I didn't know the Christian name of most of them. They called me, 'Sir!' I took the view that everybody in a tank crew is inter-dependent – and everybody has got to do the job as best they can. On one occasion they had 'liberated' something like seventeen eggs and we were going to have them for breakfast. Just as they were cooking nicely, I was called off to an 'O' Group which took rather a long time. And when I came back my driver had eaten all the eggs that were left – I didn't even get one. I am happy to say he suffered for it![44]

Lieutenant Thomas Heald, 2 Troop, 'A' Squadron, 2nd F&FY

Heald had also begun to master his tactical role in command of 2 Troop. Again, he was travelling the well-trodden path to becoming a capable and trusted officer. In any given action it was his job to understand exactly what it was they were meant to achieve, how they were to do it, and what support they could call on in case of emergency. If in doubt, he had to speak out; silence could mean disaster for his men – or an avoidable failure in whatever operation they were undertaking.

I was a troop commander. I had to attend Order Groups, I had to control the other tanks in the troop, and I was responsible that all the troop was working efficiently. 'A' Squadron 'O' Group was held nearly every morning, led by Major Hutchison, where the orders for the day were given out: you were told what the tactical situation was and what it was intended you should do, where you should go, and which troop should lead. Each day you had to get your codes; all the map references had to be in code. You had to deal with such questions as when you were going to be refuelled, what route one was taking, what would happen in certain circumstances. There was no objection to asking intelligent questions. It may be you didn't like what you were being asked to do, but at least you'd ask questions as to how you should do it. We weren't the sort of people who would be quiet if we didn't like something! Everybody realised that everybody depended on everybody else. Then you had to relate that to your own troop. I would have a small 'O' Group of my own, with the troop sergeant and troop corporal – and I would tell them what we were doing. If we were the leading troop, I would then have to decide how we were to proceed – and which order we should proceed in. One tank has to lead, I think I always put myself the second tank. I felt it was a bit unfair that I didn't lead on occasions, but I took the view that if anything happened to the first tank, I was in a position to assist. Whereas if I was the first tank and something happened to me, everybody else was in difficulties. I think that was generally accepted and it worked out well.

Lieutenant Thomas Heald, 2 Troop, 'A' Squadron, 2nd F&FY

And of course, he had by this time fully grasped the most important tenets of tank warfare – keep out of sight, and hence the direct line of fire, as much as possible.

If you are hull-down, all that is visible is the turret. If you are turret-down, nothing is visible, except the commander's head. The ideal is to approach the crest of a hill and be in such a position that any enemy beyond the hill are not aware that there is a tank there. On the other hand, if you are going to start firing, you really have to move into hull-down position, with the hull below the ground, because the gunner needs to be able to observe his target through his telescope. One could in fact shoot from right down behind a hill, with an observer or the

tank commander observing where the shots fell, like a field gun
– that would be HE.[45]

Lieutenant Thomas Heald, 2 Troop, 'A' Squadron, 2nd F&FY

In Germany, the preoccupation was nearly always with these
often deadly panzerfausts. Len Harkins was in a Comet that was
hit by a panzerfaust. In the confusion that followed, the ever-
pugilistic Harkins came face to face with one of the attackers.
The story also shows the blurred border between murder and
acceptable behaviour in amidst the terrors, chaos and confusion
of war.

Jimmy King was driving down this lane. I was dozing off
because I'd just come off two-hours' guard. We'd gone only 200
yards away from where we'd been in laager. All of a sudden, I
heard him say, 'There it is! There it is! King, turn!' They could
see a bazooka coming. They didn't travel fast, they had a hollow
charge, they burnt their way through! I woke up and I could
see five Jerries running out of some houses and across fields.
I turned the co-axial gun round, telling King to put the right
hand down so it would bring me in line! He did it, but as I was
just going to fire, the big gun hit them – they'd gone! When he
pulled the stick, he hit a house, the house came down on the
tank! I thought we were hit, and I was opening the hatch to
get out! He was telling me not to, because he knew we'd hit the
house. All panic stations. After ten minutes, quarter of an hour,
I got out of the tank. Our infantry had gone into the houses
where these Jerries were. I could hear somebody shouting, 'Is
that Harkins?' across the other side. Somebody was out of the
top of our tank. 'Send him over!' Quite a long walk – could be
100 yards. Walking across to where they were there was a very
big ditch, and I mean a big ditch 15 to 20 feet deep! With a lot
of reeds in. All of sudden, a Jerry came up with a bazooka in his
hand! I didn't have even a pistol on me! I told him to get out.
As he came up, I kicked the bazooka out of his hand. He was

a big bloke – 6 foot 2 or 3 – Jerry Marine Commando. I took
him back to the tank. I said, 'I've got a prisoner here, boys!
What shall I do with him?' 'Shoot the bugger!' Well, I don't
happen to have a pistol!' I said, 'A head came out and they slid
one down over the front of the Comet.' I just put the pistol in
the Jerry's back and pulled the trigger. You'd never believe it,
duff round! It had struck the base of the round and never went
off! I thought, 'This bugger deserves to live!' King got out,
he was a rough hand, he said, 'He's a big bugger isn't he! Turn
him round!' With that King jumped up and hit him – because
King was very short! He belted him – it was a bit rough on the
man, but quarter of an hour before he was trying to kill us! An
infantry officer came over and said, 'Did you pull that trigger?' I
said, 'Yes!' I broke the pistol and showed him. He said, 'I'd have
had you court martialled!' I said, 'Well its lucky it was a duff
round then, wasn't it!' And with this the officer did the same,
he belted him and sent him back down the line![46]

Trooper Len Harkins, 'A' Squadron, 2nd F&FY

On some occasions their Comet main armaments would be used
to blast away any possible opposition in a town or village. Civilian casualties were just collateral damage in the brutal thinking
of the time. If chances were to be taken, then they could be taken
by the 'other' side. It was a cruel, hard business.

One town, there were about sixty tanks, we were all lined
up, got our guns pointed – and we hit it with everything we
had. Sixty guns firing HE shells. Into this town. It made an
awful mess of it. When we went through the town, it was
in a shambles. There were people running about. I'll always
remember this woman with her child in her arms – and the
child was obviously dead. But that was war – and they were
Germans, so we weren't too put out. They said that their town
had been 'open', the Germans had pulled out and left the town

open, but we weren't to know that. Just one of these things in wartime. [47]

Trooper John Buchanan, 4 Troop, 'A' Squadron, 2nd F&FY

Most of the men were keen to collect 'souvenirs' or, more accurately, loot, from the prisoners they took and the villages they captured.

When we passed through villages, you found things you considered 'spoils of war'. Most people looked for watches and cameras. When you got prisoners, they usually offered you their watches, they were so glad they were finished with fighting. They knew you were going to take it from them anyway! We weren't supposed to do this – it was against all regulations – but most officers turned a blind eye – I think some of them were busy looting away themselves. There was a nice big blonde farmer's wife came and said to one of the boys who understood German. He spread the news that she had some cows she was going to service with this bull. Everybody dashed into the farmyard and got into places where they could observe. While we were all watching this ridiculous thing some criminals in the trucks of the 'B' Echelon went into all the tanks and pinched all the loot. I lost several watches and two cameras![48]

Trooper Ron Forbes, 4 Troop, 'B' Squadron, 2nd F&FY

Terry Boyne remembered one amusing incident.

We were going down these houses; there was ever such a noisy action taking place, and the co-driver, Len, says, 'Won't be a minute!' And with that he dived out of the Comet and he ran over to a shop. On the shelves, very high, were bottles; he dived into the shop and he took a couple of these bottles, stuck them under his arm and he dived into this Comet headfirst. 'Cor, look what I've got!' 'Great!' When we opened one of these bottles it was vinegar! All that effort for vinegar![49]

Trooper Terry Boyne, 4 Troop, 'A' Squadron, 2nd F&FY

However, looting was widespread and in some cases men would take an appalling advantage of their position as invaders of a conquered land.

> As we went round, we were picking loot up – shops, villages. Anything blokes had picked up and we were carrying it for them. Watches – and more watches! Cameras. Just take it. We didn't rape anybody – and yet it went on. You couldn't have that number of men and not have somebody among you somewhere that wouldn't find a woman and rape her. It would be pointless to say we didn't do it. I'm sure it went on. If it wasn't rape it then it was certainly next to it. A packet of fags, a bar of chocolate and 'jiggy-jig' behind the bushes. To me that's rape the same as anything else. These people were hungry, they were desperate and starving. Some of them had kids, they would do anything for it. As far as I'm concerned it was rape.[50]
>
> Trooper John Gray, Recce Troop, HQ Squadron, 2nd F&FY

War layered brutalities on brutalities as men were desensitised by the fighting and the terrible things they had witnessed – and done – to survive. It seemed to have been going on for ever.

> The infantry were becoming very difficult! They realised the war was ending and it was very difficult to get them to do anything. It was very clear that the quality of the infantry was not what it had been earlier on. You are less vulnerable [in a tank]. You aren't vulnerable to the rifle shot. What I disliked more than anything was walking down the street and never being sure which direction the next shot was coming from. In a tank, you've got 4 inches of armour all round you, if anything is going to happen to you it's got to be an anti-tank gun or bazooka. There weren't many anti-tank guns or tanks about then. Some tank commander would hang back more than others. Dereck Collis, for instance, my troop sergeant, he'd

been in the war for six years. I don't think he would have 'stuck his neck out' at that stage, but one accepted that.[51]

Lieutenant Thomas Heald, 2 Troop, 'A' Squadron, 2nd F&FY

The Germans were doomed to defeat, but most of them kept on fighting. The days muddled together, but men were still dying, still being maimed.

17

HOW MUCH LONGER?

The Germans were not really fighting any more. They were tending to surrender. After all, we had got up to the Elbe by this stage. The question was where we would meet the Russians really. One realised it was near the end of the war.[1]

Lieutenant Thomas Heald, 2 Troop, 'A' Squadron, 2nd F&FY

IT WAS ALL OVER BAR THE SHOUTING. In fact, both sides seemed to have lost their enthusiasm for a war that was ending soon but might yet outlive them. They knew plenty more men would die, they just hoped not to be among that sorry number. By 10 April, the Twelfth Army Group had completed their subjugation of the economic powerhouse of the Ruhr. Now Montgomery and Bradley were required to launch a concerted drive for the Elbe, with the British edging north towards Hamburg. For many of the men this was a depressing period. The 2nd F&FY remained at Esperke for a couple of days, as there was considerable concern over the proximity of the Belsen Concentration Camp some 10–15 miles to the north-east. Here there were some 40,000 emaciated inmates, in a camp designed for 8,000, many of whom were afflicted with typhus, with an additional 10,000 unburied corpses to pose a further serious health hazard. This triggered negotiations, where the Germans claimed their only concern was that the inmates might spread the disease widely. In the end a limited neutral zone was granted immediately around the camp. In view of what was found there, the German authorities were really only intent on gaining time to hide their crimes against humanity. Whatever the case, some precautions were instituted among the men of the 2nd F&FY.

> We were issued with insect powder, because of this camp where typhus was raging. We didn't know it was Belsen at the time. We were told to sprinkle inside our clothing and inside our blankets. I couldn't have a bath, but we had a canvas bucket and I filled it with some water and got undressed and had a washdown. As I got dressed, I sprinkled this insect powder inside my shirt, pants and uniform as I redressed. Sprinkled some inside my three blankets.[2]
>
> Trooper Jack Edwards, 'B' Squadron, 2nd F&FY

The bridge over the Aller had been demolished by the Germans, but the Royal Engineers had soon built at new bridge at Essel. Once Winsen en der Aller had been captured by the 15/19th Hussars and Cheshires, they were able to resume the advance on 15 April, taking it in turns with the Hussars to lead the advance. It was just another day, but it proved to be a day packed full of dramatic action.

> Up at 05.30 again, in a grey mist, and ate a rotten breakfast on the move. This was always an unpleasant experience: things like cold greasy bacon or soya sausages out of a mess-tin, lukewarm compo tea in a mug, bread and butter sometimes, or hard biscuits, all being handed up in instalments from somewhere down in the tank. It was still better than being in the infantry. In Winsen [en der Aller] there were all the dreary remnants of a battle. We waited in a field for the Herefords, took them on our backs, and set off in the lead.[3]
>
> Captain William Steel Brownlie, Headquarters, 'A' Squadron, 2nd F&FY

Occasionally there would be a brisk exchange of fire, but nothing seriously impeded their progress as a regiment, although some tanks were knocked out of action. When they were leading, as usual, if in any doubt, they would blaze away at the hedges and woods that surrounded them. But at first progress was quick.

> We went flat out through thick woods, firing ahead and to the flanks, occasionally seeing a few enemy and booby-traps – panzerfausts tied to trees with tripwires across the road: ineffective. The usual pall of smoke rose behind us.[4]

Captain William Steel Brownlie, Headquarters, 'A' Squadron, 2nd F&FY

They encountered serious opposition at Wolthausen, which lay on the main Soltau–Celle road.

> We met a roadblock. The Herefords dismounted to make an assault, and I went round to the left to find a good fire position. From here I blazed away with HE and tracer to help the infantry forward, and the attack went in, past the wrecked roadblock and into the blazing streets. I followed, ploughing through burning debris. At one point the house on my left collapsed, showering the tank with embers. I got out and kicked away anything that might have set fire to our precious possession, the bedding, stowed on the back of the tank. The Herefords, with our close support, forced the defenders to retreat, but a few snipers were left. They killed or wounded several of the infantry, and we tank commanders ducked up and down to present as small a target as possible, while still seeing what was going on. We could not pinpoint the snipers, but we were able to identify the area from where their fire was coming. It was decided to burn them out. Tom Heald and I crashed through the gardens, surrounded the offending area, and poured in maximum fire till within ten minutes, all the houses were ablaze. The snipers were silent. House-to-house fighting like that in Wolthausen was always exhilarating: imminent danger from any direction, and the closeness of the destruction caused by one's own guns.[5]

Captain William Steel Brownlie, Headquarters, 'A' Squadron, 2nd F&FY

In Wolthausen there occurred an incident which represented a close escape for Colonel Alec Scott, something that triggered initial concern, dissolving into amusement.

> We sat in the street with the infantry reorganising round us and saw 'Dusty' [Miller] blocking the road a mile away. Desmond therefore reported the road clear, and Colonel Alec at the head of regimental headquarters bowled round the corner towards 'Dusty'. He had gone less than 100 yards when there was an almighty explosion that shook the town and knocked some of us off our feet. The CO's tank disappeared in a cloud of smoke and dust. Silence. At length Alec came on the air, inviting Desmond to walk up for a chat, or words to that effect. His point probably was that a road was never 'clear' until someone had actually driven up it – not normally the commanding officer! The cause of the explosion was a mine linked to an aerial bomb buried nearby, which had gone off before the first tank drew level with it. In the opposite ditch was another bomb, about 500lb size, with its nose blown off and its brown explosive exposed, which had failed to go off. I felt sorry for Desmond – we all make mistakes.[6]
>
> Captain William Steel Brownlie, Headquarters, 'A' Squadron, 2nd F&FY

The advance resumed, with Norman Miller and Scott Brownlie leading the way. They made good progress, passing through Sulze, Diesten and Huxahl with minimal opposition. Then they reached the village of Beckedorf.

> Shots were fired at the leading tanks, by troops dug in on the fields. Fire was returned, they fell silent, but made no sign of surrender, so Tom Heald got among them with his troop. Still no response, so he got out and hauled a few from their trenches, which was taking a chance.[7]
>
> Captain William Steel Brownlie, Headquarters, 'A' Squadron, 2nd F&FY

They could have posed a real threat had the 'German' soldiers not proved to be broken men who had had more than they could take of the war.

> Suddenly two hands appeared out of the ground. Looking at it we realised this ploughed field was full of slit trenches. This was obviously somebody wanting to surrender. Well, there were some of our infantry about, but I couldn't persuade them to do anything about it, so I got out and hauled this poor chap – who was a 17-year-old Hungarian – out of the ground and put him on the tank. So, I drove the tank over the trenches, really to frighten people, I made quite sure the tracks were on either side of the trenches. The infantry followed and got them out of the ground – that's how we got seventy or eighty prisoners.[8]
>
> Lieutenant Thomas Heald, 2 Troop, 'A' Squadron, 2nd F&FY

On and on they went, pushing down to Hermannsburg, to Baven, then down a long stretch of road to Müden at the junction of the Wietze and Örtze rivers, with 'B' Squadron now having taken the lead. At Müden, Major David Voller was ordered to check on whether the bridge across the Wietze was still extant. If it was passable, he was to advance across it to secure the village. Advancing with 'B' Squadron was Captain W. G. Lucas of the 151st Field Regiment (Ayrshire Yeomanry) ensconced in a Cromwell tank, acting as a forward observation post, with wireless communication back to his trusty 25-pounders. His driver, Gunner 'Tam' Steven, left an account of their experiences.

> As we raced towards the bridge, we found it to be protected by a single roadblock of tree-trunks and earth, set in a defile with high banks and trees on either side, which screened from view both the bridge and the town beyond. But as the column halted, no time was lost, and a few well-placed rounds of 77mm sent the block skywards in a shower of shattered timber and stones. In a matter of minutes, we were driving through and over the bridge into the town of Müden itself, where we sat in the middle of the high street, two troops of Comets, being

regarded with some surprise by about a hundred or more
German infantry, complete with their transport. Our jubilation
was short-lived, however, as the bridge behind us disappeared
in a terrific explosion and columns of dust, leaving us cut off
from the tail of our squadron and, for that matter, from the rest
of the brigade.[9]

Gunner 'Tam' Stevens, 151st Field Regiment (Ayrshire Yeomanry) Royal
Artillery

This could have been a disaster – they were cut off and surrounded by Germans, with no infantry support to fend them
off. From the other side of the Wietze, the 2nd F&FY intelligence officer, Lieutenant Harry Axton, was sent forward with
his driver, Ken Watson, to examine what remained of the bridge.

Harry Axton and I were told to go up and inspect the blown
bridge and report back the circumstances. To inspect the
bridge, we had to get out of the scout car. Some shells landed
– they exploded all around the scout car. I got down with my
head at the back of the wheel of the scout car, hands over my
head, nevertheless I got hit by a bit of shrapnel in the leg, which
hit the sciatic nerve. Harry Axton once again was lucky! I
didn't feel the wound – the sciatic nerve was dead, and my foot
went numb. I thought I was hit in the foot! I said to the chaps
who came to assist me, 'I've been hit in the foot!' They took
my boot off and they said, 'Well we can't find anything here!'
Then they looked around and found a hole in my battledress
trousers.[10]

Lance Corporal Ken Watson, HQ Squadron, 2nd F&FY

In Müden, Major David Voller and 'B' Squadron had sprung
into a frenzied burst of action to defend themselves, spraying
77mm shells and Besa machine-gun fire liberally at anything
that moved to break out of the close confines of the town and
escape into the surrounding fields. 'Tam' Stevens recalled what
happened.

The air was filled with urgent enquiries and excited commands, and the tanks went into action individually, firing at the enemy transports and into the buildings, and within half an hour of our arrival Müden was reduced to a burning shambles of lorries and equipment of all kinds, while we now found ourselves in the gathering dusk, firing at bazooka-men in doorways and front gardens – not a healthy spot for tanks after dark, though there was some light from the fires we had started. It was at this point that Major Voller ordered us to break out of the town to the open country beyond. This we set out to do, but the leading tank unfortunately took a wrong turning and was immediately knocked out by bazooka fire. The remainder kept going at top speed, however, still firing at houses as they passed, our own two Besas by now seized solid from continuous firing. I remember my co-driver and myself firing Stens through our hatches as we went along, whenever a target offered.[11]

Gunner 'Tam' Stevens, 151st Field Regiment (Ayrshire Yeomanry) Royal Artillery

They wanted to get into open country, where they would have a chance of preventing the German infantry from getting to close grips with them.

We were joined later by the Fife and Forfar tanks, as it turned out we had halted on the only piece of high ground in the area. So we settled down to spend the night, having counted our blessings. We were seven in number and had about 300 rounds of Besa per tank, and about five rounds of 77mm. We, in the Cromwell, were rather better off as our Besas had jammed earlier, and we had quite a lot of Besa ammunition and rather more 75mm due to our extra capacity. Tight laager was formed, with most of the ammunition in four sentry tanks, and two attacks were made during the night by patrols of infantry, who fired bazookas from a distance before being driven off by concentrated Besa fire. The morning of the 16th dawned bright and clear, and we were delighted and surprised to hear on the

'A' set that the engineers had completed a bridge during the night.[12]

Gunner 'Tam' Stevens, 151st Field Regiment (Ayrshire Yeomanry) Royal Artillery

The Herefords and Royal Engineers excelled themselves in coming to the rescue. During the night, the Herefords crossed the river and established a small tight bridgehead, which had allowed the sappers to get to work and throw up a replacement bridge. Next morning, the rest of the regiment would surge across the new bridge to relieve the isolated 'B' Squadron. Before they set off that morning, Steel Brownlie liberated a group of slave-workers to his immense personal satisfaction. This really was 'making the difference'.

> Near the farm where I was sitting was a sort of barbed-wire cage, surrounding a hut. I broke down part of the fence and was amazed to find over a dozen men and women of various nationalities, some French, ragged and in squalid conditions. They were slave workers who had been there for two or three years, and they 'belonged' to the farmer, who locked them in at the end of each day's work. They then ate what was passed through the wire. I got all this out of them, astonished at their casual and matter-of-fact description of their lot: they were totally dispirited and submissive, but I felt quite otherwise. I hauled out the farmer and his family, and made them tear all the wire down, no tools allowed. The ex-slaves sat and watched, smoking our cigarettes after eating a hot meal from our rations, and visibly came alive again.[13]

Captain William Steel Brownlie, Headquarters, 'A' Squadron, 2nd F&FY

After crossing the new Müden bridge, they headed off north to Poitzen. Here Steel Brownlie and Tom Heald were ordered forward to make sure the next wood was clear to assist the 23rd Hussars, who were taking over the lead role. This triggered a tragic incident.

The wood was half a mile away, astride the road. A German halftrack had just emerged from it and been destroyed. We had no infantry, so the best tactic was to go flat out, and circle the wood just out of panzerfaust range: all quiet. I got permission to go further and had a good view of a smaller wood to the right. There were movements and two tiny white dots appearing at ground level: evidently men in slit trenches. I put in four or five HE, then a stream of machine gun. The place took fire. Figures emerged waving white cloths, and I motored nearer. To my horror, they were civilians, followed by a horse and cart on which were piled all kinds of household goods. I halted 100 yards from them, not knowing what else to do. Two figures came towards me. They were children, a boy and a girl, holding hands and running as hard as they could over the rough ploughed earth. They came right up to the tank, looked up at me, and the small boy said in English, 'You have killed my father.' There was nothing I could say. The only thing to do was to get on with the job.[14]

Captain William Steel Brownlie, Headquarters, 'A' Squadron, 2nd F&FY

From liberating slave labourers to killing innocent civilians in just a few hours. It was a cruel war.

Little did he know it, but Steel Brownie's war was almost over. With Tom Heald following up, he decided to check the woods were clear before waving through the 23rd Hussars for the next leg of the advance.

On the edge facing Poitzen was a heavily camouflaged 75mm anti-tank in a pit, with an AP round up the spout, pointing at the squadron area. Roundabout were piles of ammunition, loaded machine guns, and the dreaded panzerfausts. As we stood talking, the crew of the gun popped up from a dugout not ten yards away, with their hands in the air. They had evidently decided not to shoot their necks out, at this stage in the war. 'Alles kaput!' Tom took them back; I stayed to destroy the gun, etc., as was the habit. Somebody else might come along and use such things.[15]

Captain William Steel Brownlie, Headquarters, 'A' Squadron, 2nd F&FY

Buchanan takes up the story.

Brownlie had a look, he said, 'I'll tell you what we'll do, we'll get a shell and we'll stick it down the muzzle! Get well back, then you fire at it!' You can turn the machine gun to single action! 'Pop! Pop!' until I hit it and that would blow it up. That was the idea, so we stuck a shell in it, he stood behind the tank, he had the telephone, 'Right, Buck, fire!' BANG! 'No, you've missed it! A wee bit to the right!' BANG! I should have waited for him, but before he could say, 'Now!' I put another bullet in – it hit it. The thing blew up and metal came back and smacked him right in chest, about an inch of shrapnel – but it hit him square about half an inch deep into his chest! Naturally, he couldn't go on, so he was sent back.[16]

Trooper John Buchanan, 4 Troop, A Squadron, 2nd F&FY

Steel Brownlie remembered the impact.

A small piece of red-hot shell-case hit me in the chest. Lying on my back looking at the sky, I put my hand inside my shirt and threw the object away. Everything rather blurred, I found myself sitting on a petrol can and McKenzie tying something tight around my chest. Soon I felt fine, and was about to stand up when the medical officer appeared. The 23rd Hussars had passed through, and their echelon was parked nearby. One of my crew had gone over to them and brought a doctor. He said I was all right, but added that, of course, I must be evacuated. I disagreed, but he insisted. If it had been our own 'Doc', I am sure that he would have let me stay in the echelon for a day or two at least to see how things went. As it was, within five minutes I was in a jeep going back the way we had come. It was then in a three-tonner uncomfortably to a dressing station,

I think in Hermannsburg. In a large barn, a medical orderly
pronounced the wound clean and gave me a jab, told me to wait
for an ambulance going back. I sat down but began to bleed, so
lay on a stretcher.[17]

Captain William Steel Brownlie, Headquarters, 'A' Squadron, 2nd F&FY

Despite his protests, Steel Brownlie was now in the grip of a very
efficient evacuation machine and he was sent back to Brussels to
recuperate.

Shortly afterwards, Tom Heald was involved in a dangerous
incident which cast further doubts in his mind as to the compe-
tence of Major Desmond Chute in command of 'A' Squadron.
The first problem was the lack of any proper tactical briefing as
the squadron moved forward in the Uelzen sector.

I was told to go up to the top of the hill – east towards Uelzen.
Nobody told me the tactical situation, that in fact our job was
to stop the defenders of Uelzen coming in a northerly direction.
I knew nothing about Uelzen, which was the training ground
for the Panzers, or SS, or something like that![18]

Lieutenant Thomas Heald, 2 Troop, 'A' Squadron, 2nd F&FY

He considered the orders he was given paid insufficient attention to the scale of opposition they were likely to encounter.

I got up to the top of this hill – there may have been the odd
shot fired at us, but we identified several guns in a wood, down
a dip and then up a slight hill on the other side. About 2,000
yards away. I must have had four tanks at the time. We shelled
the front of the wood, with perhaps sixty to seventy shells. As
far as we could see we had cleared it, we couldn't see any anti-
tank guns left. We were ordered by Desmond Chute to advance
down this hill. I said, quite clearly, 'Well, can you send a troop
to support us?' I didn't mind advancing down the hill, but if
something went wrong, I wanted some firepower at the top!
'No! Go down!' Well, I hadn't been told what there was at

Uelzen, and if we were stopping them advancing north, there
was no point in us going south. Anyhow, I started going down
the hill: Sergeant Anderson's tank was on the left, about 200
yards to the left; Derick Collis' tank was about 150 yards to my
right, slightly forward. I was going down in the centre. I'm sure
I left a fourth tank at the top of the hill – there should have
been a whole troop up there to provide covering fire.[19]

Lieutenant Thomas Heald, 2 Troop, 'A' Squadron, 2nd F&FY

His fears were justified, as several German anti-tank guns opened
up on them as they started to move down the hill.

We got about 200 yards down and we were fired at. The second
shot fired at Sergeant Anderson's tank hit it. I reported that
it was brewing up. I reported it so quickly that their radio
operator heard me reporting it, before he got out of the tank! I
could see flames and smoke. It wasn't a very bad fire, but there
was a fire.[20]

Lieutenant Thomas Heald, 2 Troop, 'A' Squadron, 2nd F&FY

Gordon Fidler was the driver in Sergeant Anderson's Comet.

The squadron is up on the top of a rise. There is an anti-tank
gun firing across. The troop are told to cross the open field on
our left, go out in open order. There was a track with a few trees
leading across. Where the shells are coming from is in front of
us. We are the lead tank, two on the flank. I don't know where
the fourth one was. We get down this track and we get hit by
this anti-tank gun – hit at the front. It starts off very gently;
with the Sherman it would probably be an eruption. It doesn't
burst into flames, but it starts flaming, not with a 'Whoosh!'
but all round. Fire starts coming up. But we're all out by now,
we've got out of the tank. Then it starts to really erupt. As we
get out, we're then machine gunned from where the anti-tank
gun was. We tried to get in the lea of the tank to avoid this.
It's burning quite fiercely now, so we can't keep too close to it!

We get out heads down, we're not going to move, we're staying where we are.[21]

Trooper Gordon Fidler, 4 Troop, 'A' Squadron, 2nd F&FY

Heald had to react quickly, using all his accumulated experience.

I ordered smoke to be put down. I ordered Derek Collis to retire. It was in a ploughed field and I took a decision that I was going to reverse up the hill – keeping the 4-inch armour facing the enemy. I hadn't realised quite how slowly a tank reverses – it does about 2 mile an hour in reverse. It must have taken about 5 minutes to get up this hill. I put down smoke with the main gun and the 2-pounder. We kept up a pretty good smokescreen. Eventually, I'd used all my smoke and the tank at the top of the hill had used all its smoke. Derek Collis tried to turn round, and he turned into a bomb crater and stalled – so they abandoned their tank. I got myself into a turret down position and I then reported back what had happened. I then set out to find out what had happened to Sergeant Anderson's crew. There was a beech wood at the top of the hill, and I went along the front edge until I came to Gordon Fidler, who was the driver. He was surprised and eternally grateful to see me! I found he and the others were all right.[22]

Lieutenant Thomas Heald, 2 Troop, 'A' Squadron, 2nd F&FY

Fidler was indeed pleased to see Heald, grateful that his officer would risk his own life to check that he and the rest of Anderson's crew were all right.

We're there probably half an hour, probably a little bit more. The machine gunning is stopped, so obviously everything's clear, but we still won't move, we stay where we are. Then who should be coming down the track, on his hands and knees is Tom Heald. He'd come out of a wood at the back of us. He comes down to us and we follow him up the track into the wood and we get on to a scout car. At the back of the squadron was a load of 5.5-inch guns. These had in the meantime been throwing shells in at the anti-tank gun.[23]

Trooper Gordon Fidler, 4 Troop, 'A' Squadron, 2nd F&FY

There was an amusing postscript when the recovery teams went to rescue the 'bogged in' Comet commanded by Derek Collis.

Later in the day, Sergeant Bennett, who was the REME sergeant, went out in the armoured recovery vehicle to the tank. Not as is suggested in the squadron diary after dark, but in the middle of the afternoon! He got out of the ARV. Pressed the starter of the tank and drove it out of the bomb crater! The REME sergeants – Sergeant Bennett in particular with the ARV – were absolutely excellent. The ARV was a Sherman hull with the turret taken out which could be used to tow a tank and could winch tanks out. They were always 'on the scene' and exceedingly useful if you were in trouble.[24]

Lieutenant Thomas Heald, 2 Troop, 'A' Squadron, 2nd F&FY

Although one tank had been knocked out and another bogged in, at least there had been no casualties. Doubts about Chute were multiplying and as a result, a couple of days later he was replaced in command of 'A' Squadron by Major William Hotblack, who was generally a better-regarded officer.

*

AS THE DAYS PASSED the routine was unrelenting. Across Germany, the three Allied Army Groups were making good progress. For the 2nd F&FY it was a case of rapid advances, hold-ups at roadblocks or blown bridges, a brief flurry of action, then a resumption in the advance. Incidents too minor to be recalled in a regimental history made a very real impression on the individuals concerned. Sometimes it was something not that important at the time, but the memory would linger on for decades after the war.

We were travelling across this country, south of the river Elbe. Market garden country. We were going on earth tracks, our tank leading. Very early morning, just after dawn. We moved into the edge of a village – and then stopped for further orders. All quiet, nothing in sight. Then along the street was a line of trees – and I could see movement coming towards us. It was a German soldier on a bike, with his rifle over his shoulder, pedalling along. I thought, 'He'll have a shock when he gets up to us – he'll have to surrender, a bit sharpish!' I wasn't going to do anything, but I just traversed the gun as the Jerry came in sight. He saw us – and he saw the gun moving. He panicked and he tried to shoot off up a side turning. I thought he was trying to escape, so I'd better get him. I gave him a quick burst – he dropped dead off his bike. Through the gun sight I got a close-up view of his face as he fell off his bike. He seemed to go grey. I can still see his face. I thought, 'What a shame, it didn't need to happen. If he'd just kept coming toward us, he would have been all right!' But I thought, 'There's 3 million German dead; another one won't make a lot of difference!'[25]

Trooper Jack Edwards, 'B' Squadron, 2nd F&FY

On 18 April, there was another terrible incident triggered by a combination of panic, stress or just sheer ruthlessness at Rottorf. Here 'C' Squadron was in the lead and 2 Troop under Lieutenant Eric Lamont had just crossed the bridge over a small stream when they heard the familiar sound of a demolition charge. Robert Nurse was a witness to what happened next.

It was blown behind, so we were in effect cut off. We pulled up the tank in the courtyard of a German farm. The farmer came out to see what was going on, and Lamont pulled his pistol from his holster, dropped it in his hatred and haste, pulled mine and put all six rounds into this guy. Which again didn't endear him to me – that side of his character I did not like. He was right; I was the one who was wrong; you've got to be ruthless in war.[26]

Trooper Robert Nurse, 2 Troop, 'C' Squadron, 2nd F&FY

There was considerable fighting in the village, before they were rescued by the rest of the squadron and a company of the Herefords, who put an end to any further resistance.

On 19 April, the regiment suffered their final fatal casualty when they were ambushed by a panzerfaust team in the woods just to the west of the village of Sangenstedt on the final approaches to the town of Winsen close to the Elbe river. This truly was a distinction that everyone wanted to avoid.

The war was rapidly approaching its end. One felt one would be unfortunate to 'catch it' at the last moment. One thought, 'Well, we've made it – almost!' You didn't volunteer for anything! A friend of mine, Corporal Bush,[27] he was killed. He'd gone right the way through from Normandy. I was just down the road. He was in the lead, and he was ordered to cross a road. As he did a German anti-tank gun fired down the road. He stopped and bailed out. The gun fired its second shot – an HE. It exploded and caught him – and killed him. I helped to bury him. It was very, very sad.[28]

Sergeant Roy Vallance, 4 Troop, 'A' Squadron, 2nd F&FY

Doug Hayes was another who helped bury Bush.

The last one I buried was Stan Bush up on the rise from the river. It came back that Stan Bush had been killed. The padre said, 'Will you come and help out on a burial? I always used to go, but it really struck me, because I knew Stan very well. He stood out as a nice guy. Very quiet and unassuming.[29]

Trooper Doug Hayes, Fitters Section, 'A' Squadron, 2nd F&FY

The same day Tom Heald had a lucky escape from the same fate, when his troop was ambushed as it passed through some woods.

We were ordered to go along the road. We proceeded in the usual way. I was the first or second tank. Certainly, I was going at a reasonable speed, probably not too fast. Probably firing. But I was hit by a bazooka. There was a flash – a big bang – I knew I'd been bazookered! One's adrenalin starts running! I ordered, 'Bazooka – driver speed up!' In fact, I was switched on to transmit, so the whole of the regiment heard I'd been bazookered! We speeded up and got through the wood. The following tank got through and I think there may have been one in front of me. When we could, we got out to see what had happened. The bazooka had hit the very end of the track pin – there was 10 or 12 inches of armour at that point! All it had done was explode on hitting – and damage the track pin slightly. So in fact we weren't bazookered 'properly'; we were terribly lucky! If it had been 6 inches higher it would have been at the base of the turret. I'm 'Lucky Tom'! Within half an hour, things had quietened down a bit. We got behind a farm building and the crew took the track off and put a fresh track pin in. [30]

Lieutenant Thomas Heald, 2 Troop, 'A' Squadron, 2nd F&FY

There was a welcome pause for the regiment in the Winsen sector, as the Elbe river was a considerable obstacle that would take a concerted effort to cross.

They were withdrawn for ten days' hard-earned rest behind the front line. Each troop took it in turns to go forward on a 24-hour standing patrol along the riverbanks of the Elbe. A panzerfaust party made a raid across the river but it was repelled with no loss. Far stranger was a session of prolonged German shelling on the night of 27 April. The first shell crashed down with awesome precision, hitting a lorry and a jeep. The rest – about fifty shells in all – landed in and around the general area the regiment was occupying, but all the rest failed to explode. This caused much speculation as to the possible reason, but no firm conclusions were reached. Perhaps the German artillery were suddenly favourably disposed to the British? Or was it sabotage of the ammunition supply?

On 1 May, they were on the move again, moving up to the Elbe, which had been crossed by their old friends in the 15th (Scottish) Division to form a bridgehead around Lauenburg. By this time the Germans really had given up the ghost and there was only very scattered token resistance. None of the men mentioned in their interviews that the day before, Adolf Hitler had committed suicide in Berlin. It was, however, good news. Peace was coming.

The 2nd F&FY was then dispatched to race as fast as possible to cut off all German communications with the Jutland peninsula. Initially the regiment were following the 23rd Hussars and 8th Rifle Brigade, but in the early afternoon it took the lead and pressed on to harbour at Wentorf and Sirksfelde. German opposition was restricted to some 'token' exchanges of fire before a grateful surrender. On 2 May, their objective was changed. It was claimed that intelligence had been received that Lübeck civilians, worried by the imminent arrival of the Russians, had removed the demolition charges laid on the bridges and were eagerly awaiting the arrival of the British. The news triggered a near instantaneous response and both the 2nd F&FY and the 23rd Hussars were ordered to proceed post-haste to Lübeck. This led to something of a race.

During that pell-mell advance, Tom Heald's troop was detached to relieve a party of some 1,600 RAF prisoners of war who were reported to be at the village of Westerau, some five to six miles from Lübeck. These former inmates of Stalag Luft 3 had been engaged in a long march under parlous conditions from the east, and had finally been set up in an impromptu wired-up POW camp in a field just outside the village.

> The reason I was chosen was that I had more fuel in the tanks than any of the other troops in the squadron. Fuel problem, because the fuel trucks hadn't been able to get over the bridge

at Lauenburg the night before, so we hadn't filled up. I went
out in the morning to find this prisoner of war camp, which we
were told was at Westerau, which was two villages in front of
our front line! I drove off with my tanks. Westerau was a small
village with about twelve houses, with almost a green in it,
which was very unusual in Germany. Not a soul about, no sign
of any prisoner of war camp. I got out of my tank and knocked
on a door. Somebody looked out of a window. I said in my
German, which was non-existent, 'Where is the prisoner of war
camp?' And they pointed down a lane. We didn't like the look
of this very much, because there were hedges down either side
of it. We went down it and after about 200 yards came to a sign
in English, 'Good pull-in for tanks 200 yards ahead'. We drove
up to the POW camp – the POWs had put the sign there. The
camp was in a farm, with a perimeter fence all the way round it.
Strangely enough, none of them had heard the tanks coming.
Therefore, they were quite unprepared; the guards opened the
gate and we drove in. No resistance at all. Then we had 800 to
1,000 RAF men descend on our three tanks! Immediately we
got there, there were then orders for us to return! Well, it's very
difficult to extract oneself from 300 men on your tank! I found
I was missing one tank.[31]

Lieutenant Thomas Heald, 2 Troop, 'A' Squadron, 2nd F&FY

Gordon Fidler, the driver of the missing Comet, picks up the
story.

We had to stop, the prisoners are coming out of the gate, they
clambered onto the tank, it was absolutely horrendous. They
put their arms round us, they were jumping on the tanks, they
wanted to ride on them, they wanted to get into the turret, they
wanted to get into every part of the tank! We were taken inside
the camp, with barbed wire all the way round. They've got a
meal of sorts, bits and pieces. So, we all got out of the tanks
and went into their messroom. Tom Heald went off with the

guards. All of a sudden, we heard a tank start up! Somebody said to me, 'Your tank's moving about out there!' I rushed out there. The co-driver had been asked by the RAF prisoners if he would knock all the wire down. That was OK – he had no right to be in there, but he did it! And he did it all wrong! He went and followed the wire along instead of going over it and back, over it and back, knocking it down. When we got out there the tank was absolutely covered with wire, all round the back sprockets, the idlers at the front, we were in a hell of a state. It took us about three to four hours – using everything to get this wire off the sprockets.[32]

Trooper Gordon Fidler, 4 Troop, 'A' Squadron, 2nd F&FY

Meanwhile, the 2nd F&FY charged up the motorway – one of the clichéd symbols of Hitler's Nazi regime turned to good use – towards Lübeck. It was a dramatic advance, one that triggered many stories.

The autobahn was a beautifully built road. It was elevated in certain parts. We were on one of these elevated parts when we saw this steam train leaving the station full of troops. We shot it up and blew up the engine. The personnel on the train all coming out and taking cover. Four or five tanks line abreast tearing up that road – flat out. If you happened to have a better tank than your neighbour, well you got ahead! It was very thrilling! You realised what tanks could do on the autobahn![33]

Trooper Ron Forbes, 4 Troop, 'B' Squadron, 2nd F&FY

There were also some strange juxtapositions. Peace was almost there, but not quite, and Doug Hayes remembered an amusing 'close shave' during these madcap advances across the German heartlands.

I was doing second man on a Bedford 3-tonner. Tony Pope was a pipe-smoker, and we could see these people moving each side of us. He said to me, 'Hey Doug, have you got any matches on you?' I said, 'No!' 'Well stick your head out and ask one of these soldiers for a match!' I opened the side door – and I said, 'You'll have to do without your smoke, Tony!' He said, 'Why?' 'Because they're all bloody Jerries that are marching each side of us! Don't say anything just keep going!' All I could see was a sea of German helmets. I thought, 'Well I'm not going to ask them for a box of matches!' They didn't realise who we were. They thought they were marching alongside their own waggons![34]

Trooper Doug Hayes, Fitters Section, 'A' Squadron, 2nd F&FY

Alex Gilchrist claimed to have been the first into Lübeck.

I was the leading tank! I got instructions from David Voller to go hell for leather. We belted along this motorway – 30–40 miles per hour. No resistance whatsoever, it was like a Sunday afternoon drive. I believe I was the first tank into Lübeck.[35]

Lieutenant Alex Gilchrist, 2 Troop, 'B' Squadron, 2nd F&FY

As far as the 2nd F&FY were concerned, trains and boats and planes were all legitimate targets as they sped through.

We were coming into Lübeck and there was an aerodrome on the right-hand side. I saw a plane, a Junkers passenger plane, taking off. I fired at it, machine-gun fire. I hit it, but what happened to it I really don't know because it was a kind of foggy, misty sort of morning. I think it must have slewed or stopped.[36]

Trooper John Buchanan, 4 Troop, 'A' Squadron, 2nd F&FY

In the mid afternoon, they reached Lübeck to find the city wide open, with no resistance. The first task was to seize control of the bridges and docks. John Buchanan was delighted to add his very own ship to his personal 'score' as a gunner of various assorted German tanks, halftracks, lorries, self-propelled guns and artillery.

We were sent down to the riverbank. No real purpose. And this ship was moving, very slowly, down the canal leading into the Baltic. The officer says, 'Fire a shot across his bow!' I think I fired an HE shell across his bow to make him stop – the damn thing didn't stop. 'Ah!' he says, 'Brass it up! Shoot at it with the machine guns!' I got the machine gun onto the bridge, and I really 'brassed it up'. All the windows were shattered. Whoever it was must have turned the wheel because the ship veered away and crashed into the bank. The ship was stopped, it slewed across the canal – it would stop anybody else. That was a ship added to my collection![37]

Trooper John Buchanan, 4 Troop, 'A' Squadron, 2nd F&FY

The Recce Troop were soon overwhelmed in their allotted task of collecting prisoners.

We were driving this Honey, we were on our own, just following the road. Some American Red Cross came up and said, 'There's some Germans that want to surrender!' We drove down the road to pick up these Germans – there were hundreds of the buggers. They had generals with them – the lot. We didn't know what to do – there was only two of us. The turret was full of loot that we were carrying for ourselves and other people! We could just get inside it – you couldn't have fired the gun if you'd wanted to! We put the generals on the back of the tank and marched them off into Lübeck. There were hundreds of them – they were armed – they'd got bazookas, rifles, machine guns! We had to cross a river coming back again, so we spoke to one of the officers who could understand English and told them to throw all these arms into the river – which is what they did. Hundreds of them! When we got to Lübeck they didn't want to know – they'd got so many of their own – so we just left them there.[38]

Trooper John Gray, Recce Troop, HQ Squadron, 2nd F&FY

All the regiment were caught up in dealing with the swarms of prisoners. By and large they were well treated.

There were prisoners all the time coming in. Most of them were bedraggled – unshaven – like tramps. They'd been days hiding. It was shocking to see what a proud army could be reduced to. Some of them were so young – they were just kids, really – 16 and that. They were crying and in complete fear. They'd been indoctrinated in that the British would shoot them. It must have been a great revelation to them when they realised that they were going to be treated fairly well.[39]

Trooper Ron Forbes, 4 Troop, 'B' Squadron, 2nd F&FY

The prisoners were disarmed and then gathered up into parties of roughly a thousand each and then dispatched off to improvised camps. In all the regiment reckoned it dealt with some 15,000 German POWs. Then there was the problem of all the German civilian refugees that were pouring into the city seeking succour from the threat from the east.

We went into Lübeck and there were thousands and thousands of German civilians, fleeing from the Russians. They were on all sorts of vehicles: lorries driving with no tyres, worn right out – gone![40]

Sergeant Roy Vallance, 4 Troop, 'A' Squadron, 2nd F&FY

At times, the rule of law collapsed as desperate civilians tried to get food from anywhere they could.

We got a call from HQ that the Swedish Red Cross were having trouble. Could we send a tank down to sort it out! There was a riot going on. I went – the Swedish bloke took me down. It was like a rough square and a load of Swedish Red Cross sheds – and German civilians were robbing it – just looting! So, we sorted them out! I couldn't speak German, but he could, I said, 'You'd better tell them that if they don't go, I shall lower the gun!' He said, 'You wouldn't, would you?' I said, 'Well, you just wait and see!' He told them – and I fired two bursts of the machine gun above their heads to emphasise it! They dropped the bloody lot – they soon scattered.[41]

Sergeant Jim Thompson-Bell, 'C' Squadron, 2nd F&FY

There was also the even more serious problem of the displaced persons, who had endured forced labour and terrible privations under the German jackboot and were now in no mood to wait for the authorities to make the 'proper' arrangements. They wanted food now. Some also wanted vengeance on any German that they might encounter.

By the end of 2 May some degree of order had been achieved, backed up by a strict curfew. Next day, the city was handed over to the tender ministrations of the 5th Division and the regiment was billeted for the next week in the nearby villages of Mönkhagen and Eckhorst, a couple of miles to the west of the city. The end of the war was nigh, and as so often happens it ended in a tremendous anti-climax. There was no heroic last battle – the German resistance so long prolonged had finally just fizzled out into a miasma of misery. On 4 May, the German High Command agreed to the surrender of all German forces in the Netherlands, north-west Germany, Schleswig-Holstein and Denmark to Montgomery – to take effect from 08.00 on 5 May 1945. The British war was effectively over. A formal military surrender was signed at 02:41 on 7 May, with the final ratification of the unconditional German surrender to the Allies finally signed at 21.20 on 8 May. The German forces would cease active operations from 23.01, remain in their current positions and accept complete disarmament. It was Victory in Europe.

They celebrated on 8 May 1945 with bonfires, drinking and general rejoicing. It was a time for mixed feelings. Relief they had survived and to finally know they were safe; a natural celebration that their war was over; but at the same time a lingering sorrow for all the friends they had lost in the year since they landed in Normandy. Some even had a kind of survivor's guilt: how had they survived when better men than them had died? It was if all the weight pressing down on them had suddenly been removed and long-suppressed thoughts forced their way to the top. Such jumbled emotions in military minds often promote a desire to seek a happy – or sad – oblivion in alcohol. And that is exactly what most of the men of the 2nd F&FY did that night.

> Then it ended – and we made a huge bonfire in the middle of a field. Believe it or not, at the centre of it was a petrol tanker! It wasn't absolutely full of petrol, but it still had some! Whatever else we could find we put on it – a huge bonfire. We had it at night with a lot of beer. We fired off all our Very pistols and whatever pyrotechnics we had. That was the end of it! I felt greatly relieved and extremely lucky![42]
>
> Sergeant Roy Vallance, 4 Troop, 'A' Squadron, 2nd F&FY

Geoff Eason remembered a truly wild bonfire blazing out of control in that farmer's field at Mönkhagen.

> We were parked in the middle of a field. Celebrations are a bit difficult to arrange – we were up to our eyeballs in muck and mud! But we did tour the countryside and towed in eight, or nine, or ten vehicles and piled them on top of a petrol tanker – and set fire to the lot. The lads who'd been to Lübeck had got all this hooch from the bonded warehouse! They were all as tight as ticks. Anybody could have taken us then! I think I was the only sober bloke there![43]
>
> Trooper Geoff Eason, Recce Troop, HQ Squadron, 2nd F&FY

Even the officers did not stand on the dignity of their rank – and they too imbibed deeply.

> I got drunk on some very unsuitable liquor! I did my drinking with the squadron – they produced this terrible liquor! It was quite potent stuff! I don't remember much else![44]
>
> Major Douglas Hutchison, RHQ Squadron, 2nd F&FY

The focus was on booze, booze and, for a 'heroic' few, even more booze. It didn't matter what kind; whatever it was, they drank it with gusto, and the results next day can well be imagined.

We celebrated with all the booze that we'd collected on the way. All different sorts in bottles. I said, 'What are we going to do?' We had a big basin we found, we put it in there – it was nearly green – we mixed it – you name it – it was in it! We had some lighting units we'd picked up on the way belonging to the Germans – we set them up. We had a good old drink up. Then we went to sleep. We all had bad heads! It was discovered in the morning that we couldn't find my driver – Smithy! We searched all around – we couldn't find him anywhere! About the second day, along come this fellow with Smithy! He says, 'I think he's one of yours!' I said, 'He's my bugger! Where have you found him?' He said, 'Well he came into us in rather a bad state – he really only woke up this morning!' Smithy looked a bit sheepish! What had happened – he went out of the barn to have a pee – turned the wrong way, didn't he, till he landed up with these people down the road. Fortunately, they were English soldiers![45]

Sergeant Jim Thompson-Bell, 'C' Squadron, 2nd F&FY

VE Day was a night to remember, celebrated in such a style that ironically ensured most of them really couldn't remember what happened! Their war was over.

EPILOGUE

When I first joined the Fifes I thought, 'What a bloody mournful lot! With the bagpipes playing. But you know in time, you get used to them. You get to like them! The Scots – they say they're mean! Are they hell! There was nobody skint in the Fifes so long as somebody had a shilling![1]

Len Harkins

OF COURSE, THEY COULDN'T all go home straight away. The 2nd F&FY were now part of an occupying army responsible for maintaining order amid the ongoing efforts to establish sound governance in war-torn Germany. They were moved to be based at Bredstedt near the east coast of Schleswig Holstein and about 15 miles from the Danish frontier. Their first major task was to receive the hordes of German soldiers as they crossed the border, falling back from their former role garrisoning Norway and Denmark. Some of the men were amazed by the defiant martial attitude of some of their erstwhile opponents.

We lined the roads just outside Bredstedt when they were coming along. We were impressed – when they came towards the town, they all came to attention. Marched at attention. And they were singing. Some of these marching songs the Germans had were very good – very inspiring! Some of the boys saluted them – I didna salute them![2]

Trooper Ron Forbes, 4 Troop, 'B' Squadron, 2nd F&FY

They also had to deal with the thousands of displaced persons who had been freed from the German forced labour camps. The squadrons took it in turns to detach men to the camps. Sadly, as was often the case among the British occupying forces in post-war Germany, there was little of the natural sympathy that might have been expected for these poor benighted victims of the German slave-labour regime, and very little real concern as to what might happen to them once they were returned to their home countries under Soviet control.

> We had to look after some large camps of displaced persons. We were supposed to entertain them; we played football against them. They were a mixture of anything from eastern Europe – they were a miscellaneous, ill-disciplined, rather tiresome lot! They were repatriated during the summer. I suppose, poor souls, that when they were returned to Russia, they had a fairly sticky response.[3]
>
> Major Douglas Hutchison, RHQ Squadron, 2nd F&FY

In the early days of the occupation, a policy of strict non-fraternisation was enforced to restrict social interaction as much as possible with the general population. It did not last.

> I was quite happy with it – I think most people were! Because I didn't really have any great love for the Germans. All these years we'd been taught to hate them, and the only good German is a dead one! But you can't really live among people and go on disliking them, particularly as they were in such a poor state. They had no food, no transport, most of their cities were bombed to smithereens. All these things start with the children – then one thing leads to another. Soldiers give children sweets, then the parents start to talk to them, and things take their natural course – you just become friendlier.[4]
>
> Sergeant Roy Vallance, 4 Troop, 'A' Squadron, 2nd F&FY

The regiment did not survive long in its wartime state. The

presence of the 'senior' regiment, the 1st F&FY, in Germany
meant that there was a large exchange of personnel, which tore
the guts out of the unit. On 17 June 1945, many of the men we
have followed for so long through these pages found themselves
packed off in drafts to join the 1st F&FY. What is more, they
were told that they were bound for the Far East and the continu-
ing war against the Japanese. An individual's fate was decided
by their demobilisation number which was calculated accord-
ing to their age and the number of months they had served in
uniform. The young ones, who had not been in the army that
long and thus had a high 'demob', were given no choice but to be
drafted. Men who had been in the army longer and who therefore had a lower number, were also given the chance to volunteer
to accompany their friends into the 1st F&FY. Not everyone was
negative about the prospect; some, like Jack Edwards, actively
welcomed the idea.

> We were told all the young men of demobilisation groups
> above a certain number had to parade in a cinema on the
> Sunday morning to be addressed by the colonel. We were all
> there, all the younger end of us, and the colonel got on the
> stage and gave us a talk to say that we were all experienced
> soldiers, who'd been in action at various times over the
> last twelve months, but that soon the regiment would be
> disbanded. But if any of us wanted to stay with the regiment
> – and stay with their friends – we could transfer to the 1st Fife
> and Forfar, which was also in Germany, but which was due to
> go to the Far East! After this talk, a gang of us in our squadron
> gathered together and we said, 'Well, the 1st Fife and Forfar
> have got Crocodiles!' We knew that! We hated the thought
> of the Japanese – their name was mud as far as we were
> concerned. We said, 'Let's go out and incinerate the yellow
> bastards!' We all volunteered to go to the 1st Fife and Forfar. A
> day or two later there was a convoy went with about a hundred
> of us from the regiment. While we were on the way there, there

was a similar number coming from the 1st Fife and Forfar, older men coming back to our regiment.[5]

Trooper Jack Edwards, 1st F&FY

One of those who 'volunteered' was Steel Brownlie, who had recovered from his minor wound and the cheerful excesses of his brief leave back in the UK. He had managed to rejoin the regiment at Bredstedt on 31 May.

Colonel Alec informed me that I had 'volunteered' to take part. The plan later unfolded. We would have Crocodiles, flame-throwing Churchills, with which to burn stubborn Japanese in their pillboxes at a range of 100 yards, as they tried to defend their homeland. We would fly to [the] UK, have thirty days leave, and then fly to [the] USA and link up with the tanks, which had gone ahead by sea.[6]

Captain William Steel Brownlie, 1st F&FY

In the end it was all cancelled when modern technology brought the war to an abrupt end.

Two atomic bombs had spared us (average age 19 years 6 months), as well as many others, another 'conventional' war. I have never had any sympathy with those who take a one-sided view of Hiroshima and Nagasaki.[7]

Captain William Steel Brownlie, 1st F&FY

Senior officers, like 'Pinkie' Hutchison, watched the drafts come and go and ultimately found himself appointed as the acting colonel of the remnants of the 2nd F&FY.

During the summer, those who were not due for early release, all the younger or more recently joined members of the regiment, were drafted into the 1st Fife and Forfar Regiment. They in turn sent us their people who, like the remainder of us, were due for early release. The idea being that having achieved this, the 2nd Fife and Forfar would be in due course disbanded.

Colonel Scott was given an appointment commanding a regiment – it may have been his own regiment, the Inniskilling Dragoons – he was a regular soldier. He left the regiment and for a few months I was paid as an acting lieutenant colonel! Which was very reasonable in the circumstances as I didn't have very much to do![8]

Major Douglas Hutchison, RHQ Squadron, 2nd F&FY

As the year wore on, and as the threat of involvement in the war against Japan evaporated, most of the men's minds turned towards demobilisation. The army was keen to help as best it could in preparing them for a renewal of civilian life.

Gradually the regiment eroded away. Demobilisation parties became the new routine, old faces disappeared, and soon hardly anyone was left. Fittingly, a Dundee recruit from 1939, then a trooper but now an officer, Alex Gilchrist, was the man charged with winding up the 2nd F&FY on the final official day of its existence, 9 January 1946.

There was only about forty to fifty of us left in the regiment. I was acting adjutant by that time and it was a matter of being in constant contact with the brigade headquarters to see what the next move was. We had to get rid of all the vehicles. I had fellows driving to Husum and Schleswig. The regiment was just being run down completely. Eventually I was told by Brigadier 'Monkey' Blacker that I had to get all the records packed up in big steel boxes and return them to Brigade HQ. The day came – that was the end of the unit. I was left with about fourteen or fifteen vehicles, and I had to get rid of them. Brigade didn't want them; Division didn't want them! I thought, 'What the hell do I do with them?' I found there was a big old quarry, not so far away, it was filled with water. I lined up those vehicles, put them in first gear and just let them simply roll into the water! Believe you me, half the farmers from all around were there within a few minutes, they had tractors and those vehicles were pulled out again within half an hour and put to their own use.[9]

Lieutenant Alex Gilchrist, 2 Troop, 'B' Squadron, 2nd F&FY

Gilchrist went off to serve the rest of his time with the Inns of Court Regiment on the Danish border and was himself demobilised in May 1946.

*

DEMOBILISATION WAS SOMETHING the men devoutly wished for, but it was not always what they wanted when they returned to civilian life. Most returned to the jobs they had left. In the harsh economic climate of the post-war world there was often little choice. They often had to bite their lips as they witnessed colleagues who had not gone to war, for whatever reason, now promoted to managerial positions far above them. They had lost several years of their working life, crucial years that were difficult to catch up.

In June 1944, I went to France weighing over 13 stone, fighting fit; I came back from there weighing barely 9 stone, a gaunt shadow of my former self. Generally, my feelings were to forget all about it, no one wanted to contact me or wanted to know, and no one cared. I had done what I had to do. I had lost six years of my life. I had expended too much of my drive. It was an awful ordeal to find my niche to pick up where I had been. I returned to the County Council; a very small fry in a big sea! No concessions were made for the six years I had been away. I was placed on a grade as if I was just starting a job with them. I did not expect much but felt a bit of a twit as a 'junior'. I had lost a lot of work experience and now the war was over I had no concessions in the professional exams. I would have to take all subjects at once and pass at the same time. Our old promotion

routes had been filled and we should have to take a back seat! I
was not welcomed back. Thus, I settled back to civilian life.[10]

John Thorpe

Often, they thrashed around, endlessly changing jobs, seeking
something they could never quite define.

I went in the army as an 18-year-old, knew nothing about
anything. Came out as a married man, who'd been away from
home for three and a half years. With great difficulty; there I
was, been away in the army for a few years. We were promised
our civvie street jobs back; could you really imagine me going
back as junior clerk at Purley's? Like a lot of people, I had a
hell of a job to settle down, I really did! I went to work on the
railway first – electrical work. Hated it! Then I went into the
offices of the railway – engineers' department – a bit better. I
think a lot of people from the services had a job to settle down.
We missed the camaraderie, the comradeship we'd got used to.
We were all reliant on each other. We looked after each other;
we were happy together. That's what we all missed.[11]

Len Newman

John Gray returned to his pre-war work behind the counter of
his local Co-operative grocers. He was a slightly strange character, but he, too, found he missed the comradeship of his army
life most of all.

You're 18, an impressionable age, you lived, you ate, you fought
and you died with these fellows. Well, they died – I lived. It was
like a big family. There was always somebody to help you, if you
needed it – if there was anything wrong at home, or anything
like that. It was an incredible thing – I think the word they use
is camaraderie – you were all mates together. When I came out
there was this feeling of emptiness. I was leaving it all behind. I
didn't really want to. It's most peculiar. It was horrible. I don't
know. You seemed to be at your wits' end all the time. You got

easily aggravated, bad tempered – it was all the things I wasn't
when I went in, I was when I came out. I think it was what
helped to ruin my first marriage.[12]

John Gray

Always on the left politically, Gray became an activist with both
his Trades Union and Labour Party, trying in some small way to
improve the quality of life for ordinary people.

We were being told all the time in the army that we were
fighting for better things. A county fit for heroes to live in –
well I was one of the heroes and I wanted it fit for me. I went
out of my way to make it like that – for me and anyone else
that required it. If people didn't have the brains to do it for
themselves, I'd do it for them.[13]

John Gray

For Len Harkins, pre-war a somewhat harum-scarum character,
the war acted as a jolt and set him on a more measured path
through life.

When I thought I was lucky enough to pull through – I never
thought I was getting out of Normandy – but when you think,
'Christ! That was near!' I said to myself then, 'If I ever come
through this, I'll bloody work day and night!' Which I did![14]

Len Harkins

Thus inspired, he would run successful enterprises in the horse
trade in the post-war years.

For William Steel Brownlie, the end of the war must have
been a real challenge. Having been rescued from the prospect of
service in the Far East, he had an inconsequential job as second in
command of a HQ Squadron with the 22nd Armoured Brigade
in Schleswig Holstein, until his demobilisation in late 1946.
Could civilian life ever really match the frenzied excitement
and challenges of leading his beloved 4 Troop of 'A' Squadron

into battle? He went back to university and graduated in French and German in 1950. Then a career as a language teacher in Renfrewshire, although he could not quite stay away from the army; he served for many years with the local territorials, the Ayrshire Yeomanry. He even wrote their regimental history, a fantastic piece of work *The Proud Trooper: The History of the Ayrshire Yeomanry from its raising in the Eighteenth Century to 1964* (London: Collins, 1964). Did he ever really settle down? Perhaps best to quote his own last words in his memoirs, *'And Came Safe Home'*, written in 1989.

> Adjustment was difficult, but also necessary, and from the back of my mind come words that were often heard during the war: 'What do you do in real life?' Well, civilian life may have been more real, but it was a lot less exciting.[15]
>
> William Steel Brownlie

There were post-war success stories: Tom Heald went back to study law at university, leading to a successful career as a barrister and then judge, while Alex Gilchrist returned to his pre-war work in the sales office of a printing firm, where he found that his war experiences had broadened his outlook and made him realise what he was capable of. His self-confidence had been boosted and he very soon found himself promoted.

For many of the wealthier officers, the war was merely an interruption in their pre-war careers. Thus, Sir John Gilmour returned to work in the brewing industry, before succeeding in becoming a Conservative Party Member of Parliament for East Fife from 1961 to 1979. He was Lord Lieutenant of Fife from 1980 to 1987, but he still found time for the F&FY, rejoining them on their re-formation as an armoured car reconnaissance unit and acting as their colonel from 1947 to 1950. 'Pinkie' Hutchison returned to his prosperous family business and became colonel of the F&FY in succession to Sir John Gilmour from 1950 to 1953.

For some, the experience of soldiering in the 2nd F&FY

really changed everything about their lives. Roy Vallance had been a printer before joining up, but the army became his life's work. He became a regular soldier and saw even more active service with the 8th King's Royal Irish Hussars in Korea in 1951. He had the honour of being the first regimental sergeant major on the amalgamation of his regiment with the 4th Queen's Own Hussars to form the Queen's Royal Irish Hussars. He was ultimately commissioned and appointed as quartermaster in 1959. Subsequently, he served in Germany, Aden and Malaya, before being medically discharged from the Army in 1971.

In contrast, for some the war extinguished all hope of becoming a regular soldier. They had enjoyed life in the army – and dared to hope that if they survived then they could make it their career.

> It was unfortunate that I was wounded, but I think had I not been wounded I would have stayed on as a soldier, I think. I did begin to enjoy it.[16]
>
> Alf Courtneidge

His hand and left hip bone had been smashed by shrapnel during Operation Goodwood in July 1944. Despite a series of operations, he was still incapacitated and as such he was not required, and was discharged on medical grounds by the army. He was given a disability pension, but he anticipated that at least he could resume his training as a bricklayer. But even that was denied him.

> I had hoped to have come out and continue as a bricklayer, because there was such a lot of war damage. It would have been a good thing to have done. But I really didn't know what one could do: there was a lot of demolition about – which I couldn't do because of my hand and my side. To be quite honest, it really did start knocking the confidence out of me. I wasn't able to play football, I couldn't play cricket. Whereas you saw other people coming out of the services and going back

and doing the normal things you do when you're 21, 22 years of age.[17]

Alf Courtneidge

Eventually he went into the fur trade, something he had worked in a little before the war, and which he knew would be lighter work. His hand was operated on and rebuilt with the aid of a skin graft, but he never really regained full use of it. However, Courtneidge was a true fighter. He studied hard to improve his qualifications and eventually had a successful career as a director of the company. But the shadow of the war remained over his whole life.

> I was not very happy. My walking was restricted as it still felt as if the hip was not a complete unit anymore. I was having nightmares – more of the pain one had suffered. Nowadays if these things happen you get counselling; well, in our day there was no counselling. It was never thought of. Fortunately, they didn't last a long while, gradually it eased off – I suppose one accepts these things – you overcome these things.[18]
>
> Alf Courtneidge

James Donovan returned to work as a driver at a laundry before a career as a coach driver. He had to cope with a lasting facial disfigurement, which despite plastic surgery was still obvious. But he had his own method of coping.

> It was a strange thing. It just depends on the person; they look at you and they see what they want to see. Children were the worst at first. They used to call you 'Rudolf', 'Raspberry Nose' or 'Strawberry Nose' but I found if you said, 'Come here and I'll tell you all about it!' They were all right once you'd told them – explained it all to them – that was the end of it! I thought the best thing I can do is not hide away, but to get among people. I got a PSV and became a coach driver – which meant I was mingling with different people every job I went

on! You met different people every day. Some people would notice it, some wouldn't. Some would say, 'Cor, you've been in the wars, mate!' And that's it! You do feel as if people look at you – stare at you! But a lot of that is in your mind. You've got to get to the stage where you think to yourself, 'I'm not going to change things, so I've got to make the best of what I've got!' I looked at people who'd lost their sight – and I think to myself, 'Thank God that wasn't me!' It never stopped me doing anything I wanted to do! Sometimes it's embarrassing because I can't feel when I've got a dewdrop![19]

James Donovan

However, Donovan, like so many of the men I interviewed, had nightmares about the war, often triggered by the prospect of oral history interviews which reawakened old memories – and old traumas.

I do get a bad night now and again – you just get a flashback! You dream about these things. I had one on Saturday night – two nights ago – that's just one of those things. Something just triggers you.[20]

James Donovan

*

THE VERY THOUGHT OF a regimental association was anathema to many of the old soldiers of the 2nd F&FY once they had got home. They were sick of the army and craved their civilian life. They may have missed the comradeship, but at the same time they did not want to be regimented, and the idea of a 'regimental association', all blazers and ties, was anathema to them, at least in the early post-war years . Many of them were also busy trying to re-establish their civilian life, studying for qualifications, and trying to ameliorate the effects of having been 'absent' from their work careers for up to six years. Unfortunately, many of the non-Scottish veterans were not even asked to join. It seems that out of sight was out of mind.

> The attitude of most of the troops when they were anxiously waiting for demobilisation was, 'When I get out of the army, I won't even join two pieces of string together!' That was the expression that sticks in my mind. During the regimental days, I'd found that because the regiment tended to exude a sort of family atmosphere to the ones that were in it right from the start, I never really felt that I would want to join an association of that type. Basically, I didn't even know there was a Scottish association! Nobody had approached me to join one.[21]
>
> Geoff Hayward

It was different for some of the Scots, particularly those who had risen through the ranks to hold responsible positions in the regiment, such as Tommy Willmott, who had risen to be regimental quartermaster sergeant. With his proven administrative skills and widespread contacts in the regiment, he was the obvious choice to be involved in setting up the association to cope with the influx of Second World War soldiers to add to the existing 'spine' of veteran members dating back to the Great War.

> When we came back in February 1946, not many had been demobbed before me, but they were starting to be demobbed quickly – and they were all coming back. There was a chap in the 1st Fife and Forfar, Captain Robertson, he was the manager of a savings bank. He says, 'There are people wanting to contact us, Tom!' Three businessmen in Dundee who were in the First World War, they got us together and said, 'What you must do is form an association now – right now! Get it organised, because the longer you wait, the harder it will be!' We formed a committee, and we had our first dinner in April 1946. The regiment came and we had a super dinner. We decided it was important to keep an annual dinner every year – and we've had

one every single year – in Dundee – right up to and including 1999. It's been invaluable. They say old soldiers never die, but there it is.[22]

Tommy Willmott

For Leslie Gibson the association became an important part of his life.

I joined the association in 1946 when it started again. I was at the very first dinner. Perhaps the six and a half years you spent in the army, you feel in many respects were six and a half years out of your life! But in many ways, it was a good six and a half years. All times during the war weren't bad! There was a lot of good times. You would never get comradeship like it anywhere else – I'm quite sure. There was something about it that gelled people together. You learnt to get on with people. You learnt you could do things. I wouldn't have swapped it. We have reunion dinners and it's so great to meet up with blokes you haven't met for a long time – and just talk about old times.[23]

Leslie Gibson

One moment at an association dinner summed up the old ties that bound them, so much so that when we interviewed the three men concerned, they all treasured the memory.

On the sixtieth anniversary of us joining the territorial regiment in April 1939, I was invited specially to come up for this. It was a marvellous thing, in Dundee on 16 April, exactly sixty years since we were attested and joined up before the war. I met people like Jock Creighton, a great friend of mine, Les Gibson, Bill Scott, all of whom I'd been in the territorials with. We were all seated at the same table – Bill stood up and said, 'Do you realise why we're all sitting together?' I said, 'No!' He said, 'Because we were the first guard the regiment ever mounted at Waitwith Camp on 14 April 1939. And here is the

four of us still alive!' We then had all our photographs taken,
'Fall in the old guard sixty years later!'[24]

Alex Gilchrist

Meanwhile, back in England, Geoff Hayward had hated the
thought of returning to work as an insurance clerk but had no
other feasible options. He got stuck in and eventually ended up
with a successful stint as a chief clerk based in Leeds and Brad-
ford. He was totally immersed in his career and his new life, but
with retirement came a long-overdue assessment of what had
been really important to him over the years – what had really
mattered. He found himself thinking more and more of his old
comrades in the 2nd F&FY.

> I had become interested in trying to trace my old tank driver,
> Alex Penman, and also Lieutenant Darke. I wanted to find out
> if there was an association in existence then that would supply
> me with this information. By putting an advert in the 'British
> Legion Journal' and a Scottish newspaper, 'Did anybody know
> of Alex Penman?' I got this reply from a chap in the Legion in
> Holland. He said, 'I see that you were in the Fife and Forfar
> Yeomanry. Do you know of anybody from the regiment,
> because the city of Antwerp is inviting 150 members of the
> 11th Armoured Division to come back for a celebration in
> September 1994.'[25]

Geoff Hayward

Through this and other replies Hayward managed to get a few
names and addresses. He began to exchange letters, gradually gathering more contacts, until eventually he had nineteen
ex-veterans to go on the Antwerp visit. He also attended the
Dundee dinner of the Scottish Fife and Forfar Yeomanry Association held in November 1995.

> It was on the train journey coming back from that dinner in 1995
> that we talked about forming some little *South of the Border*

group that could meet occasionally for all those who couldn't afford or want to go to the Scottish 'dos' because of the distance. I said, 'I'll start the ball rolling. I'll write a letter to all the people I know in England that can't get up to these Scottish dinners!' This idea grew from very small beginnings. We thought the best we could hope for was perhaps a dozen, but it has now grown, and we've got eighty. It is important to get people weaving, with the idea of preserving their memories. And this theme has come out – to try and get people to put their memories down – and not to let their family throw them away if they die – to get them preserved. We're very, very pleased with the reaction we're getting from the members of our group![26]

Geoff Hayward

There were many like Terry Boyne, who had returned to his career as a fitter and lathe machinist after the war, but who was inspired to respond as soon as he saw the adverts.

The *South of the Border* put an advert in the Legion paper. I'd had no links with anybody. I'd joined nothing at all, it had all dropped away. The bulk of the people were Scots and to go up there to make contact was too much effort. But *South of the Border* meant that there were some that I would have known. So I wrote off. They sent me a directory of who was already on there and sure enough names started popping up that I remembered. Roy Vallance, Len Hatchings and these others. I'm pleased that I did. Since then, it generated an awful lot of interest. When we get together it's, 'Do you remember?' It drives the wives barmy I expect! They must have heard it all before! 'Do you remember this, that and everything else?' It's a lovely few hours! It really is! People never understand the bond that you generate in the service. It's always there; it's your family at the time! It's a link that forms and you're part of it – like it or not! You are part of it![27]

Terry Boyne

John Gray was another who responded positively to this unexpected reminder of a joint past from out of the blue.

> After that, nothing. Suddenly I'm looking at the 'freebie' newspaper and down in the corner was this little notice, '*South of the Border, 2nd F&FY*'. I've never moved so fast in all my life as to get on to that phone number. Speaking to the [association] secretary, I said, 'I thought everyone was dead; I thought I was the last one alive!' It was absolutely incredible after all those years that there were still Fife and Forfars going. Although I don't know any of them! The problem is, I might well have sat in a tank with them, sat and ate my food with them. But then when you look at my photograph [back then] and you look at me now – I don't look anything like it. I'm still handsome, suave and debonair, but I certainly don't look like that! I've got a few wrinkles now – and they're the same![28]
>
> John Gray

People often trot out the tired old cliché that old soldiers 'didn't like to talk about it'. For some relatives this serves the dual purpose in excusing their failure to listen to the 'tedious' repetition of old war stories, while at the same time implying that the veterans had seen 'too much' and generating a spurious second-hand glamour. Then again, many veterans recognised that their families would not be interested, or that their stories were not suitable for their young kids. But they did like to talk about it, when given half a chance, to fellow veterans at the British Legion, or best of all to their old comrades in the regimental associations. A chance to relive their youth, refight old battles and remember old friends dead before their time. Most of them never forgot what they had experienced together.

> Out of all the mish-mash of memories, I have one that is vivid when I walk the dog of an evening. If the wind is blowing quietly through the trees, and everything else is still, I physically

feel what it was like to be in a field in Normandy at the end of a day. Not mentally, just physically. It is a strange feeling.[29]

William Steel Brownlie

The voices of most, if not all, of the 2nd F&FY men featured in this book have now been silenced. But we will remember them. Collectively they were proud but not boastful of what they had achieved together. Let the last word be from one of these amazing ordinary yet extraordinary men.

I can say that I met the enemy face to face, and I fired a machine gun at him for more days than I care to think about. But it was all chance. My country was fighting for her life; it could have happened to any man in Britain. It was my fate. I was a conscript. I did not object; someone had to fight this war. I did what I had to do. I did not want to dodge the issue.[30]

John Thorpe

NOTES

1. Fleeting Impressions

1. IWM SOUND: Charles Workman, AC 20318, Reel 8.
2. IWM SOUND: Charles Workman, AC 20318, Reel 10.
3. IWM SOUND: Charles Workman, AC 20318, Reel 9.
4. Major Christopher Nicholls died aged 30 on 18 July 1944. He is commemorated on the Bayeux Memorial.
5. IWM SOUND: Charles Workman, AC 20318, Reel 9.
6. IWM SOUND: Charles Workman, AC 20318, Reels 9 & 10.

2. Start at the Beginning

1. IWM SOUND: Ron Forbes, AC 19818, Reel 1.
2. IWM SOUND: John Gilmour, AC 19809, Reel 1.
3. IWM SOUND: John Gilmour, AC 19809, Reel 1.
4. IWM SOUND: John Walker, AC 19803, Reel 1.
5. IWM SOUND: Douglas Hutchison, AC 20315, Reel 1.
6. IWM SOUND: John Gilmour, AC 19809, Reel 1 and 2.
7. IWM SOUND: Alexander Frederick, AC 19804, Reel 1.
8. IWM SOUND: Ron Forbes, AC 19818, Reel 1.
9. IWM SOUND: Tommy Willmott, AC 19806, Reel 1.
10. IWM SOUND: Jack Wann, AC 20399, Reel 1.
11. IWM SOUND: Alex Gilchrist, AC 20149, Reel 1.
12. IWM SOUND: Alex Gilchrist, AC 20149, Reel 2.
13. IWM SOUND: Alexander Frederick, AC 19804, Reel 1.
14. IWM SOUND: Jack Wann, AC 20399, Reel 2.

3. Tiny Steps

1. IWM SOUND: Douglas Hutchison, AC 20315, Reel 2.
2. IWM SOUND: Jack Wann, AC 20399, Reel 2.
3. IWM SOUND: James Dowie, AC 19808, Reel 1.
4. IWM SOUND: Jack Wann, AC 20399, Reel 2.
5. IWM SOUND: Jack Wann, AC 20399, Reel 3.
6. R. J. B. Sellar, *The Fife and Forfar Yeomanry, 1919–1956* (Edinburgh & London: William Blackwood & Sons Ltd, 1960), p. 131.

7.   IWM SOUND: Douglas Hutchison, AC 20315, Reel 2.
8.   J. Grimond, *Memoirs* (London: William Heinemann, Ltd, 1979), p. 91.
9.   J. Grimond, *Memoirs* (London: William Heinemann, Ltd, 1979), pp. 51–2.
10. IWM SOUND: Alex Gilchrist, AC 20149, Reel 2.
11. IWM SOUND: Ron Forbes, AC 19818, Reel 4.
12. IWM SOUND: Ron Forbes, AC 19818, Reel 2.
13. IWM SOUND: Douglas Hutchison, AC 20315, Reel 2.
14. IWM SOUND: Ron Forbes, AC 19818, Reel 2.
15. IWM SOUND: Harold Brown, AC 19800, Reel 1.
16. IWM SOUND: Douglas Hutchison, AC 20315, Reel 3.
17. IWM SOUND: Alex Gilchrist, AC 20149, Reel 3.
18. J. Grimond, *Memoirs* (London: William Heinemann, Ltd, 1979), p. 92.
19. IWM SOUND: John Gilmour, AC 19809, Reel 2.
20. IWM SOUND: James Dowie, AC 19808, Reel 2 and 3.
21. IWM SOUND: Douglas Hutchison, AC 20315, Reel 3.
22. IWM SOUND: Douglas Hutchison, AC 20315, Reel 6.
23. IWM SOUND: Jack Wann, AC 20399, Reel 7.
24. IWM SOUND: Douglas Hutchison, AC 20315, Reel 3.
25. IWM SOUND: Alex Gilchrist, AC 20149, Reel 3.
26. IWM SOUND: Ron Forbes, AC 19818, Reel 3.
27. IWM SOUND: Leslie Gibson, AC 19811, Reel 2.

4. Why are we Waiting?

1.   IWM SOUND: John Gilmour, AC 19809, Reel 3.
2.   IWM SOUND: Ron Forbes, AC 19818, Reel 4.
3.   IWM SOUND: Alex Gilchrist, AC 20149, Reel 4.
4.   IWM SOUND: Douglas Hutchison, AC 20315, Reel 4.
5.   IWM SOUND: Alex Gilchrist, AC 20149 Reel 4.
6.   IWM SOUND: Geoff Hayward, AC 18706, Reel 6.
7.   IWM SOUND: Alex Gilchrist, AC 20149 Reel 5.
8.   IWM SOUND: Roy Vallance, AC 19074, Reel 3.
9.   IWM SOUND: Charles Workman, AC 20318, Reels 2 and 3.
10. IWM SOUND: Charles Workman, AC 20318, Reel 3.
11. IWM SOUND: Charles Workman, AC 20318, Reel 3.
12. IWM SOUND: Geoff Hayward, AC 18706, Reel 8.
13. IWM SOUND: Len Newman, AC 18705, Reel 4.
14. IWM SOUND: John Gray, AC 20202, Reel 3.
15. IWM SOUND: John Gray, AC 20202, Reel 5.
16. IWM SOUND: John Gray, AC 20202, Reel 6.
17. IWM SOUND: Jack Edwards, AC 22629, Reel 4.
18. IWM SOUND: Len Harkins, AC 21109, Reel 1.
19. IWM SOUND: Charles Workman, AC 20318, Reel 3.
20. IWM SOUND: Charles Workman, AC 20318, Reel 3.
21. IWM SOUND: Roy Vallance, AC 19074, Reel 3.
22. IWM SOUND: Jack Wann, AC 20399, Reel 7.
23. IWM SOUND: Leslie Gibson, AC 19811, Reel 3.

24. R. J. B. Sellar, *The Fife and Forfar Yeomanry, 1919–1956* (Edinburgh: William Blackwood & Sons Ltd, 1960), p. 147.
25. IWM SOUND: Ron Forbes, AC 19818, Reel 4.
26. IWM SOUND: Geoff Hayward, AC 18706, Reel 8.
27. IWM SOUND: James Dowie, AC 19808, Reel 3.
28. IWM SOUND: Roy Vallance, AC 19074, Reel 3.

5. Sherman Training

1. IWM SOUND: Ron Forbes, AC 19818, Reel 5.
2. IWM SOUND: Roy Vallance, AC 19074, Reel 3 and 4.
3. IWM SOUND: Gordon Fidler, AC 18785, Reel 4.
4. IWM SOUND: Charles Workman, AC 20318, Reel 5.
5. IWM SOUND: Charles Workman, AC 20318, Reel 8.
6. IWM SOUND: Charles Workman, AC 20318, Reel 5.
7. Roscoe Harvey, quoted by Tim Fitzgeorge-Parker, *Roscoe the Bright Shiner: The biography of Brigadier Roscoe Harvey DSO* (London: Severn House Publishers, 1987).
8. Musée Percée du Bocage: William Steel Brownlie, '*And Came Safe Home*'.
9. Musée Percée du Bocage: William Steel Brownlie, '*And Came Safe Home*'.
10. IWM SOUND: James Donovan, AC 20316, Reel 4.
11. IWM SOUND: Charles Workman, AC 20318, Reel 6.
12. IWM SOUND: Jack Edwards, AC 22629, Reel 4.
13. IWM SOUND: Douglas Hutchison, AC 20315, Reel 6.
14. IWM SOUND: John Gray, AC 20202, Reel 7.
15. IWM SOUND: George Cozens, AC 20201, Reel 5.
16. IWM SOUND: Douglas Hutchison, AC 20315, Reel 5.
17. IWM SOUND: Charles Workman, AC 20318, Reel 6.
18. IWM SOUND: Charles Workman, AC 20318, Reel 6.
19. IWM SOUND: Roy Vallance, AC 19074, Reel 5.
20. IWM SOUND: Jack Edwards, AC 22629 Reel 4.

6. On Their Way at Last

1. IWM SOUND: Peter Young, AC 20319, Reel 3.
2. Musée Percée du Bocage: William Steel Brownlie, '*And Came Safe Home*'.
3. IWM SOUND: James Donovan, AC 20316, Reel 4.
4. IWM SOUND: Gordon Fidler, AC 18785, Reel 5.
5. IWM SOUND: Geoff Hayward, AC 18706, Reel 10.
6. IWM SOUND: Roy Vallance, AC 19074, Reel 5.
7. IWM SOUND: Doug Hayes, AC 19097, Reel 5.
8. IWM SOUND: John Gray, AC 20202, Reel 7.
9. IWM SOUND: Charles Workman, AC 20318, Reel 7.
10. IWM SOUND: John Gray, AC 20202, Reel 7.
11. IWM SOUND: Ron Forbes, AC 19818, Reel 5.
12. IWM SOUND: Charles Workman, AC 20318, Reel 7.
13. Trooper David Sutherland died aged 26 on 29 August 1944. He is buried at Etrepagny Cemetery.

14. IWM SOUND: James Donovan, AC 20316, Reel 5.

15. Roscoe Harvey, quoted by Tim Fitzgeorge-Parker, *Roscoe the Bright Shiner: The biography of Brigadier Roscoe Harvey DSO* (London: Severn House Publishers, 1987), pp. 205–6.

16. IWM SOUND: Ron Forbes, AC 19818, Reel 6.

17. IWM SOUND: Jack Edwards, AC 22629, Reel 5.

18. IWM SOUND: Doug Hayes, AC 19097, Reel 5.

7. Calm before the Storm

1. Musée Percée du Bocage: William Steel Brownlie, '*And Came Safe Home*'.

2. IWM SOUND: Roy Vallance, AC 19074, Reel 5.

3. IWM SOUND: Gordon Fidler, AC 18785, Reel 6.

4. IWM SOUND: Andrew Dewar, AC 20845, Reel 2 and 3.

5. IWM SOUND: Bill Knights AC 21015, Reel 2.

6. IWM SOUND: Ron Forbes, AC 19818, Reel 6.

7. IWM SOUND: Roy Vallance, AC 19074, Reel 6.

8. IWM SOUND: George Cozens, AC 20201, Reel 6.

9. IWM SOUND: Roy Vallance, AC 19074, Reel 6.

10. IWM SOUND: Jack Edwards, AC 22629, Reel 5.

11. IWM SOUND: Ron Forbes, AC 19818, Reel 6.

12. IWM SOUND: Robert Nurse, AC 22196, Reel 2.

13. IWM SOUND: Jack Edwards, AC 22629, Reel 5.

14. IWM SOUND: Roy Vallance, AC 19074, Reel 6.

15. IWM SOUND: Geoff Hayward, AC 18706, Reel 11.

16. IWM SOUND: Roy Vallance, AC 19074, Reel 6.

17. IWM SOUND: Roy Vallance, AC 19074, Reel 6.

18. IWM SOUND: Gordon Fidler, AC 18785, Reel 6.

19. IWM SOUND: James Donovan, AC 20316, Reel 4.

20. IWM SOUND: Gordon Fidler, AC 18785, Reel 6.

21. IWM SOUND: Jack Edwards, AC 22629, Reel 5.

22. IWM SOUND: John Gilmour, AC 19809, Reel 4.

8. Operation Epsom

1. IWM SOUND: Douglas Hutchison, AC 20315, Reel 7.

2. IWM SOUND: Charles Workman, AC 20318, Reels 7 and 8.

3. CRA is Commander Royal Artillery.

4. Pip Roberts, *From the Desert to the Baltic* (London: William Kimber, 1987), p. 162.

5. IWM SOUND: Alf Courtneidge, AC 19078, Reel 3 and 5.

6. IWM SOUND: Tommy Willmott, AC 19806, Reel 6.

7. IWM SOUND: Geoff Hayward, AC 18706, Reel 12.

8. IWM SOUND: Geoff Hayward, AC 18706, Reel 12 and 13.

9. Musée Percée du Bocage: William Steel Brownlie, '*And Came Safe Home*'.

10. IWM SOUND: John Gilmour, AC 19809, Reel 4.

11. IWM SOUND: Jack Edwards, AC 22629, Reel 5.

12. IWM SOUND: Ron Forbes, AC 19818, Reel 6.

13. IWM SOUND: Jack Edwards, AC 22629, Reel 5.

14. IWM SOUND: Jack Edwards, AC 22629, Reel 5.

15. IWM SOUND: John Gray, AC 20202, Reel 8.

16. Lieutenant Cecil Pritchard died 26 June 1944. Commemorated on Bayeux Memorial.

17. IWM SOUND: Charles Workman, AC 20318, Reel 8.

18. Ron Cox, quoted by Ian Dalglish, *Over the Battlefield: Operation Epsom* (Barnsley: Pen & Sword Military, 2015), p. 67

19. Musée Percée du Bocage: William Steel Brownlie, '*And Came Safe Home*'.

20. IWM SOUND: Gordon Fidler, AC 18785, Reel 7.

21. IWM SOUND: John Buchanan, AC 19867, Reel 3.

22. IWM SOUND: John Buchanan, AC 19867, Reel 5.

23. IWM SOUND: Terry Boyne, AC 18786, Reel 7.

24. IWM SOUND: Douglas Hutchison, AC 20315, Reel 6.

25. IWM SOUND: Tommy Willmott, AC 19806, Reel 7.

26. IWM SOUND: John Hunter, AC 19818, Reel 3 and 4.

27. IWM SOUND: Roy Vallance, AC 19074, Reel 6.

28. IWM SOUND: John Buchanan, AC 19867, Reel 5.

29. IWM SOUND: John Buchanan, AC 19867, Reel 5.

30. Musée Percée du Bocage: William Steel Brownlie, '*And Came Safe Home*'.

31. IWM SOUND: John Buchanan, AC 19867, Reel 6.

32. IWM SOUND: Douglas Hutchison, AC 20315, Reel 7.

33. Thomas Morgan died aged 28 on 26 June 1944. Buried in the St. Manvieu War Cemetery, Cheux.

34. Edward Crowley died aged 20 on 26 June 1944. Commemorated on the Bayeux Memorial.

35. IWM SOUND: Robert Nurse, AC 22196, Reel 2.

36. IWM SOUND: Roy Vallance, AC 19074, Reel 7.

37. Musée Percée du Bocage: William Steel Brownlie, '*And Came Safe Home*'.

38. Hans Siegel, quoted by Herbert Meyer, *The 12th SS Volume One: The History of the Hitler Youth Panzer Division* (Mechanicsburg: Stackpole Books, 2005), pp. 394–5.

39. Hans Siegel, quoted by Herbert Meyer, *The 12th SS Volume One: The History of the Hitler Youth Panzer Division* (Mechanicsburg: Stackpole Books, 2005), p. 395.

40. Musée Percée du Bocage: William Steel Brownlie, '*And Came Safe Home*'.

41. IWM SOUND: John Buchanan, AC 19867, Reel 7.

42. Trooper Stanley Thomson died aged 26 on 26 June 1944. Commemorated on Bayeux Memorial. Official date of death appears to be wrong.

43. Trooper Harold Sykes died aged 28 on 26 June 1944. Commemorated on Bayeux Memorial. Official date of death appears to be wrong.

44. Trooper William Harper died in hospital aged 30 on 5 July 1944. Buried in Kendall Parkside Cemetery.

45. Musée Percée du Bocage: William Steel Brownlie, '*And Came Safe Home*'.

46. Hans Siegel, quoted by Herbert Meyer, *The 12th SS Volume One: The History*

of the Hitler Youth Panzer Division (Mechanicsburg: Stackpole Books, 2005), pp. 395–6.

47. Sergeant John Hepburn died aged 26 on 27 June 1944. Buried at St. Manvieu War Cemetery, Cheux.
48. Musée Percée du Bocage: William Steel Brownlie, '*And Came Safe Home*'.
49. Musée Percée du Bocage: William Steel Brownlie, '*And Came Safe Home*'.
50. Musée Percée du Bocage: William Steel Brownlie, '*And Came Safe Home*'.
51. Musée Percée du Bocage: William Steel Brownlie, '*And Came Safe Home*'.
52. IWM SOUND: Douglas Hutchison, AC 20315, Reel 7.
53. IWM SOUND: Douglas Hutchison, AC 20315, Reel 7.

9. Hill 112

1. IWM SOUND: John Buchanan, AC 19867, Reel 5.
2. IWM SOUND: Norman Bradley, AC 19077, Reel 4.
3. IWM SOUND: Douglas Hutchison, AC 20315, Reel 7.
4. Willy Kretzschmar, quoted by Herbert Meyer, *The 12th SS Volume One: The History of the Hitler Youth Panzer Division* (Mechanicsburg: Stackpole Books, 2005), pp. 412–13.
5. IWM SOUND: Charles Workman, AC 20318, Reel 8.
6. IWM SOUND: Roy Vallance, AC 19074, Reel 7.
7. IWM SOUND: Robert Nurse, AC 22196, Reel 3.
8. IWM SOUND: Harold Wilson, AC 21567, Reel 9.
9. IWM SOUND: Terry Boyne, AC 18786, Reel 8.
10. IWM SOUND: Terry Boyne, AC 18786, Reel 8.
11. Edgar Palamountain, *Taurus Pursuant: A History of the 11th Armoured Division* (Printing and Stationery Service: British Army of the Rhine, 1945), p. 5.
12. IWM SOUND: Douglas Hutchison, AC 20315, Reel 7.
13. IWM SOUND: Charles Workman, AC 20318, Reels 7 and 8.
14. IWM SOUND: Douglas Hutchison, AC 20315, Reel 7.
15. Musée Percée du Bocage: William Steel Brownlie, '*And Came Safe Home*'.
16. IWM SOUND: Jack Edwards, AC 22629, Reel 6.
17. IWM SOUND: Jack Edwards, AC 22629, Reel 6.
18. IWM SOUND: Jack Rex, AC 20945, Reel 4.
19. IWM SOUND: John Buchanan, AC 19867, Reel 6.
20. IWM SOUND: John Buchanan, AC 19867, Reel 6.
21. IWM SOUND: Robert Nurse, AC 22196, Reel 4.
22. IWM SOUND: Geoff Hayward, AC 18706, Reel 14.
23. IWM SOUND: Geoff Hayward, AC 18706, Reel 14 and 15.
24. IWM SOUND: Geoff Hayward, AC 18706, Reel 15.
25. IWM SOUND: John Gray, AC 20202, Reel 8.
26. Musée Percée du Bocage: John Thorpe, *A Soldier's Tale. To Normandy and Beyond*, p. 92.
27. IWM SOUND: Terry Boyne, AC 18786, Reel 8.
28. IWM SOUND: Douglas Hutchison, AC 20315, Reel 7.
29. IWM SOUND: John Gray, AC 20202, Reel 8.

10. Operation Goodwood

1. IWM SOUND: James Donovan, AC 20316, Reel 5.
2. Pip Roberts, *From the Desert to the Baltic* (London: William Kimber, 1987), pp. 169–71.
3. I am indebted to the calculations of Stephen Napier in *The Armoured Campaign in Normandy, June – August 1944* (Stroud: The History Press, 2017), pp. 202–3.
4. IWM SOUND: Douglas Hutchison, AC 20315, Reel 7.
5. IWM SOUND: John Gilmour, AC 19809, Reel 6.
6. IWM SOUND: Len Hutchings, AC 19076, Reel 2.
7. IWM SOUND: Gordon Fidler, AC 18785, Reel 8.
8. IWM SOUND: John Buchanan, AC 19867, Reel 6.
9. Musée Percée du Bocage: William Steel Brownlie, '*And Came Safe Home*'.
10. IWM SOUND: Jack Edwards, AC 22629, Reel 6.
11. IWM SOUND: John Gilmour, AC 19809, Reel 5.
12. Musée Percée du Bocage: William Steel Brownlie, '*And Came Safe Home*'.
13. Richard Freiherr von Rosen, quoted by Ian Daglish, *Over the Battleground – Goodwood* (Barnsley: Pen & Sword Military,2013), pp. 64–5.
14. IWM SOUND: Douglas Hutchison, AC 20315, Reel 8.
15. IWM SOUND: Douglas Hutchison, AC 20315, Reel 8.
16. IWM SOUND: Jack Edwards, AC 22629, Reel 6.
17. Trooper John Keightley died aged 25 on 18 July 1944. Buried at Hermanville War Cemetery.
18. IWM SOUND: Robert Nurse, AC 22196, Reel 4.
19. Major Chris Nicholls died aged 30 on 18 July 1944. Commemorated on Bayeux Memorial.
20. IWM SOUND: Charles Workman, AC 20318, Reels 8, 9 and 10.
21. Trooper Dennis Stone died aged 21 on 18 July 1944. Buried in Banneville la Campagne War Cemetery.
22. IWM SOUND: Harold Wilson, AC 21567, Reel 8.
23. Musée Percée du Bocage: John Thorpe, *A Soldier's Tale. To Normandy and Beyond*, p. 97.
24. Musée Percée du Bocage: John Thorpe, *A Soldier's Tale. To Normandy and Beyond*, pp. 97–8.
25. IWM SOUND: Jack Edwards, AC 22629, Reel 6.
26. IWM SOUND: Jack Edwards, AC 22629, Reel 6.
27. IWM SOUND: Roy Vallance, AC 19074, Reel 8.
28. Philip Noakes, quoted by Christopher Dunphie, *Pendulum of Battle: Operation Goodwood July 1944* (Barnsley: Leo Cooper, 2004), pp. 76–7.
29. Corporal William Truslove died aged 25 on 18 July 1944. Commemorated on the Bayeux Memorial.
30. Trooper Stanley Haddock died aged 20 on 18 July 1944. Commemorated on the Bayeux Memorial.
31. Trooper Edwin Belsham died aged 20 on 18 July 1944. Buried in Ranville War Cemetery.
32. Trooper Ronald York died aged 25 on 18 July 1944. Commemorated on the Bayeux Memorial.

33. J. Sedgebeer, quoted by Christopher Dunphie, *Pendulum of Battle: Operation Goodwood July 1944* (Barnsley: Leo Cooper, 2004), p. 77.

34. 'Pip' Roberts, quoted by Christopher Dunphie, *Pendulum of Battle: Operation Goodwood July 1944* (Barnsley: Leo Cooper, 2004), pp. 80–1.

35. Don Gillate (edited Ronald Jeltes), *With the 8th Rifle Brigade from Normandy to the Baltic: June 1944–May 1945* (Hamburg: Tredition GmbH, 2019), pp. 64–8.

36. Don Gillate (edited Ronald Jeltes), *With the 8th Rifle Brigade from Normandy to the Baltic: June 1944–May 1945* (Hamburg: Tredition GmbH, 2019), pp. 64–8.

37. IWM SOUND: John Gilmour, AC 19809, Reel 5 and 6.

38. Jack Frost, quoted by Christopher Dunphie, *Pendulum of Battle: Operation Goodwood July 1944* (Barnsley: Leo Cooper, 2004), pp. 105–6.

39. Trooper Kenneth Gillmore died aged 30 on 18 July 1944. Buried in Ranville War Cemetery.

40. Trooper Claude Marchant died aged 20 on 18 July 1944. Buried in Ranville War Cemetery.

41. Corporal Douglas Bostwick died aged 25 on 18 July 1944. Buried in Ranville War Cemetery

42. IWM SOUND: Norman Bradley, AC 19077, Reel 5.

43. IWM SOUND: Charles Workman, AC 20318, Reels 8, 9 and 10.

44. IWM SOUND: Douglas Hutchison, AC 20315, Reel 8.

45. IWM SOUND: Terry Boyne, AC 18786, Reel 9.

46. IWM SOUND: James Donovan, AC 20316, Reel 5.

47. IWM SOUND: James Donovan, AC 20316, Reel 5.

48. IWM SOUND: James Donovan, AC 20316, Reel 5.

49. IWM SOUND: Alf Courtneidge, AC 19078, Reel 6.

50. IWM SOUND: John Gilmour, AC 19809, Reel 5 and 6.

51. Robert Clark, quoted by Christopher Dunphie, *Pendulum of Battle: Operation Goodwood July 1944* (Barnsley: Leo Cooper, 2004), p. 102.

52. Pip Roberts, *From the Desert to the Baltic* (London: William Kimber, 1987), p. 177.

53. This would be James Bowes-Lyon who was serving with the Grenadier Guards. He was the first cousin of Queen Elizabeth (The Queen Mother).

54. IWM SOUND: Charles Workman, AC 20318, Reels 8, 9 and 10.

55. IWM SOUND: Geoff Hayward, AC 18706, Reel 15.

56. IWM SOUND: Bill Scott, AC 19802, Reel 4.

57. IWM SOUND: Bill Scott, AC 19802, Reel 4.

58. Lance Sergeant James Watson died aged 22 on 18 July 1944. No known grave and commemorated on Bayeux Memorial.

59. IWM SOUND: John Gray, AC 20202, Reel 8–9.

60. IWM SOUND: Jack Edwards, AC 22629, Reel 6.

61. IWM SOUND: Geoff Hayward, AC 18706, Reel 15.

62. IWM SOUND: John Gray, AC 20202, Reel 9.

63. IWM SOUND: Gordon Fidler, AC 18785, Reel 8.

64. IWM SOUND: James Donovan, AC 20316, Reel 6.

65. IWM SOUND: Ron Forbes, AC 19818, Reel 7 and 8.

66. IWM SOUND: Norman Bradley, AC 19077, Reel 5.

67. Trooper George Wooldridge died aged 21 on 19 July 1944. Buried in Ranville War Cemetery.
68. IWM SOUND: Jack Rex, AC 20945, Reel 4.
69. IWM SOUND: James Donovan, AC 20316, Reel 6.
70. Sergeant Eric Asher died aged 26 on 19 July 1944. Buried at Bayeux War Cemetery.
71. IWM SOUND: Peter Young, AC 20319, Reel 4 and 5.
72. Robert Clark, quoted by Christopher Dunphie, *Pendulum of Battle: Operation Goodwood July 1944* (Barnsley, Leo Cooper, 2004), p. 148.
73. IWM SOUND: Terry Boyne, AC 18786, Reel 9.
74. IWM SOUND: Roy Vallance, AC 19074, Reel 8.
75. IWM SOUND: Terry Boyne, AC 18786, Reel 10.
76. Major John Powell died aged 32 on 19 July 1944. Buried at Banneville la Campagne War Cemetery.
77. IWM SOUND: Alf Courtneidge, AC 19078, Reel 6.
78. IWM SOUND: Robert Nurse, AC 22196, Reel 4.
79. IWM SOUND: Roy Vallance, AC 19074, Reel 8.
80. IWM SOUND: Robert Nurse, AC 22196, Reel 4.
81. Musée Percée du Bocage: Graeme Hutchison, in document compiled by John Thorpe in 'Accounts of a Battle: Operation Goodwood'.
82. IWM SOUND: Jack Edwards, AC 22629, Reel 7.

11. Operation Bluecoat

1. IWM SOUND: Roy Vallance, AC 19074, Reel 8.
2. IWM SOUND: Tommy Willmott, AC 19806, Reel 8.
3. IWM SOUND: John Gilmour, AC 19809, Reel 6.
4. IWM SOUND: Tommy Willmott, AC 19806, Reel 8.
5. IWM SOUND: Roy Vallance, AC 19074, Reel 8.
6. IWM SOUND: Douglas Hutchison, AC 20315, Reel 9.
7. IWM SOUND: John Gilmour, AC 19809, Reel 6.
8. IWM SOUND: Jack Edwards, AC 22629, Reel 7.
9. IWM SOUND: Roy Vallance, AC 19074, Reel 9.
10. IWM SOUND: Jack Edwards, AC 22629, Reel 7.
11. Musée Percée du Bocage: William Steel Brownlie, '*And Came Safe Home*'.
12. IWM SOUND: Charles Workman, AC 20318, Reel 10.
13. Musée Percée du Bocage: William Steel Brownlie, '*And Came Safe Home*'.
14. IWM SOUND: John Buchanan, AC 19867, Reel 7.
15. Musée Percée du Bocage: William Steel Brownlie, '*And Came Safe Home*'.
16. IWM SOUND: Douglas Hutchison, AC 20315, Reel 9.
17. Sounds like Trooper John Thistlethwaite died aged 20 on 31 July 1944. Buried at Banneille La Campagne War Cemetery.
18. IWM SOUND: Gordon Fidler, AC 18785, Reel 9.
19. Musée Percée du Bocage: William Steel Brownlie, '*And Came Safe Home*'.
20. IWM SOUND: Jack Edwards, AC 22629, Reel 7.
21. Musée Percée du Bocage: William Steel Brownlie, '*And Came Safe Home*'.
22. IWM SOUND: Terry Boyne, AC 18786, Reel 10.

23. IWM SOUND: Douglas Hutchison, AC 20315, Reel 9 and 10.

24. IWM SOUND: John Buchanan, AC 19867, Reel 7.

25. IWM SOUND: Terry Boyne, AC 18786, Reel 11.

26. IWM SOUND: Douglas Hutchison, AC 20315, Reel 10.

27. IWM SOUND: Andrew Dewar, AC 20845, Reel 4.

28. Musée Percée du Bocage: William Steel Brownlie, '*And Came Safe Home*'.

29. Musée Percée du Bocage: William Steel Brownlie, '*And Came Safe Home*'.

30. Musée Percée du Bocage: William Steel Brownlie, '*And Came Safe Home*'.

31. Major William Hotblack

32. IWM SOUND: Douglas Hutchison, AC 20315, Reel 10.

33. Musée Percée du Bocage: John Thorpe, *A Soldier's Tale. To Normandy and Beyond*, p. 107.

34. Musée Percée du Bocage: John Thorpe, *A Soldier's Tale. To Normandy and Beyond*, pp. 108–9.

35. Captain Richard Carrick died aged 26 on 6 August 1944. He is buried at Tilly sur Seulles War Cemetery

36. Musée Percée du Bocage: Graeme Hutchison, in document compiled by John Thorpe in 'Accounts of a Battle: Operation Goodwood'.

37. IWM SOUND: Douglas Hutchison, AC 20315, Reel 10 and 13.

38. IWM SOUND: Bill Scott, AC 19802, Reel 5.

39. IWM SOUND: Jack Edwards, AC 22629, Reel 8.

40. Trooper Charles Mclaren died aged 20 on 7 August 1944. Buried at Bayeux War Cemetery.

41. Trooper John Smith died aged 36 on 7 August 1944. Buried at Tilly sur Seulles War Cemetery.

42. No reference to this casualty in CWGC or in regimental history – perhaps Thorpe has mis-remembered.

43. Trooper Henry Skelton died aged 20 on 6 August 1944. Commemorated on Bayeux Memorial.

44. Musée Percée du Bocage: John Thorpe, *A Soldier's Tale. To Normandy and Beyond*, p. 109.

45. Will Fey, *Armour Battles of the Waffen SS, 1943–45* (Mechanicsburg: Stackpole Books, 2003), pp. 144–5.

46. IWM SOUND: John Gilmour, AC 19809, Reel 6 and 7.

47. R. J. B. Sellar, *The Fife and Forfar Yeomanry, 1919–1956* (Edinburgh & London: William Blackwood & Sons Ltd, 1960), p. 184.

48. IWM SOUND: Ron Forbes, AC 19818, Reel 8.

49. Will Fey, *Armour Battles of the Waffen SS, 1943–45* (Mechanicsburg: Stackpole Books, 2003), pp. 147–8.

50. IWM SOUND: Jack Edwards, AC 22629, Reel 8.

51. IWM SOUND: Jack Edwards, AC 22629, Reel 8.

52. IWM SOUND: Bill Scott, AC 19802, Reel 5.

53. IWM SOUND: Jack Edwards, AC 22629, Reel 8.

54. IWM SOUND: John Buchanan, AC 19867, Reel 7.

12. What's It Like?

1. IWM SOUND: Charles Workman, AC 20318, Reel 10.
2. IWM SOUND: John Gilmour, AC 19809, Reel 3 and 4.
3. IWM SOUND: Charles Workman, AC 20318, Reel 10.
4. IWM SOUND: John Buchanan, AC 19867, Reel 7.
5. IWM SOUND: Douglas Hutchison, AC 20315, Reel 5.
6. IWM SOUND: Charles Workman, AC 20318, Reel 9.
7. IWM SOUND: Roy Vallance, AC 19074, Reel 3 and 4.
8. IWM SOUND: Roy Vallance, AC 19074, Reel 7.
9. IWM SOUND: Charles Workman, AC 20318, Reel 10.
10. IWM SOUND: James Donovan, AC 20316, Reel 3.
11. IWM SOUND: Roy Vallance, AC 19074, Reel 8 and 9.
12. IWM SOUND: John Buchanan, AC 19867, Reel 6.
13. IWM SOUND: John Buchanan, AC 19867, Reel 3.
14. IWM SOUND: John Buchanan, AC 19867, Reel 2 and 5.
15. IWM SOUND: John Buchanan, AC 19867, Reel 8.
16. IWM SOUND: Terry Boyne, AC 18786, Reel 3 and 10–11.
17. IWM SOUND: Jack Rex, AC 20945, Reel 4.
18. IWM SOUND: Ron Forbes, AC 19818, Reel 5.
19. IWM SOUND: Len Harkins, AC 21109, Reel 6.
20. IWM SOUND: James Donovan, AC 20316, Reel 6.
21. IWM SOUND: Charles Workman, AC 20318, Reels 11 and 15.
22. IWM SOUND: Charles Workman, AC 20318, Reel 10.
23. IWM SOUND: John Buchanan, AC 19867, Reel 5.
24. IWM SOUND: Gordon Fidler, AC 18785, Reel 8.
25. IWM SOUND: Charles Workman, AC 20318, Reel 8.
26. IWM SOUND: James Donovan, AC 20316, Reel 5.
27. IWM SOUND: John Buchanan, AC 19867, Reel 4.
28. IWM SOUND: John Buchanan, AC 19867, Reel 7.
29. IWM SOUND: Terry Boyne, AC 18786, Reel 11.
30. IWM SOUND: Charles Workman, AC 20318, Reel 10.
31. IWM SOUND: Doug Hayes, AC 19097, Reel 6.
32. IWM SOUND: Jack Rex, AC 20945, Reel 7.
33. IWM SOUND: Doug Hayes, AC 19097, Reel 7.
34. IWM SOUND: John Buchanan, AC 19867, Reel 6.
35. IWM SOUND: Ron Forbes, AC 19818, Reel 9.
36. IWM SOUND: Douglas Hutchison, AC 20315, Reel 8 and 10.
37. IWM SOUND: Charles Workman, AC 20318, Reel 6.

13. Advance through France and Belgium

1. Philip Roberts, quoted by Tim Fitzgeorge-Parker, *Roscoe the Bright Shiner: The biography of Brigadier Roscoe Harvey DSO* (London: Severn House Publishers, 1987), p. 215.
2. IWM SOUND: Jack Edwards, AC 22629, Reel 8.
3. IWM SOUND: Jack Edwards, AC 22629, Reel 8.

4. Lieutenant Colonel Alec Scott was evacuated only locally for medical treatment and a much-needed few days of rest and recuperation, before rejoining the unit on 18 August 1944.

5. Sergeant Eric Gale died aged 28 on 14 August 1944. Buried in St. Charles de Percy War Cemetery.

6. IWM SOUND: Douglas Hutchison, AC 20315, Reel 11.

7. IWM SOUND: Douglas Hutchison, AC 20315, Reel 11.

8. IWM SOUND: John Buchanan, AC 19867, Reel 8.

9. IWM SOUND: Jack Edwards, AC 22629, Reel 8.

10. IWM SOUND: Cliff Pember, AC 21278, Reel 3.

11. Lieutenant Alexander Munro died aged 21 on 17 August 1944. Buried at Banneville La Campagne War Cemetery.

12. IWM SOUND: Jack Edwards, AC 22629, Reel 8.

13. IWM SOUND: Cliff Pember, AC 21278, Reel 3.

14. IWM SOUND: Cliff Pember, AC 21278, Reel 3.

15. IWM SOUND: Jack Edwards, AC 22629, Reel 8.

16. IWM SOUND: Jack Edwards, AC 22629, Reel 8.

17. This is probably a mistake by Edwards. Holden's wife was Dorothy Georgina Beatrice Holden, of Byfleet, Surrey.

18. IWM SOUND: Jack Edwards, AC 22629, Reel 8.

19. Trooper Vivian Holden died aged 32 on 17 August 1944. Buried at Banneville La Campagne War Cemetery.

20. IWM SOUND: Jack Edwards, AC 22629, Reel 8.

21. IWM SOUND: Jack Edwards, AC 22629, Reel 9.

22. On holiday in France several years later, Hutchison found the broken pieces of this sign just lying propped up against the post. He regretted not just popping into the boot of his car to take home as a souvenir!

23. IWM SOUND: Douglas Hutchison, AC 20315, Reel 11.

24. IWM SOUND: Ken Watson, AC 19096, Reel 7.

25. IWM SOUND: Leslie Gibson, AC 19811, Reel 4 and 5.

26. IWM SOUND: Leslie Gibson, AC 19811, Reel 5.

27. R. J. B. Sellar, *The Fife and Forfar Yeomanry, 1919–1956* (Edinburgh & London: William Blackwood & Sons Ltd, 1960), p. 186.

28. IWM SOUND: Reginald Osgerby, AC 17967, Reel 3.

29. Pip Roberts, *From the Desert to the Baltic* (London: William Kimber, 1987), pp. 201–2.

30. Musée Percée du Bocage: William Steel Brownlie, '*And Came Safe Home*'.

31. IWM SOUND: Roy Vallance, AC 19074, Reel 9.

32. R. J. B. Sellar, *The Fife and Forfar Yeomanry, 1919–1956* (Edinburgh & London: William Blackwood & Sons Ltd, 1960), p. 186.

33. IWM SOUND: John Buchanan, AC 19867, Reel 8.

34. IWM SOUND: Douglas Hutchison, AC 20315, Reel 11.

35. IWM SOUND: Ron Forbes, AC 19818, Reel 9.

36. IWM SOUND: John Buchanan, AC 19867, Reel 8.

37. IWM SOUND: Jim Thompson-Bell, AC 21016, Reel 4–5.

38. IWM SOUND: Ken Watson, AC 19096, Reel 7.

39. Edgar Palamountain, *Taurus Pursuant: A History of the 11th Armoured Division* (Printing and Stationery Service, British Army of the Rhine, 1945), p. 51.
40. IWM SOUND: Gordon Fidler, AC 18785, Reel 9.
41. IWM SOUND: Bill Knights, AC 21015, Reel 3.
42. IWM SOUND: Jack Rex, AC 20945, Reel 5.
43. IWM SOUND: Roy Vallance, AC 19074, Reel 9.
44. Musée Percée du Bocage: William Steel Brownlie, '*And Came Safe Home*'.
45. IWM SOUND: John Buchanan, AC 19867, Reel 8.
46. IWM SOUND: Geoff Easton, AC 21276, Reel 3.
47. IWM SOUND: Roy Vallance, AC 19074, Reel 9.
48. Musée Percée du Bocage: William Steel Brownlie, '*And Came Safe Home*'.
49. IWM SOUND: Roy Vallance, AC 19074, Reel 10.
50. IWM SOUND: Terry Boyne, AC 18786, Reel 12.
51. IWM SOUND: Harold Wilson, AC 21567, Reel 10.
52. IWM SOUND: Douglas Hutchison, AC 20315, Reel 13.
53. IWM SOUND: Roy Vallance, AC 19074, Reel 10.
54. IWM SOUND: Roy Vallance, AC 19074, Reel 10.
55. IWM SOUND: James Donovan, AC 20316, Reel 7.
56. IWM SOUND: James Donovan, AC 20316, Reel 7.
57. IWM SOUND: James Donovan, AC 20316, Reel 7.
58. IWM SOUND: James Donovan, AC 20316, Reel 7.
59. IWM SOUND: James Donovan, AC 20316, Reel 7.
60. IWM SOUND: James Donovan, AC 20316, Reel 7.
61. IWM SOUND: James Donovan, AC 20316, Reel 7.
62. IWM SOUND: James Donovan, AC 20316, Reel 7.
63. IWM SOUND: James Donovan, AC 20316, Reel 7.
64. IWM SOUND: James Donovan, AC 20316, Reel 7.
65. IWM SOUND: James Donovan, AC 20316, Reel 7.
66. IWM SOUND: James Donovan, AC 20316, Reel 7.
67. IWM SOUND: James Donovan, AC 20316, Reel 8.
68. IWM SOUND: James Donovan, AC 20316, Reel 8.
69. Musée Percée du Bocage: William Steel Brownlie, '*And Came Safe Home*'.
70. Musée Percée du Bocage: William Steel Brownlie, '*And Came Safe Home*'.
71. IWM SOUND: John Buchanan, AC 19867, Reel 8.
72. James Milne died aged 28 on 11 September 1944. Buried at Leopoldsburg Cemetery.
73. IWM SOUND: Tommy Willmott, AC 19806, Reel 8.

14. Adventures in Holland

1. IWM SOUND: Don Fairweather, AC 20283, Reel 3.
2. Frank Moppet, quoted by Patrick Delaforce, *The Black Bull: From Normandy to the Baltic with the 11th Armoured Division* (London: Chancellor Press, 2000), p. 155.
3. Musée Percée du Bocage: William Steel Brownlie, '*And Came Safe Home*'.
4. IWM SOUND: Douglas Hutchison, AC 20315, Reel 12.
5. Musée Percée du Bocage: William Steel Brownlie, '*And Came Safe Home*'.

6. IWM SOUND: Ken Watson, AC 19096, Reel 8.
7. Musée Percée du Bocage: William Steel Brownlie, '*And Came Safe Home*'.
8. IWM SOUND: John Buchanan, AC 19867, Reel 9.
9. Lieutenant Don Bulley died aged 22 on 22 September 1944. Buried in the Mierlo War Cemetery.
10. Sergeant David McMahon died aged 36 on 22 September 1944. Buried in the Mierlo War Cemetery.
11. IWM SOUND: John Buchanan, AC 19867, Reel 9.
12. IWM SOUND: Douglas Hutchison, AC 20315, Reel 12.
13. Trooper Harry Gregory died aged 20 on 22 September 1944. Buried in the Mierlo War Cemetery.
14. IWM SOUND: Geoff Easton, AC 21276, Reel 4.
15. Musée Percée du Bocage: William Steel Brownlie, '*And Came Safe Home*'.
16. IWM SOUND: John Buchanan, AC 19867, Reel 9.
17. IWM SOUND: John Buchanan, AC 19867, Reel 9.
18. IWM SOUND: John Buchanan, AC 19867, Reel 9.
19. IWM SOUND: John Buchanan, AC 19867, Reel 9.
20. Musée Percée du Bocage: William Steel Brownlie, '*And Came Safe Home*'.
21. IWM SOUND: Don Fairweather, AC 20283, Reel 3.
22. Lance Corporal Clifford Colley died aged 20 on 24 September 1944. Buried at Nederweert War Cemetery.
23. IWM SOUND: Robert Nurse, AC 22196, Reel 4.
24. IWM SOUND: Harold Wilson, AC 21567, Reel 11.
25. IWM SOUND: John Gilmour, AC 19809, Reel 7.
26. Musée Percée du Bocage: William Steel Brownlie, '*And Came Safe Home*'.
27. IWM SOUND: Geoff Easton, AC 21276, Reel 4.
28. Musée Percée du Bocage: John Thorpe, *A Soldier's Tale. To Normandy and Beyond*, pp. 123 and 135.
29. Captain Roger Fairweather died aged 29 on 18 October 1944. Buried at Venray War Cemetery.
30. IWM SOUND: Don Fairweather, AC 20283, Reel 3.
31. IWM SOUND: Ron Forbes, AC 19818, Reel 10.
32. IWM SOUND: John Buchanan, AC 19867, Reel 9.
33. IWM SOUND: Ron Forbes, AC 19818, Reel 10.
34. IWM SOUND: Jim Thompson-Bell, AC 21016, Reel 5.
35. Lieutenant Oliver Davies died 1 November 1944. Buried at Venray Military Cemetery.
36. R. J. B. Sellar, *The Fife and Forfar Yeomanry, 1919–1956* (Edinburgh & London: William Blackwood & Sons Ltd, 1960), pp. 212–3.
37. IWM SOUND: Harold Wilson, AC 21567, Reel 11.
38. IWM SOUND: Harold Brown, AC 19800, Reel 3.
39. IWM SOUND: Alex Gilchrist, AC 20149, Reel 6.
40. IWM SOUND: Alex Gilchrist, AC 20149, Reel 7.
41. IWM SOUND: Thomas Heald, AC 19075, Reel 3.
42. IWM SOUND: Harold Wilson, AC 21567, Reel 11.
43. IWM SOUND: John Buchanan, AC 19867, Reel 9.

44. IWM SOUND: Ron Forbes, AC 19818, Reel 10.
45. IWM SOUND: Alex Gilchrist, AC 20149, Reel 7.
46. IWM SOUND: Geoff Hayward, AC 18706, Reel 18.
47. Trooper William Tyrie died 16 December 1944. Buried in Schoonselhof Cemetery.
48. IWM SOUND: Alex Gilchrist, AC 20149, Reel 7.
49. IWM SOUND: Geoff Hayward, AC 18706, Reel 18.
50. IWM SOUND: Geoff Hayward, AC 18706, Reel 19.

15. Ardennes Interruption

1. IWM SOUND: Roy Vallance, AC 19074, Reel 10.
2. IWM SOUND: Douglas Hutchison, AC 20315, Reel 13.
3. Musée Percée du Bocage: William Steel Brownlie, *'And Came Safe Home'*.
4. IWM SOUND: Ron Forbes, AC 19818, Reel 10.
5. IWM SOUND: Jim Thompson-Bell, AC 21016, Reel 6.
6. Musée Percée du Bocage: William Steel Brownlie, *'And Came Safe Home'*.
7. IWM SOUND: Douglas Hutchison, AC 20315, Reel 13.
8. IWM SOUND: Alex Gilchrist, AC 20149, Reel 8.
9. IWM SOUND: Ron Forbes, AC 19818, Reel 11.
10. IWM SOUND: Alex Gilchrist, AC 20149, Reel 8.
11. IWM SOUND: Thomas Heald, AC 19075, Reel 6.
12. IWM SOUND: Thomas Heald, AC 19075, Reel 6.
13. IWM SOUND: Roy Vallance, AC 19074, Reel 10.
14. IWM SOUND: John Buchanan, AC 19867, Reel 10.
15. IWM SOUND: George Davidson, AC 18978, Reel 2.
16. IWM SOUND: Ron Forbes, AC 19818, Reel 10.
17. IWM SOUND: Geoff Hayward, AC 18706, Reel 19.
18. Trooper Leslie Lines died aged 23 on 4 January 1944. Buried in Hotton War Cemetery.
19. IWM SOUND: Robert Nurse, AC 22196, Reel 4.
20. Musée Percée du Bocage: William Steel Brownlie, *'And Came Safe Home'*.
21. IWM SOUND: John Buchanan, AC 19867, Reel 10.
22. IWM SOUND: Ron Forbes, AC 19818, Reel 11.
23. Musée Percée du Bocage: William Steel Brownlie, *'And Came Safe Home'*.
24. IWM SOUND: George Cozens, AC 20201, Reel 7.
25. IWM SOUND: Ron Forbes, AC 19818, Reel 11.
26. IWM SOUND: Charles Workman, AC 20318, Reel 15.
27. IWM SOUND: Charles Workman, AC 20318, Reel 11.
28. IWM SOUND: Charles Workman, AC 20318, Reel 12.
29. IWM SOUND: Doug Hayes, AC 19097, Reel 9.
30. IWM SOUND: Alex Gilchrist, AC 20149, Reel 8.
31. IWM SOUND: Charles Workman, AC 20318, Reel 12.
32. IWM SOUND: Ron Forbes, AC 19818, Reel 11.
33. IWM SOUND: Doug Hayes, AC 19097, Reel 9.
34. IWM SOUND: John Buchanan, AC 19867, Reel 10.
35. IWM SOUND: Alex Gilchrist, AC 20149, Reel 9.

36. IWM SOUND: John Buchanan, AC 19867, Reel 10.
37. IWM SOUND: Jack Edwards, AC 22629, Reel 9.
38. IWM SOUND: Ken Watson, AC 19096, Reel 9.
39. Musée Percée du Bocage: William Steel Brownlie, *And Came Safe Home*.
40. IWM SOUND: Charles Workman, AC 20318, Reel 12.

16. Into Germany

1. IWM SOUND: Charles Workman, AC 20318, Reel 12.
2. Musée Percée du Bocage: William Steel Brownlie, *And Came Safe Home*.
3. IWM SOUND: Ron Forbes, AC 19818, Reel 11.
4. IWM SOUND: Douglas Hutchison, AC 20315, Reel 14.
5. IWM SOUND: Douglas Hutchison, AC 20315, Reel 14.
6. Pip Roberts, *From the Desert to the Baltic* (London: William Kimber, 1987), p. 214.
7. Robin Hastings, quoted by Tim Fitzgeorge-Parker, *Roscoe the Bright Shiner: The biography of Brigadier Roscoe Harvey DSO* (London: Severn House Publishers, 1987), pp. 221–2.
8. IWM SOUND: Terry Boyne, AC 18786, Reel 13.
9. IWM SOUND: Ron Forbes, AC 19818, Reel 11.
10. IWM SOUND: Charles Workman, AC 20318, Reel 12.
11. IWM SOUND: Charles Workman, AC 20318, Reel 12.
12. IWM SOUND: Ron Forbes, AC 19818, Reel 11.
13. IWM SOUND: Charles Workman, AC 20318, Reels 12 and 13.
14. Corporal Alfred Wedderburn died aged 27 on 30 March 1945. Buried at Reichswald Forest War Cemetery.
15. IWM SOUND: Ken Watson, AC 19096, Reel 10.
16. Musée Percée du Bocage: William Steel Brownlie, *And Came Safe Home*.
17. IWM SOUND: John Buchanan, AC 19867, Reel 11.
18. IWM SOUND: Roy Vallance, AC 19074, Reel 11.
19. Musée Percée du Bocage: William Steel Brownlie, *And Came Safe Home*.
20. IWM SOUND: Charles Workman, AC 20318, Reel 13.
21. Musée Percée du Bocage: William Steel Brownlie, *And Came Safe Home*.
22. Musée Percée du Bocage: William Steel Brownlie, *And Came Safe Home*.
23. Lieutenant Frank Fuller died aged 33 on 5 April 1945. Buried in Hanover War Cemetery.
24. Lance Corporal Arthur Axtell died aged 34 on 5 April 1945. Buried in Hanover War Cemetery.
25. Lance Corporal Herbert Grossmith died aged 30 on 5 April 1945. Buried in Hanover War Cemetery.
26. Lance Corporal Frederick Marris died aged 21 on 5 April 1945. Buried in Hanover War Cemetery.
27. IWM SOUND: Jim Thompson-Bell, AC 21016, Reel 6.
28. Musée Percée du Bocage: William Steel Brownlie, *And Came Safe Home*.
29. Musée Percée du Bocage: William Steel Brownlie, *And Came Safe Home*.
30. Major Arthur Loram (Peter was a nickname) died on 7 April 1945. Buried Hanover War Cemetery.

31. IWM SOUND: Alex Gilchrist, AC 20149, Reel 9.
32. IWM SOUND: Thomas Heald, AC 19075, Reel 7.
33. Musée Percée du Bocage: William Steel Brownlie, '*And Came Safe Home*'.
34. IWM SOUND: Jack Edwards, AC 22629, Reel 10.
35. IWM SOUND: Jack Edwards, AC 22629, Reel 10.
36. Musée Percée du Bocage: William Steel Brownlie, '*And Came Safe Home*'.
37. IWM SOUND: John Gilmour, AC 19809, Reel 8.
38. Trooper Thomas Smith died aged 29 on 10 April 1945. Buried in Becklingen War Cemetery.
39. IWM SOUND: Thomas Heald, AC 19075, Reel 7.
40. IWM SOUND: Gordon Fidler, AC 18785, Reel 10.
41. IWM SOUND: John Gilmour, AC 19809, Reel 8.
42. IWM SOUND: Douglas Hutchison, AC 20315, Reel 14.
43. IWM SOUND: John Buchanan, AC 19867, Reel 11.
44. IWM SOUND: Thomas Heald, AC 19075, Reel 8.
45. IWM SOUND: Thomas Heald, AC 19075, Reel 4.
46. IWM SOUND: Len Harkins, AC 21109, Reel 3.
47. IWM SOUND: John Buchanan, AC 19867, Reel 10.
48. IWM SOUND: Ron Forbes, AC 19818, Reel 11.
49. IWM SOUND: Terry Boyne, AC 18786, Reel 14.
50. IWM SOUND: John Gray, AC 20202, Reel 10.
51. IWM SOUND: Thomas Heald, AC 19075, Reel 8.

17. How Much Longer?

1. IWM SOUND: Thomas Heald, AC 19075, Reel 8.
2. IWM SOUND: Jack Edwards, AC 22629, Reel 10.
3. Musée Percée du Bocage: William Steel Brownlie, '*And Came Safe Home*'.
4. Musée Percée du Bocage: William Steel Brownlie, '*And Came Safe Home*'.
5. Musée Percée du Bocage: William Steel Brownlie, '*And Came Safe Home*'.
6. Musée Percée du Bocage: William Steel Brownlie, '*And Came Safe Home*'.
7. Musée Percée du Bocage: William Steel Brownlie, '*And Came Safe Home*'.
8. IWM SOUND: Thomas Heald, AC 19075, Reel 7.
9. W. Steel Brownlie, *The Proud Trooper: The History of the Ayrshire Yeomanry from its raising in the Eighteenth Century to 1964* (London: Collins, 1964), p. 450.
10. IWM SOUND: Ken Watson, AC 19096, Reel 10.
11. T. Stevens, quoted by W. Steel Brownlie, *The Proud Trooper: The History of the Ayrshire Yeomanry from its raising in the Eighteenth Century to 1964* (London: Collins, 1964), pp. 450–51.
12. T. Stevens, quoted by W. Steel Brownlie, *The Proud Trooper: The History of the Ayrshire Yeomanry from its raising in the Eighteenth Century to 1964* (London: Collins, 1964), p. 451.
13. Musée Percée du Bocage: William Steel Brownlie, '*And Came Safe Home*'.
14. Musée Percée du Bocage: William Steel Brownlie, '*And Came Safe Home*'.
15. Musée Percée du Bocage: William Steel Brownlie, '*And Came Safe Home*'.
16. IWM SOUND: John Buchanan, AC 19867, Reel 11.
17. Musée Percée du Bocage: William Steel Brownlie, '*And Came Safe Home*'.

18. IWM SOUND: Thomas Heald, AC 19075, Reel 7 and 8.
19. IWM SOUND: Thomas Heald, AC 19075, Reel 7 and 8.
20. IWM SOUND: Thomas Heald, AC 19075, Reel 7 and 8.
21. IWM SOUND: Gordon Fidler, AC 18785, Reel 11.
22. IWM SOUND: Thomas Heald, AC 19075, Reel 7 and 8.
23. IWM SOUND: Gordon Fidler, AC 18785, Reel 11.
24. IWM SOUND: Thomas Heald, AC 19075, Reel 8.
25. IWM SOUND: Jack Edwards, AC 22629, Reel 11.
26. IWM SOUND: Robert Nurse, AC 22196, Reel 5.
27. Corporal Stanton Bush died aged 33 on 19 April 1944. Buried in Becklingen Cemetery, Niedersachsen.
28. IWM SOUND: Roy Vallance, AC 19074, Reel 11.
29. IWM SOUND: Doug Hayes, AC 19097, Reel 10.
30. IWM SOUND: Thomas Heald, AC 19075, Reel 8.
31. IWM SOUND: Thomas Heald, AC 19075, Reel 8.
32. IWM SOUND: Gordon Fidler, AC 18785, Reel 11.
33. IWM SOUND: Ron Forbes, AC 19818, Reel 11 and 12.
34. IWM SOUND: Doug Hayes, AC 19097, Reel 10.
35. IWM SOUND: Alex Gilchrist, AC 20149, Reel 10.
36. IWM SOUND: John Buchanan, AC 19867, Reel 11.
37. IWM SOUND: John Buchanan, AC 19867, Reel 11.
38. IWM SOUND: John Gray, AC 20202, Reel 10.
39. IWM SOUND: Ron Forbes, AC 19818, Reel 12.
40. IWM SOUND: Roy Vallance, AC 19074, Reel 11.
41. IWM SOUND: Jim Thompson-Bell, AC 21016, Reel 7.
42. IWM SOUND: Roy Vallance, AC 19074, Reel 12.
43. IWM SOUND: Geoff Easton, AC 21276, Reel 6.
44. IWM SOUND: Douglas Hutchison, AC 20315, Reel 15.
45. IWM SOUND: Jim Thompson-Bell, AC 21016, Reel 7.

Epilogue

1. IWM SOUND: Len Harkins, AC 21109, Reel 10.
2. IWM SOUND: Ron Forbes, AC 19818, Reel 12.
3. IWM SOUND: Douglas Hutchison, AC 20315, Reel 15.
4. IWM SOUND: Roy Vallance, AC 19074, Reel 12.
5. IWM SOUND: Jack Edwards, AC 22629, Reel 11.
6. Musée Percée du Bocage: William Steel Brownlie, '*And Came Safe Home*'.
7. Musée Percée du Bocage: William Steel Brownlie, '*And Came Safe Home*'.
8. IWM SOUND: Douglas Hutchison, AC 20315, Reel 15.
9. IWM SOUND: Alex Gilchrist, AC 20149, Reel 10.
10. Musée Percée du Bocage: John Thorpe, *A Soldier's Tale. To Normandy and Beyond*, pp. 135–6.
11. IWM SOUND: Len Newman, AC 18705, Reel 8.
12. IWM SOUND: John Gray, AC 20202, Reel 11.
13. IWM SOUND: John Gray, AC 20202, Reel 11.
14. IWM SOUND: Len Harkins, AC 21109, Reel 10.

15. Musée Percée du Bocage: William Steel Brownlie, '*And Came Safe Home*'.
16. IWM SOUND: Alf Courtneidge, AC 19078, Reel 8.
17. IWM SOUND: Alf Courtneidge, AC 19078, Reel 7 and 8.
18. IWM SOUND: Alf Courtneidge, AC 19078, Reel 8.
19. IWM SOUND: James Donovan, AC 20316, Reel 8.
20. IWM SOUND: James Donovan, AC 20316, Reel 8.
21. IWM SOUND: Geoff Hayward, AC 18706, Reel 22.
22. IWM SOUND: Tommy Willmott, AC 19806, Reel 9.
23. IWM SOUND: Leslie Gibson, AC 19811, Reel 5.
24. IWM SOUND: Alex Gilchrist, AC 20149, Reel 10.
25. IWM SOUND: Geoff Hayward, AC 18706, Reel 22.
26. IWM SOUND: Geoff Hayward, AC 18706, Reel 22.
27. IWM SOUND: Terry Boyne, AC 18786, Reel 15.
28. IWM SOUND: John Gray, AC 20202, Reel 11.
29. Musée Percée du Bocage: William Steel Brownlie, '*And Came Safe Home*'.
30. Musée Percée du Bocage: John Thorpe, *A Soldier's Tale. To Normandy and Beyond*, p. 6.

PICTURE CREDITS

The author and publisher would like to thank the Imperial War Museum for permission to reproduce the following images: page 2 (H 8463); page 3, top (H 21016); bottom (B 6187); page 4 (B 8483); page 5, top (B 9184); bottom (B 9528); page 6, bottom (BU 4946); page 8, top (BU 2919). All images © Imperial War Museums. All other images were kindly provided by Geoff Hayward, for which many thanks.

ACKNOWLEDGMENTS

FIRST OF ALL, I WOULD like to thank all the men of the 2nd F&FY that I had the pleasure of interviewing. This is their book; I hope they would have enjoyed it. I am also indebted to all my colleagues at the Imperial War Museum, who gave me the opportunity to record all these veterans. I would particularly thank Bryn Hammond, Margaret Brooks, Tony Richards, Conrad Wood and Richard McDonough. Then I must thank all those who have helped me in the technicalities of writing the book: Andrew Franklin has been a wonderfully patient editor; lovely Penny Gardiner, who always manages to copy edit my text without causing any irritation; Martin Lubikowski for the maps; and overseeing everyone and everything the rather wonderful and slightly scary Penny Daniel. I would also express my gratitude to my idiot friends Gary Bain, John Paylor and Phil Wood who were all kind enough to check the manuscript to discover many errors. Gareth Davies helped keep me on the straight and narrow with the arcane complexities of armoured warfare. Lastly, but never least, I was glad to be able to call on the assistance of my brilliant literary agent Ian Drury, who seems to have an unrivalled expertise in all aspects of military history!

In our internet world, a bibliography is a waste of time in a footnoted book, more an exercise in specious 'boasting' than a serious list of what the author has read. However, these books were particularly useful. I urge you to buy them all: Anon, *Taurus Pursuant: A History of 11th Armoured Division* (Printing and Stationery Service British Army of the Rhine, 1946); John Buckley, *British Armour in the Normandy Campaign 1944* (London & New York: Routledge, 2004); Ian Dalglish, *Over the Battlefield Operation Epsom* (Barnsley: Pen & Sword Military, 2015); Ian Dalglish, *Over the Battlefield Operation Goodwood* (Barnsley: Pen & Sword Military, 2013); Ian Dalglish, *Over the Battlefield Operation Bluecoat* (Barnsley: Pen & Sword Military, 2009), Christopher Dunphie, *Pendulum of Battle: Operation Goodwood July 1944* (Barnsley: Leo Cooper, 2004); Lionel Ellis, with G. R. G. Allen, A. E. Warhurst, and Sir James Robb, *Victory in the West: The Battle of Normandy* (London: HM Stationery Office, 1962); Lionel Ellis, *Victory in the West: The Defeat of Germany* (London: HM Stationery Office, 1968); Stephen Napier, *The Armoured Campaign in Normandy, June–August 1944* (Stroud: The History Press, 2017).

INDEX

Page references in *italics* indicate images.